TRIGONOMETRY
USING
CALCULATORS

TRIGONOMETRY USING CALCULATORS

JOSEPH ELICH
Utah State University, Logan, Utah

CARLETTA J. ELICH
Logan High School, Logan, Utah

 ADDISON-WESLEY PUBLISHING COMPANY

Reading, Massachusetts • Menlo Park, California
London • Amsterdam • Don Mills, Ontario • Sydney

ABOUT THE COVER

The abacus is one of the oldest computing devices known. It is a forerunner to the calculator and is still widely used in many countries. The number displayed on the abacus on the cover of this book is 2,345,347. It is the product of three prime numbers. If you are curious, find them. Using an abacus or a calculator might be helpful.

Library of Congress Cataloging in Publication Data

Elich, Joseph, 1918-
Trigonometry using calculators.

Includes index.
1. Trigonometry. 2. Calculating machines.
I. Elich, Carletta J. 1935-   joint author. II. Title.
QA531.E44   516'.24'0285   79-18934
ISBN 0-201-03186-8

ISBN 0-201-03186-8
BCDEFGHIJK-DO-89876543210

*To our parents
Anna and Dan Elich,
Jessie Mae and the late James E. Johnson*

PREFACE

One of the truly significant technological achievements of the twentieth century is the development of high-speed computing devices, including the hand-held calculator. These machines permit not only rapid and accurate computations of complicated numerical problems but they have great potential in all phases of the educational curriculum. In this book we give a complete treatment of the topics traditionally covered in a trigonometry course. Full advantage is taken of the capabilities of scientific calculators, not merely as computational tools but also as an aid to motivating and reinforcing basic concepts.

Some of the prominent features in this book are:

1. Emphasis is on basic definitions and ideas throughout the text. As in most mathematical textbooks, problem sets are included primarily for the purpose of providing the student with an opportunity to apply definitions of fundamental concepts, thus leading to a better understanding of basic ideas. In most of the problems involving numerical answers the student is asked to give results in exact form or in approximate decimal form. In general, the first precludes the use of calculators while the second almost always requires their use. Expressing answers in exact form involves application of definitions and/or basic concepts, while in giving results in decimal form the student becomes familiar with numbers as they occur in real-life applications (for example, one does not ordinarily encounter numbers such as $\sqrt{2}$ or π on a blueprint).

2. The traditional approach to solving triangles has been to formulate solutions (whenever possible) so that logarithms can be used to carry out the final computations. In this book we are freed from such constraints since calculators can perform additions and subtractions as easily as multiplications and divisions. Thus the Law of Cosines has a higher priority than it does in other trigonometry books.

3. The numbers used in application problems are more realistic; calculators can handle such numbers just as easily as the carefully selected simple numbers chosen for the sole purpose of avoiding even slightly cumbersome computations. The calculator adds the dimension of approximate numbers often ignored in mathematics books.

4. Appendix A contains a relatively complete introduction to the use of calculators for those students who have had no previous experience with them. Included in separate sections is a discussion of AOS calculators based on algebraic entry and RPN calculators based on Reverse Polish Notation. The basic calculator keys are carefully described; this is followed by several detailed examples and practice problems. In most cases, the student can master this material on his or her own. In addition to the treatment included in Appendix A, further instruction on special function keys is given throughout the text proper, as needed and when appropriate.

5. Appendix B includes a relatively detailed treatment of computation with approximate numbers.

6. Although logarithms may no longer be popular for computational purposes, they are important as functions that occur in applications and in theoretical mathematics. Their study is needed in preparation for subsequent courses (such as calculus). Therefore, included in Chapter 10 is a fairly complete treatment in which basic properties of logarithmic functions are emphasized. This chapter is independent of the others and can be included at any point in the course. As in the earlier chapters, the treatment here is calculator oriented.

7. Throughout the entire book, presentations of topics follows the pattern: a) introduction of basic ideas; b) illustration of these by several examples worked in detail; c) set of problems carefully designed to give practice with the concepts being discussed and to stimulate related ideas. Also included are chapter review exercises which utilize any of the concepts studied up to that point.

8. A concept, a technique, or a fact can best be learned by encountering it frequently and in a variety of settings. We exploit this by including problems in exercise sets that repeatedly use ideas introduced in earlier sections. For instance, one of the most difficult topics in trigonometry for a student to master is that of identities. Basic identities are introduced in Chapter 4, and in subsequent chapters several problems have been designed specifically to show that the application of an appropriate identity greatly simplifies solution of the given problem. In this way the student sees that a knowledge of identities can be helpful and there is no need to wait until calculus to justify their importance.

9. The exercise sets include a large number of problems ranging from simple to challenging. In each section the student will find several easy-to-follow examples that illustrate the various types of problems included as exercises. In some cases, the use of calculators allows us to present problem solving methods that are not part of a traditional course.

10. Although calculators make tables obsolete for computational purposes, we recognize that learning to read tables may be an integral part of some trigonometry courses. Therefore, we have included tables of trigonometric functions and common logarithms in Appendix C. These can be incorporated in solving problems at appropriate places throughout the text.

This book is designed for a one-semester or one-quarter course in trigonometry. A prerequisite of high-school geometry and intermediate algebra is assumed. Although basic concepts are covered in sequential order throughout the first nine chapters, it is not necessary to study all sections of a given chapter. Each chapter contains sufficient material, so that a careful selection can be made to fit the needs of any course.

It is assumed that many students have had some experience with calculators. Therefore, instruction in use of calculators is included in Appendix A as optional material. It can be formally introduced when the group of students is uniformly inexperienced. AOS and RPN systems are treated separately to allow the individual student to follow only the portion corresponding to the logic of a given calculator.

A summary of formulas for quick reference is included inside the covers. Inside the front cover is a listing of formulas from algebra and geometry which the student has probably seen in previous courses. Identity equations and formulas from trigonometry are collected inside the back cover.

The authors are grateful to the mathematics staffs at Utah State University and Logan High School for their willingness to teach from experimental versions of this book and to their students who provided the essential link with reality. We are particularly indebted to Wanda C. Sayer for her patience and understanding in typing the various versions of the manuscript. We extend our appreciation to the following persons who reviewed the manuscript at various stages: Laura Cameron from the University of New Mexico in Albuquerque, Robert T. Fair from the Kankakee Community College in Illinois, Steven D. Kerr from Weber State College in Ogden, Utah, and Michael Windham from Utah State University in Logan, Utah. The resulting product reflects their many helpful suggestions. Finally, we wish to express our sincere gratitude to the entire editorial staff of Addison-Wesley, especially to our editor Patricia Mallion for her vision and encouragement, and to Rima Zolina for her superb editing.

Logan, Utah   J.E.
November 1979   C.J.E.

CONTENTS

CHAPTER ONE

INTRODUCTORY CONCEPTS

1.1 INTRODUCTION

As the name indicates, *trigonometry* pertains to the study of measurements related to triangles. Approximately 3000 years ago the Egyptians and Babylonians used properties of triangles to establish land boundaries and explore astronomy. In modern times the ideas related to solution of triangles are still important in several areas of application. Trigonometric functions are also important in the study of calculus and in physics, engineering, and most fields in which mathematics is applied. Two main goals of this book are: 1) the study of problems related to the solution of plane triangles (in which calculators will be essential); 2) the study of basic concepts of trigonometric functions needed for further study of mathematics, particularly calculus (in which calculators are used when appropriate).

1.2 ANGLES AND ANGLE MEASURE

The study of *plane trigonometry* implies that we begin with a given plane. All of the geometric figures discussed (lines, rays, angles, triangles, and so on) are subsets of this plane. In geometry, a *ray* is defined as a half line together with its endpoint, and an *angle* is the union of two rays with a common endpoint. Also the idea of *measure of an angle* is introduced but usually limited to angles with measures less than or equal to 180°.

It now becomes necessary to extend the notion of angle and angle measure beyond that studied in geometry. Eventually we shall express the angle measure as a real number (*radian* measure), and it will be useful to have a correspondence between the angles in the plane and the set of real numbers. In order to do this, it is convenient to think of an angle as being generated by a ray that is rotated about its endpoint from its initial position to a final position. The ray corresponding to the initial position is called the *initial side* of the angle, while that in the final position is called the *terminal side* of the angle. The point about which rotation takes place is called the *vertex* of the angle. The definition of an angle is now extended to be the union of two rays together with the rotation. Measure of an angle is then described in terms of amount of rotation. This allows us to have angles with measures greater than 180° (indeed greater than 360°) and also angles with negative measures, by using direction of rotation. A *directed angle* will have positive measure if the rotation is counterclockwise and negative measure if the rotation is clockwise. For purposes of brevity we shall frequently say "the angle is positive" to mean "the measure of the angle is positive"; similarly for negative.

In Fig. 1.1(a) angle *A* is shown with initial and terminal sides labeled, as well as with an arrow indicating direction of rotation. It is common to use the arrow notation. Figure 1.1(b) illustrates angle *B* in which the rotation is more than a complete revolution. Angles *A* and *B* are positive, while angle *C* is negative.

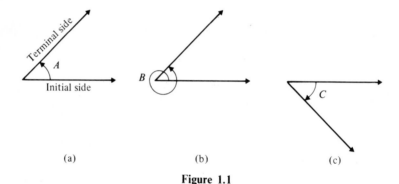

(a)   (b)   (c)

Figure 1.1

1.3 UNITS OF ANGLE MEASURE

There are two units of angle measure that are widely used: 1) degrees-minutes-seconds, 2) radians. Scientific calculators frequently include a third unit of angle measure, that is, the *grad.** Since this unit is rarely encountered, it will not be used in this text.

1. Degrees, Minutes, Seconds

If the initial side of an angle is rotated counterclockwise one complete revolution, the measure of the corresponding angle is defined to be 360 degrees, denoted by 360°. Thus an angle of 1° is one in which the initial side

---

* A grad is 1/100 of a right angle; that is, 400 grads is equivalent to a complete revolution.

is rotated counterclockwise 1/360 of a revolution. For more refined measurements, the units of minutes and seconds are used, which are defined by:

60 minutes equals one degree, denoted by $60' = 1°$,
60 seconds equals one minute, denoted by $60'' = 1'$.

> When a calculator is used, minutes and seconds must be entered as a decimal part of a degree.

For example, $30°15' = 30.25°$ and $42°12'45'' = 42.2125°$.

    Figure 1.2 illustrates degree measure of several angles. For brevity we write $A = 90°$ to denote that the measure of angle A is 90°, and similarly for other angles.

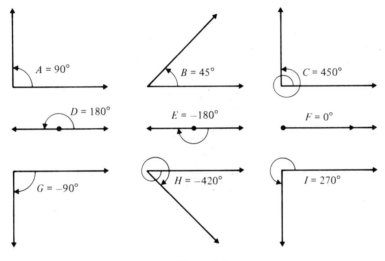

Figure 1.2

2. Radians

Although the measure of angles in degrees is useful in some fields of application (such as surveying and navigation), it is more convenient to use another unit of measure for theoretical work in mathematics as well as applied areas. This unit is the *radian* and is defined as follows:

> An angle (with its vertex at the center of a circle) subtending an arc whose length is equal to the radius of the circle, has a measure of one radian.

An angle of measure 1 radian is shown in Fig. 1.3(a). In this case we write $\theta = 1$ rad.*

In general, the radian measure of any angle is defined as follows:

If α is an angle (with vertex at the center of a circle of radius r) that subtends an arc of length s (where r and s are measured in the same units), then the radian measure of α is defined as $\alpha = s/r$ radians.†

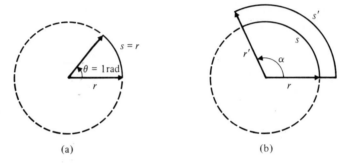

(a)   (b)

Figure 1.3

Examples

⚠1 If $r = 4$ cm and $s = 3$ cm, then $\alpha = 3\text{cm}/4\text{cm} = \frac{3}{4}$. Since the centimeters units cancel, the result is a real number and it is not necessary to write "radians" after $\frac{3}{4}$. In this text we shall write $\alpha = \frac{3}{4}$ ($\alpha = 0.75$ in calculator display form) or $\alpha = \frac{3}{4}$ rad to mean α is an angle having radian measure $\frac{3}{4}$. ∎

When the measure of an angle is given as a real number (with no unit designation), it will be understood that the unit of measure is the radian.

For example, $\theta = 15$ means that θ is an angle whose measure is 15 radians.

⚠2 Express $36°16'23''$ in decimal form correct to four decimal places.

---

* In trigonometry angles are frequently indicated by Greek letters: α (alpha), β (beta), γ (gamma), θ (theta), ϕ (phi), and so on.

†Note that this definition is independent of the size of circle used; that is, in Fig. 1.3(b) the two ratios s/r and s'/r' are equal (this is a fact from geometry).

Solution. Since $60' = 1°$, then $16' = 16/60$ degrees. Also $3600'' = 1°$, then $23'' = 23/3600$ degrees. Therefore

$$36°16'23'' = \left(36 + \frac{16}{60} + \frac{23}{3600}\right)° = 36.2731°.$$

The computation involved in getting the final result is easily done by using a calculator.* ∎

△3 Express 64.276° in degrees, minutes, and seconds (to the nearest second).

Solution.

$$64.276° = 64° + (0.276)(60') = 64° + 16.56'$$
$$= 64° + 16' + (0.56)(60'') = 64°16'34''.$$

Note. In order to get maximum accuracy we suggest the following steps: Record 64°, enter 0.276 into the calculator and multiply by 60, then record the whole number part of the result (16); then subtract 16 from the display, multiply the result by 60 and this gives the number of seconds. ∎

EXERCISE 1.3

1. Illustrate by a sketch the following angles. A protractor may be useful but if one is not available, a reasonably approximate drawing will be sufficient.

   a) $A = 135°$ b) $B = 720°$ c) $C = -60°$ d) $D = -540°$
   e) $E = 210°$ f) $F = 10°$ g) $G = -300°$ h) $H = 22°30'$

2. Determine the measure (in degrees) of the angles shown in Fig. 1.4. Use a protractor or make a reasonable estimate in each case.

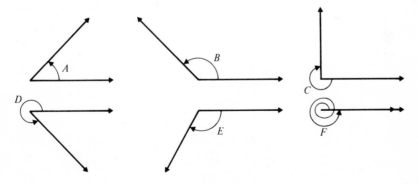

Figure 1.4

---

*Throughout the entire text it is assumed that a calculator is used to do most of the arithmetic computations. Appendix A includes calculator instructions for those who need them.

3. Note that an angle corresponding to one complete revolution has degree measure of $360°$ and radian measure of $s/r = 2\pi r/r = 2\pi$ rad. From this we see that $180°$ and π rad are equivalent. Illustrate by a sketch the following angles given in radian measure:

a) $A = 2\pi$
b) $B = \dfrac{17\pi}{6}$
c) $C = \dfrac{\pi}{2}$
d) $D = \dfrac{\pi}{4}$

e) $E = -\dfrac{7\pi}{2}$
f) $F = -\dfrac{3\pi}{2}$
g) $G = \dfrac{9\pi}{4}$
h) $H = \dfrac{\pi}{3}$

4. Determine the measure (in radians) of the angles shown in Fig. 1.5. Express answers in terms of π, as suggested in Problem 3. Estimate if necessary.

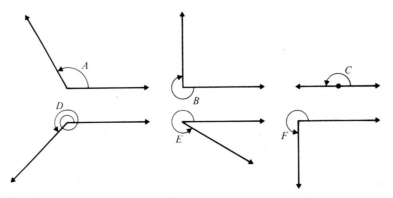

Figure 1.5

5. Sketch an angle that satisfies the given conditions:

a) $0 < \theta < \dfrac{\pi}{2}$
b) $\pi < \theta < \dfrac{3\pi}{2}$
c) $-\pi < \theta < -\dfrac{\pi}{2}$

d) $\dfrac{3\pi}{4} < \theta < \pi$
e) $\dfrac{9\pi}{4} < \theta < \dfrac{11\pi}{4}$
f) $\theta > 2\pi$

6. Express the given angles as a decimal number of degrees correct to three decimal places:

a) $156°37'$
b) $215°18'36''$

7. Express the given angles as a decimal number of degrees correct to four decimal places:

a) $48°39'42''$
b) $-75°12'41''$

8. Express the given angles in degrees and minutes correct to the nearest minute:

a) $24.36°$
b) $149.375°$

9. Express the given angles in degrees, minutes, and seconds correct to the nearest second:

a) $37.583°$
b) $321.5764°$

1.4 DEGREE–RADIAN RELATIONSHIPS

Problem 3 of Exercise 1.2 suggests a relationship between the degree and radian units of angle measure. We now give a formal treatment so that the different units can be used interchangeably. If the initial side of an angle is rotated counterclockwise one complete revolution, the measure in degrees of the corresponding angle is 360°. The same angle in radians has measure s/r, where in this special case s is the circumference of the circle with radius r; that is,

$$s = 2\pi r \text{ and so } \frac{s}{r} = \frac{2\pi r}{r} = 2\pi.$$

Thus we have 360° and 2π radians as the measures of the same angle and we write

$$360° = 2\pi \text{ rad.}$$

Dividing both sides of this equality by 2 gives

$$\boxed{180° = \pi \text{ rad.}} \tag{1.1}$$

From Eq. (1.1) we get the following:

$$\boxed{\begin{aligned} 1° &= \frac{\pi}{180} = 0.017453 \text{ rad,} \\ 1 \text{ rad} &= \frac{180°}{\pi} = 57.296° = 57°17'45''. \end{aligned}} \tag{1.2}$$

Equations (1.2) can be used to convert the measure of an angle from one unit to the other. However, the decimal numbers involved are difficult to memorize and we suggest that the student remember the equality stated in Eq. (1.1) and use it as a starting point for conversions.

Examples

⚠️1 Change 30° to an equivalent measure in radians.

Solution. Since $1° = \pi/180$ rad, 30° must be 30 times $\pi/180$ rad; that is, $30° = 30 \cdot (\pi/180)$ rad $= \pi/6$ rad $= 0.5236$ (to four decimal places). ∎

⚠️2 Express 147°32′ in radian measure correct to four decimal places.

Solution. We first convert 147°32′ to a decimal number of degrees, and then similar to Example 1 we have:

$$147°32' = \left(147 + \frac{32}{60}\right)° = \left(147 + \frac{32}{60}\right) \cdot \left(\frac{\pi}{180}\right) \text{rad} = 2.5749 \text{ rad.} \quad \blacksquare$$

⚠️3 Express 2.5 rad in terms of degrees (to three decimal places).

Solution. Since 1 rad $= (180/\pi)°$, we have 2.5 rad $= 2.5(180°/\pi) = 143.239°$.
∎

△4 Convert $13\pi/4$ rad to degree measure.

Solution. This is similar to Example 3 and so

$$\frac{13\pi}{4} = \left(\frac{13\pi}{4}\right)\left(\frac{180}{\pi}\right)^\circ = 585^\circ.$$

∎

It should be clear from the above examples that we have the following two rules:

> 1. To convert from degrees to radians, multiply by $\pi/180$.
> 2. To convert from radians to degrees, multiply by $180/\pi$.

The Number Pi

The number π occurs frequently in mathematics. Although the student may have some familiarity with this number, it is worthwhile recalling some facts about it. More than 2000 years ago the Greeks were aware of an interesting property of circles. That is, in any two given circles (one with diameter d_1 and circumference c_1, and the other with diameter d_2 and circumference c_2), the ratios c_1/d_1 and c_2/d_2 are equal (Fig. 1.6). The common ratio is denoted by π (the Greek letter pi).

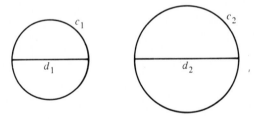

Figure 1.6

Scientific calculators have a key labeled $\boxed{\pi}$. When this key is pressed, the display shows 3.141592654. Actually, this is an approximation to the value of π that is correct to nine decimal places. The number 22/7 is frequently used as a value of π. It is important that the student realize that this is also an approximation. In decimal form, 22/7 is given by the repeating decimal $3.\overline{142857}$, which approximates π correctly to two decimal places.

Another approximation to π is $333/106 = 3.1415094339\ldots$ We see that this agrees with π (as given in (1.3) below) in the first four decimal digits. However, in rounded-off form it is correct to three decimal places. (See Appendix B for a discussion of approximate numbers.)

Even though approximations to π by fractions or decimals are useful in practical applications, it is important that the student realize that it is impossible to represent π exactly as a rational number, that is, a quotient of two integers; π is an irrational number, that is, its decimal representation is nonterminating and nonrepeating. Calculating π correctly to several decimal places requires a representation of it in terms of an infinite process (such as an infinite series), and discussion of this must be delayed until the study of calculus. The decimal approximation correct to 24 decimal places is

$$\pi = 3.1415\ 92653\ 58979\ 32384\ 62643. \qquad (1.3)$$

Note. In this text we shall frequently ask for an answer in (a) exact form and (b) decimal approximation form. When the number pi is involved, the only way we shall represent it in exact form is by the symbol π. To avoid cumbersome statements, we frequently take some liberties with notation. For example, we write $\pi = 3.1416$ and we understand that the "equal to" symbol used here actually means "approximately equal to," which is correct to the number of decimal places used.* As another example, a number whose square is 2 can be represented by $\sqrt{2}$ and this is an exact form for that number; $\sqrt{2}$ cannot be written in finite decimal form, and when we write $\sqrt{2} = 1.414$ we mean that 1.414 is a decimal approximation to $\sqrt{2}$, which is correct to three decimal places.

EXERCISE 1.4

1. Express the given angles in radian measure. Write your answer in two forms: exact (using π) and as a decimal correct to three places.

   a) 60° b) −135° c) 225° d) 720°

2. Follow instructions of Problem 1 for

   a) 120° b) 315° c) 22.5° d) −330°

3. Express the given angles in radian measure correct to three decimal places:

   a) 23.53° b) −48.635° c) 237°48′ d) 121°40′31″ e) 437°23′

4. Convert to radian measure correct to two decimal places:

   a) 64.431° b) 229°47′30″ c) −36°23′08″ d) 148.012° e) 472.37°

5. The following numbers represent the measure of an angle in radians. Convert to the corresponding measure in degrees and express the result in exact form.

   a) $\dfrac{\pi}{6}$ b) $\dfrac{2\pi}{3}$ c) $\dfrac{3\pi}{2}$ d) $\dfrac{23\pi}{45}$ e) $\dfrac{7\pi}{18}$

6. Follow instructions of Problem 5 for

   a) $\dfrac{3\pi}{4}$ b) $-\dfrac{7\pi}{2}$ c) $\dfrac{11\pi}{18}$ d) -17π e) $\dfrac{15\pi}{4}$

---

* When we say that 3.1416 approximates π correctly to four decimal places we mean that the actual value of π has been rounded off to four decimal places (see Appendix B for a discussion of approximate numbers).

7. The given numbers represent angles in radian measure. Convert to degrees and express the results in two forms: decimal number correct to three decimal places and degrees, minutes, and seconds correct to the nearest second.

   a) 1.15   b) 2.48   c) 0.0493   d) −5.76   e) 64

8. Follow instructions of Problem 7 for

   a) 1.37   b) 0.0034   c) $\dfrac{1+\sqrt{5}}{2}$ d) −3.45   e) 30

9. Use your calculator to express the fraction 355/113 as a decimal; obtain a sufficient number of decimals to determine how closely it approximates π.

10. Follow the instructions of Problem 9 for the rational number 208341/66317. It will be necessary to get more decimal digits than given in the full display of your calculator. Find a way of getting at least 12 decimal digits using your calculator.

1.5   APPLICATIONS INVOLVING RADIAN MEASURE

The use of radians for angular measure is helpful in solving applied problems in physics, engineering, and other fields as well as in theoretical developments in mathematics. In this section we consider examples that illustrate applications of radian measure.

1. Arc Length

In Section 1.2 radian measure of an angle is defined as follows:

$$\theta = \frac{s}{r},$$ (1.4)

where the angle has its vertex at the center of a circle of radius r and s is the length of the intercepted arc, as shown in Fig. 1.7. Equation (1.4) can be written in equivalent form as

$$s = r\theta$$ (1.5)

Figure 1.7

Examples

⚠ Find the arc length of a circle with radius 64.87 m that is intercepted by a central angle 23°37′.

Solution. We first express the given angle in radians,

$$\theta = 23°37' = \left(23 + \frac{37}{60}\right) \cdot \left(\frac{\pi}{180}\right) \text{ rad};$$

substituting into Eq. (1.5) we get

$$s = 64.87\left(23 + \frac{37}{60}\right) \cdot \left(\frac{\pi}{180}\right) = 26.74 \text{ m}.$$

The final computations are done by calculator and then rounded to two decimal places.   ∎

⚠ The distance from the Earth to the Moon is approximately 384,000 km. If the angle subtended by the Moon from a point on the Earth is measured as 30′50″, then we can approximate the diameter of the Moon by assuming it to be the arc of a circle, as shown in Fig. 1.8. That is, the diameter of the Moon is approximately equal to s, where

$$s = r\theta = 384\ 000 \cdot \left(\frac{30}{60} + \frac{50}{3600}\right) \cdot \frac{\pi}{180} \text{ km} = 3444 \text{ km}.$$

Figure 1.8

∎

2. Velocity of Rotation

Suppose we have a circular wheel of radius $r = 10$ cm rotating about its center O, and P is a point on the circumference (Fig. 1.9). Suppose also that point P

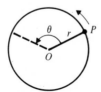

Figure 1.9

travels a distance of $s = 20$ cm each second. We say the *linear velocity* of P is 20 cm per second and write $v = 20$ cm/sec. During each second the radial line $\overline{OP}$ rotates through an angle $\theta = s/r = 20$ cm/10 cm $= 2$ rad. We say that the *angular velocity* of rotation is 2 radians per second, and denote this by $\omega = 2$ rad/sec (ω is the Greek letter omega).

The above example illustrates the problem of a point P moving in a circular path. We distinguish two types of velocity: linear velocity v tells us how fast P is moving, while angular velocity ω tells us how fast the central angle θ is changing (that is, how fast the radial line $\overline{OP}$ is rotating). Both v and ω are measures of how fast P is moving at any given instant. In general, v and ω are functions of time. In the special case when P is moving at a constant speed, we call such a motion *uniform circular motion*. We shall limit our discussion to this case and leave the general case when v varies with time, for calculus.

We wish to determine the equation that gives the relationship between v and ω. Suppose that point P moves to point Q, covering distance s in time t (see Fig. 1.10). Then $v = s/t$. During the same time, the radial line $\overline{OP}$ rotates through a central angle θ, and so $\omega = \theta/t$. Since $s = r\theta$, we get

$$v = \frac{s}{t} = \frac{r\theta}{t} = r \cdot \frac{\theta}{t} = r\omega.$$

Thus we have

$$v = r\omega, \tag{1.6}$$

where ω is in *radians per unit of time.*

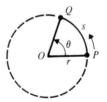

Figure 1.10

Examples

⚠ The wheel of a turbine rotates at the rate of 648 revolutions per minute and the distance from the center to a point P on the outer edge is 96.3 cm. What is the linear velocity of point P?

Solution. Since 1 rev $= 2\pi$ rad, $\omega = 648$ rev/min $= 648 \cdot 2\pi$ rad/min. Substituting into Eq. (1.6), we get

$$v = 648 \cdot 2\pi \cdot 96.3 \frac{\text{cm}}{\text{min}} = \frac{648 \cdot 2\pi \cdot 96.3}{100} \frac{\text{m}}{\text{min}} = 3921 \frac{\text{m}}{\text{min}}.$$

∎

⚠ The diameter of each wheel of a bicycle is 70 cm. Suppose a person riding the bicycle travels at a constant speed and is timed at 3 min over a distance of two city blocks, where the length of a block is 200 m. Find the angular velocity of a spoke of a wheel.

Solution. Each time the wheel (or a spoke) makes one revolution, the bicycle moves forward a distance equal to the circumference of the wheel, that is, 70π cm. Therefore when the bicycle travels two blocks (400 m or 40,000 cm), the number of revolutions of a wheel is $40000/(70\pi)$. It takes 3 min to make this number of revolutions, and so

$$\omega = \frac{40000}{70\pi} \div 3 = 60.63 \frac{\text{rev}}{\text{min}} .$$

Expressing ω in radians per second, we have

$$\omega = 60.63 \cdot 2\pi \div 60 = 6.35 \frac{\text{rad}}{\text{sec}}.$$

∎

3. Area of a Sector of a Circle

A sector of a circle is defined as a region bounded by two radial lines and the intercepted arc of the circle. Figure 1.11 shows two regions bounded by the same radial lines. In order to distinguish between these two, we always indicate the central angle of the sector. In Fig. 1.11(a) the sector has central angle α, while in Fig. 1.11(b) the central angle is β.

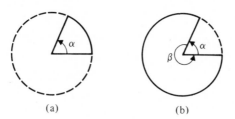

(a)   (b)

Figure 1.11

From the study of geometry we know that in any given circle the areas of two sectors are proportional to the corresponding central angles. That is, in the diagrams shown in Fig. 1.12,

$$\frac{\text{Area of sector } AOB}{\theta} = \frac{\text{Area of sector } COD}{\alpha}$$

In particular, if we let sector COD be the entire circle, so that $\alpha = 2\pi$, and the area is πr^2, we get

$$\frac{\text{Area of sector } AOB}{\theta} = \frac{\pi r^2}{2\pi} = \frac{r^2}{2} .$$

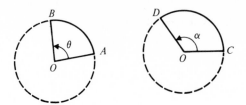

Figure 1.12

That is, area of sector AOB is $\theta r^2/2$.

Therefore, the area of the sector of a circle of radius r and central angle θ in *radians* is

$$\boxed{\text{Area} = \theta r^2/2} \qquad (1.7)$$

Example. Find the area of the sector of a circle of radius 2.54 cm and central angle $73°24'$.

Solution. We first convert $73°24'$ to radians and then substitute into Eq. (1.7):

$$73°24' = \left(73 + \frac{24}{60}\right) \cdot \frac{\pi}{180} \text{ rad.}$$

Therefore,

$$\text{Area} = \frac{1}{2} \cdot \left(73 + \frac{24}{60}\right) \cdot \frac{\pi}{180} \cdot 2.54^2 = 4.13 \text{ cm}^2. \qquad \blacksquare$$

EXERCISE 1.5

1. Suppose the radius of a circle is 37.43 cm. Find the length of arc intercepted by the given central angle. Give answers correct to two decimal places.

   a) $36°$ b) $73°23'$ c) 3.58

2. The radius of a circle is 75.23 cm. Find the length of arc intercepted by the given central angle. Give answers correct to two decimal places.

   a) $187°15'$ b) $17\pi/12$ c) $18°15'35''$

3. If the radius of a circle is 25.32 cm, find the central angle that subtends the given arc. Give answers in radians correct to two decimal places.

   a) $s = 12.47$ cm   b) $s = 60.53$ cm   c) $s = 29.45$ cm

4. If a central angle of $68°35'$ subtends an arc of a circle of length 47.53 cm, find the radius of the circle. Give your answer in centimeters correct to two decimal places.

5. Suppose point P moves along a circular path with a radius of 3.57 m and center at O. Find the total distance traveled by P if the radial line $\overline{OP}$ sweeps out the given angle. Give two-decimal-place answers.

   a) $257°$ b) $1440°$ c) $9\pi/2$ d) 35π

6. In Problem 5, the point P travels a distance of 47.55 m. Through what angle does $\overline{OP}$ sweep? Give your answer in radians (correct to two decimal places) and in degrees (correct to two decimal places).

7. Find the velocity v of a point on the rim of a wheel of radius 24.37 cm if it is rotating at the given angular velocity:

   a) $\omega = 5.4$ rad/sec

   b) $\omega = 1247$ rad/min

   c) $\omega = 63.5$ rev/min

   d) $\omega = 124$ deg/sec

8. A wheel of diameter 127.48 cm is rotating at a constant rate. Find the angular velocity if a point on the rim is moving at the given speed. Give answers correct to two decimal places in rad/sec and in rev/sec.

   a) $v = 348$ cm/sec

   b) $v = 2.75$ m/sec

9. Find the angular velocity of the minute hand of a clock in each of the following units:

   a) rev/hr   b) rev/min   c) deg/min   d) rad/min

10. Find the angular velocity of the second hand of a watch in

    a) rev/min   b) deg/hr   c) rad/sec

11. If the length of the minute hand of a clock from the pivot point to the tip is 6.5 cm, find the linear velocity of its tip in each of the following units:

    a) cm/hr   b) cm/min   c) cm/sec

12. If the length of the hour hand of a clock from the pivot point to the tip is 5.2 cm, find how far its tip will travel in the given time:

    a) 2 hr   b) 3 hr 40 min   c) 16 hr 32 min

13. Find the linear velocity of the tip of a propeller blade that is 2.48 m from the pivot point and is rotating at 640 rev/min. Express your answer in m/min correct to two decimal places.

14. The length of the minute hand of a clock is 8.5 cm and the length of the hour hand is 6.1 cm. Give answers in meters and find the ratio of the distance in (a) to that in (b). Give two-decimal-place answers.

    a) How far will the tip of the minute hand travel in a year? Assume 365 days in a year.

    b) How far will the tip of the hour hand travel in a year?

15. Assume that the Earth is spherical with radius 6400 km and that its period of rotation about an axis passing through the north and south poles is 24 hours. How fast is a point on the equator moving in km/hr due to rotation?

16. A *trundle wheel* is an instrument used to measure distance (Fig. 1.13). It consists of a wheel pivoted at one end of the handle, so that it can turn freely. The operator holds the other end of the handle and rolls the wheel (without slipping) along the path whose distance is to be measured. A *meter trundle wheel* is one whose circumference is equal to one meter. Suppose Diane wishes to measure the length of a Logan city block. She rolls her meter trundle the length of the block and counts 196 clicks (indicating 196 revolutions). She moves at a constant speed and it takes her 3 minutes and 36 seconds. Give two-decimal-place answers.

Figure 1.13

a) What is the length of the block in meters?

b) What is her linear velocity?

c) What is the angular velocity of the wheel in rev/sec; in rad/sec?

17. A satellite travels around the Earth and makes one revolution every 4.5 hours. Assuming that the orbit is a circle of radius 7240 km, find how fast it is traveling in km/hr. Give answer correct to the nearest whole number.

18. A circle has a radius 17.3 cm. Find the area (correct to two decimal places) of the sector of the circle with the given central angle:

    a) 24°   b) 37°53′   c) $\frac{\pi}{3}$ d) 3.56

19. If the radius of a circle is 1.26 m and the area of a sector is 0.8764 m², find the central angle (to two decimal places) in

    a) radians   b) degrees

20. What is the measure in radians of the smaller angle between the hour and minute hands of a clock at

    a) 1:15 A.M.   b) 1:45 P.M.

21. A pulley of diameter 31.64 cm is driven by a belt. If 32 meters of belt passes around the pulley (without slipping), through what angle does a radial line $\overline{OP}$ on the pulley turn? Express the answer (correct to two decimal places) in

    a) degree measure   b) radian measure

22. In Problem 21, suppose it takes 24 seconds for the 32 meters of belt to pass around the pulley; find the angular velocity of the pulley in

    a) deg/sec   b) rad/sec

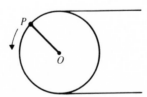

Figure 1.14

23. Assume that the Earth travels about the Sun in a circular orbit (actually it is a nearly circular ellipse), and the distance between the Earth and Sun is 149 million kilometers. A radial line is drawn from the Sun through the Earth.

   a) What is the angle (in radians) swept out by that line in a day? (Assume that it takes 365.25 days to travel once around the Sun.)

   b) What is the angular velocity of the radial line in radians per hour?

   c) What is the linear velocity of the Earth in kilometers per hour?

24. A treadle sewing machine is driven by two wheels with a belt passing around them, as shown in Fig. 1.15. The sewing machine used by Motl, the tailor, has the following measurements: the diameter of the larger wheel is 31 cm, while that of the smaller wheel is 7 cm. If Motl treadles his machine at a fixed rate, so that in 45 seconds the larger wheel turns through 63 revolutions, find the angular velocity of each wheel (assume the belt does not slip). Express each answer in

   a) rev/sec   b) rad/sec

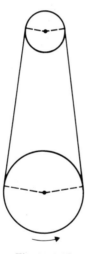

Figure 1.15

25. Using the information of Problem 24, find the linear velocity of point P on the belt, in centimeters per second. Also determine, how far point P travels when the sewing machine is operated at the given rate for 8 seconds.

26. If the area of a given sector of a circle is 265.78 cm² and the length of the arc is 36.3 cm, find

   a) the radius of the circle   b) the central angle of the sector

27. If the area of a circular sector is 24.32 m² and the radius is 6.47 m, find the length of arc bounding the sector. Give answer in meters correct to two decimal places.

28. The front wheel of a tricycle is 51.4 cm in diameter and each of the rear wheels has a diameter of 23.5 cm. If the tricycle travels along a straight path for a distance of 48 m, through how many revolutions will each wheel turn? Also express each answer in number of radians the wheel will turn.

29. The time is between one and two o'clock and the angle measured clockwise from the hour hand to the minute hand is 64°15′. What time is it? Give the answer correct to the nearest minute.

30. a) A certain pickup truck comes factory equipped with standard-size tires. The diameter of such a tire is 29 in. The speedometer is calibrated with this size tire. If the truck travels for 1 hr at a constant speed with the speedometer reading 55 mi/hr, how many revolutions will a wheel make?

    b) The owner of the truck prefers larger tires and replaces the originals with tires of 30.75 in. diameter. Now he travels for 1 hr at a constant speed with the speedometer reading 55 mi/hr (thus each wheel will make the same number of revolutions as in (a)). How far does he go during that hour? By how many miles per hour is he violating the 55 mi/hr speed limit?

31. A spherical water tank is located 0.8 km from point P, and the angle it subtends at P is measured to be 17.5 minutes. (See Fig. 1.16.) Using this information, obtain a reasonable approximation to the volume of the tank in cubic meters.

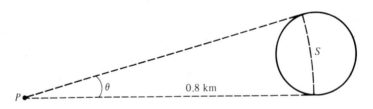

Figure 1.16

Hint. The diagram shows a vertical plane through the center of the tank and P. Assume that P is the center of a circle of radius 0.8 km and that θ is a central angle of measure 17.5′. Calculate the arc length S and use this as an approximation to the diameter D of the tank. The formula for calculating the volume of a sphere is $V = \left(\pi/6\right)D^3$.

REVIEW EXERCISE

1. Express the following angles in decimal number of degrees correct to two decimal places:

    a) 37°42′   b) −321°17′40″   c) 1.43 rad   d) $15\pi/23$ rad

2. Give the following angles in radian measure correct to two decimal places:

    a) 175°   b) 23°16′   c) 327.48°   d) 137°16′37″

3. Make a sketch illustrating the given angles (a reasonable approximation is sufficient):

    a) 150°   b) –250°   c) $2\pi/3$ d) $7\pi/5$ e) 3.58   f) 8.4

4. The central angle of a circular sector is 64°27′. If the radius of the circle is 24.6 cm, find the length of arc of the sector in centimeters correct to one decimal place.

5. In Problem 4, find the area of the circular sector in square centimeters correct to one decimal place.

6. The measures of three angles α, β, and γ are: $\alpha = 0.935$, $\beta = 5\pi/17$, $\gamma = 3\pi/10$. Determine which is the largest angle and which is the smallest angle.

7. The measures of four angles α, β, γ, and θ are:

    $\alpha = 126°27′$, $\beta = 126.43°$, $\gamma = 2.21$, $\theta = 7\pi/10$.

    Order these according to size from the smallest to the largest.

8. An arc of a circle of radius 37.63 m has length equal to 12.37 m. Find the measure of the central angle subtended by this arc in degree measure correct to the nearest minute.

9. Find the area of the circular sector described in Problem 8. Give answer in square meters correct to two decimal places.

10. Determine the smaller angle between the hour and minute hands of a clock when the time is 3:45. Express your answer in degree measure correct to two decimal places.

11. The area of a circular sector is 35.61 cm² and its central angle is 34.63°. Find the length of arc of the sector in centimeters correct to two decimal places.

12. A particle travels in a circular path of radius 3.45 cm at a constant speed. It takes 1 min 36 sec to make 84.75 revolutions.

    a) Find its angular velocity in radians per second.

    b) If it travels at the given rate for 3 min 20 sec, what is the total distance traveled? Give answer in centimeters correct to two decimal places.

13. If both the radius and central angle of a circular sector are doubled, by what factor is the area increased?

14. The diagram illustrates part of a machine in which the larger wheel drives the smaller wheel by a belt around the two wheels (Fig. 1.17). The diameter of the

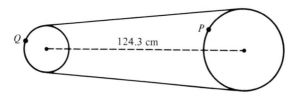

Figure 1.17

larger wheel is 63.4 cm, while that of the smaller wheel is 25.8 cm; the distance between their centers is 124.3 cm.

a) If the larger wheel rotates at a constant rate of 250 rev/min, find the rate at which the smaller wheel rotates (in rev/min) correct to the nearest whole number.

b) If P is a point on the circumference of the larger wheel, what is the linear speed of P in m/min? Give answer to one decimal place.

c) If Q is a point on the circumference of the smaller wheel, find the linear velocity of Q in m/min correct to one decimal place.

d) If T is a point on the belt, how far will T travel in 1.5 minutes? Give answer in meters.

15. A circular pizza is cut into four pieces by making two straight cuts across through the center. Two of the pieces are smaller, each having a central angle 10° narrower than that of each larger piece. Find the ratio of the area of the larger piece to that of the smaller piece.

CHAPTER TWO

TRIGONOMETRIC FUNCTIONS

2.1 TRIGONOMETRIC FUNCTIONS FOR ACUTE ANGLES

In this chapter we introduce six basic trigonometric functions. We define these in two phases: first for angles whose measures are between 0° and 90° (acute angles), and then in Section 2.4 we extend these definitions to the general case of angles of any measure.

At this point the student may profit from a review of functions as studied in algebra. There the idea of a function was introduced as a correspondence between elements of two sets (usually sets of numbers); the first set is called the *domain D* of the function and the second set the *range R* of the function. If f denotes the function (in which the rule of correspondence is frequently given by an equation, or by a verbal statement, or a table), then for each element x of D there is a single corresponding element of R denoted by $f(x)$. That is, every element x of D has a unique mate $f(x)$ in R. The symbol x is called the *independent variable*, while $f(x)$ is called the *dependent variable*, and we usually write $y = f(x)$.

For example, equation $y = x^2$, along with the domain (the set of real numbers) describes a function, since for each real number x there is exactly one value of y (the square of x) paired with it. The range of this function is the set of nonnegative real numbers.

We now define the six trigonometric functions—the building blocks of trigonometry. These functions are basic and the student should master them.

In mathematics, when a particular function occurs frequently, it is given a special name for easy reference (rather than using letters such as f, g, etc.). The names of the functions that we are about to introduce are: sine and cosine, tangent and cotangent, secant and cosecant; these are abbreviated as sin, cos, tan, cot, sec, csc, respectively.

To define these functions, we consider a *right triangle* with standard notation, as shown in Fig. 2.1.

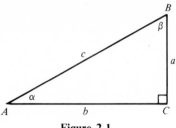

Figure 2.1

The two acute angles are denoted by α and β, and the two sides (or *legs*) opposite these angles are labeled a and b, correspondingly. The side opposite the right angle (c in the figure) is called the *hypotenuse*. A special property of right triangles involving the legs and the hypotenuse is stated in the *Pythagorean theorem:*

$$a^2 + b^2 = c^2.$$

Note that we take liberties with language and notation here as well as throughout the text. For example, we say "side b" when we really mean that the letter b represents the length of the side opposite angle β.

We now give the following definitions, where "opp(α)" and "adj(α)" represent "side opposite" and "side adjacent angle α":

$$\sin \alpha = \frac{\text{opp }(\alpha)}{\text{hyp}} = \frac{a}{c}, \quad \cos \alpha = \frac{\text{adj }(\alpha)}{\text{hyp}} = \frac{b}{c}, \quad \tan \alpha = \frac{\text{opp }(\alpha)}{\text{adj }(\alpha)} = \frac{a}{b},$$

$$\cot \alpha = \frac{\text{adj }(\alpha)}{\text{opp }(\alpha)} = \frac{b}{a}, \quad \sec \alpha = \frac{\text{hyp}}{\text{adj }(\alpha)} = \frac{c}{b}, \quad \csc \alpha = \frac{\text{hyp}}{\text{opp }(\alpha)} = \frac{c}{a}.$$

Similarly for angle β we have:

$$\sin \beta = \frac{\text{opp }(\beta)}{\text{hyp}} = \frac{b}{c}, \quad \cos \beta = \frac{\text{adj }(\beta)}{\text{hyp}} = \frac{a}{c}, \quad \tan \beta = \frac{\text{opp }(\beta)}{\text{adj }(\beta)} = \frac{b}{a},$$

$$\cot \beta = \frac{\text{adj }(\beta)}{\text{opp }(\beta)} = \frac{a}{b}, \quad \sec \beta = \frac{\text{hyp}}{\text{adj }(\beta)} = \frac{c}{a}, \quad \csc \beta = \frac{\text{hyp}}{\text{opp }(\beta)} = \frac{c}{b}.$$

The following observations can be made from the above definitions:

1. There are many right triangles which contain a given angle, such as α in Fig. 2.1, and so it may appear that the above definitions depend upon the particular right triangle used. However, this is not the case since we recall from geometry that any two such triangles are similar and the ratios of corresponding sides are always equal. For example, in Fig. 2.2 we have two similar right triangles, and so $a_1/c_1 = a_2/c_2$. Thus $\sin \alpha$ is equal to a_1/c_1 or a_2/c_2.

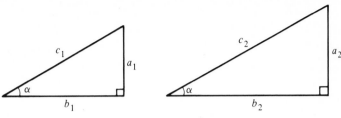

Figure 2.2

2. It should be clear that the definitions given above describe six functions. For example, to each acute angle the sine function attributes a unique real number a/c. The situation is similar for each of the other five relations.

3. There is an obvious reciprocal relationship between pairs of the six functions. For example, $\csc \alpha = c/a$ and $\sin \alpha = a/c$, therefore $\csc \alpha = 1/\sin \alpha$. Similarly the sec, cos and cot, tan functions are reciprocals of each other:

$$\csc \alpha = \frac{1}{\sin \alpha}, \qquad \sec \alpha = \frac{1}{\cos \alpha}, \qquad \cot \alpha = \frac{1}{\tan \alpha}.$$

4. We know from geometry that $\beta = 90° - \alpha$. Since $\cos \alpha$ and $\sin \beta$ are both equal to b/c, then we have $\sin \beta = \cos \alpha$, or $\sin (90° - \alpha) = \cos \alpha$. Thus we have complementary-angle identities:

$$\sin(90° - \alpha) = \cos \alpha, \qquad \cos(90° - \alpha) = \sin \alpha, \qquad \tan(90° - \alpha) = \cot \alpha,$$
$$\cot(90° - \alpha) = \tan \alpha, \qquad \sec(90° - \alpha) = \csc \alpha, \qquad \csc(90° - \alpha) = \sec \alpha.$$

5. The domain of each of the six functions is a set of angles (actually, measures of angles) defined as

$$D = \{\theta \,|\, 0° < \theta < 90°\}.$$

The range of each function is a subset of the real numbers; for example, the range of the sine and cosine functions is $\{y \,|\, 0 < y < 1\}$, while the range of the tangent and cotangent functions is $\{y \,|\, y > 0\}$, and that of the secant and cosecant functions is $\{y \,|\, y > 1\}$. These statements should be intuitively clear from the definitions of the six functions.

We remind the student that the above statements are limited to the special case we are considering, that of acute angles. In Section 2.4 we shall extend the above definitions to include angles of any measure.

1. Trigonometric Functions for Special Angles: $30°, 45°, 60°$

There are two right triangles in which the sides are related in a simple manner, and so the trigonometric functions for the angles of these triangles can be expressed in exact form. The student is reminded of the following properties encountered in the study of geometry.

1. If one angle of a right triangle is 45°, then the other is also 45°, and the triangle is *isosceles.* Therefore the lengths of the two sides are equal. If both are taken to be one unit in length, as shown in Fig. 2.3(a), then by the Pythagorean theorem the hypotenuse will have length $\sqrt{1^2 + 1^2} = \sqrt{2}$. This triangle can be used to find the trigonometric functions of 45°. For example,

$$\sin\ 45° = \frac{1}{\sqrt{2}} = \frac{1 \cdot \sqrt{2}}{\sqrt{2} \cdot \sqrt{2}} = \frac{\sqrt{2}}{2}.$$

Thus $\sin\ 45° = \sqrt{2}/2$. Using the calculator to evaluate $\sqrt{2}/2$, we get $\sin\ 45° = 0.7071$ (to four decimal places). We say that $\sqrt{2}/2$ is an exact form for $\sin\ 45°$, while 0.7071 is a decimal approximation.

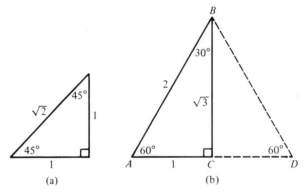

Figure 2.3

2. In a right triangle with one angle equal to 30° and the other 60°, the hypotenuse is twice as long as the shorter side (the side opposite the 30° angle). This property can be seen from Fig. 2.2(b), where triangle ABD is equilateral and triangles ACB and DCB are congruent. Thus if we take the length of the hypotenuse as 2, then the side opposite the 30° angle must be 1. By the Pythagorean theorem, the length of the other side is $\sqrt{2^2 - 1^2} = \sqrt{3}$. Using right triangle ABC we can find the trigonometric function values for 30° and for 60°. For example, $\sin\ 30° = 1/2$ and $\sin\ 60° = \sqrt{3}/2$ in exact form, while $\sin\ 60° = 0.8660$ is a decimal approximation correct to four places.

2. Exact Form vs. Decimal Form

In many problems throughout this textbook the student is asked to express numerical answers in *exact form* or in *decimal form correct to a given number of places.* In general, the exact form is obtained by applying definitions or basic results, while the decimal answer is a rounded-off approximation of the exact form. In most cases, answers obtained by using a calculator are approximate decimal numbers with accuracy limited by the capacity of the machine.

Examples

⚠ If θ is an angle for which $\sin \theta = \frac{1}{3}$, find $\tan \theta$ and $\sin (90° - \theta)$:

    a) in exact form   b) in decimal form (to four places)

Solution. Consider a right triangle with θ as an acute angle. Since $\sin \theta = \frac{1}{3}$, we can use the side opposite θ as one unit and the hypotenuse as three units, as shown in Fig. 2.4. The length of the third side will be $\sqrt{3^2 - 1^2} = \sqrt{8} = 2\sqrt{2}$.

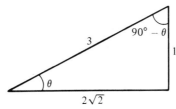

Figure 2.4

Therefore,

    a) $\tan \theta = \dfrac{\text{opp } (\theta)}{\text{adj } (\theta)} = \dfrac{1}{2\sqrt{2}} = \dfrac{\sqrt{2}}{4}$,

       $\sin (90° - \theta) = \dfrac{\text{opp } (90° - \theta)}{\text{hyp}} = \dfrac{2\sqrt{2}}{3}$

    b) $\tan \theta = 0.3536$, $\sin (90° - \theta) = 0.9428$ ▌

⚠ In a right triangle, $a = 5.24$ cm and $c = 16.36$ cm (Fig. 2.5). Find:

    a) the length of side b (to two decimal places),

    b) $\tan \alpha$ (remember, α is the angle opposite side a).

Figure 2.5

Solution.

a) From the Pythagorean theorem,

$$b = \sqrt{16.36^2 - 5.24^2} = 15.50 \text{ cm}.$$

b) $\tan \alpha = \dfrac{a}{b} = \dfrac{5.24}{\sqrt{16.36^2 - 5.24^2}} = 0.3381.$ ∎

3 If $\sin \theta = 0.47$, find the remaining five trigonometric functions of θ (correct to two decimal places):

Solution. Since $\sin \theta = 0.47/1$, we can use a right triangle with hypotenuse 1 and side opposite θ as 0.47 (Fig. 2.6). Let x represent the length of the adjacent side; then $x = \sqrt{1^2 - (0.47)^2} = 0.8827.$ Thus,

$$\cos \theta = 0.88 \qquad \tan \theta = 0.53 \qquad \cot \theta = 1.88$$
$$\sec \theta = 1.13 \qquad \csc \theta = 2.13$$

∎

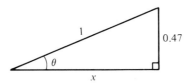

Figure 2.6

4 In a right triangle we are given that $c = 15.72$ and $\sin \beta = 3/5$ (Fig. 2.7). Find (correct to two decimal places):

a) the length of side a b) $\tan \alpha$

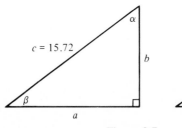

Figure 2.7

Solution.

a) Since $\cos \beta = a/15.72$, we have $a = 15.72 \cos \beta$. Thus we need to determine $\cos \beta$.

Since $\sin \beta = 3/5$, we draw a second triangle as shown in Fig. 2.7, in which we first determine $x = \sqrt{5^2 - 3^2} = 4$. From this triangle we have $\cos \beta = 4/5$. Therefore,

$$a = 15.72 \cos \beta = (15.72)\left(\frac{4}{5}\right) = 12.58.$$

b) From the second triangle we have: $\tan \alpha = 4/3 = 1.33.$ ∎

EXERCISE 2.1

1. Determine the following and give answers in exact form:
   a) $\cos 45°$ b) $\tan 45°$ c) $\cot 45°$ d) $\sec 45°$ e) $\csc 45°$

2. Complete the following table by entering in exact form the function values for the given angles:

	sin	cos	tan	cot	sec	csc
30°						
60°						

3. If $\cos \theta = 3/5$, find in exact form
   a) $\tan \theta$ b) $\cot \theta$ c) $\csc \theta$

4. If $\tan \alpha = 4/3$, find in exact form
   a) $\sin \alpha$ b) $\cos \alpha$ c) $\sec \alpha$

5. If $\sin \theta = 3/4$, find the answers correct to two decimal places:
   a) $\cos \theta$ b) $\tan \theta$

6. If $\sin \alpha = 2/7$, determine each of the following in exact form:
   a) $\cos \alpha$ b) $\sin (90° - \alpha)$ c) $\tan \alpha$ d) $\sec(90° - \alpha)$

7. If $\cos \theta = 8/17$, find in exact form:
   a) $\tan \theta$ b) $\tan (90° - \theta)$ c) $\sec(90° - \theta)$ d) $\csc \theta$

8. If $\sec \theta = 1.5$, find in exact form:
   a) $\sin \theta$ b) $\tan \theta$ c) $\cos(90° - \theta)$

9. If $\cos \theta = 0.63$, find the remaining five trigonometric functions of θ. Give results correct to two decimal places.

10. A cat stranded on a telephone pole has found secure footing at a point where the guy wire meets the pole. If the distance from the foot of the pole to the foot of the guy wire is 3 m and the wire makes an angle of 60° with the ground, how high above the ground is the cat?

11. In a right triangle $a = 2.36$, $b = 5.63$. Find (to two places)
    a) the length of c b) $\sin \alpha$
    c) $\cot \beta$

12. In a right triangle we are given that $c = 6.47$ and $\sin \alpha = 5/17$. Find correct to two decimal places:
    a) the length of a b) the length of b c) $\tan \beta$

13. Find the height of the Washington Monument if it casts a shadow of 290 m when the sun is 30° above the horizon. Give the answer to the nearest meter.

14. Lighthouse BC is located on the edge of a cliff, as shown in Fig. 2.8. From point A (which is 67 m from the base of the cliff D) angles α and β are measured and found to be 60° and 45°, respectively. Find the height h of the lighthouse.

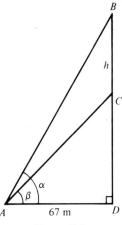

Figure 2.8

2.2. USING THE CALCULATOR TO FIND VALUES OF TRIGONOMETRIC FUNCTIONS*

In the preceding section we saw examples of special angles for which we could evaluate the trigonometric functions in exact form. In the general situation, however, this is not possible. It therefore becomes necessary to find other means than ratios of sides of right triangles to determine the values of the trigonometric functions. For example, if we want to determine sin 37°, we could draw a right triangle with a 37° angle, as shown in Fig. 2.9; then $\sin 37° = a/c$.

However, there is no simple relationship between a, b, and c, as in the case for 45° or 30° − 60° right triangles. We could measure the lengths a and c, and evaluate a/c, but such a technique could produce only an approximation, which would probably be very crude.

In the study of calculus the student is introduced to methods (infinite series) for evaluating trigonometric functions accurately to any desired number

_____
* See Appendix A for basic calculator instruction.

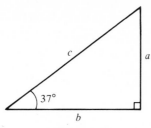

Figure 2.9

of decimal places. Earlier textbooks in trigonometry included several pages of tables listing such values (usually to four or five decimal places), and the student was expected to master the art of reading these tables. With the availability of the scientific hand-held calculator, such tables are no longer necessary. Each calculator has built into it the capacity to quickly evaluate any trigonometric function accurately to several (usually seven to nine) decimal places. Since tables are not necessary, there is no longer a need to study interpolation techniques to evaluate trigonometric functions for angles not included in tables.

All scientific calculators have keys labeled $\boxed{\text{sin}}$, $\boxed{\text{cos}}$, $\boxed{\text{tan}}$. Also, there is a key (or keys) that will allow the operator to put the calculator in degree, radian, or grad mode. The owner's manual which comes with the purchase of a calculator describes this feature and should be consulted to make certain it is understood.

To illustrate the use of the calculator for determining values of trigonometric functions we consider some examples.

Examples

△1 Evaluate sin 37°.

Solution. First be certain that your calculator is in degree mode. Then merely press the following keys: 3, 7, $\boxed{\text{sin}}$. The display will read 0.60 for many calculators, and if greater decimal accuracy is desired, the operator can have the calculator display a larger number of decimal digits (the owner's manual has instructions for doing this). Thus we can get, accurate to nine decimal places, sin 37° = 0.601815023.￭

△2 Evaluate cot 64°.

Solution. The calculator does not have a key labeled $\boxed{\text{cot}}$. However, as we observed in Section 2.1, the cotangent function is the reciprocal of the tangent, and so we have cot 64° = 1/tan 64°. Therefore, with the calculator in degree mode, press the following keys: 6, 4, $\boxed{\text{tan}}$, $\boxed{\text{1/x}}$. The display will give cot 64° = 0.487732589. The student should note at this point that 1/tan 64°

and tan(1/64)° are not equal. That is, the 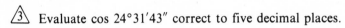 key should be pressed after the ⏍tan⏍ key.

Alternative solution. As was pointed out in Section 2.1, cot $\theta = \tan(90° - \theta)$, and so we have cot 64° = tan(90°− 64°) = tan 26°. Thus pressing the keys 2, 6, ⏍tan⏍ gives cot 64° = 0.487732589.   ▌

△3 Evaluate cos 24°31′43″ correct to five decimal places.

Solution. We first convert 24°31′43″ into a decimal number of degrees as follows:

$$24°31'43'' = \left(24 + \frac{31}{60} + \frac{43}{3600}\right)°.$$

Be sure your calculator is in degree mode and carry out the following sequence of steps: evaluate 24 + 31/60 + 43/3600; then press ⏍cos⏍ and the answer will appear in the display. That is, cos 24°31′43″ = 0.90975.   ▌

△4 Evaluate sin 1.2 correct to four decimal places.

Solution. Note that sin 1.2 means sine of 1.2 rad. Place the calculator in radian mode; then press 1.2, ⏍sin⏍, and the value will appear in the display:

$$\sin\ 1.2 = 0.9320.$$ ▌

△5 Evaluate tan $(3\pi/11)$ correct to eight decimal places.

Solution. Place the calculator in radian mode; calculate $3\pi/11$ (use the ⏍π⏍ key on the calculator), then press ⏍tan⏍ : tan $(3\pi/11) = 1.15406152$.   ▌

EXERCISE 2.2

In each of the following use a calculator to evaluate the given function and express your answer correct to four decimal places:

1. sin 28°	**2.** tan 49°	**3.** cos 72°
4. cot 78°	**5.** sec 35°	**6.** csc 17°
7. sin 43°21′	**8.** sec 57°16′	**9.** cos 12°37′41″
10. sin 0.4	**11.** cos 1.25	**12.** tan $\pi/3$
13. cot $3\pi/8$	**14.** sec $\pi/4$	**15.** tan $\pi/4$

In each of the following use a calculator to evaluate the given expression. Give answers correct to two decimal places. (If necessary, see Appendix A for a review.)

16.   (2.48) sin 73°16′   **17.** $\dfrac{3.56 \sin\ 24°17'}{\sin\ 47°21'}$

18. $\dfrac{2 \tan 35°12'}{1 - (\tan 35°12')^2}$ 19. 65.48 csc 43°18'

20. $\tan \dfrac{3\pi}{13}$ 21. sec 1.47

22. $\cos \dfrac{7\pi}{17}$ 23. $\dfrac{8.54 \sin (5\pi/11)}{\sin (3\pi/7)}$

24. $(\sin 23°48')^2 + (\cos 23°48')^2$ 25. sec $(31°12'36'')$

26. cot $(72°15'41'')$ 27. $\dfrac{1}{\csc (3\pi/8)} + \dfrac{1}{\sec (3\pi/8)}$

28. $\sin \left(\dfrac{1 + \sqrt{2}}{5} \right)$ 29. $\sin 37° \cos 56° - \sin 56° \cos 37°$

30. $\left(\dfrac{1 + \sqrt{5}}{3} \right) \sin \left(\dfrac{5\pi}{12} \right)$

31. How tall is a flagpole that casts a shadow of 23 m when the sun is 37° above the horizon?

32. The distance from the base to the top of the Leaning Tower of Pisa is 54.6 m and it makes an angle of 84°45' with the horizontal. How far does the top overhang the base?

2.3 ANGLES IN STANDARD POSITION

In Section 2.1 we defined six trigonometric functions which applied to angles with a measure between 0° and 90°. We are interested in extending those definitions to angles of any size. In order to do this, it is convenient to use a coordinate system for labeling points in the plane. We first recall some properties of rectangular coordinates.

The plane is divided into four regions (called *quadrants*) by a horizontal line (*x*-axis) and a vertical line (*y*-axis), as shown in Fig. 2.10(a). The point of intersection of these two lines is called the *origin*. We associate points on each of the axes with the set of real numbers in a one-to-one manner, the positive numbers corresponding to the points on the *x*-axis located to the right of the origin (called the *positive x-axis*) and the negative numbers corresponding to points to the left of the origin (called the *negative x-axis*). Similarly for the *y*-axis, up is the positive direction and down is negative.

Each point *P* in the plane can now be identified by a pair of names (a first name and a second name) that are labeled (*x*,*y*), where *x* denotes the directed distance of *P* from the *y*-axis and *y* is the directed distance from the *x*-axis. This gives a one-to-one correspondence between points of the plane and ordered pairs of real numbers. For example, the ordered pair (−3, 2) indicates a point that is three units to the left of the *y*-axis and two units above the *x*-axis. Similarly for the other points plotted in Fig. 2.10(b).

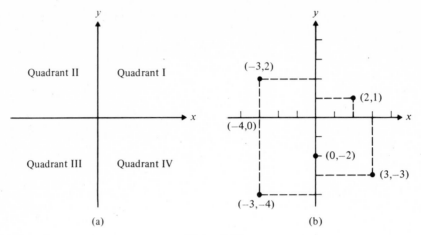

Figure 2.10

1.   The Distance Formula

Let $P : (x_1, y_1)$ and $Q : (x_2, y_2)$ be any two points in the plane and let d represent the distance from P to Q (Fig. 2.11). Then it follows from the Pythagorean theorem that $d^2 = (x_2 - x_1)^2 + (y_2 - y_1)^2$. Thus,

$$d = \sqrt{(x_2 - x_1)^2 + (y_2 - y_1)^2}.$$

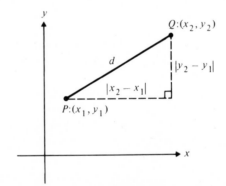

Figure 2.11

2. Angles in Standard Position

In order to define the trigonometric functions for angles of any size, it is convenient to consider angles in a standard position. We shall say that *an angle is in standard position* when the vertex of the angle coincides with the origin of a rectangular coordinate system and the initial side coincides with the positive x-axis. Figure 2.12 is an illustration of angles in standard position. Angles α, β, and γ are positive and δ is negative.

When the terminal side of an angle in standard position is located in a given quadrant, we say that the angle is in that quadrant. For example, in Fig. 2.12, angle α is in quadrant I, β is in quadrant III, γ is in quadrant II,

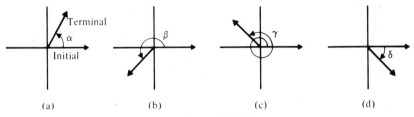

Figure 2.12

and δ is in quadrant IV. If the terminal side of angle θ coincides with an axis, then θ is called a *quadrantal angle* and is not said to be in any quadrant.

When two angles are placed in standard position (in a given coordinate system) and their terminal sides coincide, we say that the *two angles are coterminal*. For example, $\alpha = 45°$ and $\beta = 405°$ are coterminal since $405° = 360° + 45°$. Similarly, $210°$ and $-150°$ are coterminal since $210° = 360° + (-150°)$; angles θ and $\theta + k \cdot 360°$, where k is any integer, are coterminal angles.

Examples

⚠ For the following angles, draw a figure with the given angle shown in standard position. Use a protractor if it is available; otherwise, an approximate free-hand sketch is sufficient.

    a) 64°   b) $-155°$ c) 248°   d) 450°   e) $-180°$

Solution. See Fig. 2.13.

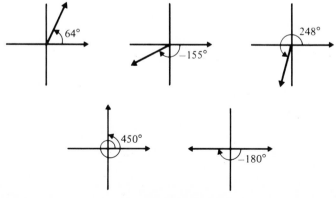

Figure 2.13

⚠️2 Sketch the given angles in standard position:

    a) $\frac{\pi}{2}$ b) $-\frac{3\pi}{4}$ c) 3.05   d) −5   e) 7.5

Solution. Note that $\pi/2 = 1.57$, $\pi = 3.14$, $3\pi/2 = 4.71$, $2\pi = 6.28$, $5\pi/2 = 7.85$. Thus:

    c) $\pi/2 < 3.05 < \pi$, and so angle 3.05 is in quadrant II;

    d) $-2\pi < -5 < -3\pi/2$, so angle -5 is in I;

    e) $2\pi < 7.5 < 5\pi/2$, so angle 7.5 is in I. (See Fig. 2.14.)

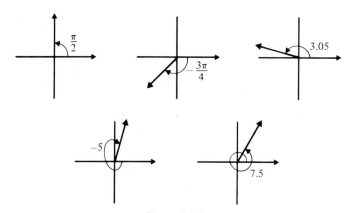

Figure 2.14

⚠️3 For each of the following determine the quadrant in which the given angle is located:

    a) 137°   b) −650°   c) $17\pi/11$ d) 6.28   e) 450°

Solution.

    a) Quadrant II, since $90° < 137° < 180°$.

    b) Quadrant I, since $-650° = -360° - 290°$.

    c) Using a calculator, we get $17\pi/11 = 4.86$, which is between $3\pi/2$ and 2π. Therefore $17\pi/11$ is in quadrant IV.

    d) Quadrant IV, since $3\pi/2 < 6.28 < 2\pi$.

    e) The terminal side coincides with the positive *y*-axis; therefore 450° is a quadrantal angle.

⚠️4 Draw the angle of measure $-48°$ in standard position (see Fig. 2.15); then draw the smallest positive angle θ that has the same terminal side as $-48°$ and determine its measure.

Solution. $\theta = 360° - 48° = 312°$.

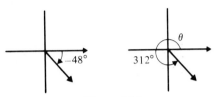

Figure 2.15

⚠️5 Follow the instructions of Example 4 for the angle of measure -2.48. (See Fig. 2.16.)

Solution. $\theta = 2\pi - 2.48 = 2(3.14) - 2.48 = 6.28 - 2.48 = 3.80$ (to two decimal places).

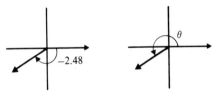

Figure 2.16

⚠️6 Find two angles coterminal with $-4\pi/3$.

Solution.

$$-\frac{4\pi}{3} + 2\pi = \frac{2\pi}{3} \quad \text{and} \quad -\frac{4\pi}{3} - 2\pi = -\frac{10\pi}{3}$$

are coterminal with $-4\pi/3$.

⚠️7 Determine all angles coterminal with $120°$.

Solution. If we add or subtract any multiple of $360°$ to $120°$ we get an angle coterminal with $120°$. Therefore, the set of all angles coterminal with $120°$ is $\{120° + k \cdot 360° \mid k$ is an integer$\}$.

EXERCISE 2.3

When drawing an angle is required, use a protractor if it is available; otherwise a reasonable freehand sketch is sufficient.

1. Draw a figure illustrating the given angles in standard position:

   a) 40°   b) 220°   c) −220°   d) 725°   e) − 460°

2. Draw a figure illustrating the given angles in standard position:

   a) $\frac{5\pi}{4}$ b) 3.41   c) −1.80   d) 8.8   e) $-\frac{17\pi}{11}$

3. Determine the quadrant in which the given angles lie (that is, the quadrant in which the terminal side is located):

   a) 37°   b) 335°   c) −125°   d) 580°   e) −480°

4. Determine the quadrant in which the given angles lie:

   a) $-\frac{3\pi}{4}$ b) $\frac{7\pi}{3}$ c) 3.56   d) 8.47   e) −5.40

5. Draw a figure of the given angles in standard position. Then draw the smallest positive angle that has the same terminal side and determine its measure:

   a) −100°   b) 540°   c) −540°   d) $-\frac{3\pi}{4}$ e) −4.32

6. For each of the given pairs of angles, determine whether or not the second one is coterminal with the first one:

   a) 60°, 240°   b) −45°, 315°   c) $-\frac{3\pi}{4}, \frac{5\pi}{4}$

   d) $\pi, -\pi$ e) 30°, 750°   f) $\frac{3\pi}{2}, -\frac{3\pi}{2}$

7. Find three angles coterminal with $\theta = 90°$.

8. Find three angles coterminal with $\theta = -\pi/6$.

9. Determine the set of all angles coterminal with $\theta = -2\pi/3$.

10. Determine the set of all angles coterminal with $\theta = 30°$.

11. Find the set of all angles coterminal with an angle whose terminal side passes through the given point:

    a) (1, 1)   b) (−3,−3)   c) (−1, $\sqrt{3}$)

12. Determine the set of all angles coterminal with the angle in standard position whose terminal side passes through the given point:

    a) (0, 3)   b) (0,−5)   c) (5, 0)   d) (−2.3, 0)

2.4 TRIGONOMETRIC FUNCTIONS OF ANGLES OF ANY SIZE

Let θ be an angle in standard position and $P : (x,y)$ be any point (other than the origin) on the terminal side of θ (Fig. 2.17). Let r be the distance from the origin to P; that is, $r = \sqrt{x^2+y^2}$ (r is always a positive number). Draw a perpendicular from P *to the x-axis* and name the point of intersection A; then right triangle PAO is called a *reference triangle* for θ.

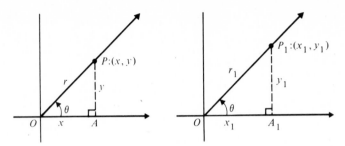

Figure 2.17

We define the six trigonometric functions of θ as follows:

$$\sin \theta = \frac{y}{r}, \qquad \cot \theta = \frac{x}{y},$$
$$\cos \theta = \frac{x}{r}, \qquad \sec \theta = \frac{r}{x}, \qquad (2.1)$$
$$\tan \theta = \frac{y}{x}, \qquad \csc \theta = \frac{r}{y}.$$

Several observations can be made:

1. The above definitions are independent of point P taken on the terminal side. That is, if $P_1 : (x_1, y_1)$ is some other point on the terminal side and $r_1 = \sqrt{x_1^2 + y_1^2}$, then the two right triangles in Fig. 2.17 are similar and hence the ratios of corresponding sides are equal.

2. If θ is an acute angle, the definitions given here agree with those given in Section 2.1.

3. The definitions stated in Eq. (2.1) define six functions; that is, each function associates each given angle θ with a unique real number by the ratio indicated in Eq. (2.1) (whenever this ratio does not involve division by zero).

4. For quadrantal angles the reference triangle becomes a line segment. However, the above definitions are in terms of x, y, r, and so we can use them in that form. For example, for $0°$ we can take the point $(1, 0)$ on the terminal side; then $r = 1$ and we have

$$\sin 0° = \frac{y}{r} = \frac{0}{1} = 0, \qquad \cos 0° = \frac{x}{r} = \frac{1}{1} = 1.$$

5. If the terminal side of θ coincides with the y-axis, then $x = 0$ and $\tan \theta = y/0$ and $\sec \theta = r/0$ are not defined. Similarly if the terminal side of θ coincides with the x-axis, then $y = 0$, and $\cot \theta = x/0$ and $\csc \theta = r/0$ are not defined.

6. From the definitions given in Eq. (2.1) we see that $\sin \theta$ and $\csc \theta$ are reciprocals of each other, $\cos \theta$ and $\sec \theta$ are also reciprocals, and so are $\tan \theta$ and $\cot \theta$. That is,

$$\csc \theta = \frac{1}{\sin \theta}, \qquad \sec \theta = \frac{1}{\cos \theta}, \qquad \cot \theta = \frac{1}{\tan \theta}.$$

7. We note that

$$(\sin \theta)^2 + (\cos \theta)^2 = \left(\frac{y}{r}\right)^2 + \left(\frac{x}{r}\right)^2 = \frac{y^2 + x^2}{r^2} = 1,$$

since $y^2 + x^2 = r^2$; thus for any angle θ we have

$$(\sin \theta)^2 + (\cos \theta)^2 = 1.$$

Examples

⚠1 Suppose θ is an angle in standard position and point $(-3, 4)$ is on the terminal side of θ. Find the values of the six trigonometric functions of θ.

Solution. The diagram in Fig. 2.18 shows a reference triangle for θ, in which point P is taken as $(-3, 4)$, and so $r = \sqrt{(-3)^2 + 4^2} = 5$. Therefore,

$$\sin \theta = \frac{4}{5}, \qquad \tan \theta = \frac{4}{-3}, \qquad \sec \theta = \frac{5}{-3}$$

$$\cos \theta = \frac{-3}{5}, \qquad \cot \theta = \frac{-3}{4}, \qquad \csc \theta = \frac{5}{4}$$

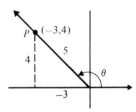

Figure 2.18

⚠2 Evaluate the six trigonometric functions for 315°. Express each answer in exact form and in decimal form (correct to four places).

Solution. In the diagram of Fig. 2.19 we see that the reference triangle for 315° is a 45° right triangle. It is therefore convenient to take $(1, -1)$ as point P, and so $r = \sqrt{1^2 + (-1)^2} = \sqrt{2}$. Thus,

$$\sin 315° = -\frac{1}{\sqrt{2}} = -\frac{\sqrt{2}}{2} \quad \text{(exact form)}.$$

Using the calculator to evaluate $-\sqrt{2}/2$, we get $\sin 315° = -0.7071$ (to four decimal places). Similarly,

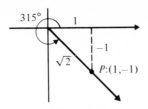

Figure 2.19

$$\cos 315° = \frac{1}{\sqrt{2}} = \frac{\sqrt{2}}{2}, \qquad \cos 315° = 0.7071,$$

$$\tan 315° = \frac{-1}{1} = -1, \qquad \tan 315° = -1.0000,$$

$$\cot 315° = \frac{1}{-1} = -1, \qquad \cot 315° = -1.0000,$$

$$\sec 315° = \frac{\sqrt{2}}{1} = \sqrt{2}, \qquad \sec 315° = 1.4142,$$

$$\csc 315° = \frac{\sqrt{2}}{-1} = -\sqrt{2}, \qquad \csc 315° = -1.4142. \qquad ∎$$

△3 Evaluate $\sin(-2\pi/3)$ and $\tan(-2\pi/3)$. Express answers in exact form.

Solution. Sketch $\theta = -2\pi/3$. The reference triangle for $\theta = -2\pi/3$ is a 30°–60° right triangle, so we can take P as $(-1, -\sqrt{3})$ (see Fig. 2.20). Thus,

$$\sin\left(-\frac{2\pi}{3}\right) = -\frac{\sqrt{3}}{2} \quad \text{and} \quad \tan\left(-\frac{2\pi}{3}\right) = \frac{-\sqrt{3}}{-1} = \sqrt{3}.$$

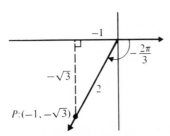

Figure 2.20

Note. In this example, as well as in the following ones, the essential steps leading to the solution are: Using the given information, 1) sketch the angle in standard position (this includes determining the quadrant in which it is located); 2) take a convenient point (x, y) on the terminal side and build a reference triangle (using the Pythagorean theorem as needed, including proper selection of " + " or " – " signs for x and y); 3) use appropriate definitions given in Eq. (2.1).   ∎

⚠4 Evaluate the following (see Fig. 2.21):

   a) sin 180°   b) cos 180°   c) tan 90°   d) sec(−540°)

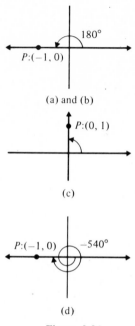

(a) and (b)

(c)

(d)

Figure 2.21

Solution.

   a) Take point P as $(-1, 0)$, so $r = 1$. Then $\sin 180° = y/r = 0/1 = 0$.

   b) Take P as in (a), then $\cos 180° = x/r = -1/1 = -1$.

   c) Let P be $(0,1)$, so $r = 1$. Then $\tan 90° = y/x = 1/0$. Since division by zero is not defined, we say that $\tan 90°$ is not defined.

   d) In the diagram of $-540°$ in standard position, we see that the terminal side coincides with the negative x-axis. Therefore we can take point P as $(-1, 0)$ and so $r = 1$. Thus

$$\sec(-540°) = \frac{r}{x} = \frac{1}{-1} = -1.$$ ∎

⚠5 If angle θ is in the second quadrant (the terminal side of θ is in quadrant II) and $\cos \theta = -0.7$, find the other five trigonometric functions of θ (see Fig. 2.22). Express each result

   a) in exact form   b) in decimal form correct to three places

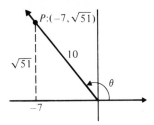

Figure 2.22

Solution. Since θ is in the second quadrant and $\cos \theta = -0.7 = -7/10$, we get a reference triangle as shown in Fig. 2.22 by taking $x = -7$, $r = 10$ (then $y = \sqrt{10^2 - (-7)^2} = \sqrt{51}$. Using definitions given in Eq. (2.1), we have:

a) $\sin \theta = \dfrac{\sqrt{51}}{10}$ $\tan \theta = \dfrac{\sqrt{51}}{-7}$ $\cot \theta = \dfrac{-7}{\sqrt{51}} = \dfrac{-7\sqrt{51}}{51}$

    $\sec \theta = \dfrac{10}{-7}$ $\csc \theta = \dfrac{10\sqrt{51}}{51}$

b) Using the calculator to evaluate the expressions in (a), we get

    $\sin \theta = 0.714$ $\tan \theta = -1.020$ $\cot \theta = -0.980$

    $\sec \theta = -1.429$ $\csc \theta = 1.400$ ∎

6   If θ is an angle in the third quadrant and $\tan \theta = 3/4$, find the remaining five trigonometric functions of θ (see Fig. 2.23).

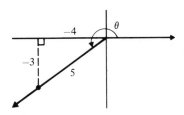

Figure 2.23

Solution. Since $\tan \theta = 3/4 = -3/-4$ and θ is in quadrant III, we can take $(-4, -3)$ as the point to determine a reference triangle as shown in the diagram; thus $r = \sqrt{(-3)^2 + (-4)^2} = \sqrt{25} = 5$. Therefore

    $\sin \theta = -\dfrac{3}{5}$, $\cos \theta = -\dfrac{4}{5}$, $\cot \theta = \dfrac{-4}{-3} = \dfrac{4}{3}$,

    $\sec \theta = -\dfrac{5}{4}$, $\csc \theta = -\dfrac{5}{3}$.   ∎

EXERCISE 2.4

1. If θ is an angle in standard position and point $(4, -3)$ is on the terminal side of θ, find each of the six trigonometric functions for θ. Express each answer in exact form and in decimal form correct to four places.

2. Point $(2,3)$ is on the terminal side of angle α. Find the six trigonometric functions for α and give answers in exact form.

In Problems 3 through 11, evaluate the given expressions and give the answers in exact form:

3. a) $\sin 60°$ b) $\cos 60°$ c) $\sin 210°$ d) $\cos 210°$

4. a) $\tan 30°$ b) $\sec 30°$ c) $\tan 300°$ d) $\sec 300°$

5. a) $\cot(-45°)$ b) $\csc(-45°)$ c) $\cot 405°$ d) $\csc 405°$

6. a) $\sin 225°$ b) $\cos 330°$ c) $\tan 135°$ d) $\cot 150°$

7. a) $\sin \dfrac{\pi}{6}$ b) $\tan \dfrac{5\pi}{6}$ c) $\cos\left(-\dfrac{\pi}{3}\right)$ d) $\cos \dfrac{2\pi}{3}$

8. a) $\cos\left(-\dfrac{5\pi}{4}\right)$ b) $\sec\left(-\dfrac{7\pi}{4}\right)$ c) $\tan \dfrac{17\pi}{3}$ d) $\sin\left(-\dfrac{17\pi}{6}\right)$

9. a) $\sin 90°$ b) $\cos 0°$ c) $\tan 270°$ d) $\sec 180°$

10. a) $\sin\left(-\dfrac{\pi}{2}\right)$ b) $\tan \pi$ c) $\cot\left(-\pi\right)$ d) $\sec\left(-4\pi\right)$

11. a) $\sec\left(-\dfrac{17\pi}{3}\right)$ b) $\cos(17\pi)$ c) $\tan\left(-\dfrac{11\pi}{6}\right)$ d) $\sin\left(\pi + \dfrac{5\pi}{6}\right)$

12. In the accompanying table write a "+" sign or a "−" sign indicating the sign of the corresponding entry:

	sin	cos	tan	cot	sec	csc
$124°$						
$-320°$						
3.04						
-1.16						

In Problems 13 through 18, give each answer in exact form and in decimal form correct to three decimal places.

13. If θ is an angle in the second quadrant and $\cos \theta = -3/5$, find the other five trigonometric functions of θ.

14. If $\sin \alpha = -3/4$ and the terminal side of α is in the fourth quadrant, find the remaining five trigonometric functions of α.

15. If $\cot \beta = 3/4$ and β is in the third quadrant, find the other five trignonometric functions of β.

16. If $\tan \gamma = -1.2$ and the terminal side of γ is in the second quadrant, find the remaining five trigonometric functions of γ.

17. If $\sin \theta = -0.25$ and $\tan \theta$ is negative, find the remaining five functions of θ.

18. If $\tan \theta = -3$ and θ is a second-quadrant angle, find the remaining five functions of θ.

19. Find the value of

$$\frac{\cos \frac{2\pi}{3} - \sin \frac{4\pi}{3} + \tan \frac{5\pi}{4}}{\sin \frac{\pi}{2} - \tan \frac{5\pi}{3} + \sec \frac{2\pi}{3}}$$

in exact form and in decimal form correct to three decimal places.

20. Verify that $\sin (\alpha - \beta) = \sin \alpha \cos \beta - \cos \alpha \sin \beta$ for each of the following pairs of values of α and β:

    a) $\alpha = \frac{2\pi}{3}, \quad \beta = \frac{\pi}{6}$ b) $\alpha = \frac{\pi}{2}, \quad \beta = \pi$

    c) $\alpha = \frac{3\pi}{2}, \quad \beta = \frac{\pi}{2}$ d) $\alpha = \frac{5\pi}{4}, \quad \beta = 3\pi$

    Hint. In each case evaluate the left-hand side and the right-hand side of the equation for the given α and β, and then verify that the two resulting numbers are equal.

21. Verify that $(\sin \theta)^2 + (\cos \theta)^2 = 1$ for each of the given values of θ:

    a) $\theta = 60°$ b) $\theta = 150°$ c) $\theta = \pi$

22. Verify that $\sin(2\theta) = 2(\sin \theta)(\cos \theta)$ for the given values of θ:

    a) $\theta = 90°$ b) $\theta = 30°$ c) $\theta = \frac{2\pi}{3}$

23. Verify that $(\sec \theta)^2 - (\tan \theta)^2 = 1$ for the given values of θ:

    a) $\theta = -\frac{3\pi}{4}$ b) $\theta = 225°$ c) $\theta = 495°$

24. For which of the given angles α and β is $\cos(\alpha + \beta) = \cos \alpha + \cos \beta$?

    a) $\alpha = \pi, \beta = 0$ b) $\alpha = 0, \beta = \frac{\pi}{2}$

    c) $\alpha = 45°, \beta = 45°$ d) $\alpha = 120°, \beta = 30°$

2.5 EVALUATING TRIGONOMETRIC FUNCTIONS

In Section 2.2 we referred to the fact that in general it is necessary to use techniques of calculus to evaluate trigonometric functions to a given degree of accuracy. For example, the sine and cosine functions can be evaluated by using the infinite series

$$\sin x = x - \frac{x^3}{3!} + \frac{x^5}{5!} - \frac{x^7}{7!} + \frac{x^9}{9!} \cdots, \tag{2.2}$$

$$\cos x = 1 - \frac{x^2}{2!} + \frac{x^4}{4!} - \frac{x^6}{6!} + \frac{x^8}{8!} \cdots, \tag{2.3}$$

where x is in *radian measure* (that is, x is a real number). Recall that $n!$ means n-factorial; for example, $4! = 1 \cdot 2 \cdot 3 \cdot 4 = 24$. Scientific calculators have a built-in capability to calculate sin, cos, or tan of any angle for which the function is defined. We first illustrate the use of Eq. (2.2) to calculate sin 10° correct to four decimal places and then compare the result with the value obtained by using the [sin] key of the calculator. The first step is to convert 10° to radian measure: $10° = 10\pi/180 = \pi/18$. Now with the use of the calculator we evaluate the following expression:

$$\sin\ 10° = \sin \frac{\pi}{18} = \frac{\pi}{18} - \frac{(\pi/18)^3}{6} + \frac{(\pi/18)^5}{120} - \dots,$$

$$\sin\ 10° = \sin \frac{\pi}{18} = 0.174532925 - 0.000886096 + 0.000001350 - \dots$$

The terms on the right side of this equation become small rapidly, and in this case (of four-place accuracy) all but the first two can be neglected. So

$$\sin\ 10° = \frac{\pi}{18} - \frac{(\pi/18)^3}{6} = 0.1736 \quad \text{(to four decimal places)}.$$

Now we place the calculator in degree mode and press 10, [sin] . The display gives sin 10° = 0.173648178 (correct to nine decimal places). We see that our calculated result agrees with that of the calculator to four decimal places. Of course, we shall not use formulas (2.2) and (2.3) to evaluate sine and cosine of a given angle since the calculator will do this for us automatically. The purpose of introducing Eqs. (2.2) and (2.3) at this time is to illustrate what occurs inside the calculator when it evaluates trigonometric functions.

Examples   Using the calculator evaluate each of the following and express the answer correct to five decimal places:

⚠️1 cos 234°

Solution. Again in degree mode, press 234, [cos] . The display reads -0.587785253; therefore, cos 234° $= -0.58779$ to five places.   ▎

⚠️2 tan (−127°)

Solution. Press 127, change sign [+/−] , [tan] , and conclude from the display that tan(−127°) = 1.32704.   ▎

⚠️3 sin 196°16′41″

Solution. In degree mode, the calculator will accept angles given in degrees as a decimal number. So it is necessary first to change

$$196°16'41'' = \left(196 + \frac{16}{60} + \frac{41}{60 \cdot 60}\right)° = 196.27806°.$$

Therefore, after using the calculator to perform this calculation, we press the [sin] key and get sin 196°16′41″ $= -0.28030$.   ▎

⚠️4 sec(−2.47)

Solution. Since the calculator does not have a [sec] key, we use observation 6 of Section 2.4 to get sec(−2.47) = 1/cos(−2.47). To evaluate this, place the calculator in radian mode, then press 2.47, [+/−] , [cos] , [1/x] . This gives sec(−2.47) = −1.27741.   ∎

 csc $\left(\dfrac{1 + \sqrt{5}}{2}\right)$

Solution. Place the calculator in radian mode, evaluate $(1 + \sqrt{5})/2$. Then with this number in the display, evaluate

$$\csc \left(\frac{1 + \sqrt{5}}{2}\right) = \frac{1}{\sin \ [(1 + \sqrt{5})/2]}$$

by pressing [sin] , [1/x] . The result is

$$\csc \left(\frac{1 + \sqrt{5}}{2}\right) = 1.00112.$$

∎

⑥ tan 450°

Solution. Place the calculator in degree mode; press 450 and [tan] ; the display will indicate "Error". If we apply observation 5 given in Section 2.4, we see that tan 450° is undefined. Some calculators give $9.9 \cdot 10^{99}$ as the value of tan 450°; such a large number should cause us to ask "What is the calculator telling us?"   ∎

EXERCISE 2.5

Using your calculator, evaluate Problems 1 through 21 and give answers correct to five decimal places:

1. sin 131°   2. cos 235°   3. tan 138°

4. sin (− 41°)   5. cot 83°   6. sec 157°

7. csc(−57°)   8. sin 204°17'31"   9. tan (−31.48°)

10. sec 148.16°   11. sin 0.08°   12. cos 251°23'53"

13. sin 0.64   14. tan (− 0.5)   15. csc 3.23

16. cos 7.25   17. cot (π + 3)   18. cos (3π/17)

19. tan $\left(-\dfrac{2\pi}{47}\right)$ 20. sin $\left[5\left(\pi + \dfrac{\pi}{9}\right)\right]$ 21. csc (2.78 + 5π)

22. Use Eq. (2.2) of this section to evaluate sin 5° correct to four decimal places; then find the value of sin 5° directly by using the [sin] key on your calculator. Compare the two answers.

23. Use Eq. (2.3) of this section to determine cos 8° correct to four decimal places; then find cos 8° using your calculator and compare answers.

24. Use the first three terms of Eq. (2.2) of this section to find sin 0.16. Compare your result with that given directly by the calculator.

25. Use the first four terms of Eq. (2.3) of this section to find cos 0.24. Compare your result with that given directly by the calculator.

2.6 CIRCULAR FUNCTIONS

Suppose θ is an angle in standard position as shown in Fig. 2.24. In Section 2.4 we formulated the definitions of the six trigonometric functions of θ by using any point P (other than the origin) on the terminal side of θ. Now suppose we take P to be the point (u, v) which is one unit from the origin; that is, $u^2 + v^2 = 1$. Since the equation $x^2 + y^2 = 1$ represents a circle with center at the origin and radius one, we call it the *unit circle*. Thus, point (u, v) is on the unit circle.

Applying the definitions given in (2.1) of Section 2.4 to the reference triangle OBP in Fig. 2.24, we get

$$\sin \theta = \frac{v}{1} = v \qquad \text{and} \qquad \cos \theta = \frac{u}{1} = u. \qquad (2.4)$$

This tells us that the coordinates of P can be written as $P : (\cos \theta, \quad \sin \theta)$.

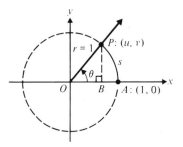

Figure 2.24

Now suppose θ is given in radians (that is, θ is a real number) and let S represent the length of arc AP of the unit circle, where A is the point $(1, 0)$. Then we write $S = s$ units, where s is a real number. For example, if the length is measured in centimeters, then $S = s$ cm and $r = \overline{OP} = 1$ cm. Using the definition of radian measure (see Section 1.2), we have

$$\theta = \frac{S}{r} = \frac{s \text{ cm}}{1 \text{ cm}} = s.$$

Thus the two real numbers θ and s are equal; then the equations in (2.4) give

$$v = \sin \theta = \sin s \qquad \text{and} \qquad u = \cos \theta = \cos s. \qquad (2.5)$$

Therefore, the point P in Fig. 2.24 is given by

$$P:(u, v) \qquad \text{or} \qquad P:(\cos\theta, \sin\theta) \qquad \text{or} \qquad P:(\cos s, \sin s).$$

The phrase "length of arc" implies a number s and an associated unit of distance measurement. We shall take liberties with language and say "s is the length of arc" when we actually mean "s is the real number associated with the length of arc." Thus in (2.5) we are talking about the *sine and cosine of a real number* s, and not of, say, s centimeters.

Since the arc length is usually given as a nonnegative number and we are interested in applying the equations in (2.5) also to negative values of s, it becomes necessary to introduce the idea of *directed arc length*. Suppose point Q starts moving along the unit circle from $A:(1, 0)$ to point P, as shown in Fig. 2.25. If Q moves in the counterclockwise direction, then the length of arc s through which it moves will be taken as positive; if the motion is in the clockwise direction, then the corresponding value of s will be negative.

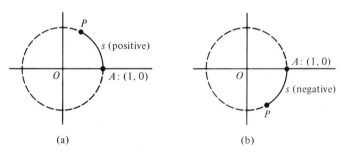

(a)   (b)

Figure 2.25

Definition. For every real number s, we consider point Q moving from point $A:(1, 0)$ on the unit circle through a directed arc of length s to a point $P:(x, y)$. We use the coordinates of P as a basis for defining the two *circular functions* sine and cosine as follows:

$$\sin s = y \qquad \text{and} \qquad \cos s = x, \tag{2.6}$$

where (x, y) are the coordinates of point P.

The remaining four circular functions are defined by using (2.6) in the following way:

$$\tan s = \frac{\sin s}{\cos s}, \qquad \cot s = \frac{\cos s}{\sin s}, \qquad \sec s = \frac{1}{\cos s}, \qquad \csc s = \frac{1}{\sin s}. \tag{2.7}$$

Examples

$\triangle 1$ Find the value of each of the six circular functions at $s = \pi/4$.

Solution. The circumference of the unit circle is $c = 2\pi r = 2\pi(1) = 2\pi$. Let (u, v) be the point P on the unit circle that corresponds to $s = \pi/4$. Since $\pi/4$ is equal to $1/8$ of 2π, triangle OBP shown in Fig. 2.26 is an isosceles triangle with $u = v$. Since (u, v) is on the unit circle, $u^2 + v^2 = 1$ and so $2u^2 = 1$. Thus we have $u = v = \sqrt{2}/2$. Therefore, the coordinates of P are $(\sqrt{2}/2, \ \sqrt{2}/2)$.

From the definitions given in (2.6) and (2.7) we have:

$$\sin\frac{\pi}{4} = v = \frac{\sqrt{2}}{2}, \qquad\qquad \cos\frac{\pi}{4} = u = \frac{\sqrt{2}}{2};$$

$$\tan\frac{\pi}{4} = \frac{\sin(\pi/4)}{\cos(\pi/4)} = \frac{\sqrt{2}/2}{\sqrt{2}/2} = 1; \qquad \cot\frac{\pi}{4} = \frac{\cos(\pi/4)}{\sin(\pi/4)} = 1;$$

$$\sec\frac{\pi}{4} = \frac{1}{\cos(\pi/4)} = \sqrt{2}; \qquad\qquad \csc\frac{\pi}{4} = \frac{1}{\sin(\pi/4)} = \sqrt{2}.$$

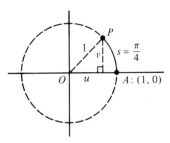

Figure 2.26

$\triangle 2$ Evaluate the six circular functions for $s = -\pi/2$.

Solution. The point P on the unit circle that corresponds to $s = -\pi/2$ is $P : (0, -1)$. Using the definitions given in (2.6) and (2.7), we get

$$\sin\left(-\frac{\pi}{2}\right) = -1; \qquad\qquad \cos\left(-\frac{\pi}{2}\right) = 0;$$

$$\tan\left(-\frac{\pi}{2}\right) = -\frac{1}{0} \text{ (undefined)}; \quad \cot\left(-\frac{\pi}{2}\right) = \frac{0}{-1} = 0;$$

$$\sec\left(-\frac{\pi}{2}\right) = \frac{1}{0} \text{ (undefined)}; \quad \csc\left(-\frac{\pi}{2}\right) = \frac{1}{-1} = -1.$$

$\triangle 3$ Suppose point P is on the unit circle and has coordinates $(-\sqrt{3}/2, 1/2)$. Find two real numbers s (one positive and one negative) that can be used as directed arc lengths corresponding to P, as described in the definition of the circular functions.

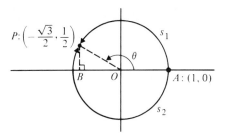

Figure 2.27

Solution. We see from Fig. 2.27 that in right triangle BOP, $\overline{BP} = \frac{1}{2}(\overline{OP})$; then angle BOP equals $30° = \pi/6$. Therefore, $\theta = 5\pi/6$. The length of arc s_1 corresponding to θ is given by

$$s_1 = r \cdot \theta = (1)\left(\frac{5\pi}{6}\right) = \frac{5\pi}{6}.$$

If point Q moves in a clockwise direction from point A to P, then the corresponding directed arc length is

$$s_2 = -\pi - \frac{\pi}{6} = -\frac{7\pi}{6}.$$

Thus $s = 5\pi/6$ and $s = -7\pi/6$ are solutions. It should be clear that if point Q moves along the unit circle from point A to P by going around the circle one or more times (in either direction), then we have other values of s corresponding to P. In fact, all values of s can be given by

$$s = \frac{5\pi}{6} + k \cdot 2\pi,$$

where k is any integer (positive, negative or zero).   ∎

Note. As can be seen from the equations given in (2.5), the circular functions defined in (2.6) are precisely the same as the corresponding trigonometric functions defined in Section 2.4. The important point is that in both cases we have defined six functions with domains consisting of a set of real numbers. It is in this setting that the student will encounter trigonometric (or circular) functions in calculus.

We shall refer to the six functions as either trigonometric functions or circular functions. One might ask: Why talk about the same thing in two different contexts? The answer is that in the setting in which trigonometric functions were introduced, it is convenient to relate the functions to triangles and apply them to solution of triangles (as will be discussed in Chapter 3), while the circular functions defined in (2.6) and (2.7) are very helpful in deriving several important properties of these functions. We illustrate this now by deriving some of the basic identities that will be useful in Chapter 4. An *identity* is an equation that is satisfied by all values of the variable (or variables) for which the function involved is defined.

1. Reciprocal Identities

The following are immediate consequences of the definitions given in (2.6) and (2.7):

$$\sin s = \frac{1}{\csc s}, \qquad \cos s = \frac{1}{\sec s}, \qquad \tan s = \frac{1}{\cot s},$$

$$\cot s = \frac{1}{\tan s}, \qquad \sec s = \frac{1}{\cos s}, \qquad \csc s = \frac{1}{\sin s}. \qquad (2.8)$$

2. Periodic Properties

1. Every point P on the unit circle has several values of s (arc lengths) associated with it. For example, if s is any real number, then the same point P is associated with arc length s and with $s + k \cdot 2\pi$, where k is any integer. Using the definitions stated in (2.6) for arc lengths s and $s + 2k\pi$, we conclude that

$$\sin(s + 2k\pi) = \sin s \qquad \text{and} \qquad \cos(s + 2k\pi) = \cos s. \qquad (2.9)$$

2. Now suppose P: (x, y) is a point on the unit circle associated with arc length s; then point M on the unit circle associated with arc length $s + \pi$ is M: $(-x, -y)$, as illustrated in Fig. 2.28. Using (2.6) for s and for $s + \pi$, we get

$$x = \cos s, \qquad y = \sin s \qquad \text{and} \qquad -x = \cos(s + \pi), \qquad -y = \sin(s + \pi).$$

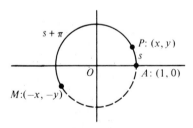

Figure 2.28

From these equations we have the identities

$$\cos(x + \pi) = -\cos s \qquad \text{and} \qquad \sin(x + \pi) = -\sin s. \qquad (2.10)$$

Using (2.7) and (2.10) we get

$$\tan(s + \pi) = \frac{\sin(s + \pi)}{\cos(s + \pi)} = \frac{-\sin s}{-\cos s} = \frac{\sin s}{\cos s} = \tan s.$$

We can get a similar result for the cotangent function, giving us the identities:

$$\tan(s + \pi) = \tan s \quad \text{and} \quad \cot(s + \pi) = \cot s. \qquad (2.11)$$

3. Other Basic Identities

1. The point P: (x, y) used in the definition of $\sin s$ and $\cos s$ in (2.6) is on the unit circle; that is, $x^2 + y^2 = 1$. Since $x = \cos s$, $y = \sin s$, we have

$$(\sin\ s)^2 + (\cos\ s)^2 = 1 \qquad (2.12)$$

for every real number s. This identity is used frequently, as we shall see in Chapters 3 and 4.

2. Suppose s is any real number and the associated arc length corresponds to P: (x, y) on the unit circle; then point M: $(x, -y)$ on the unit circle corresponds to the directed arc length $-s$, as illustrated in Fig. 2.29. Using the definitions for s and $-s$ stated in (2.6), we get

$$x = \cos\ s,\ y = \sin s \quad \text{and} \quad x = \cos(-s),\ -y = \sin(-s).$$

From these we get the following relations for each real number s:

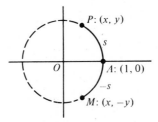

Figure 2.29

$$\sin(-s) = -\sin s \quad \text{and} \quad \cos(-s) = \cos s. \qquad (2.13)$$

Using the definitions given in (2.7) and the results from (2.13), we get for each real number s:

$$\begin{array}{ll} \tan(-s) = -\tan s; & \cot(-s) = -\cot s; \\ \sec(-s) = \sec s; & \csc(-s) = -\csc s. \end{array} \qquad (2.14)$$

Definition. A function f is said to be an *odd function* if $f(-x) = -f(x)$ for every x in $D(f)$. If $f(-x) = f(x)$ for each x in $D(f)$, then f is said to be an *even function*.

From the identities given in (2.13) and (2.14) we conclude that:

> The sine, tangent, cotangent and cosecant are odd functions; the cosine and secant functions are even functions.

In Exercise 2.6 the student is asked to derive other indentities using the definitions of circular functions.

EXERCISE 2.6

In Problems 1 through 12, s is a real number corresponding to an arc length and associated with a point P on the unit circle, as described in this section. In each case, use the given value of s to

   a) draw a diagram showing the point P,

   b) give the coordinates of P,

   c) find the values of the six circular functions for the given number s. Provide answers in exact form.

1. $s = \dfrac{\pi}{2}$ 2. $s = \dfrac{\pi}{6}$ 3. $s = -\dfrac{3\pi}{4}$ 4. $s = -\pi$

5. $s = \dfrac{9\pi}{4}$ 6. $s = 3\pi$ 7. $s = \dfrac{3\pi}{2}$ 8. $s = \dfrac{5\pi}{6}$

9. $s = \dfrac{17\pi}{4}$ 10. $s = -\dfrac{15\pi}{4}$ 11. $s = \dfrac{7\pi}{3}$ 12. $s = \dfrac{4\pi}{3}$

In Problems 13 through 20, follow the instructions of the preceding Problems 1 through 12 except in part (b). Use Eq. (2.5) of this section and a calculator to find the coordinates of P to three decimal places; in part (c) give answers to two decimal places.

13. $s = 1$ 14. $s = -2.5$ 15. $s = 7.3$ 16. $s = 16.4$

17. $s = \sqrt{2}$ 18. $s = \sqrt{\pi}$ 19. $s = -12$ 20. $s = \pi - 8$

In Problems 21 through 26, point P is given on the unit circle. Find three real numbers s (two positive and one negative) representing arc lengths associated with P, as described in this section.

21. $P : \left(-\dfrac{1}{2}, \dfrac{\sqrt{3}}{2}\right)$ 22. $P : (-1, 0)$ 23. $P : \left(-\dfrac{\sqrt{2}}{2}, -\dfrac{\sqrt{2}}{2}\right)$

24. $P : \left(\dfrac{\sqrt{3}}{2}, -\dfrac{1}{2}\right)$ 25. $P : (1, 0)$ 26. $P : \left(-\dfrac{\sqrt{2}}{2}, \dfrac{\sqrt{2}}{2}\right)$

In Problems 27 through 32, use the definitions of circular functions given in (2.6) and (2.7) and any of the results obtained in the Examples to prove that the given equations are identities:

27. a) $\sin(\pi - s) = \sin s$ b) $\cos(\pi - s) = -\cos s$

28. a) $\sin\left(\dfrac{\pi}{2} - s\right) = \cos s$ b) $\cos\left(\dfrac{\pi}{2} - s\right) = \sin s$

29. a) $\sin\left(\dfrac{\pi}{2} + s\right) = \cos\ s$ b) $\cos\left(\dfrac{\pi}{2} + s\right) = -\sin\ s$

30. a) $\sec(s + \pi) = -\sec\ s$ b) $\csc(s + \pi) = -\csc\ s$

31. a) $\tan\left(s + \dfrac{\pi}{2}\right) = -\cot\ s$ b) $\cot\left(s + \dfrac{\pi}{2}\right) = -\tan\ s$

32. a) $\sin\left(s - \dfrac{\pi}{2}\right) = -\cos\ s$ b) $\cos\left(s - \dfrac{\pi}{2}\right) = \sin\ s$

In Problems 33 through 40, determine whether the given equation is an identity:

33. a) $\sin\left(s + \dfrac{3\pi}{2}\right) = -\cos\ s$ b) $\cos\left(s + \dfrac{3\pi}{2}\right) = \sin\ s$

34. a) $\tan\left(s + \dfrac{5\pi}{2}\right) = \tan\ s$ b) $\cot\left(s + \dfrac{5\pi}{2}\right) = \cot\ s$

35. a) $\sin\left(\dfrac{5\pi}{2} - s\right) = \sin\ s$ b) $\cos\left(\dfrac{5\pi}{2} - s\right) = \cos\ s$

36. a) $\sin(s + 3\pi) = -\sin\ s$ b) $\cos(s + 3\pi) = -\cos\ s$

37. a) $\tan(s - 3\pi) = \tan\ s$ b) $\cot(s - 3\pi) = \cot\ s$

38. a) $\sec(s + 4\pi) = \sec\ s$ b) $\csc(s + 4\pi) = \csc\ s$

39. a) $\tan\left(s - \dfrac{7\pi}{2}\right) = -\cot\ s$ b) $\cot\left(s - \dfrac{7\pi}{2}\right) = \cot\ s$

40. a) $\sin(s + 23\pi) = -\sin\ s$ b) $\cos(s + 23\pi) = -\cos\ s$

2.7 PERIODIC PROPERTIES AND GRAPHS OF TRIGONOMETRIC FUNCTIONS

In Section 2.6 we saw that if g represents any one of the six circular functions, then $g(s + 2\pi) = g(s)$ for every real number s for which $g(s)$ is defined. This tells us that each of the trigonometric functions repeats itself infinitely with a cycle of 2π. Any function repeating itself over consecutive intervals of fixed length is said to be a periodic function. Many scientific investigations involve phenomena of a cyclic nature which can be described in terms of periodic functions. It is an interesting and important fact that practically all periodic functions can be expressed as a linear combination of sine and cosine functions.* It is this fact that makes trigonometry extremely useful in applications of mathematics to many real-life problems.

Definition. If f is any function with the property that there is a positive number p such that

$$f(x + p) = f(x) \qquad (2.15)$$

for all values of x in the domain of f, then f is said to be a *periodic function*. If p is the *smallest positive number* for which Eq. (2.15) holds, then p is called the *period* of the function.

We shall now draw the graphs of the trigonometric functions and use them to determine the periods of those functions.

---

* This is the basis for a broad topic in advanced mathematics called Fourier analysis.

1. Graph of the Sine Function

We could make a table of x, y values that satisfy the equation $y = \sin x$ and then use the corresponding (x, y) points to draw the graph. However, we can gain considerable insight into the behavior of the sine function by treating it as a circular function, as we did in the preceding section. There each real number s was associated with an arc length and a point Q that moved along the unit circle from point $A : (1, 0)$ to point P covering a directed distance s; then we defined $\sin s$ as the second coordinate of point P.

In drawing a graph in the x, y rectangular system of coordinates, it is customary to call x the independent variable; that is, we draw a graph of $y = \sin x$. Thus in our definition of the sine function we shall replace s by x and think of x as being associated with the arc length (not as the x-coordinate of P). So as not to get the variables confused, we shall denote the coordinates of P by (u, y), as illustrated in Fig. 2.30.

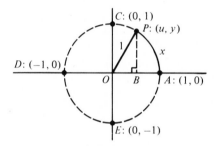

Figure 2.30

Therefore, from (2.6) we have: $y = \sin x$, where x is any real number associated with the directed arc length of a point moving from A to P.

We can proceed to draw the graph of $y = \sin x$ by letting point $P : (u, y)$ move along the unit circle (counterclockwise for $x \geq 0$) starting at A and record the corresponding points $T : (x, y)$ on the graph shown in Fig. 2.31.

When P is at A, then $x = 0$, $y = 0$; so T is at $A_1 : (0, 0)$. As P moves from A to C, the arc length x increases from 0 to $\pi/2$ and the corresponding values of y increase from 0 to 1; then point T moves from $A_1 : (0, 0)$ to $C_1 : (\pi/2, 1)$. As P moves from C to D, x increases from $\pi/2$ to π and the corresponding values of y decrease from 1 to 0; this gives the points of the graph from C_1 to D_1. As P moves from D to E, x increases from π to $3\pi/2$ and y decreases from 0 to -1; this gives the points on the graph between D_1 and E_1. As P moves from E to A, x increases from $3\pi/2$ to 2π and y increases from -1 to 0, giving the corresponding points T between E_1 and A_2 in Fig. 2.31.

The above gives us one complete cycle of the sine curve. Since we know that $\sin(x + 2\pi) = \sin x$ for each real number x, we can continue the graph as indicated by the broken portion of the curve in Fig. 2.31.

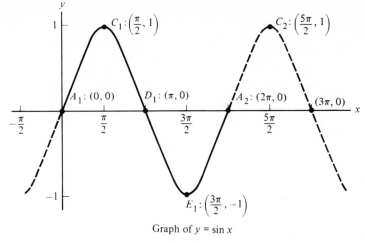

Graph of $y = \sin x$

Figure 2.31

From the graph in Fig. 2.31 we see that $p = 2\pi$ is the smallest positive number p such that $\sin(x + p) = \sin x$ for each real number x. Thus we can conclude the following from the graph:

a) The sine function is periodic with period 2π.

b) The domain and range of the sine function are given by

$$D(\sin) = \{x \mid x \text{ is any real number}\},$$
$$R(\sin) = \{y \mid -1 \le y \le 1\}.$$

2. Graph of the Cosine Function

We can draw a graph of $u = \cos x$ by following a procedure similar to that used to draw the graph of the sine function. In Fig. 2.30 the first coordinate of $P : (u, y)$ yields the value of $\cos x$ for any given real number x; thus, $u = \cos x$. We omit the details and draw the curve shown in Fig. 2.32 with the solid portion corresponding to the points (x, u) which we get as point P moves counterclockwise along the unit circle from point A in Fig. 2.30.

From the curve in Fig. 2.32 we see that $p = 2\pi$ is the smallest positive number p such that $\cos(x + p) = \cos x$ for every real number x. Therefore, we conclude that:

a) The cosine function is periodic with period 2π.

b) The domain and range of the cosine function are given by

$$D(\cos) = \{x \mid x \text{ is any real number}\},$$
$$R(\cos) = \{u \mid -1 \le u \le 1\}.$$

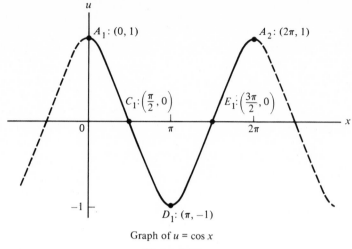

Graph of $u = \cos x$

Figure 2.32

3. Graph of the Tangent Function

We shall draw a graph of the tangent function by first making a table of x, y values that satisfy $y = \tan x$; then we plot these points and draw the curve shown in Fig. 2.33. In selecting what values of x to use in the table, we recall that $\tan(x + \pi) = \tan x$ for each real number x for which $\tan x$ is defined. Thus, it is sufficient to make a table where x is between $-\pi/2$ and $\pi/2$. Also, in Section 2.6 it was noted that $\tan(-x) = -\tan x$ for each x in $D(\tan)$; this tells us that the graph of $y = \tan x$ is symmetric about the origin. Therefore, it is sufficient to make a table $0 \le x < \pi/2$. Since $\tan(\pi/2)$ is not defined, we include values of x near $\pi/2 = 1.570796\ldots$

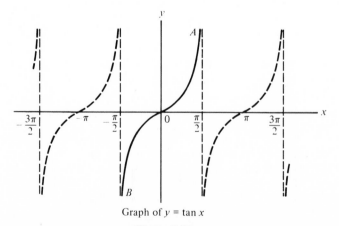

Graph of $y = \tan x$

Figure 2.33

x	0	0.25	0.50	0.75	1.00	1.25	1.50	1.52	1.55	1.56	1.57
y	0	0.26	0.55	0.93	1.56	3.01	14.1	19.7	48.1	92.6	1256

In Fig. 2.33 the portion of the curve between 0 and A corresponds to the points in the table. Since the curve is symmetric about the origin (that is, $\tan(-x) = -\tan x$), the portion of the curve from 0 to B is obtained by reflecting the points from 0 to A about the origin. The remaining branches (broken portions of the curve) follow from the periodic property given by $\tan(x + \pi) = \tan x$. From the graph in Fig. 2.33 we conclude that:

a) The tangent function is periodic with period π.

b) The domain and range of the tangent function are given by

$$D(\tan) = \{x \mid x \neq \tfrac{\pi}{2} + k\pi, \ k \text{ is any integer}\},$$

$$R(\tan) = \{y \mid y \text{ is any real number}\}.$$

We also note from the graph that the curve gets closer and closer to the vertical broken lines passing through

$$x = \frac{\pi}{2}, \ \frac{3\pi}{2}, \ \ldots, \ -\frac{\pi}{2}, \ -\frac{3\pi}{2}, \ \ldots$$

These lines are called *vertical asymptotes* to the curve.

4. Graph of the Cotangent Function

We can draw a graph of $y = \cot x$ by following a procedure similar to that used in drawing the graph of the tangent function. We omit the details and give the graph shown in Fig. 2.34. From the graph we conclude the following:

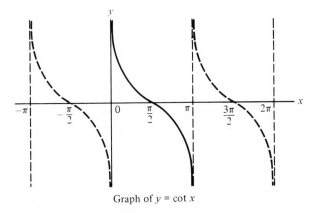

Graph of $y = \cot x$

Figure 2.34

   a) The cotangent function is periodic with period π.

   b) The domain and range of the tangent function are given by

$$D(\cot) = \{x \mid x \neq k\pi, \ \ k \text{ is any integer}\}$$
$$R(\cot) = \{y \mid y \text{ is any real number}\}.$$

We also note that the cotangent curve has vertical asymptotes given by $x = k\pi$, where k is any integer.

5. Graph of the Secant Function

From the discussion of circular functions in Section 2.6 we recall that $\sec(x + 2\pi) = \sec x$ for every real number x for which $\sec x$ is defined. Thus in making a table of x, y values that satisfy $y = \sec x$, it is sufficient to include values of x in the interval $-\pi$ to π. Also, from Section 2.6 we have that $\sec(-x) = \sec x$ for every x in $D(\sec)$; thus the graph is symmetric about the y-axis, and so it is sufficient to include in our table values of x between 0 and π. Since the secant function is not defined at $\pi/2$, we include values of x near $\pi/2 = 1.57\ldots$

x	0	0.25	0.50	0.75	1.00	1.25	1.50	1.56	1.57	1.58
y	1	1.03	1.14	1.37	1.85	3.17	14.1	92.6	1256	-109

1.60	1.75	2.00	2.25	2.50	2.75	3.00	π
-34.2	-5.61	-2.40	-1.59	-1.25	-1.08	-1.01	-1

We now plot the points given in this table and draw the curve for x between 0 and π; then from the symmetry about the y-axis, we draw the curve for x between 0 and $-\pi$. This gives us the solid portion of the curve in Fig. 2.35. The remainder of the curve (broken portion) can now be drawn by using the identity $\sec(x + 2\pi) = \sec x$. From Fig. 2.35 we conclude the following:

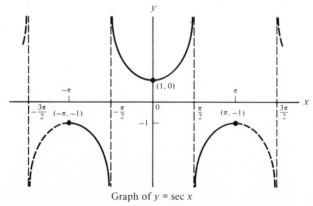

Graph of $y = \sec x$

Figure 2.35

a) The secant function is periodic with period 2π.

b) The domain and range are given by

$$D(\sec) = \{x \mid x \neq \tfrac{\pi}{2} + k\pi, \ \ k \text{ is any integer}\},$$

$$R(\sec) = \{y \mid y \leq -1 \ \text{ or } \ y \geq 1\}.$$

We also note that the vertical lines given by $x = (2k + 1)\pi/2$, where k is any integer, are vertical asymptotes of the secant curve.

6. Graph of the Cosecant Function

We can follow a procedure similar to that used to draw the graph of the secant function; omitting the details, we draw the graph shown in Fig. 2.36 and conclude that:

a) The cosecant function is periodic with period 2π.

b) The domain and range are given by

$$D(\csc) = \{x \mid x \neq k\pi, k \text{ is any integer}\},$$

$$R(\csc) = \{y \mid y \leq -1 \text{ or } y \geq 1\}.$$

Also, we see that $y = \csc x$ has infinitely many vertical asymptotes given by $x = k\pi$, where k is any integer.

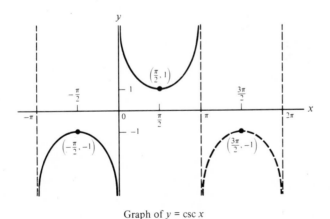

Graph of $y = \csc x$

Figure 2.36

EXERCISE 2.7

1. Draw a graph of sine function by first making a table of x, y values that satisfy the equation $y = \sin x$; plot these points and then draw the curve. Use the identities $\sin(x + 2\pi) = \sin x$ and $\sin(-x) = -\sin x$ to convince yourself that it is sufficient to include in the table values of x in $0 \leq x \leq \pi$. For values of x use 0, 0.25, 0.50, 0.75, . . .

2. Follow instructions similar to those in Problem 1 but for $y = \cos x$.

3. In Subsection 4 of this section we suggested a procedure for drawing the graph of $y = \cot x$ but omitted the details. Supply the details by making a table of x, y values; use the identities $\cot(x + \pi) = \cot x$ and $\cot(-x) = -\cot x$. Show that it is sufficient to include in your table values of x between 0 and $\pi/2$. Check whether the (x, y) points from your table are on the graph in Fig. 2.34.

4. In Subsection 6 of this section the details of drawing the graph of $y = \csc x$ were omitted. Supply them by making a table of x, y values. Use the identities $\csc(x + 2\pi) = \csc x$ and $\csc(-x) = -\csc x$ in deciding what values of x to include in your table. Check whether the (x, y) points given in your table are on the graph in Fig. 2.36.

REVIEW EXERCISE

1. Make a sketch showing the given angles in standard position (a reasonable approximation is sufficient):

   a) 135°   b) $-240°$ c) $\frac{5\pi}{2}$

   d) $-137°$ e) -2.34 f) $\frac{17\pi}{6}$

2. Determine the quadrant in which the given angles are located:

   a) 235°   b) 4.705   c) -2.47

   d) $-640°$ e) 841°   f) 30

In Problems 3 through 10, give the answers in exact form.

3. Evaluate the following:

   a) $\sin 90°$ b) $\tan 30°$ c) $\sec 150°$ d) $\cos(-240°)$

   e) $\tan(-180°)$ f) $\csc 450°$ g) $\cot(-315°)$ h) $\sin 270°$

4. Evaluate the following:

   a) $\cos 3\pi$ b) $\cot(-\pi)$ c) $\sin \frac{5\pi}{3}$ d) $\cos\left(-\frac{7\pi}{3}\right)$

   e) $\tan \frac{7\pi}{6}$ f) $\sec \frac{3\pi}{2}$ g) $\sec\left(\pi - \frac{\pi}{6}\right)$ h) $\csc\left(\frac{\pi}{3} + \frac{5\pi}{6}\right)$

5. If θ is an angle in the third quadrant and $\tan \theta = 4/3$, determine the following:

   a) $\sin \theta$ b) $\sec \theta$ c) $\cos(\theta + \pi)$

   d) $\tan(\theta - \pi)$ e) $\csc\left(\theta - \frac{\pi}{2}\right)$ f) $\cos\left(\theta + \frac{\pi}{2}\right)$

6. Determine θ from the given information:

   a) $\sin \theta = -\frac{\sqrt{2}}{2}$ and $\pi < \theta < \frac{3\pi}{2}$ b) $\cos \theta = -\frac{1}{2}$ and $0 < \theta < \pi$

   c) $\tan \theta = -1$ and $-2\pi < \theta < -\pi$ d) $\sec \theta = -1$ and $0 < \theta < 2\pi$

7. Determine α from the given information:

   a) $\sin \alpha = -1$ and $0° \le \alpha \le 360°$ b) $\csc \alpha = 2$ and $-90 < \alpha < 90°$

   c) $\cos \alpha = -\frac{1}{\sqrt{2}}$ and $0 \le \alpha \le 180°$ d) $\tan \alpha = -1$ and $-90° \le \alpha \le 90°$

8. If $\alpha = 3\pi/2$, $\beta = \pi/3$, and $\gamma = 5\pi/6$, evaluate the following:

   a) $\sin \alpha$ b) $\tan \gamma$ c) $\cos(\alpha - \beta)$

   d) $\sec(\beta + \gamma)$ e) $\sec(\gamma - \alpha)$ f) $\cos(\alpha + \gamma - \beta)$

9. If $\alpha = 30°$, $\beta = 90°$, and $\gamma = 210°$, evaluate the following:

   a) $\sin(\alpha + \gamma)$ b) $\sin \alpha + \sin \gamma$ c) $\cos(\alpha - \beta)$

   d) $\cos \alpha - \cos \beta$ e) $\tan 2\gamma$ f) $2 \tan \gamma$

10. If $\cos \theta = -0.75$ and $\tan \theta$ is negative, determine the following:

    a) $\sin \theta$ b) $\cot \theta$ c) $\sec\left(\theta - \dfrac{\pi}{2}\right)$ d) $\tan(\theta + \pi)$

In Problems 11 through 16, evaluate the given expressions and give answers correct to four decimal places:

11. a) $\sin 43°$ b) $\tan 154°$ c) $\cos 57°16'$

    d) $\cot 48°$ e) $\sec 327°12'$ f) $\sin(-231°)$

12. a) $\cos 1.43$ b) $\sin 3.86$ c) $\tan(5\pi/12)$ d) $\cot(12/5\pi)$

13. a) $\sin(53° + 75°)$ b) $\sin 53° + \sin 75°$

14. a) $\tan(1.36 + 2.14)$ b) $\tan 1.36 + \tan 2.14$

15. a) $(\sin 153°)^2 + (\cos 153°)^2$ b) $(\sin 1.5)^2 + (\cos 1.5)^2$

16. a) $2\left(\sin \dfrac{\pi}{12}\right)\left(\cos \dfrac{\pi}{12}\right)$ b) $\left(\cos \dfrac{\pi}{3}\right)^2 - \left(\sin \dfrac{\pi}{3}\right)^2$

17. Determine whether the given statements are true or false:

    a) π and $-\pi$ are coterminal angles

    b) $-\dfrac{3\pi}{2}$ and $-\dfrac{\pi}{2}$ are coterminal angles

    c) $210°$ and $-\dfrac{5\pi}{6}$ are coterminal angles

    d) An angle in standard position with terminal side passing through point $(-1, 2)$ is coterminal with $150°$.

18. Draw a graph of $y = 2 \sin x$ by first making a table of several (x, y) pairs that satisfy the given equation. Use degree measure for the x-values.

19. Same as Problem 18 for $y = 2 \cos x$.

20. If $y = -\tan x$, make a table of (x, y) values that satisfy the equation, starting with $x = -2.0$ and then increasing by 0.2 for successive values of x up to $x = 2.0$. Plot the corresponding points and draw a graph of $y = -\tan x$.

CHAPTER THREE

SOLVING TRIANGLES

As we noted earlier, the word *trigonometry* implies the study of measurements related to triangles. Historically, the development of the subject was indeed motivated by the practical needs of surveying, navigation, and architecture (among other things), and these involved problems of determining certain unknown parts of a triangle from known information about it.

We first describe a problem that involves triangles for its solution. Suppose we wish to determine the height of a mountain peak and there is no convenient way to measure it directly. One approach is to locate two points A and B on the ground, as shown in Fig. 3.1, and measure the distance between them. Also we can measure the angles α and β. With this much information we can determine the height h by using trigonometric properties of triangles that will be developed in this chapter. We postpone further discussion of this example until such properties are at our disposal (see Problem 30 of this section).

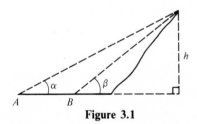

Figure 3.1

A triangle has six parts—three angles and three sides. When we say "angle of a triangle," we mean the angle formed by the two rays that contain two sides of the triangle and have the vertex as their common endpoint. To "solve a triangle" means that measurements of some of these parts are given (usually sufficient to determine a unique triangle) and we determine the remaining parts from the given information. In this chapter we develop the topic in two steps: First we study the problem involving right triangles only and then we consider general triangles.

3.1 RIGHT TRIANGLES

Figure 3.2 illustrates a right triangle in which we label the parts using standard notation. Note that side a is opposite α, and side b is opposite angle β. As in the first two chapters, we shall use a letter (b, for example) interchangeably to denote a side (line segment) of the triangle or to represent the length of that side; similarly for "angle α" and "measure α of the angle."

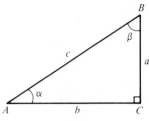

Figure 3.2

If, in addition to the right angle, the measures of two of the remaining five parts are known and at least one of these is a, b or c, then a unique triangle is determined and we can find the remaining parts. This will involve only the use of the definitions of trigonometric functions (as given in Section 2.1), the Pythagorean theorem, and the calculator. We illustrate by considering some examples. Solution of the first example is discussed in some detail. The others involve similar considerations, not all of which are recorded. In each case a calculator is used for numerical computations.

Examples

⚠ In a right triangle, $a = 32.4$ cm, $\alpha = 40°$. Find b, c and β.

Solution. We draw a right triangle and denote the given parts (a and α), as shown in Fig. 3.3. To determine side b, the first step is to look for an equation that involves b and the given parts. We could use either $\tan \alpha = a/b$, which gives $b = a/\tan \alpha$, or $\cot \alpha = b/a$ to get $b = a \cot \alpha$. Since the calculator does not have a ⌷ cot key, we shall choose the first equation:

$$b = \frac{a}{\tan \alpha} = \frac{32.4}{\tan 40°} = 38.6 \text{ cm.}$$

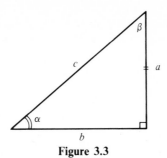

Figure 3.3

To determine the hypotenuse c we could use any of the three equations: $\sin \alpha = a/c$; $\csc \alpha = c/a$; $c = \sqrt{a^2 + b^2}$. In general, it is good practice to use a relationship that involves only the given parts, if possible. That is, the third option has a slight disadvantage in case we make an error in solving for b. The second has the disadvantage of involving cosecant, and our calculator does not have a ⌜csc⌟ key. Therefore we decide upon the first expression:

$$c = \frac{a}{\sin \alpha} = \frac{32.4}{\sin 40°} = 50.4 \text{ cm.}$$

We know from geometry that the sum of the three angles of a triangle is 180°: $\alpha + \beta + 90° = 180°$. Therefore we have

$$\beta = 180° - 90° - \alpha = 90° - 40° = 50°. \qquad ▮$$

Given $\alpha = 15°21'23''$ and $c = 3.587$ m, find a, b, and β (Fig. 3.4).

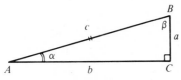

Figure 3.4

Solution. Since $\sin \alpha = a/c$, then $a = c \sin \alpha$, and

$$a = 3.587 \cdot \sin \ 15°21'23'' = 0.95 \text{ m.}$$

For b we use $\cos \alpha = b/c$, and so $b = c \cos \alpha$:

$$b = 3.587 \cdot \cos \ 15°21'23'' = 3.46 \text{ m.}$$

To find β we use $\beta = 90° - \alpha$:

$$\beta = 89°59'60'' - 15°21'23'' = 74°38'37''. \qquad ▮$$

⚠️3 Given $c = 16.25$ cm and $\beta = 68°24'$, find the area of the triangle (Fig. 3.5).

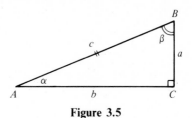

Figure 3.5

Solution. The area is equal to $ab/2$, so we first need to find sides a and b. From $\sin \beta = b/c$ we get $b = c \sin \beta$, and from $\cos \beta = a/c$ we get $a = c \cos \beta$. Therefore,

$$\text{Area} = \frac{1}{2} (c \cos \beta)(c \sin \beta) = \frac{c^2 \sin \beta \cos \beta}{2}$$

$$= \frac{(16.25)^2 (\sin 68°24' \cos 68°24')}{2} = 45.19 \text{ cm}^2. \qquad ▌$$

⚠️4 Given $a = 37.4$ cm, $b = 63.3$ cm, find c, α, and β (Fig. 3.6).

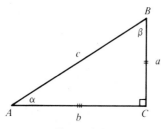

Figure 3.6

Solution. $c = \sqrt{a^2 + b^2} = \sqrt{(37.4)^2 + (63.3)^2} = 73.5$ cm. For angle α we use $\tan \alpha = a/b = 37.4/63.3 = 0.59084$.

We are now confronted with the problem of finding α when we know $\tan \alpha$. This is the inverse of the problem of finding $\tan \alpha$ when α is given. The subject of inverse trigonometric functions will be discussed formally in Chapter 5; here we shall merely point out that scientific calculators can be used to find an angle corresponding to a given value of a trigonometric function. Calculator keys for inverse functions are usually labeled as $\boxed{\sin^{-1}}$, $\boxed{\cos^{-1}}$, $\boxed{\tan^{-1}}$; or there is an $\boxed{\text{INV}}$ key that is to be followed by the appropriate $\boxed{\sin}$, $\boxed{\cos}$,

⬚tan⬚ key. We illustrate by completing the above problem where we know that
$\tan \alpha = 0.59084$ and we wish to determine α.

If the calculator has an ⬚INV⬚ key, then enter the number 0.59084 into the
display and, with calculator in degree mode, press the ⬚INV⬚ , ⬚tan⬚ keys in that
order. The display will read 30.5762° (to four decimal places).

If the calculator has a ⬚tan⁻¹⬚ key, then, with 0.59084 in the display and the
calculator in degree mode, press ⬚tan⁻¹⬚ . The display will read 30.5762°. Thus
$\alpha = 30.5762° = 30°34'24''$. To find β, we use $\beta = 90° - \alpha$ and so
$$\beta = 59°25'36''. \qquad \blacksquare$$

⑤ a) If $\sin \alpha = 0.4835$, find α in degrees correct to two decimal places.

  b) If $\cos \alpha = 0.6897$, find α in radians correct to three decimal places.

Solution.

  a) Place the calculator in degree mode, enter the number 0.4835 into the
     display and then press ⬚sin⁻¹⬚ or ⬚INV⬚ , ⬚sin⬚ . The display will show
     28.91°. Thus $\alpha = 28.91°$.

  b) Place the calculator in radian mode, enter the number 0.6897 into the
     display and then press ⬚cos⁻¹⬚ or ⬚INV⬚ , ⬚cos⬚ . The display will show
     0.810. That is, $\alpha = 0.810$ rad. $\qquad \blacksquare$

⑥ If $a = 8.31$ cm and $\beta = 21.63°$, find the area of the right triangle
(Fig. 3.7).

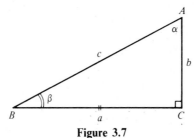

Figure 3.7

Solution. The area is equal to $ab/2$ and since $b = a \tan \beta$, we have

$$\text{Area} = \frac{1}{2} \cdot a^2 \tan \beta = \frac{1}{2} (8.31)^2 \tan 21.63° = 13.69 \ \text{cm}^2. \qquad \blacksquare$$

In certain applications it is necessary to measure angles from a horizontal
line of sight. An angle formed by a horizontal ray and the observer's line of
sight to an object above the horizontal is called the *angle of elevation*. If the
object is below the horizontal, the angle between the horizontal and the line of
sight is called the *angle of depression* (Fig. 3.8).

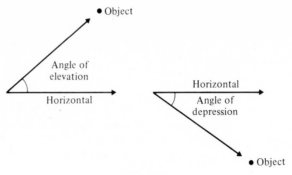

Figure 3.8

⑦   From a window 25 meters above the ground the angle of elevation to the top of a nearby building is 24°20′ and the angle of depression to the bottom of the building is 14°40′ (Fig. 3.9). Find the height of the building.

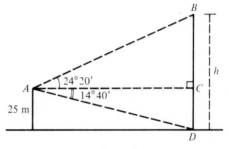

Figure 3.9

Solution. In the diagram we wish to find $h = \overline{BC} + \overline{CD}$. We know that $\overline{CD} = 25$ m, so $h = \overline{BC} + 25$ m. By using triangle ACD, we have

$$\overline{AC} = \overline{CD} \cot 14°40' = 25 \cot 14°40'.$$

Therefore, from triangle ABC, we get $\overline{BC} = (25 \cot 14°40' \tan 24°20')$m. Thus

$$h = 25 + 25 \cot 14°40' \tan 24°20'$$

$$= 25 + \frac{25 \tan 24°20'}{\tan 14°40'} = 68.20 \text{ m.} \qquad \blacksquare$$

Accuracy of Measurements

It should be noted that angle β in Example 3 was determined to the nearest second. This was done primarily to illustrate the technique for getting such accuracy. In applied work the degree of accuracy of computed values (as well as measured values) will depend upon several factors, including the ultimate use of the results. It is pointless to calculate the height of a mountain peak in meters to four decimal places and use such a number on a map.

In practical applications involving computations of angles and lengths, one of the first questions is: What degree of accuracy should be used? Naturally, the answer depends upon the particular problem and upon the subsequent application of the results. We cannot expect the computed values to have a greater number of reliable decimal digits than the starting data, which in applications are usually physical measurements.

In Appendix B we discuss the accuracy of computation in problems involving approximate numbers. It should be understood that the rules stated there are to be used in applied problems as a practical guide. *In this text* (as well as in most mathematics texts) *no effort is made to be completely consistent with these rules.* Most of our problems are mathematical in nature and our primary goal is to provide the student with examples that will lead to a better understanding of the basic mathematical concepts discussed. Thus, in most of the problems involving computations, the student is asked to find a result correct to a given number of decimal places, or to a given number of significant digits. Also in many problems we say, for example, that the length of a side of a triangle is 24.3, and we do not even specify the units. In practical applications (such as in physics, chemistry, engineering, etc.) the units will be specified and there should be no problem in following the rules given in Appendix B for computations with approximate numbers.

EXERCISE 3.1

In the problems of this exercise, give answers involving lengths and areas correct to two decimal places, and angle measures in degrees and minutes correct to the nearest minute.

Problems 1 through 15 refer to right triangles in which the letters used to denote sides and angles are as described in this section.

1. $\alpha = 35°24'$; $a = 3.27$ cm;   find b, c, β.

2. $a = 56$ cm, $b = 33$ cm;   find c, α, β.

3. $a = 175$ cm, $c = 337$ cm;   find b, α, β.

4. $\beta = 65.72°$, $a = 32.5$ m;   find b, c, α and the area of the triangle.

5. $\alpha = 27°17'$, $c = 56.5$ cm;   find a, b, β and the area of the triangle.

6. $b = 2730$ m, $c = 4666$ m;   find a, α, β.

7. $a = 24208$ m, $b = 10575$ m;   find c, α, β.

8. $\beta = 42°30'$, $b = 3.25$ cm;   find a, c, α.

9. $a = 288$ km, $\beta = 31.2845°$;   find b, c, α.

10. $a = 241.1$ cm, $b = 125.3$ cm;   find c, α, β.

11. $a = 5.36$ cm, $c = 12.48$ cm;   find b, α, β and the area of the triangle.

12. $b = 73.56$ cm, $c = 131.42$ cm;   find a, α, β and the area of the triangle.

13. $\alpha = 37.43°$, $c = 64.56$ cm;   find a, b, β and the area of the triangle.

14. $a = 0.143$ mm, $\alpha = 16.47°$;   find b, c, β.

15. $a = 2.53$ cm, $b = 1.48$ cm;   find c, α, β.

16. Assuming that the Earth is a sphere with a radius of 6400 km, find the minimum height of an airplane above the surface, at which the pilot will be able to see an object on the ground 100 km away. In Fig. 3.10 point B is the center of the Earth, A is the position of the plane, and object C is on the horizon ($\overline{AC} = 100$ km).

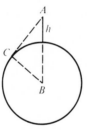

Figure 3.10

17. A line passes through two points (5, 2) and (8, 15). Find the angle between this line and the x-axis.

18. From a tower 27 meters tall the angle of depression of a boat on a lake is 56°. How far is the boat from the base of the tower? Assume that the base of the tower is in the same horizontal plane as the lake.

19. You wish to fence a triangular piece of land with dimensions $a = 236$ m and $\alpha = 70°$ (Fig. 3.11). Find the total amount of fencing you must purchase.

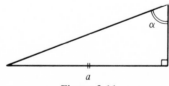

a

Figure 3.11

20. Find the area of an equilateral triangle with a side of length 12.56 cm.

21. Find the area of an isosceles triangle with equal sides 2.47 m long and an angle 41°37′ opposite one of them.

22. You wish to mount an antenna and have purchased a tower 12.48 meters tall. The tower is to be anchored from the top by three guy wires at a distance of 7.36 meters from the base (Fig. 3.12). How much guy wire do you need?

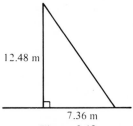

12.48 m

7.36 m

Figure 3.12

23. The sides of a parallelogram are 38.4 cm and 64.8 cm, and an interior angle is 115.65°. Find the area of the parallelogram.

24. A regular polygon is inscribed in a circle of radius 57 cm. Find the area of the polygon if it has

   a) four sides (a square)   b) six sides (a hexagon)
   c) eight sides (an octagon)   d) n sides

25. In Fig. 3.13, line segment $\overline{AB}$ is a diameter of the circle with radius 24 cm, C is a point on the circle, arc $\overarc{AC}$ is 27.3 cm long. Find the length of chord $\overline{AC}$. *Hint.* Let θ be the central angle shown in the diagram; use definition of radian measure to find θ. Recall facts from geometry about measures of central and inscribed angles in a circle.

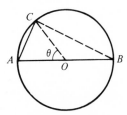

Figure 3.13

26. If the altitude of the sun is 17.48° at 5 P.M. on December 21, how far east of a retaining wall 5.48 meters tall should one locate plants requiring year-round full sun?

27. If figure $ABCD$ is a square with length of side 37.41 meters and angle $\theta = 36°15'$, find the lengths of $\overline{CF}$ and $\overline{CE}$ (Fig. 3.14).

28. A segment of a circle of radius 4.56 cm is shown as the shaded region between chord $\overline{AB}$ and arc $\overset{\frown}{AB}$ (Fig. 3.15). If the central angle θ is 1.15 radians, find the area of the segment.

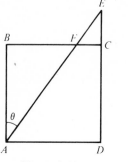

Figure 3.14

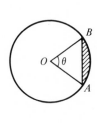

Figure 3.15

29. In Fig. 3.16, side a and angles α and β are given. Show that $x = a \sin \alpha \sin \beta$.

30. A surveyor wishes to determine the height of a mountain top above the horizontal ground. He observes the angles of elevation from two points A and B on the ground and in line with the mountain top. He measures the distance from A to B. These measurements are: $\alpha = 43°30'$, $\beta = 32°20'$, $AB = 256$ m. Find the height of the mountain top above the horizontal ground level (Fig. 3.17).

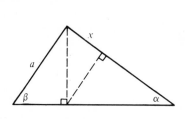

Figure 3.16

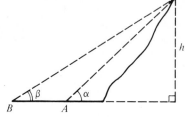

Figure 3.17

31. In Fig. 3.18 line segments $\overline{AD}$ and $\overline{BC}$ are parallel, the length of $\overline{AD}$ is 8.47 cm and $\theta = 41°36'$. Find the lengths of $\overline{BC}$ and $\overline{CD}$.

32. A triangular piece of land is bounded by two farm roads intersecting at right angles and a highway intersecting one of the roads at an angle of 24.5°, as shown in Fig. 3.19. You wish to purchase the property and know that the previous owner required 843 meters of fencing to enclose it. Land sells at $2.50 per square meter in this region. How much does the property cost?

33. From point A that is 8.1 meters above the horizontal level of the ground, the angle of elevation of the top of a tower (point B) is $\alpha = 32°30'$ and the angle of depression of its base (point C) is $\beta = 16°40'$ (Fig. 3.20). Find the height of the tower.

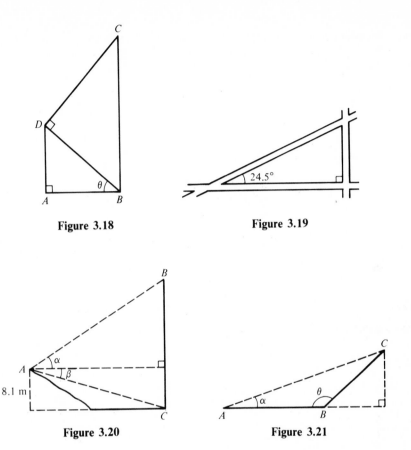

Figure 3.18

Figure 3.19

8.1 m

Figure 3.20

Figure 3.21

34. A surveyor starts at point A and measures $\overline{AB} = 41.32$ m, $\overline{BC} = 37.53$ m, $\theta = 137.44°$ (Fig. 3.21). Find the distance from A to C and angle α.

35. A sector with central angle $72°$ is cut out of a circular piece of tin of radius 16.48 cm. The edges of the remaining piece are joined together to form a cone. Find the volume of the cone (see inside front cover for volume formula).

36. Suppose A, B, C are vertices of a right triangle and α is the acute angle at A, as shown in Fig. 3.22. Also suppose the length of $\overline{AB}$ is 1. Extend side CA to point D so that the length of $\overline{AD}$ is also 1.

a) Show that the angle CDB is equal to $\alpha/2$.

b) Use right triangle BCD to find $\tan \alpha/2$. Specifically, show that it can be expressed in the form $\tan \alpha/2 = (\sin \alpha)/(1 + \cos \alpha)$. This useful identity will be seen again in Chapter 4.

37. In Problem 24 of Exercise 1.4, Motl's treadle sewing machine was described (Fig. 3.23). The radii of the two wheels are $r_1 = 3.5$ cm and $r_2 = 15.5$ cm. The distance between the centers is $\overline{EF} = 56$ cm. Find the length of the belt that goes

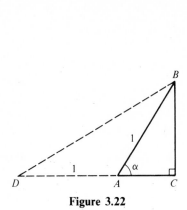

Figure 3.22

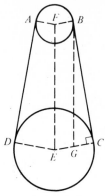

Figure 3.23

around the two wheels. In the diagram, E and F are centers of the wheels, points A, B, C, and D are points at which the belt is tangent to the respective wheels, and we construct line BG through B parallel to EF.

38. A right triangle is inscribed in a circle of radius 5.6 cm. One angle of the triangle is 64°. Find the lengths of the two sides.

39. The area of a right triangle is 6.73 cm² and one of its angles is 36°. Find the length of the hypotenuse.

40. The perimeter of a right triangle is 8.56 m and one of its angles is 23°30′. Find the lengths of the two sides.

41. One angle of a right triangle is 47°30′ and its perimeter is 15.48 cm. Determine the area of the triangle.

3.2 LAW OF COSINES

Techniques used in the preceding section apply to solution of right triangles. We now consider the general case in which triangles are not necessarily right triangles. Although it is true that solving a general triangle can be reduced to problems involving right triangles, it is desirable to have formulas that can be applied directly.

Suppose A, B, C are vertices of a triangle, as shown in Fig. 3.24. We shall use Greek letters α, β, γ to denote the three angles and a, b, c to represent the

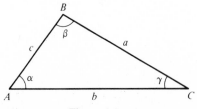

Figure 3.24

three sides. As indicated in Fig. 3.24, angle α has vertex at A and side a is opposite α; likewise for B, β, b and C, γ, c.

Thus a triangle has six parts—three angles and three sides. In general, if three parts are known (at least one of which is a side), then a fixed triangle is determined and our problem is to solve for the remaining three parts. We shall discuss two sets of formulas that will be useful; these are called *Law of cosines* and *Law of sines.*

In this section we develop the Law of cosines; the Law of sines will be discussed in the next section.

Figure 3.25 shows triangle ABC, where D is the base of the altitude from vertex A. Let $h = \overline{AD}$ and $x = \overline{CD}$. From right triangle ADC we get

$$x = b \cos \gamma \qquad \text{and} \qquad h = b \sin \gamma.$$

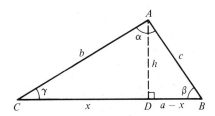

Figure 3.25

Applying the Pythagorean theorem to right triangle ADB, we have

$$c^2 = h^2 + (a - x)^2 = h^2 + a^2 - 2ax + x^2.$$

Substituting $x = b \cos \gamma$ and $h = b \sin \gamma$ gives

$$\begin{aligned} c^2 &= (b \sin \gamma)^2 + a^2 - 2a(b \cos \gamma) + (b \cos \gamma)^2 \\ &= a^2 + b^2[(\sin \gamma)^2 + (\cos \gamma)^2] - 2\,ab \cos \gamma \\ &= a^2 + b^2 - 2ab \cos \gamma, \end{aligned}$$

where in the last step we replaced $(\sin \gamma)^2 + (\cos \gamma)^2$ by 1 (see Eq. (2.12)). Thus we have

$$c^2 = a^2 + b^2 - 2ab \cos \gamma.\text{*}$$

In a similar manner we can develop analogous formulas for a^2 and b^2. The three equations are listed in (3.1) and these are called the *Law of cosines* for triangle ABC:

$$\boxed{\begin{aligned} a^2 &= b^2 + c^2 - 2bc \cos \alpha, \\ b^2 &= a^2 + c^2 - 2ac \cos \beta, \\ c^2 &= a^2 + b^2 - 2ab \cos \gamma. \end{aligned}} \qquad (3.1)$$

---

*In the derivation of this formula the acute angle γ of Fig. 3.25 was used. Actually the final result holds if γ is any angle between $0°$ and $180°$ (see Problem 15 of Exercise 3.2).

The technique used to solve a triangle depends upon the given information. We classify all problems into the following four cases according to the three given parts:

1. three sides,
2. two sides and the included angle,
3. two sides and an angle opposite one of them,
4. one side and two angles.

The Law of cosines is particularly suitable for solving triangles described by cases 1 and 2, while the Law of sines is better suited for case 4. Case 3 presents a special problem in that it is possible for the given information to describe either one triangle, two triangles, or no triangle (as illustrated by Examples 3 through 5 of this section). For this reason, case 3 is usually referred to as the *ambiguous case*. We shall illustrate through examples how to handle this case by using the Law of cosines. This involves solution of a quadratic equation, but with the aid of a calculator the computation of answers becomes easy.

Examples

⚠ *Given two sides and the included angle.* Suppose $a = 33.24$, $b = 47.37$, and $\gamma = 38°15'$. Find c, α and β (Fig. 3.26).

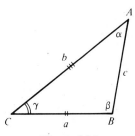

Figure 3.26

Solution. To find c we use the third equation of (3.1):

$$c^2 = (33.24)^2 + (47.37)^2 - 2(33.24)(47.37)\cos\ 38°15'.$$

Using a calculator to evaluate the right-hand side and then pressing the $\boxed{\sqrt{x}}$ key, we get

$$c = 29.59.$$

Hint. To get maximum calculator accuracy, store the full decimal value of c in the calculator and then use that value in subsequent computations involved in determining α and β.

We now determine α by using the first equation of (3.1) in the form

$$\cos \alpha = \frac{b^2 + c^2 - a^2}{2bc}.$$

This gives

$$\alpha = 44.0589° = 44°04'.$$

Similarly, we can use the second equation of (3.1) to determine β:

$$\cos \beta = \frac{a^2 + c^2 - b^2}{2ac}$$

and we get

$$\beta = 97°41'.$$

We could have determined β by using $\beta = 180° - (\alpha + \beta)$ but we prefer to use this as a check of our computations. That is, we see that

$$\alpha + \beta + \gamma = 44°04' + 97°41' + 38°15' = 180°,$$

and so we can be reasonably certain that our computations are correct. ▮

2. *Given three sides.* Suppose $a = 56.84$, $b = 83.45$, and $c = 51.63$. Find angles α, β, and γ.

Solution.

$$\cos \alpha = \frac{b^2 + c^2 - a^2}{2bc} = \frac{(83.45)^2 + (51.63)^2 - (56.84)^2}{2(83.45)(51.63)}.$$

This gives

$$\alpha = 42.0491° = 42°03',$$

$$\cos \beta = \frac{a^2 + c^2 - b^2}{2ac} = \frac{(56.84)^2 + (51.63)^2 - (83.45)^2}{2(56.84)(51.63)}.$$

Thus

$$\beta = 100.4788° = 100°29',$$

$$\cos \gamma = \frac{a^2 + b^2 - c^2}{2ab} = \frac{(56.84)^2 + (83.45)^2 - (51.63)^2}{2(56.84)(83.45)}.$$

We get

$$\gamma = 37.4721° = 37°28'.$$

As a check, we add the computed values of α, β, γ and get

$$\alpha + \beta + \gamma = 42°03' + 100°29' + 37°28' = 180°. \qquad ▮$$

3. *Given two sides and an angle opposite one of them.* This is the so-called ambiguous case in which there may be two solutions, one solution, or no solution, depending upon the given data. In the following three examples we illustrate each of the three possibilities (see Problem 32 of this section for further discussion of this case).

Suppose $a = 17.48$, $b = 25.63$, and $\alpha = 37°48'$. Find c, β, and γ.

Solution. If we substitute the given values of a, b, α into the first expression of (3.1)

$$a^2 = b^2 + c^2 - 2bc \cos \alpha,$$

the resulting equation will be quadratic in c:

$$c^2 - (2b \cos \alpha)c + (b^2 - a^2) = 0.*$$

Applying the quadratic formula from algebra, we have

$$c = \frac{1}{2}\left[2b \cos \alpha \pm \sqrt{(-2b \cos \alpha)^2 - 4(b^2 - a^2)}\right]$$

$$= b \cos \alpha \pm \sqrt{a^2 - b^2[1 - (\cos \alpha)^2]}.$$

Since $1 - (\cos \alpha)^2$ is identically equal to $(\sin \alpha)^2$ (see Eq. (2.12)), we get

$$\boxed{c = b \cos \alpha \pm \sqrt{a^2 - (b \sin \alpha)^2}.} \qquad (3.2)$$

Substituting the given values of a, b, and α into Eq. (3.2) gives

$$c = 25.63 \cos 37°48' \pm \sqrt{(17.48)^2 - (25.63)^2(\sin 37°48')^2}.$$

We can evaluate this result by calculator. To avoid recording any intermediate computations, we can first evaluate the square-root part and store it by using the ⌊STO⌋ key (and recall it when we wish by using the ⌊RCL⌋ key).† Thus we get two answers:

$$c_1 = 27.91873 \qquad \text{and} \qquad c_2 = 12.58462.$$

To be consistent with the given data, we round off to two decimal places:

$$c_1 = 27.92 \qquad \text{and} \qquad c_2 = 12.58.$$

In this example we see that there are two solutions; these are illustrated in Fig. 3.27. The second triangle can be obtained from the first by rotating side a

---

*Substituting the values of a, b, and α at this point gives

$$c^2 - [2(25.63)\cos 37°48']c + (25.63^2 - 17.48^2) = 0.$$

That is,

$$c^2 - 40.5033c + 351.3465 = 0.$$

This is the quadratic equation that determines c but it is not necessary to record the intermediate numbers appearing as the coefficient of c and the constant term. It is simpler to solve the quadratic equation for the general case and then substitute the values of a, b, and α into the final result shown in Eq. (3.2).

†The ⌊STO⌋ and ⌊RCL⌋ keys may be labeled differently on some calculators (see Appendix A or owner's manual).

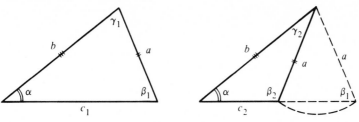

Figure 3.27

clockwise about the top vertex, as indicated in the diagram. We now proceed to find β_1 and γ_1 by using

$$\cos \beta_1 = \frac{a^2 + c_1^2 - b^2}{2ac_1} \qquad \text{and} \qquad \cos \gamma_1 = \frac{a^2 + b^2 - c_1^2}{2ab}.$$

This gives

$$\beta_1 = 63°59' \qquad \text{and} \qquad \gamma_1 = 78°13'.$$

As a check we add the three angles:

$$\alpha + \beta_1 + \gamma_1 = 37°48' + 63°59' + 78°13' = 180°.$$

To find β_2 and γ_2 we note that

$$\beta_2 = 180° - \beta_1 = 180° - 63°59' = 116°01',$$
$$\gamma_2 = 180° - (\alpha + \beta_2) = 26°11'.$$

$\boxed{4}$ $a = 32$, $b = 25$, and $\alpha = 43°$. Find c (Fig. 3.28).

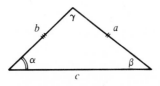

Figure 3.28

Solution. This problem is similar to that of Example 3 and so we can find c by substituting into Eq. (3.2):

$$c = 25 \cos 43° \pm \sqrt{(32)^2 - (25)^2 (\sin 43°)^2}.$$

This gives

$$c_1 = 45.36 \qquad \text{and} \qquad c_2 = -8.80.$$

Since c_2 is negative, we do not get a triangle corresponding to it. Therefore there is only one solution with $c = 45.36$.

5 $a = 27$, $b = 64$, and $\alpha = 68°$. Find c (Fig. 3.29).

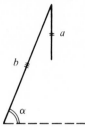

Figure 3.29

Solution. Applying Eq. (3.2) gives

$$c = 64 \cos 68° \pm \sqrt{(27)^2 - (64)^2(\sin 68°)^2}.$$

When a calculator is used to evaluate this result, it indicates "Error". The reason for this is that the number under the square root is negative (-2792.21), and so the roots of the quadratic equation for c are imaginary. Thus there is no triangle corresponding to the given data. In the diagram we see that side a is not long enough to reach the third side. ∎

EXERCISE 3.2

In Problems 1 through 14 use the given data to find the remaining three parts of the triangle. Give answers involving length correct to the same number of significant digits as the given data, and calculate angles correct to the nearest minute.

1. $a = 36$, $b = 67$, $\gamma = 43°$.

2. $b = 24$, $c = 73$, $\alpha = 130°$.

3. $a = 85$, $c = 42$, $\beta = 83°24'$.

4. $a = 41.32$, $b = 57.56$, $\gamma = 61°12'$.

5. $a = 1.47$, $c = 2.16$, $\alpha = 124.75°$.

6. $a = 17$, $b = 45$, $c = 50$.

7. $a = 288$, $b = 175$, $c = 337$.

8. $a = 31.5$, $b = 63.4$, $c = 41.6$.

9. $a = 6.743$, $b = 4.567$, $c = 8.125$.

10. $a = 17$, $b = 25$, $\alpha = 37°$.

11. $a = 24.57$, $b = 34.63$, $\alpha = 31°15'$.

12. $c = 4666$, $a = 2730$, $\alpha = 32°$.

13. $b = 35$, $c = 31$, $\beta = 68°$.

14. $a = 1.45$, $b = 3.54$, $\beta = 53°$.

15. In this section the Law of cosines was derived using Fig. 3.25, where angle γ was acute. Suppose γ is obtuse as in Fig. 3.30. Derive the Law of cosines for this case by showing that

$$c^2 = a^2 + b^2 - 2ab \cos \gamma.$$

16. If triangle ABC is a right triangle with $\gamma = 90°$, show that the third expression of Eq. (3.1) can be reduced to the Pythagorean theorem.

17. A ship sails due east form point A for a distance of 48.6 km; then it changes direction southward by an angle of $16°40'$, as shown in Fig 3.31. After sailing 37.8 km in the new direction, how far is the ship from point A?

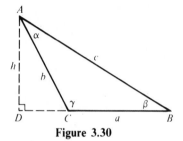

Figure 3.30

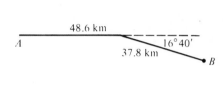

Figure 3.31

18. If $a = 32.6$, $b = 56.3$, $c = 36.8$, find the measure of the smallest angle of the triangle correct to the nearest minute.

19. If $a = 39,098$, $b = 17,160$, and $c = 42,698$, find the measure of the largest angle of the triangle correct to the nearest minute.

20. If $a = 3.76$, $b = 5.34$, and $\gamma = 48°50'$, find the altitude to side b and then determine the area of the triangle correct to two decimal places.

21. If $b = 34.52$, $c = 76.81$, and $\alpha = 121°30'$, find the altitude to c and then find the area of the triangle correct to two decimal places.

22. An equilateral triangle is inscribed in a circle of radius 4.56. Find the perimeter of the triangle.

23. A square is inscribed in a circle of radius 4.56. Find the area of the square.

24. A dime, a nickel, and a quarter are placed on a table so that they just touch each other, as shown in Fig. 3.32. The diameters of the dime, nickel, and quarter are 1.75 cm, 2.25 cm, and 2.50 cm, respectively. Find the length of the smaller part of the circumference of the quarter between the two points where it touches the dime and the nickel. (In the diagram, D, N, and Q are respective centers.)

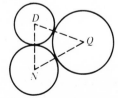

Figure 3.32

25. In Problem 24, the centers of the coins form a triangle. Find the measure of the smallest angle to the nearest degree.

26. Use the Law of cosine equations given in (3.1) as follows: Replace term b^2 in the first equation by that given by the right side of the second equation, and then simplify to get

$$a \cos \beta + b \cos \alpha = c.$$

In a similar manner, if we use the first and third, and then the second and third equations of (3.1), we can get

$$c \cos \alpha + a \cos \gamma = b,$$
$$b \cos \gamma + c \cos \beta = a.$$

27. In Example 3 of this section, after determining c_1 we solved for β_1 by using the Law of cosines. As an alternative method for finding β_1, use the first equation derived in Problem 26 in the form

$$\cos \beta_1 = \frac{c_1 - b \cos \alpha}{a}$$

and solve for β_1. Similarly find γ_1 by using the second equation given in Problem 26. Check your results with those given in the example.

28. In Example 4 of this section, use the given data and the result for c to find β by applying the equation derived in Problem 26.

29. A vertical tower BC is located on a hill whose slope is $12°$ steep (Fig. 3.33). From point A (43 meters down the hill from base B of the tower) the angle of elevation of point C at the top of the tower is $\alpha = 37°$. Find the height of the tower.

30. A triangular slab of marble has sides of length 120 cm, 156 cm, and 173 cm. If it is placed vertically, so that the longest edge is on the ground, how high from the ground will it reach?

31. Consider a regular pentagon $ABCDE$ with sides of unit length, as shown in Fig. 3.34. Let r be the length of a diagonal (such as CE).

   a) Show that each of two angles α is equal to $36°$, and each of the angles β is $72°$. Thus triangles ACE and BCF are similar.

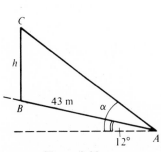

Figure 3.33

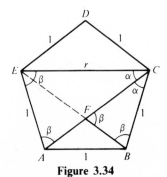

Figure 3.34

b) Show that $\overline{CF} = 1$ and $\overline{BF} = r - 1$; then, using the corresponding-ratios property of similar triangles, prove that r satisfies the equation $r^2 - r - 1 = 0$. Solve this equation and get

$$r = \frac{1 + \sqrt{5}}{2} .$$

This is a well-known number called the *golden ratio.*

c) Apply the Law of cosines to triangle BCF to find cos $72°$ and show that

$$\cos 72° = \frac{1}{2r} = \frac{1}{1 + \sqrt{5}}.$$

Thus we have expressed cos $72°$ in exact form (in fact, in simple terms involving the golden ratio). As a check, evaluate cos $72°$ directly with your calculator and then evaluate $1/(1 + \sqrt{5})$, and see if the two numbers are equal.

32. In Examples 3 through 5 we gave solutions of problems in which the given parts of a triangle are two sides and an angle opposite one of them. Suppose a, b, and α are the given parts. What conclusions can be drawn concerning the number of solutions in each of the situations listed below? In each case draw a diagram starting with α and b — for example,

—and show how a fits into the picture. Use Eq. (3.2) to support your conclusions. Suppose α *is an acute angle* and

    a) $a = b \sin \alpha$ b) $a < b \sin \alpha$
    c) $b \sin \alpha < a < b$ d) $a \geq b$

Examine the problem for the case when α *is an obtuse angle* and when $\alpha = 90°$. Draw diagrams to illustrate your conclusions.

3.3 LAW OF SINES

In triangle ABC of Fig. 3.35 the sides and angles are labeled as in the preceding section, and point D is the base of altitude h from vertex B. From the two right triangles we have

$$\sin \alpha = \frac{h}{c} \quad \text{and} \quad \sin \gamma = \frac{h}{a}.$$

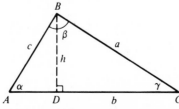

Figure 3.35

Eliminating h in these two equations, we get $c \sin \alpha = a \sin \gamma$. This can be written as

$$\frac{\sin \alpha}{a} = \frac{\sin \gamma}{c}.$$

In a similar manner (see Problem 24 of this section), we can show that

$$\frac{\sin \alpha}{a} = \frac{\sin \beta}{b} \quad \text{and} \quad \frac{\sin \beta}{b} = \frac{\sin \gamma}{c}.$$

The three equations given here are called the *Law of sines* and are written as:

$$\boxed{\frac{\sin \alpha}{a} = \frac{\sin \beta}{b} = \frac{\sin \gamma}{c}} \qquad (3.3)$$

Note. To derive this formula we used a diagram in which angles α and β were both acute. The result still holds if one of the angles is obtuse (see Problem 27 of this section).

In the preceding section we listed four cases to be considered in solving triangles and indicated that case 4 (in which one side and two angles are given) can be solved by using the Law of sines. We now illustrate this case.

Examples

△1 Suppose $b = 5.834$, $\alpha = 64°12'$, and $\gamma = 47°47'$. Find a, c and β (Fig. 3.36).

Solution. To find β, we use $\beta = 180° - (\alpha + \gamma)$ and get $\beta = 68°01'$. To determine a we use the Law of sines in the form

$$a = \frac{b \sin \alpha}{\sin \beta} = \frac{5.834 \sin 64°12'}{\sin 68°01'}.$$

This gives $a = 5.664$. Similarly,

$$c = \frac{b \sin \gamma}{\sin \beta} = \frac{5.834 \sin 47°47'}{\sin 68°01'} = 4.659. \qquad ∎$$

△2 Given $\alpha = 42°23'$, $a = 74.51$, $b = 71.35$, find the area of triangle ABC (Fig. 3.37).

Solution. We use the formula for area of a triangle:

$$\text{Area} = \frac{1}{2} \text{ Base} \times \text{Altitude}.$$

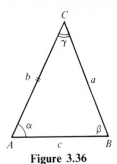

Figure 3.36

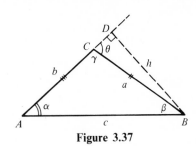

Figure 3.37

As shown in the diagram, let h be the altitude to side b. Thus Area $= \frac{1}{2}\, bh$.
First we find β by using the Law of sines:

$$\sin \beta = \frac{b \sin \alpha}{a} = \frac{71.35 \sin 42°23'}{74.51}.$$

This gives $\beta = 40°12'$. Since $\theta = \alpha + \beta$ (exterior angle of a triangle is the sum of the opposite interior angles), we have

$$\theta = 42°23' + 40°12' = 82°35'.$$

From right triangle BDC we get

$$h = a \sin \theta = 74.51 \sin 82°35' = 73.89.$$

Therefore

$$\text{Area} = \frac{1}{2}\, bh = \frac{1}{2}\, 71.35 \cdot 73.89 = 2635.91. \qquad \blacksquare$$

EXERCISE 3.3

In Problems 1 through 8, use the given data to find the remaining three parts of the triangle. Give answers involving length correct to the same number of significant digits as the given data, and calculate angles correct to the nearest minute.

1. $\alpha = 27°$, $\beta = 73°$, $a = 16$.

2. $\beta = 67°$, $\gamma = 26°$, $a = 463$.

3. $\alpha = 47°$, $\gamma = 112°$, $c = 81$.

4. $\alpha = 51°$, $\beta = 70°$, $c = 133$.

5. $\alpha = 32°17'$, $\beta = 55°12'$, $a = 32.5$.

6. $\beta = 61°47'$, $\gamma = 82°15'$, $b = 63.54$.

7. $\alpha = 73.46°$, $\beta = 25.75°$, $c = 4.875$.

8. $\alpha = 35.48°$, $\gamma = 73.54°$, $b = 3.754$.

9. A surveyor wishes to find the distance from point A to a point C on the opposite side of the river. He locates a point B on his side of the river and measures the distance $\overline{AB}$ and the two angles α and β, as shown in Fig. 3.38. The measurements are $\overline{AB} = 132.4$ m, $\alpha = 78°$, $\beta = 53°$. Find the distance $\overline{AC}$.

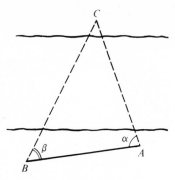

Figure 3.38

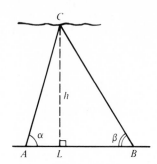

Figure 3.39

10. In order to measure the height of clouds at night, two observers are located 126 meters apart at points A and B; the spotlight is at point L in line with A and B. A vertical beam of light from L is reflected from the bottom of the clouds at point C and the angles of elevation are measured from A and B. These are $\alpha = 74°$ and $\beta = 58°$, as shown in Fig. 3.39. How far above the ground is the bottom of the clouds?

11. Triangle ABC has measurements $a = 41.3$ cm, $\alpha = 43.5°$, $\beta = 73.4°$. Find the length of the longest side.

12. From point A on top of a building the angle of depression of point C on the ground is observed to be $\alpha = 54°$, while from a window at point B (15 meters directly below A) the angle of depression is $\beta = 42°$. Find the height of the building (Fig. 3.40).

13. Find the area of the triangle described by $\alpha = 47°31'$, $\beta = 67°50'$, $a = 16.36$.

14. Find the area of the triangle where $\beta = 36°28'$, $a = 37.54$, $b = 41.63$.

15. Use the Law of sines as an alternative method to solve Problem 11 of Exercise 3.2, in which $a = 24.57$, $b = 34.63$, $\alpha = 31°15'$; find β, γ, and c.

16. If, in triangle ABC, $c = 4666$, $a = 2730$, $\alpha = 35.82°$, find angle γ.

17. A surveyor wishes to find the width of a river. He notices a tree T on the opposite bank, so he takes two points A and B along the bank on his side of the river. He

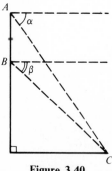

Figure 3.40

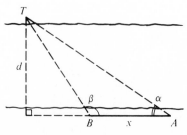

Figure 3.41

measures the distance x between A and B, and the two angles α and β, as shown in Fig. 3.41. He finds $x = 19.8$ meters, $\alpha = 33°$, $\beta = 124°$. From these measurements calculate the width d of the river.

18. A technique for determining the height of an inaccessible point is the following: a surveyor locates two points A and B and measures the distance between them. Then the angles α, β, θ are measured. This is illustrated by Fig. 3.42 in which points A, B, C are in the plane of the ground, D is directly above C, angle θ is the angle of elevation of point D from B, and α and β are angles of triangle ABC. Show that

$$a = \frac{d \sin \alpha}{\sin[180° - (\alpha + \beta)]} \quad \text{and} \quad h = \frac{d \sin \alpha \tan \theta}{\sin[180° - (\alpha + \beta)]}.$$

19. In Problem 18, suppose that we wish to determine the height h of a mountain peak, and points A and B are such that $d = 463$ meters, $\beta = 63°10'$, $\alpha = 46°40'$, $\theta = 47°20'$. Find h.

20. From point C located on a hill $21°$ steep, the elevation angle of the top A of a nearby building is observed to be $\alpha = 25°$ and the angle of depression of the base B is $\beta = 12°$. If the distance between C and the bottom of the hill D is 24 meters, find the height of the building (Fig. 3.43).

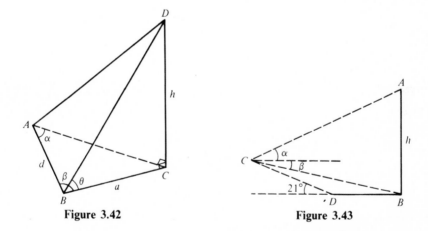

Figure 3.42   Figure 3.43

21. Points A and B are located on opposites sides of a lake (Fig. 3.44). From point C on a nearby hill the angles of depression of A and B are observed to be $\alpha = 12°$ and $\beta = 17°$, respectively. If the hill is $27°$ steep, and point D at the base of the hill is 48 meters from C, find the width of the lake.

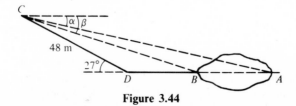

Figure 3.44

22. On a rectangular set of coordinates the locations of two forest-ranger stations are given as A: (15, 32), B: (84, 15). A fire is spotted at point C and angles $\alpha = 20°$, $\beta = 117°$ are measured, as shown in Fig. 3.45. Locate the fire by finding the coordinates of C.

23. Suppose a triangle ABC is inscribed in a circle, as shown in Fig. 3.46. Show that the ratios appearing in the Law of sines

$$\frac{a}{\sin\ \alpha} = \frac{b}{\sin\ \beta} = \frac{c}{\sin\ \gamma}$$

are equal to the diameter of the circle, that is,

$$\text{Diameter} = \frac{a}{\sin\ \alpha}.$$

Hint. Point D is selected so that side DB passes through the center O of the circle. Recall from geometry that angle CDB is equal to angle CAB (angle α). Also, angle DCB is a right angle and DB is a diameter.

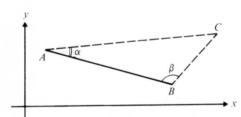

Figure 3.45

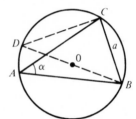

Figure 3.46

24. To complete the proof of the Law of sines given in this section, it is necessary to show that

$$\frac{\sin\ \alpha}{a} = \frac{\sin\ \beta}{b}.$$

Hint. Adjust the diagram in Fig. 3.35 as shown in Fig. 3.47.

25. A surveyor wishes to determine the distance between points A and B on opposite sides of a lake. He does this by taking points C and D (Fig. 3.48) and gets the following measurements: $\overline{AC} = 205$ m, $\overline{CD} = 263$ m, $\overline{DB} = 185$ m, $\alpha = 126°$, and $\beta = 104°$. Using this information, find (to the nearest meter) the distance across the lake.

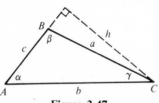

Figure 3.47

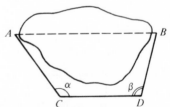

Figure 3.48

26. A railroad crosses the highway at point C at an angle of 40°, as shown in Fig. 3.49.
   An observer at point A on the highway (1.5 km from C) notices that it takes a train
   20 seconds to travel from P to Q and that the angles α and β are $\alpha = 45°$, $\beta = 75°$.
   How fast is the train traveling?

27. In the derivation of the Law of sines, Fig. 3.35 was used, in which both angles α and
   γ are acute. Derive the same law using a diagram in which angle α is obtuse
   (Fig. 3.50). Use the fact that $\sin(180° - \alpha) = \sin \alpha$.

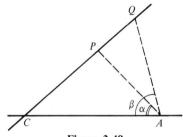

Figure 3.49

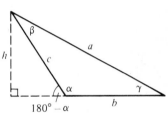

Figure 3.50

3.4 AREA OF A TRIANGLE

In some problems of Sections 3.2 and 3.3 the student was asked to find areas
of triangles. In each case the approach was to find the altitude of the triangle,
then use the formula Area = ½ Base × Altitude. In this section we develop
general formulas for finding areas of triangles.

1. Given Two Angles and a Side

Suppose α, γ, and, a are given as shown in Fig. 3.51. Using the Law of sines,
we obtain

$$c = \frac{a \sin \gamma}{\sin \alpha}.$$

The altitude h can be determined from the right triangle involving β:

$$h = a \sin \beta.$$

Therefore,

$$\text{Area} = \frac{1}{2} \frac{a \sin \gamma}{\sin \alpha} a \sin \beta.$$

Using $\beta = 180° - (\alpha + \gamma)$, we get

$$\text{Area} = \frac{a^2 \sin \gamma \sin [180° - (\alpha + \gamma)]}{2 \sin \alpha}. \qquad (3.4)$$

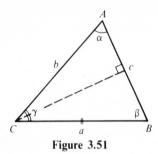

Figure 3.51

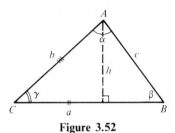

Figure 3.52

2. Given Two Sides and the Included Angle

Suppose a, b, and γ are given. Let h be the altitude to $\overline{CB}$, as shown in Fig. 3.52. From the right triangle containing angle γ, we have $h = b \sin \gamma$. Therefore,

$$\text{Area} = \frac{1}{2}\, ab\, \sin \gamma. \tag{3.5}$$

If γ is an obtuse angle, the diagram shown in Fig. 3.52 is different, but the formula still holds (see Problem 10 of Exercise 3.4).

3. Given Three Sides

In this case we derive the famous Heron's formula, named after the Greek philosopher-mathematician Heron (also known as Hero) of Alexandria (75 B.C.).

Suppose a, b, and c are given. We wish to derive a formula for area in terms of the three sides. We can use Eq. (3.5) given above, provided $\sin \gamma$ can be expressed in terms of a, b, and c. In observation 7 of Section 2.4 we stated that $(\sin \gamma)^2 + (\cos \gamma)^2 = 1$. This can be used to find $(\sin \gamma)^2$ in terms of $\cos \gamma$, as follows:

$$(\sin \gamma)^2 = 1 - (\cos \gamma)^2 = (1 + \cos \gamma)(1 - \cos \gamma). \tag{3.6}$$

We now get $\cos \gamma$ in terms of a, b, and c by using the Law of cosines:

$$\cos \gamma = \frac{a^2 + b^2 - c^2}{2ab}. \tag{3.7}$$

By substituting Eqs. (3.6) and (3.7) into Eq. (3.5), we get

$$\text{Area} = \frac{1}{2}\, ab \sqrt{\left(1 - \frac{a^2 + b^2 - c^2}{2ab}\right)\left(1 + \frac{a^2 + b^2 - c^2}{2ab}\right)}. \tag{3.8}$$

This result can be written in compact form by introducing the quantity s denoting one-half the perimeter of the triangle (called the *semiperimeter*), that is,

$$s = \frac{1}{2}\,(a + b + c).$$

Then, as a result of a good exercise in algebra (see Problem 7 of this section), we get *Heron's formula:*

$$\text{Area} = \sqrt{s(s - a)\ (s - b)\ (s - c)}. \tag{3.9}$$

Examples

1. Find the area of the triangle that has $b = 3.57$, $c = 4.83$, and $\alpha = 49°38'$.

Solution. Using an equivalent form of Eq. (3.5), we obtain

$$\text{Area} = \frac{1}{2}\,bc\,\sin\,\alpha = \frac{1}{2}\cdot 3.57\cdot 4.83\cdot\sin\,49°38' = 6.57.\qquad\blacksquare$$

2. If $a = 34.75$, $b = 48.38$, and $c = 28.46$, find the area of the triangle.

Solution. Use Heron's formula stated in Eq. (3.9):

$$\text{Area} = \sqrt{s(s - a)\ (s - b)\ (s - c)},$$

where $s = \frac{1}{2}\,(a + b + c) = \frac{1}{2}\,(34.75 + 48.38 + 28.46)$. Put this result in the memory of the calculator (press STO or appropriate key). The remaining calculation can be carried out by using the RCL key to recall s when needed. Evaluate:

$$\text{Area} = \sqrt{s(s - 34.75)\ (s - 48.38)\ (s - 28.46)} = 487.85.\qquad\blacksquare$$

EXERCISE 3.4

In Problems 1 through 6 find the area of the given triangle. Express each answer correct to the same number of decimal places as that of corresponding length measurements.

1. $\alpha = 37°14'$, $\beta = 65°24'$, $a = 34.6$.

2. $\alpha = 42°15'$, $\gamma = 96°32'$, $b = 483$.

3. $a = 32.7$, $b = 73.2$, $\gamma = 57°34'$.

4. $b = 73.6$, $c = 87.6$, $\alpha = 124°47'$.

5. $a = 73.5$, $b = 84.8$, $c = 58.5$.

6. $a = 0.433$, $b = 0.632$, $c = 0.543$.

7. In the development of Heron's formula we introduced the quantity $s = \frac{1}{2}(a + b + c)$ and indicated that, after some algebraic manipulation, Eq. (3.8) can be written in the form given by Eq. (3.9). To do this, we go through the following steps:

$$1 - \cos\,\gamma = 1 - \frac{a^2 + b^2 - c^2}{2ab} = \frac{c^2 - (a-b)^2}{2ab} = \frac{(c - a + b)(c + a - b)}{2ab}$$

$$= \frac{(a + b + c - 2a)(a + b + c - 2b)}{2ab} = \frac{2(s - a)(s - b)}{ab}.$$

Complete the problem by going through similar steps for $1 + \cos\,\gamma$, and then obtain the formula given in Eq. (3.9).

8. Suppose a circle is inscribed in a triangle with sides a, b, c (Fig. 3.53). Show that the radius of the circle is given by

$$r = \sqrt{\frac{(s - a)\,(s - b)\,(s - c)}{s}}.$$

Hint. From geometry recall that the bisectors of the three angles of a triangle are concurrent and their point of intersection is the center of the circle.

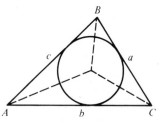

Figure 3.53

9. Given a circle of radius 8.435 and a central angle $\theta = 52°35'$, find the area of the shaded region between the chord and arc, as shown in Fig. 3.54.

10. In this section we derived a formula for the area of a triangle when two sides a, b, and the included angle γ are given. A triangle with an obtuse angle γ is shown in Fig. 3.55. Prove the area formula Area $= \frac{1}{2}\,ab \sin\,\gamma$.

Figure 3.54

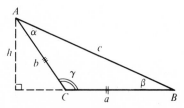

Figure 3.55

11. A farm consists of a triangular plot of land bounded on three sides by roads, in which $\gamma = 47°$, $a = 254$ m, and $b = 531$ m (Fig. 3.56). Find the area of the farm and also the amount of fencing required to completely enclose it.

12. A level lot is in the shape of a quadrilateral with dimensions shown in Fig. 3.57. If land sells for $3.50 per square meter, find the cost of the lot.

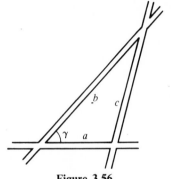

Figure 3.56

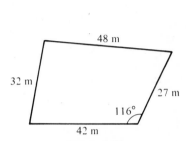

Figure 3.57

13. A farm is triangular; the rectangular coordinates of its vertices are A: (247, 123), B: (72, 411), C: (328, 483), and the unit of measurement is the meter. Find the area correct to three significant digits.

14. The area of triangle ABC is 246.3 m², $a = 31.4$ m, and $b = 17.5$ m. Find angle γ to the nearest minute.

15. If the area of triangle ABC is 25.46 m², $\alpha = 46°$, and $\beta = 82°$, find the lengths of the three sides. Give answers in meters correct to two decimal places.

16. The area of triangle ABC is 254.6 cm². Find the area of the new triangle if
    a) Each side of ABC is doubled;
    b) Each side of ABC is tripled.

17. Suppose that $\alpha = 53°$, $c = 35$ cm, and the area of triangle ABC is 387 cm². Find b and a.

18. Quadrilateral $OABC$ is inscribed in a quarter circle, as shown in Fig. 3.58, where

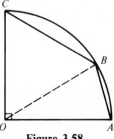

Figure 3.58

$|\overline{AB}| = 2$ and $|\overline{BC}| = 4$. Find the area of $OABC$ and express the answer as $a + b\sqrt{c}$, where a, b, and c are positive integers. *Hint.* If you think you are a good mathematics student, you should try this one. You do not need any more information (such as the radius of the circle), and you should first convince yourself that angle BOC is *not* twice angle AOB.

3.5 VECTORS: GEOMETRIC APPROACH

In order to introduce the concept of scalar and vector quantities, we first consider a simple example. Suppose a particle travels from point A to point B, as shown in Fig. 3.59. We ask two questions:

a) How far did the particle travel?

b) What is its displacement at B from A?

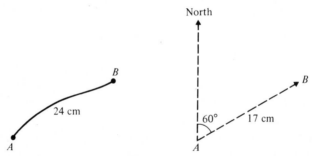

Figure 3.59

The answer to question (a) depends upon the path taken by the particle in going from A to B. In any case, the answer will be given as a distance (that is, a number accompanied by a unit of measure, such as 24 cm).

In question (b) we are actually asking: "How far and in what direction is B from A?" We say that B is displaced from A by 17 cm in the direction of 60° east of north. When we talk about displacement, we ignore the actual path taken by the particle and focus our attention on the change in position.

This example illustrates two types of quantities that occur frequently in applications. The distance actually traveled can be described by giving a number and a unit of measure; such a quantity is called a scalar. Displacement requires a number (with the unit of measure) and the direction for its description; such a quantity is called a vector.

In general, any quantity that can be described in terms of *magnitude only* (a number with a unit) is called a *scalar* quantity. Examples of scalar quantitites are: distance, mass, time, temperature, area, volume, and so on. We shall also include real numbers as scalars; for example, 3, π, $\sqrt{2}$, 17, ... will be called scalars even though there is no unit of measurement involved.

Quantities that can be described by *magnitude and direction* are called *vector quantities*. Examples of vectors are: displacement, force, velocity, acceleration, electric field, magnetic field, and so on.

1. Notation

To distinquish a vector quantity from a scalar, it is customary to write the symbol for a vector in boldface type or with an arrow; thus V or $\vec{V}$ will denote a vector. In the example above we can use the symbol $\overrightarrow{AB}$ as a vector to represent the displacement of B from A.

    In most problems it is convenient to draw a diagram in which a vector is represented by a directed line segment whose length is equal to the magnitude of the vector (drawn to scale). The magnitude (or length) of a vector is called the *absolute value* of a vector and is denoted by $|V|$.

2. Algebra of Vectors

We are already familiar with the algebra of scalars since they are essentially real numbers. The algebra of vectors is different; for example, we do not get the sum of two vectors by merely adding their magnitudes, and so it will be necessary to define addition of vectors. However, we first ask the question: "When are two vectors equal?"

    We can get some insight for defining equality and sum of two vectors by returning to the example given at the beginning of this section, in which a particle travels from A to B (see Fig. 3.59). The displacement of B from A is denoted by AB and described as a vector of magnitude 17 cm in the direction 60° east of north.

    Now suppose a second particle travels from C to D, as shown in Fig. 3.60; its displacement is denoted by CD—a vector described as having magnitude 17 cm in the direction 60° east of north. We see that the descriptions of both

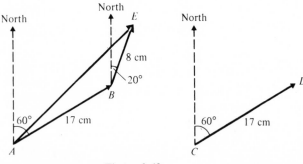

Figure 3.60

AB and *CD* are exactly the same. Therefore, we shall say that they are equal and write:

$$AB = CD.$$

In general, we say that *two vectors are equal* (regardless of their location in the plane) if they have the same magnitudes and the same directions.

To define the sum of two vectors, we let our particle travel from *A* to *B* and then from *B* to *E*, as shown in Fig. 3.60. The displacement of *E* from *A* can be described in terms of the two displacements, *B* from *A* and *E* from *B;* and we say that the resultant vector *AE* is the sum of vectors *AB* and *BE*, and write:

$$AB + BE = AE.$$

In general, we define the *sum of two vectors* geometrically as follows: Suppose *V* and *U* are two vectors, as shown in Fig. 3.61; move *U* parallel to itself until its initial point coincides with the terminal point of *V* (Fig. 3.61, a).

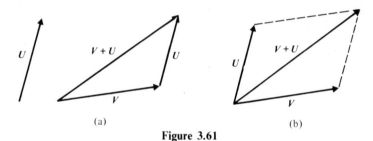

(a)   (b)

Figure 3.61

Then the vector drawn from the initial point of *V* to the terminal point of *U* is the sum of *V* and *U*, and is represented by *V* + *U*.

Equivalently, we can move *U* parallel to itself, so that its initial point coincides with the initial point *V*, and then draw the parallelogram (Fig. 3.61, b). The sum *V* + *U* will be represented by the diagonal, as shown.

This method of adding vectors geometrically is referred to as the *parallelogram law*. It should be clear that vector addition is commutative, that is

$$V + U = U + V.$$

Also, the associative property holds for addition of vectors (see Problem 17 of this section); that is,

$$(U + V) + W = U + (V + W).$$

In this book we are not interested in a complete discussion of vector algebra.* However, we do introduce the idea of a vector multiplied by a scalar through the following examples:

---

*In a more advanced study of vector analysis, two types of vector multiplication are defined: *dot product* and *vector product*. The collection of vectors, scalars, and algebraic operations with these constitute a so-called *vector space*.

$2V$ denotes a vector of magnitude $2|V|$ in the same direction as V,
$-2V$ denotes a vector of magnitude $2|V|$ in the opposite direction of V,
$(-1)V$ will be denoted by $-V$,
$0 \cdot V$ is a vector of zero magnitude and no specific direction. It is called the *zero (or null) vector* and is written as O.

We define the *subtraction* of vectors in terms of addition as follows:

$$U - V = U + (-V).$$

Examples

⚠ In Fig. 3.62 find the sum of AB and BE.

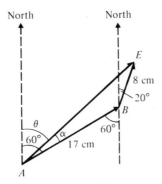

Figure 3.62

Solution. We can describe the sum $AB + BE = AE$ by giving the length of line segment AE and the angle θ. Thus we need to solve triangle ABE for side AE and angle α. Using the Law of cosines, we get

$$(AE)^2 = 8^2 + 17^2 - 2 \cdot 8 \cdot 17 \cos 140°,$$
$$AE = 23.69 \text{ cm.}$$

To find angle α we use the Law of sines:

$$\sin \alpha = \frac{8 \sin 140°}{23.69}.$$

This gives $\alpha = 12.54° = 12°32'$; and so $\theta = 60° - \alpha = 47°28'$.

Thus the sum of AB and BE can be described as a vector having magnitude 23.69 cm in the direction of $47°28'$ east of north.   ▋

⚠ Suppose vectors U and V are as follows: U has magnitude 3.5 units in direction 20° east of south, V has magnitude 5.1 units in direction 76° west of north. Find

    a) $U + V$ b) $-3U$ c) $2U - V$.

Solution.

a) We first draw a diagram showing U, V, and $U + V$ (Fig. 3.63). We can describe $U + V$ in terms of the length of line segment $\overline{CB}$ and angle θ. Thus we isolate triangle ABC. Using the Law of cosines, we get

$$(\overline{CB})^2 = (3.5)^2 + (5.1)^2 - 2 \cdot 3.5 \cdot 5.1 \cos 56°, \quad \overline{CB} = 4.3.$$

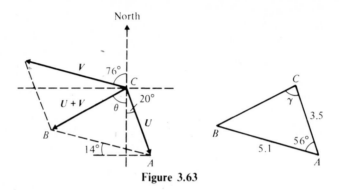

Figure 3.63

Using the Law of sines, we get

$$\sin \gamma = \frac{5.1 \sin 56°}{4.3}$$

This gives $\gamma = 81°$. Therefore, $\theta = 81° - 20° = 61°$. Thus $U + V$ is a vector with magnitude 4.3 units in the direction 61° west of south.

b) $-3U$ is a vector with magnitude $3 \cdot 3.5 = 10.5$ units and the direction opposite to U, that is 20° west of north.

c) $2U - V = 2U + (-V)$. To describe $2U - V$ we first solve triangle CDE for $\overline{CE}$ and angle α (Fig. 3.64):

$$(\overline{CE})^2 = (7.0)^2 + (5.1)^2 - 2 \cdot 7.0 \cdot 5.1 \cos 124°, \quad \overline{CE} = 10.7,$$
$$\sin \alpha = \frac{5.1 \sin 124°}{10.7}, \quad \alpha = 23°.$$

Thus $2U - V$ is a vector with magnitude 10.7 units in the direction of $20° + \alpha = 43°$ east of south.   ∎

⟨3⟩ Using the map given in Fig. 3.66, find the displacement of Reno from Los Angeles.

Solution. The coordinates of Reno and Los Angeles are $R : (-649, -175)$, $L : (-618, -828)$. Thus the relative positions of R and L are as shown in Fig. 3.65. We wish to find vector $\mathbf{LR}$. In the right triangle we have

$$\overline{RC} = |-649 - (-618)| = 31, \quad \overline{LC} = |-175 - (-828)| = 653.$$

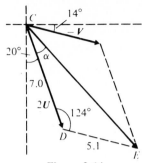

Figure 3.64

Figure 3.65

Therefore,

$$|LR| = \sqrt{31^2 + 653^2} = 653.74,$$

$$\tan \theta = \frac{31}{653}, \qquad \theta = 2.72°.$$

Thus, the displacement of Reno from Los Angeles is 654 km in the direction 2.72° west of north.

EXERCISE 3.5

1. A man walks 2.4 km north and then 1.5 km west. Construct a vector diagram and describe his displacement from the starting point.

2. A car travels 60 km east and then 83 km northeast. Draw a vector diagram and describe its displacement from the starting point.

3. Vectors U and V are as follows: U has magnitude 1.5 cm in direction of 60° east of north, V has magnitude 2.0 cm in direction of 75° east of north. Using a protractor and ruler determine (by measurements) each of the following vectors:
   a) $U + V$ b) $U - 2V$ c) $3U + 2V$

4. Do Problem 3 by computing the vectors, and then compare with the answers obtained in Problem 3.

5. Using the map in Fig. 3.66, find the displacement of Phoenix from Logan.

6. Using the map in Fig. 3.66, find the displacement of Las Vegas from Denver.

7. Point B is displaced north of point A by 24 m, and point C is displaced from B by 15 m in the northeast direction. Find the displacement of C from A; then describe the displacement of A from C.

8. A boat travels east 47 km and then turns 25° toward the south and travels 65 km. Find its displacement from the starting point.

9. A golfer takes two putts to get his ball into the hole. The first one rolls the ball 3.4 m in the northeast direction and the second putt sends the ball north 1.2 m into

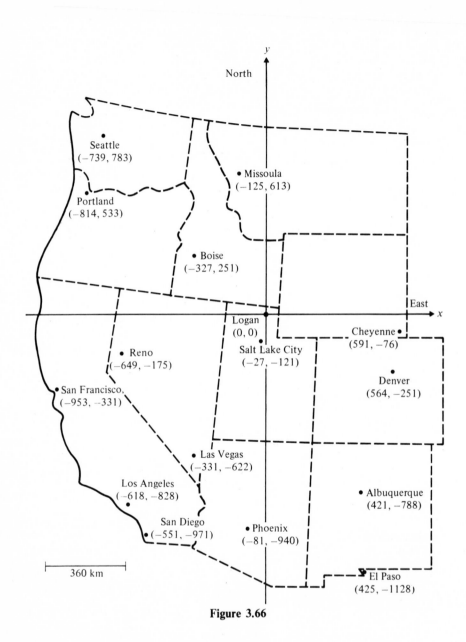

Figure 3.66

the hole. How far and in what direction should he have aimed the first putt to get the ball into the hole with one stroke?

10. A girl walks 1 km southeast, then 3 km in the direction 30° west of south, and then 4 km in the direction 50° west of north. Using a protractor and ruler, draw a vector diagram (to scale) and determine (by measuring) the distance and direction in which she should walk to return to the starting point.

11. Points A and B are two points in the plane with rectangular coordinates A: (2,5), B: (3,7). If O is the origin and vectors A and B are defined as $A = OA, B = OB$, find
    a) $|A|$ b) $|B|$ c) $|A + B|$

12. Points A and B are on the opposite ends of a lake. Starting at A, a man walks to B by taking the route shown in Fig. 3.67: A to C (56 m in a southeast direction), C to D (40 m due east), D to B (85 m due north). If he went by boat directly from A to B, how far and in what direction would he go?

13. Consider two displacements of magnitudes 8 m and 15 m. Deterɪ. ine directions in which they should be taken so that you get a resultant displacement of
    a) 23 km   b) 7 m   c) 17 m

14. Vectors A and B both have magnitude 40 km. If they are oriented as shown in Fig. 3.68, find the direction and magnitude of $A + B$.

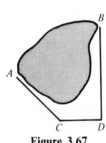

Figure 3.67

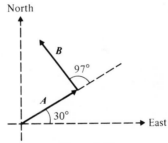

Figure 3.68

15. Using the map in Fig. 3.66, find the coordinates of a point that is 200 km southeast of Cheyenne.

16. A plane travels from Seattle to Denver, and then continues in the same direction for another 400 km. Using the map in Fig. 3.66, find the coordinates of its position.

17. Using a geometrical argument, prove that addition of vectors is commutative and associative; that is, show that

$$U + V = V + U \quad \text{and} \quad (U + V) + W = U + (V + W).$$

3.6 VECTOR ALGEBRA: ANALYTIC APPROACH

In the preceding section we introduced the concept of vector addition as a geometric operation (the parallelogram rule). As may be apparent from the problems in Exercise 3.5, the process of adding vectors geometrically is awkward. In this section we introduce an analytic technique that simplifies addition of vectors.

In all of the examples of Section 3.5 the description of vectors was given relative to a compass orientation. We now introduce a rectangular coordinate system in which the positive x-axis is in the east direction and the positive y-axis is in the north direction. The direction of any vector V can now be described by giving the angle θ (measured counterclockwise) between it and the positive x-axis.

Let i and j be unit vectors (of length one) in the positive x- and y-directions respectively, as shown in Fig. 3.69. Any vector in the plane can be expressed as a linear combination of these two unit vectors, as shown in the diagram, where (v_x, v_y) represents the coordinates of the terminal point of V.

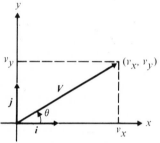

Figure 3.69

Thus we have two vectors $V_x = v_x i$ and $V_y = v_y j$ such that their sum is V. That is,

$$V = V_x + V_y = v_x i + v_y j.$$

Vectors V_x and V_y are called the *components* of V in the x- and y-directions, respectively. The process of expressing V as the sum of V_x and V_y is known as *resolution* of V into its x- and y-components (or i- and j-directions). The magnitude of V is given by $|V| = \sqrt{v_x^2 + v_y^2}$.

Using $\cos \theta = v_x/|V|$ and $\sin \theta = v_y/|V|$, we see from the right triangle shown in Fig. 3.69 that

$$v_x = |V| \cos \theta \qquad \text{and} \qquad v_y = |V| \sin \theta.$$

Thus, any vector V can be written in the form

$$\boxed{V = (|V| \cos \theta)\, i + (|V| \sin \theta)\, j.}$$

Addition of Vectors

Suppose vectors U and V are expressed in terms of i, j as

$$U = u_x i + u_y j, \quad V = v_x i + v_y j.$$

Vector addition is associative and commutative (see Problem 17 of Exercise 3.5), and so we have

$$U + V = (u_x i + u_y j) + (v_x i + v_y j) = (u_x + v_x) i + (u_y + v_y) j.$$

Therefore, to add two vectors we merely add their corresponding components.

Examples

⚠1   Suppose V is a vector with magnitude 4 and direction $\theta = 120°$. Resolve V into its x- and y-components.

Solution.

$$v_x = |V| \cos \theta = 4 \cos 120° = -2,$$
$$v_y = |V| \sin \theta = 4 \sin 120° = 2\sqrt{3}.$$

Thus

$$V = -2i + 2\sqrt{3}\,j. \qquad\qquad ▮$$

⚠2   Suppose U is a vector of length 5 in the direction of 70° east of north, and V has length 3 in the direction of 20° west of south (Fig. 3.70). Find the sum of U and V; then find $|U + V|$.

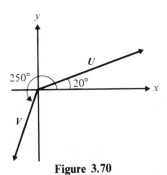

Figure 3.70

Solution. We first express U and V in i, j form:

$$U = 5 \cos 20° \, i + 5 \sin 20° \, j = 4.70 \, i + 1.71 \, j,$$
$$V = 3 \cos 250° \, i + 3 \sin 250° \, j = -1.03 \, i - 2.82 \, j.$$

Therefore,

$$U + V = 3.67 i - 1.11 j.$$

To find $|U + V|$ we write:

$$|U + V| = \sqrt{(3.67)^2 + (-1.11)^2} = 3.83.$$

▲3 Suppose $A = 2i + 3j$ and $B = 4i - j$. Find the vector $3A - 5B$.

Solution.

$$3A - 5B = 3(2i + 3j) - 5(4i - j) = (6i + 9j) + (-20i + 5j).*$$

Thus

$$3A - 5B = -14i + 14j.$$

▲4 If the displacement of Havre from Las Vegas is given by the vector $LH = 541\,i + 1383\,j$, find the coordinates of Havre on the map of Fig. 3.66 (p. 100). The given distances are in kilometers.

Solution. We wish to find the coordinates of H as shown in Fig. 3.71. We can do this by finding vector

$$OH = OL + LH.$$

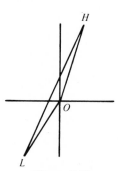

Figure 3.71

From information given on the map, we have

$$OL = -331i - 622\,j$$

Therefore,

$$OH = (-331\,i - 622\,j) + (541\,i + 1383\,j) = 210\,i + 761\,j.$$

The coordinates of Havre are (210, 761).

---

*Note that in replacing $3(2\,i + 3\,j)$ by $6\,i + 9\,j$ we used the distributive property
$$3(2\,i + 3\,j) = 3(2\,i) + 3(3\,j),$$
and the associative property
$$3(2\,i) = (3 \cdot 2)\,i \qquad \text{and} \qquad 3(3\,i) = (3 \cdot 3)\,j.$$
These properties hold in general and are basic in the study of *vector spaces*.

EXERCISE 3.6

In Problems 1 through 10, vectors U, V, and W are given by

$$U = i + j, \qquad V = 2i - 5j, \qquad W = -2i + j.$$

In each case draw a diagram illustrating the problem geometrically and then determine the given vector in i, j form:

1. $U + V$
2. $U - V$
3. $2U + 3W$
4. $U + V + W$
5. $3U - 2V + 4W$

6. Find a vector that gives W when added to U.

7. Find a vector that gives V when subtracted from W.

8. Find
   a) $|U|$
   b) $|V|$
   c) $|U + V|$

9. Find $|2U - 3V|$
10. Find $|3U + 2V - 5W|$

In Problems 11 through 14, suppose the x, y-coordinate system corresponds to compass directions and the direction angle θ is measured as described in this section. Let A and B be given as follows: A has magnitude 1.5 cm in direction 60° east of north, B has magnitude 3.2 cm in direction 20° west of north.

11. Draw a diagram illustrating vectors A and B, and then give the direction of each in terms of the corresponding θ angle.

12. Resolve A and B into their x, y-components.

13. Find the sum of A and B and describe the resultant in terms of compass direction.

14. Find $2A - B$ and give the result in terms of its magnitude and compass direction.

In Problems 15 through 19 use information from the map given in Fig. 3.66 (p. 100).

15. Find the displacement of Boise from Portland as a vector in i, j-form.

16. Point P is 200 km from Albuquerque in the direction of 54° east of north. Find the coordinates of P.

17. Find the displacement vector of El Paso from Missoula in i, j-form. Get an approximate check on your result by using a ruler and protractor on the map.

18. The displacement of point P from San Diego is given by the vector

$$DP = 321i + 175j.$$

Find the displacement vector of P from Logan.

19. Determine the direction in which a plane should fly to travel directly from Los Angeles to Salt Lake City (assuming no wind effect).

20. Find the magnitude and direction of a vector whose x-component is 32 units and y-component is 24 units.

21. A girl walks 2 km in the southwest direction, then 1.5 km east, and then 3 km in the direction 30° east of north. Find her displacement from the starting point. Give the answer in terms of distance and compass direction.

22. What are the x- and y-components of a vector with magnitude 16 cm and the direction given by $\theta = 210°$?

23. Find a unit vector with the same direction as $A = 3\,i + j$.

24. Find a unit vector perpendicular to vector $A = 3\,i + j$.

25. If $A = 3\,i - 2\,j$ and $B = 2\,i + j$, find
    a) the angle between A and B b) the angle between $A + B$ and $A - B$.

26. Find a unit vector parallel to the line through points $(3, 5)$ and $(2, -1)$.

27. Express vector $V = 3\,i + 4\,j$ as the sum of two vectors with directions shown by broken lines in Fig. 3.72.

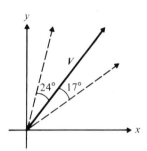

Figure 3.72

28. Find the coordinates of point P whose displacement from point $(3, 1)$ is of magnitude 4 in the direction of $136°$ with the positive x-axis.

29. A particle moving in the x, y-plane is photographed each second and its x, y-components for the first five seconds are given by the following table:

t (sec)	0	1	2	3	4	5
x (cm)	10	14	21	27	16	31
y (cm)	0	5	8	12	22	30

    a) Draw a diagram that illustrates the displacements for successive seconds.
    b) Find the displacement from $t = 0$ to $t = 4$ sec.
    c) Find the displacement from $t = 1$ to $t = 5$ sec.

30. Suppose that the coordinates of a particle moving in the x, y-plane are given by

$$x = 3t - 5t^2, \qquad y = -4t^2 + t^3,$$

where t is in seconds and x, y are in centimeters. Find

a) the displacement of the particle from $t = 0$ to $t = 4$ sec,

b) the displacement of the particle from $t = 2$ to $t = 4$ sec.

31. A plane travels from Seattle to Missoula and then 450 km in the southeast direction. Using the map in Fig. 3.66 (p. 100) find how far and in what direction the plane is from Seattle.

32. On a par 4 hole a golfer scores a birdie with the following three strokes:

the first travels 84 m at an angle of 54° east of south;
the second goes 21 m in the direction 10° west of south;
the third is a putt of 2.5 m in the northwest direction.

How far and in what direction should he have hit his drive to get a hole in one?

3.7 APPLICATION OF VECTORS TO VELOCITY PROBLEMS

Relative Velocities

We illustrate the idea of relative velocity by considering the following example. The compass of an airplane shows that the plane is pointed due north. Ground information indicates that there is a wind blowing due east. The result is that the plane will not fly due north but that its direction will be affected by the wind and its actual course will be shifted toward the northeast. We discuss details of this situation by introducing three vectors:

V_a represents the velocity of the plane relative to the air (this is given by the airspeed* and compass on the instrument panel and would be the actual velocity of the plane if there were no wind);

V_g represents the velocity of the plane relative to the ground (this is what an observer on the ground would see as the actual speed and direction of the plane);

U represents the velocity of the wind (that is, the velocity of the air relative to the ground).

These vectors are shown in Fig. 3.73, where V_g is the resultant (or sum) of V_a and U. That is,

$$V_g = V_a + U. \tag{3.10}$$

Examples

⚠ Suppose the instrument panel of a plane indicates an airspeed of 350 km/hr and a direction due north; the wind is 80 km/hr in a due east direction.

---

*The word *speed* is used to denote the magnitude of velocity. Thus speed is a scalar quantity associated with velocity, which is a vector quantity.

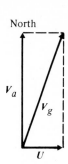

Figure 3.73

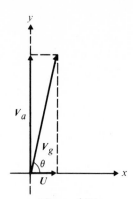

Figure 3.74

What is the actual velocity of the plane with respect to the ground? How far has the plane traveled after 50 min in flight?

Solution. (Fig. 3.74): $V_a = 350\,j$ and $U = 80\,i$, therefore,

$$V_g = V_a + U = 350\,j + 80\,i.$$

The actual speed of the plane is

$$|V_g| = \sqrt{350^2 + 80^2}\ \text{km/hr} = 359.03\ \text{km/hr}.$$

The direction of the plane is given by

$$\tan\theta = \frac{350}{80}, \qquad \theta = 77.12°.$$

Thus the actual velocity of the plane is 359 km/hr in the direction of

$$90° - 77.12° = 12.88°\ \text{east of north}.$$

In this example the plane will always be pointed north (that is, the compass reading will indicate north) and the airspeed will show 350 km/hr even though the wind causes the plane to drift.

Recall that

$$\text{Distance} = \text{Rate} \times \text{Time}$$

and so after 50 min in flight the plane actually travels a distance of $359(50/60) = 299.17$ km. ∎

△2 Suppose in Example 1 the pilot actually wants to travel due north. Find the direction in which he should point the plane and the actual ground speed.

Solution. Here we want the resultant V_g to be in the north direction. Thus V_a will have to be in the northwesterly direction, as shown in Fig. 3.75:

$$V_a = (350\ \cos\ \theta)\,i + (350\ \sin\ \theta)\,j,$$
$$V_g = |V_g|\,j, \qquad U = 80i.$$

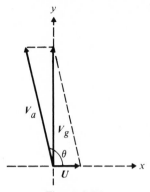

Figure 3.75

Our problem is to find θ and $|V_g|$. Substituting into equation $V_g = V_a + U$, gives

$$|V_g| \, j = (350 \cos \theta) \, i + (350 \sin \theta) \, j + 80 \, i$$
$$= (350 \cos \theta + 80) \, i + (350 \sin \theta) \, j.$$

If two vectors are equal, then their x- and y-components must be respectively equal. That is,

$$350 \cos \theta + 80 = 0, \qquad 350 \sin \theta = |V_g|.$$

Solving these two equations simultaneously for θ and $|V_g|$ gives

$$\theta = 103.21°, \qquad |V_g| = 340.73 \text{ km/hr.}$$

Thus the plane should head in the direction of 13.21° west of north and its ground speed will be 340.73 km/hr. ∎

EXERCISE 3.7

In Problems 1 through 4, the airspeed and direction of a plane and the wind velocity are given.

    a) Find the actual ground speed and direction of the plane.

    b) Determine the actual distance covered by the plane after 45 min in flight.

1. V_a is 300 km/hr due east; U is 60 km/hr from the west.

2. V_a is 350 km/hr due south; U is 50 km/hr from the south.

3. V_a is 300 km/hr in direction 40° east of north; U is 80 km/hr in direction of 10° west of south.

4. V_a is 400 km/hr in southeast direction; U is 70 km/hr from the north.

5. If the pilot of an airplane wishes to travel due north with an airspeed of 400 km/hr, in what direction should he point the plane if there is a wind of 80 km/hr blowing in the due east direction?

6. In Problem 5, how far will the plane actually travel in 1 hr 25 min?

7. In Problem 5, how long will it take the plane to travel 540 km?

8. A pilot wishes to have his plane travel due east with an airspeed of 350 km/hr. There is a head wind given by $U = -40\,i - 30\,j$. In what direction should he point the plane and what will be the ground speed?

9. In Problem 8, how long will it take the plane to travel 800 km?

10. A ship is traveling due north at a speed of 24 km/hr. A man walks east across the deck at a speed of 3.5 km/hr. Describe his velocity (speed and direction) relative to the surface of the ocean.

11. According to instrument readings, a destroyer is steaming due east at 40 km/hr. The ocean current is known to be toward the southwest at the rate of 8 km/hr. In what direction and at what speed is the ship actually traveling?

12. A pilot heads his plane so that the compass reading is 40° east of north. A wind is blowing in the direction 50° east of north. Find the airspeed of the plane and the speed of the wind if the resulting ground speed is $V_g = 200\,i + 223\,j$.

13. A river flows from north to south at the rate of 2 km/hr and is 0.4 km wide. A man starts from the west bank and rows across the river keeping his boat constantly pointed east. If he can row (in still water) at the rate of 4.5 km/hr and point A is directly across the river from his starting point, how far down the river from point A will he land?

14. Using the information given in Problem 13, find the direction in which the man should point his boat to reach point A.

15. A plane traveling at an airspeed of 400 km/hr is over San Francisco and is headed in a direction with compass reading 57° east of north. In 55 min it passes over Reno. Using information from the map in Fig. 3.66 (p. 100) find the velocity of the wind (assuming it to be the same for the entire trip).

16. A plane travels from Reno to Salt Lake City. Assuming that the wind velocity for the entire trip is 32 km/hr from the northwest, at what airspeed and compass direction should the plane travel to get to Salt Lake City in exactly 2 hr? Use information from the map in Fig. 3.66 (p. 100).

3.8 APPLICATION OF VECTORS TO FORCE PROBLEMS

Concurrent Forces in Equilibrium

If a body is at rest (or is moving at a constant velocity), it is said to be in *equilibrium*. If a body is in equilibrium and a force is applied to it, then the equilibrium will be disturbed. Thus if forces are applied and the net, or resultant, force is nonzero, then the body will not be in equilibrium. This is equivalent to saying that if a body is to remain in equilibrium, then the resultant of any forces acting on it must be zero. This implies that the sum of the x-components of the forces must be zero and the sum of the y-components must equal zero. We thus have the following *basic principle for a body to be in equilibrium:*

> For a set of forces to be in equilibrium,* it is necessary that the sum of their components in any two mutually perpendicular directions in the plane be zero.

If the body is not moving, then it is said to be in *static equilibrium*. The problems considered in this section will all be of this type.

If all of the forces acting on a body pass through a common point, then they are said to be *concurrent* forces. If there are nonconcurrent forces, then it is necessary to introduce the concept of *torque* (or moments of forces) in the above stated basic principle. For example, two tangential forces applied to opposite points of a wheel are not concurrent.

In this section we deal only with bodies in static equilibrium and concurrent forces. Thus the basic principle stated above will be sufficient to give us solutions.

Examples

⚠️ A 50-kg weight is suspended by two ropes as shown in Fig. 3.76 (a), where $\alpha = 50°$ and $\beta = 24°$. Find the tension in each rope.

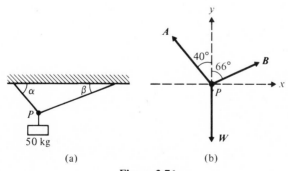

Figure 3.76

---

*It is common to speak of forces being in equilibrium meaning that the body to which these forces are applied is in equilibrium.

Solution. In solving a problem of this type, we first fix our attention on a point where several of the forces are applied, and then draw a vector diagram showing all of the forces. In our problem it is natural to isolate point P where three forces given by vectors A, B, and W are acting.

We wish to determine the tension in the two ropes, that is, we want to find the magnitudes of A and B. If we choose our x, y-system of coordinates with origin at P as shown in Fig. 3.76 (b), we have

$$A = (|A| \cos 130°)i + (|A| \sin 130°)j,$$
$$B = (|B| \cos 24°)i + (|B| \sin 24°)j,$$
$$W = -50j.$$

Since our system is in equilibrium, we can apply the basic principle stated above and get

Sum of x-components: $|A| \cos 130° + |B| \cos 24° = 0$
Sum of y-components: $|A| \sin 130° + |B| \sin 24° - 50 = 0.$

Solving these equations simultaneously for $|A|$ and $|B|$ gives

$$|A| = 47.52 \text{ kg} \qquad \text{and} \qquad |B| = 33.43 \text{ kg}.$$

Note that in applying the basic principle of equilibrium we essentially determined two forces A and B, such that their resultant $(A + B)$ just balances W, thus leaving the system in equilibrium (Fig. 3.77).

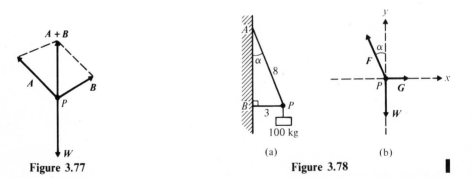

Figure 3.77   Figure 3.78

2. A weight of 100 kg is suspended from a wall as shown in Fig. 3.78(a). Find the tension on the portion of the rope AP (8 m long) and the force on the bar BP (3 m long).

Solution. We isolate P as the point where three forces are acting; we denote them by F (pull by the rope), G (force on the bar), and W (force of gravity on the weight), as shown in Fig. 3.78(b).

First we determine angle α; from the triangle in Fig. 3.78(a) we have

$$\tan \alpha = \frac{3}{8}, \qquad \alpha = 20.55°.$$

Therefore we can write the three vectors as follows:

$$W = -100\,j, \qquad G = |G|\,i,$$
$$F = (\,|F|\ \cos\ 110.55°)\,i + (\,|F|\ \sin\ 110.55°)\,j.$$

Applying the basic principle of equilibrium, we get:

Sum of x-components: $|G| + |F|\ \cos\ 110.55° = 0,$
Sum of y-components: $|F|\ \sin\ 110.55° - 100 = 0.$

Solving these two equations simultaneously, we get

$$|F| = 106.80\ \text{kg},$$
$$|G| = 37.49\ \text{kg}.$$

Thus the tension in the rope is 106.80 kg and the bar is pushing against P with a force of 37.49 kg.   ∎

$\boxed{3}$ A weight of 25 kg is being held on an inclined plane by a rope PA, as shown in Fig. 3.79(a). If the angle of inclination to the horizontal is 36°, what is the tension in the rope? Neglect any force caused by friction.

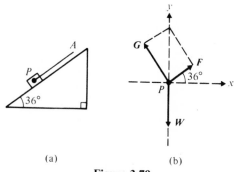

(a)   (b)

Figure 3.79

Solution. We isolate point P and note that there are three forces acting on it. We denote these by F (pull by the rope), G (push by the incline against the weight in the direction perpendicular to the incline), and W (force of gravity on the weight). These forces are shown in Fig. 3.79(b) and are given by

$$F = (\,|F|\ \cos\ 36°)\,i + (\,|F|\ \sin\ 36°)\,j,$$
$$G = (\,|G|\ \cos\ 126°)\,i + (\,|G|\ \sin\ 126°)\,j,$$
$$W = -25\,j.$$

Since the system is in equilibrium, we can apply the basic principle and get

Sum of x-components: $|F|\ \cos\ 36° + |G|\ \cos\ 126° = 0,$
Sum of y-components: $|F|\ \sin\ 36° + |G|\ \sin\ 126° - 25 = 0.$

We solve these two equations simultaneously for $|F|$:

$$|F| = \frac{25 \cos 126°}{\sin 36° \cos 126° - \sin 126° \cos 36°} = 14.69 \text{ kg.}$$

Thus it will require a pull of 14.69 kg on the rope to keep the 25 kg weight in place.   ∎

EXERCISE 3.8

1. A 120 kg weight is suspended by two ropes, as shown in Fig. 3.80. What is the tension in each rope?

2. A weight of 80 kg is suspended from a wall, as shown in Fig. 3.81. The bar BP is perpendicular to the wall. Find the tension in the rope AP.

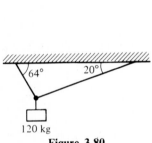

120 kg

Figure 3.80

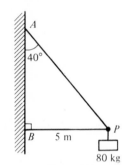

80 kg

Figure 3.81

3. An 80-kg weight is suspended from the wall, as shown in Fig. 3.82. The bar BP is inclined at 80° to the wall. Find the tension in the rope AP.

4. A weight of 100 kg is being held on a ramp by a rope from P to A, as shown in Fig. 3.83. If the ramp is inclined 25° to the horizontal, find the tension in the rope. Neglect any friction forces.

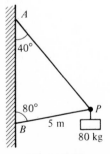

Figure 3.82

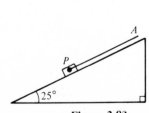

Figure 3.83

5. A weight of 100 kg is being held on an inclined plane by a rope PA, as shown in Fig. 3.84. Find the tension in the rope.

6. Two forces, one of 100 kg and the other of 160 kg, act on an object with an angle of 64° between them. What is the magnitude of a third force that will keep the object in equilibrium?

7. Two men are holding a weight suspended between them on a rope, as shown in Fig. 3.85. One exerts a force of 45 kg in the direction of 30° from the horizontal, while the other exerts a force in the direction of 40° with the horizontal. How heavy is the weight?

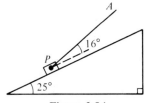

Figure 3.84

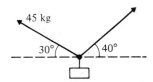

Figure 3.85

8. A girl gymnast hangs from a horizontal bar with her arms outstretched so that each makes an angle of 36° with the bar. If she weighs 55 kg, what is the tension in each arm?

9. Two forces, each of 55 kg with an angle of 72° between them, act on an object. What additional force is required to keep the object in equilibrium?

10. A boat weighing 600 kg is being pulled up a loading ramp inclined 20° to the horizontal. What force is required? Neglect any friction forces.

11. A weight of 62 kg is suspended by two ropes, as shown in Fig. 3.86. What is the tension on each rope?

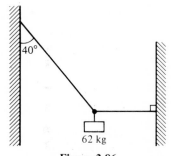

Figure 3.86

12. A force of 160 kg is required to hold a weight on an inclined plane with an angle of 24° to the horizontal. How heavy is the weight? Neglect any friction forces.

13. A boom *AP*, 4.5 m long, holds a weight of 86 kg away from a vertical wall. The weight is anchored to the wall by a rope *BP,* as shown in Fig. 3.87. What is the tension in the rope?

14. Suppose that in Problem 13 the rope makes an angle of 12° with the horizontal, as shown in Fig. 3.88. What is the tension in the rope?

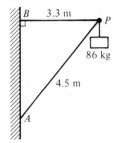

Figure 3.87

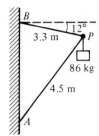

Figure 3.88

15. A balloon filled with helium is anchored by two ropes, as shown in Fig. 3.89. If the tension of the rope inclined at 40° is 120 kg, find the buoyancy force of the balloon.

16. Janet is sitting in the center of a hammock suspended from two trees with ropes that make an angle of 64° with the vertical. If she weighs 52 kg, what is the tension in each rope? Neglect the weight of the hammock.

17. If each rope in Problem 16 can support a pull of at most 100 kg before breaking, what angle with the vertical can each make for Janet to be safe in the hammock?

18. An archer pulls back on his bow with a force of 10 kg before releasing the arrow, as shown in Fig. 3.90. With what force is the string pulling on the bow ends?

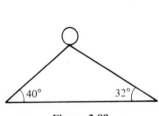

Figure 3.89

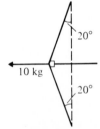

Figure 3.90

19. An inclined plane is 5 m long and one end is 2 m above the other. A weight of 48 kg is held in place by a rope *AP* tied to a building, as shown in Fig. 3.91. What is the tension in the rope? Neglect any friction forces.

20. A boy is being pulled up an icy hill by a rope tied to his sled. If the child and sled weigh a total of 36 kg, the angle of the hill slope with the horizontal is 15°, and the rope is inclined at 24° to the hill, what force is required to pull the sled?

21. A weight of 64 kg hangs vertically supported by a rope tied to the top of the building. The rope is strong enough to support at most 128 kg. A second rope (sufficiently strong) is tied to the weight and is pulled always horizontally, so that the first rope makes an angle of θ with the building (as shown in Fig. 3.92). How large can θ be before the first rope breaks?

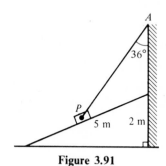

Figure 3.91

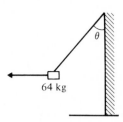

Figure 3.92

REVIEW EXERCISE

1. The hypotenuse of a right triangle is 37.42 cm and one angle is 48°12′. Find the lengths of the two sides. Give answers correct to four significant digits.

2. If ABC is an isosceles triangle with $|\overline{AB}| = |\overline{AC}| = 4.73$ and the angle opposite AB is 52°14′, find the length of the altitude from A to $\overline{BC}$. Then find the area of the triangle. Give answers correct to two decimal places.

3. If the hypotenuse of a right triangle is 24.3 cm and one of the sides is 15.4 cm, find the length of the other side correct to three significant digits. Determine the angles correct to the nearest minute.

4. In Fig. 3.93, $ABCD$ is a square with length of side 18.76 cm. If $|\overline{EC}| = 8.43$ cm, find the length of $\overline{AF}$.

5. In Fig. 3.94, $\alpha = 34°$, $\beta = 120°$, and $|\overline{CD}| = 15$ cm. Find the length of $\overline{AB}$ correct to two significant digits.

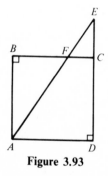

Figure 3.93

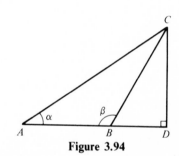

Figure 3.94

In Problems 6 through 14, parts of a triangle are given (using conventional notation as described in this chapter). First, decide whether the given information is sufficient to determine a triangle. If it is, find the remaining parts. Give answers correct to the accuracy you think is consistent with the given information.

6. $b = 32$, $c = 47$, $\alpha = 18°$.

7. $a = 15$, $b = 20$, $c = 40$.

8. $\alpha = 62.5°$, $\beta = 23.6°$, $c = 3.47$.

9. $a = 3.4$, $b = 4.6$, $c = 3.7$.

10. $\beta = 64°12'$, $b = 32.5$, $c = 23.8$.

11. $\alpha = 30°$, $\beta = 60°$, $\gamma = 90°$.

12. $\alpha = 48°$, $\beta = 74°$, $\gamma = 58°$, $a = 436$

13. $\alpha = 36°$, $\beta = 65°$, $a = 36.4$, $b = 25.3$.

14. $\beta = 32°14'$, $\gamma = 64°18'$, $a = 42.53$.

15. In Fig. 3.95, the length of $\overline{CD}$ and angles α and β are measured and found to be

$$|\overline{CD}| = 137 \text{ m}, \qquad \alpha = 44°, \qquad \beta = 123°.$$

Find the distance from A to B and from A to C.

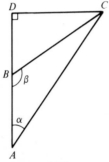

Figure 3.95

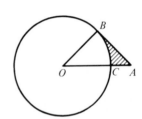

Figure 3.96

16. In Fig. 3.96, the center of the circle is O, $\overline{AB}$ is a tangent to the circle at B, and C is a point on the circle and on $\overline{OA}$. If the radius of the circle is 12 cm and the length of arc $\overset{\frown}{BC}$ is 9 cm, find the area of the shaded region.

17. Each side of a regular pentagon has length 24 cm. The five diagonals of this pentagon intersect in five points forming another regular pentagon inside the given one. Find the length of side of this pentagon.

18. Find the areas of each of the pentagons described in Problem 17. Then find the ratio of the larger area to the smaller area.

19. The three sides of a triangle are $a = 3.4$, $b = 5.6$, $c = 4.8$. Find the area of the triangle correct to one decimal place.

20. The lengths of two sides of a triangle are 32.6 cm and 43.5 cm, and the angle between them is 55°40'. Find the area of the triangle correct to three significant digits.

In Problems 21 through 24, vectors *A*, *B*, and *C* are given by

$$A = 3\,i + 4\,j, \qquad\qquad B = -2\,i + 5\,j, \qquad\qquad C = 2\,i - 3\,j.$$

21. Find: a) $2A - 3B$ b) $B + 3C$

22. Determine: a) $|A|$ b) $|4B - C|$ c) $|A - B|$

23. Find a) the angle between *A* and *B*, b) the angle between *A* + *B* and *B* + *C*.

24. Find the unit vectors perpendicular to vector *A*.

25. Using information from the map given in Fig. 3.66 (p. 100), find
    a) the vector describing the displacement of Reno from El Paso;
    b) the direction and distance from Denver to Salt Lake City.

26. The pilot of an airplane encounters a wind of velocity 60 km/hr in the due east direction. If his instruments indicate an airspeed of 360 km/hr in the due south direction, what is his ground speed and in what direction is the plane actually flying?

27. If the pilot in Problem 26 wishes to have the plane actually fly in the due south direction with the airspeed indicator still showing 360 km/hr, in what direction should he point his plane? How far will he fly in 1 hr 20 min?

28. A weight of 100 kg is suspended from a wall by a rope $\overline{AP}$ and held out from the building by a bar $\overline{BP}$, as shown in Fig. 3.97. Find the tension in the rope.

29. Two forces with magnitudes of 50 kg and 80 kg are acting on an object with an angle of 64° between them. Find the magnitude of the force required to keep the object from moving.

30. An object weighing 80 kg is being held in place on an incline by a rope $\overline{AP}$ tied to the object and a building, as shown in Fig. 3.98. Find the tension in the rope. Neglect friction force.

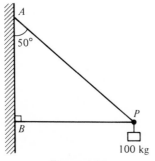

Figure 3.97

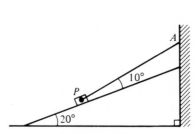

Figure 3.98

CHAPTER FOUR

IDENTITIES

Problem-solving in mathematics frequently involves a sequence of steps in which the problem is restated in a different but equivalent form until ultimately it is reduced to a form that can be solved by familiar techniques. For example, in algebra the student learns to solve the equation $x^2 - x - 6 = 0$ by replacing its left-hand side with $(x - 3)(x + 2)$, so that the problem then becomes one of solving $(x - 3)(x + 2) = 0$. In this form the problem can be solved by resorting to a theorem stating that if the product of two numbers is zero, then at least one of the two numbers must be zero. That is, $x - 3 = 0$ or $x + 2 = 0$; so $x = 3$ and $x = -2$ are the solutions.

In this example we call the equation $x^2 - x - 6 = (x - 3)(x + 2)$ an identity, because it is satisfied by every real number. That is, if we replace x by any given real number in the expression on the left-hand side of the equality sign and in the expression on its right-hand side, the two resulting numbers will be equal. However, the equation $x^2 - x - 6 = 0$ does not have this property since it is satisfied by only two real number values of x. We call such an equation a *conditional equation.*

An *identity* is defined as an equation satisfied by all values of the variable (or variables) for which both the left-hand side and the right-hand side are defined. For example,

$$\frac{x^2 - 4}{x - 2} = x + 2$$

is an identity since it is satisfied by all real numbers except $x = 2$, a value for which the left side is not defined. The student has already encountered several identities in algebra, such as the factoring formulas

$$x^2 - y^2 = (x + y)(x - y), \qquad x^2 + 2xy + y^2 = (x + y)^2,$$

$$x^3 + y^3 = (x + y)(x^2 - xy + y^2), \dots$$

Presently we are interested in developing a collection of identities involving trigonometric functions. We have already used one such identity,

$$(\sin \gamma)^2 + (\cos \gamma)^2 = 1,$$

in Section 3.4 when we derived Heron's formula for the area of a triangle. In the process we replaced $(\sin \gamma)^2$ by $1 - (\cos \gamma)^2$; then we replaced $1 - (\cos \gamma)^2$ by $(1 + \cos \gamma)(1 - \cos \gamma)$. This is the form that allowed us to complete the derivation.

This chapter will include a large number of identities with which the student should become familiar. These may be difficult to memorize but through frequent encounters in solving a large number of problems, the student will eventually come to know them. In subsequent chapters of this book, the usefulness of identities will become apparent.

4.1 BASIC IDENTITIES

The following equations are satisfied by each value of θ for which both sides of the given equation are defined. That is, they are identities.

(I.1)
$$\csc \theta = \frac{1}{\sin \theta}$$

(I.2)
$$\sec \theta = \frac{1}{\cos \theta}$$

(I.3)
$$\cot \theta = \frac{1}{\tan \theta}$$

(I.4)
$$\sin (-\theta) = -\sin \theta$$

(I.5)
$$\cos(-\theta) = \cos \theta$$

(I.6)
$$\tan(-\theta) = -\tan \theta$$

(I.7)
$$\tan \theta = \frac{\sin \theta}{\cos \theta}$$

(I.8)
$$\cot \theta = \frac{\cos \theta}{\sin \theta}$$

(I.9)
$$\sin^2 \theta + \cos^2 \theta = 1*$$

(I.10)
$$1 + \tan^2 \theta = \sec^2 \theta$$

(I.11)
$$1 + \cot^2 \theta = \csc^2 \theta$$

---

*Notation $\sin^2\theta$ means $(\sin \theta)^2$; that is, we first get $\sin \theta$ and then square the result. Not to be confused with $\sin \theta^2$, where we first square θ, then get the sine of the result.

Note. Trigonometric identities (I.1) through (I.11) (as well as subsequent identities) are listed inside the back cover for easy reference.

Identities I.1 through I.9, as well as others, have already been introduced in Section 2.6. Proofs of I.10 and I.11 are left to the student (see Problem 1 of Exercise 4.1).

Examples

△1 Prove that $\cos x \tan x = \sin x$ is an identity.

Solution. Let LHS and RHS stand for "left-hand side" and "right-hand side" of the given equation, respectively:

$$\text{LHS} = \cos x \tan x = \cos x \,\frac{\sin x}{\cos x} \qquad \text{(by (I.7))}$$

$$= \sin x \qquad \text{(by algebra).}$$

Therefore LHS = RHS, and so the given equation is an identity.   ■

△2 Prove that $\dfrac{1-\sec x}{1+\sec x} = \dfrac{\cos x - 1}{\cos x + 1}$ is an identity.

Solution.

$$\text{LHS} = \frac{1-\sec x}{1+\sec x} = \frac{1 - 1/\cos x}{1 + 1/\cos x} \qquad \text{(by (I.2))}$$

$$= \frac{\cos x - 1}{\cos x} \div \frac{\cos x + 1}{\cos x} = \frac{\cos x - 1}{\cos x + 1} \quad \text{(by algebra)}$$

$$= \text{RHS.}$$

     ■

△3 Prove that $(\sin x + \cos x)^2 = \dfrac{\sec x \csc x + 2}{\sec x \csc x}$ is an identity.

Solution.

$$\text{LHS} = (\sin x + \cos x)^2 = \sin^2 x + 2 \sin x \cos x + \cos^2 x$$
$$= (\sin^2 x + \cos^2 x) + 2 \sin x \cos x \qquad \text{(by algebra)}$$
$$= 1 + 2 \sin x \cos x \qquad \text{(by (I.9));}$$
$$\text{RHS} = \frac{\sec x \csc x + 2}{\sec x \csc x} = \frac{\sec x \csc x}{\sec x \csc x} + \frac{2}{\sec x \csc x} \qquad \text{(by algebra)}$$
$$= 1 + 2 \,\frac{1}{\sec x} \cdot \frac{1}{\csc x} \qquad \text{(by algebra)}$$
$$= 1 + 2 \cos x \sin x. \qquad \text{(by (I.2) and (I.1)).}$$

Therefore, by the transitive property, LHS = RHS and so the given equation is an identity.   ■

Technique for Proving Identities

The student will notice that in the above examples we did *not* begin our proof with the given equation and manipulate it until we got an obvious equality. Here we emphasize an important point of logic. A proof consists of a logical sequence of statements in which the final statement is the statement to be proved.

We illustrate our point with an obvious example. Suppose we wish to prove that $1 = 2$. If we are allowed to start with this equality as the first step, then our "proof" could proceed as follows:

$$1 = 2,$$

multiply both sides by zero:

$$0 \cdot 1 = 0 \cdot 2;$$

hence,

$$0 = 0.$$

Since $0 = 0$ is an obvious equality, can we conclude that $1 = 2$? Clearly NOT! The only conclusion we can make from the above is that "if $1 = 2$, then $0 = 0$," which is a true statement.

The important point illustrated by this example is that it is not logically acceptable to begin a proof with the statement you wish to prove, perform algebraic manipulations on it, obtain an obvious equality, and then conclude that the starting statement is true. If such a procedure is followed and if it can be shown that these steps are reversible, then the proof is valid. However, the steps in reverse are a necessary part of the proof and should be included. What step or steps in the above faulty proof are not reversible?

Note. As illustrated in Examples 1 through 3 above, we believe that the best technique in communicating a proof is to *work independently* with either or both of the left- and right-hand sides of the given equation to show that each reduces to the same expression. The final statement of LHS = RHS then follows from the transitive property of the equals relation.

EXERCISE 4.1

1. Use I.9 to derive I.10 and I.11.

In Problems 2 through 40 prove that the given equation is an identity.

2. $\sin \theta \cot \theta = \cos \theta$

3. $\dfrac{\tan \theta}{\sin \theta} = \sec \theta$

4. $\cot \theta = \csc \theta \cos \theta$

5. $\cos x \sec x = 1$

6. $\cos x \tan x = \sin x$

7. $1 - \cos^2 x = \cos^2 x \tan^2 x$

8. $\cot x \sec x = \csc x$

9. $\sin^2 x = (1 - \cos x)(1 + \cos x)$

10. $\dfrac{\cot x}{\sec x} = \csc x - \sin x$

11. $\dfrac{\sin x \csc x}{\cot x} = \tan x$

12. $\dfrac{\sin(-\theta)}{\cos \theta} = \tan(-\theta)$

13. $\sec \theta \csc \theta = \tan \theta + \cot \theta$

14. $\sec \theta(\csc \theta - \sin \theta) = \csc \theta \cos \theta$

15. $\dfrac{1 - \cos x}{1 + \cos x} = (\cot x - \csc x)^2$

16. $\dfrac{\sin \theta}{1 + \cos \theta} = \dfrac{1 - \cos \theta}{\sin \theta}$

17. $\tan x + \cot x = \dfrac{\csc x}{\cos x}$

18. $\dfrac{1 + \tan \theta}{\sec \theta} = \dfrac{1 + \cot \theta}{\csc \theta}$

19. $\cot \alpha \csc \alpha = \dfrac{1}{\sec \alpha - \cos \alpha}$

20. $\dfrac{1}{1 - \sin x} + \dfrac{1}{1 + \sin x} = 2 \sec^2 x$

21. $\sec^2 x + \csc^2 x = \sec^2 x \csc^2 x$

22. $\dfrac{\sin \theta}{1 + \cos \theta} + \dfrac{1 + \cos \theta}{\sin \theta} = \dfrac{2}{\sin \theta}$

23. $(\cos x + 1)(\sec x - 1) = \sec x - \cos x$

24. $\sec \theta - \cos \theta = \sin(-\theta)\tan(-\theta)$

25. $\sin^4 x - \cos^4 x = \sin^2 x - \cos^2 x$

26. $1 + \tan^2 x = \tan x \sec x \csc x$

27. $\dfrac{\tan \theta + \sec \theta}{\sin \theta \cot \theta} = \dfrac{1 + \sin \theta}{\cos^2 \theta}$

28. $\cot(-x)\cos(-x) = \sin x - \csc x$

29. $\dfrac{\cos \theta}{\sin \theta} + \dfrac{\sin \theta}{\cos \theta} = \sec \theta \csc \theta$

30. $\dfrac{1 - \sin(-x)}{\cos x} = \tan x + \sec x$

31. $\dfrac{1 - \cos x}{1 + \cos x} = \dfrac{\sec x - 1}{\sec x + 1}$

32. $1 - (\sin x - \cos x)^2 = 2 \sin x \cos x$

33. $\dfrac{\csc(-x)}{\cot(-x) + \tan(-x)} = \cos x$

34. $\dfrac{\cos x}{1 - \sin x} = \dfrac{1 + \sin x}{\cos x}$

35. $\sec^4 x - \tan^4 x = \sec^2 x(\sin^2 x + 1)$

36. $\tan^2 x - \sec^2 x = -1$

37. $\tan^4 x + \tan^2 x = \sec^4 x - \sec^2 x$

38. $\dfrac{1}{\sec \theta - \tan \theta} = \sec \theta + \tan \theta$

39. $\dfrac{\cot x + \tan x}{\sec x \csc x} = 1$

40. $\sin^2 x \tan^2 x + \sin^2 x = \tan^2 x$

4.2 BASIC IDENTITIES (CONTINUED)

All problems of the preceding section are of the form "Prove that the given equation is an identity." In this section our problems are similar except that we ask "Is the given equation an identity?" Thus we have the additional burden of trying to decide whether or not the equation is an identity. If we think it is, then we must prove it. If not, we must exhibit at least one value of the variable for which both sides of the equation are defined and for which the two sides are not equal. We illustrate the procedure through the following examples.

Examples

$\triangle 1$ Determine whether or not equation $\sin^4 x + \cos^4 x = 1$ is an identity.

Solution. If we have no advance information or insight as to whether or not an equation is an identity, then it is probably wise to first try a few values of x to see whether the equation is satisfied by these values. If we find one value that does not satisfy it, then the given equation is not an identity. In our problem we try

$$x = 0: \qquad \sin^4 0 \;+ \cos^4 0 \;= 0^4 + 1^4 \quad = 1;$$

$$x = \frac{\pi}{2}: \qquad \sin^4 \frac{\pi}{2} + \cos^4 \frac{\pi}{2} = 1^4 + 0^4 \quad = 1;$$

$$x = \pi: \qquad \sin^4 \pi \;+ \cos^4 \pi \;= 0^4 + (-1)^4 = 1.$$

Thus the given equation is satisfied by each of the three values of x, and so by now we begin to suspect that it is an identity. However, it is worth noting that the tested values $(0, \pi/2, \pi)$ of x are special; and in many cases these will satisfy a given equation while others will not. It is wise to try (after 0) a number such as $x = 1$; with the calculator (in radian mode), it is easy to evaluate and get $(\sin 1)^4 + (\cos 1)^4 = 0.5866$. Therefore, $\sin^4 x + \cos^4 x = 1$ is *not* an identity since it is not satisfied by $x = 1$. ∎

⚠ Determine whether equation $\dfrac{1}{1 - \cos x} = \dfrac{1 + \cos x}{\sin^2 x}$ is an identity.

Solution. We first try a few values of x and evaluate the LHS and RHS for these values:

$$x = 0: \qquad \text{LHS} = \frac{1}{1 - \cos 0} = \frac{1}{1 - 1} = \frac{1}{0},$$

thus the LHS is undefined, and so $x = 0$ is not in the domain of discussion for this problem;

$$x = \frac{\pi}{2}: \qquad \text{LHS} = \frac{1}{1 - \cos (\pi/2)} = \frac{1}{1 - 0} = 1,$$

$$\text{RHS} = \frac{1 + \cos (\pi/2)}{\sin^2 (\pi/2)} = \frac{1 + 0}{1^2} = 1;$$

$$x = 1: \qquad \text{LHS} = \frac{1}{1 - \cos 1} = 2.175342651,$$

$$\text{RHS} = \frac{1 + \cos 1}{\sin^2 1} = 2.175342650.$$

Although the LHS and RHS given by the calculator for $x = 1$ differ slightly, it is a good guess that $x = 1$ does satisfy the given equation (the discrepancy is probably due to round-off error within the calculator).

   At this point it is reasonable to suspect that the given equation is an identity, and so we attempt to prove it:

$$\text{LHS} = \frac{1}{1-\cos x} = \frac{1+\cos x}{(1-\cos x)(1+\cos x)} = \frac{1+\cos x}{1-\cos^2 x} \quad \text{(by algebra)}$$

$$= \frac{1+\cos x}{\sin^2 x} \quad \text{(by (I.9))}.$$

Therefore, LHS = RHS, and so the given equation is an identity. ∎

△3 In algebra, symbol "$\sqrt{}$" is introduced as the nonnegative square root of a nonnegative number. For example, $\sqrt{4} = 2$ (and not $\sqrt{4} = \pm2$). Thus $\sqrt{a^2} = a$ is correct only if $a \geq 0$, but $\sqrt{a^2} = |a|$ is true for every real number a. Therefore, $\sqrt{1-\sin^2 x} = \cos x$ is not an identity since it is not satisfied by any value of x for which $\cos x < 0$ (for example, if $x = \pi$, then $\sqrt{1-\sin^2\pi} = \sqrt{1-0^2} = \sqrt{1} = 1$, while $\cos \pi = -1$). However, equation $\sqrt{1-\sin^2 x} = |\cos x|$ is an identity. Thus we can replace $\sqrt{1-\sin^2 x}$ by $|\cos x|$ in any problem; however when we replace $\sqrt{1-\sin^2 x}$ by $\cos x$, we must make certain that the discussed x-values are such that $\cos x \geq 0$. ∎

△4 Is $\sqrt{\tan^2 x - \sin^2 x} = \sin x \tan x$ an identity?

Solution. We first try a few values of x:

$x = 0$: $\text{LHS} = \sqrt{\tan^2 0 - \sin^2 0} = 0,$

$\qquad\quad \text{RHS} = \sin 0 \tan 0 = 0 \cdot 0 = 0;$

$x = \frac{\pi}{4}$: $\text{LHS} = \sqrt{\tan^2 \frac{\pi}{4} - \sin^2 \frac{\pi}{4}} = \sqrt{1 - \left(\frac{1}{\sqrt{2}}\right)^2} = \sqrt{1 - \frac{1}{2}} = \frac{1}{\sqrt{2}},$

$\qquad\quad \text{RHS} = \sin \frac{\pi}{4} \cdot \tan \frac{\pi}{4} = \frac{1}{\sqrt{2}} \cdot 1 = \frac{1}{\sqrt{2}};$

$x = 1$: $\text{LHS} = \sqrt{(\tan 1)^2 - (\sin 1)^2} = 1.310513411,$

$\qquad\quad \text{RHS} = (\tan 1)(\sin 1) = 1.310513411.$

It now appears that the given equation is an identity. Suppose we attempt to "prove" it by starting with the given equation. If we square both sides, we get

$$\tan^2 x - \sin^2 x = (\sin x \tan x)^2.$$

Using algebra and some of the basic identities, we can write the following steps:

$\dfrac{\sin^2 x}{\cos^2 x} - \sin^2 x = \sin^2 x \tan^2 x; \qquad \sin^2 x \sec^2 x - \sin^2 x = \sin^2 x \tan^2 x;$

$\sin^2 x(\sec^2 x - 1) = \sin^2 x \tan^2 x; \qquad \sin^2 x \tan^2 x = \sin^2 x \tan^2 x.$

Can we now conclude that $\sqrt{\tan^2 x - \sin^2 x} = \sin x \tan x$ is an identity? The answer is NO. Actually it is not an identity, as we can show by trying $x = 3\pi/4$:

$$\text{LHS} = \sqrt{\tan^2 \frac{3\pi}{4} - \sin^2 \frac{3\pi}{4}} = \sqrt{1 - \frac{1}{2}} = \frac{1}{\sqrt{2}},$$

$$\text{RHS} = \left(\tan \frac{3\pi}{4}\right)\left(\sin \frac{3\pi}{4}\right) = -1 \cdot \frac{1}{\sqrt{2}} = -\frac{1}{\sqrt{2}}$$

This example illustrates a *faulty proof*, in which we began by squaring both sides of the given equation. This step is not reversible.   ▌

EXERCISE 4.2

Determine whether the given equations are identities. Give good reasons for your conclusions.

1. $\dfrac{\sin^2 x}{\cos x} = \sec x - \cos x$ **2.** $\sin x \cot x = \cos x$

3. $\sin x \tan x = 1 - \cos x$ **4.** $(\sin \theta + \cos \theta)^2 = 1$

5. $(\sin x - \cos x)^2 = \sin^2 x - \cos^2 x$ **6.** $\dfrac{\sin \theta + \cos \theta}{\cos \theta} = 1 + \tan \theta$

7. $(\cos x + \sin x)(\sec x + \csc x) = 1$ **8.** $\cot x \sec x = \cos x$

9. $\sin x \cos x(\sin x \sec x + \cos x \csc x) = 1$

10. $[\cos(-x) + \sin(-x)]^2 = 1 - 2 \sin x \cos x$

11. $(\sin x + \cos x)^3 = \sin^3 x + \cos^3 x$ **12.** $\sin^4 x - \cos^4 x = 2 \sin^2 x - 1$

13. $\sqrt{1 - \cos^2 \theta} = \sin \theta$

14. $\sin^3 x - \cos^3 x = (\sin x - \cos x)(1 + \sin x \cos x)$

15. $(\tan \theta + \cot \theta)^2 = \tan^2 \theta + \cot^2 \theta$ **16.** $\sqrt{\cot^2 x - \cos^2 x} = \cos x \cot x$

17. $\sqrt{\sin^2 x + \cos^2 x} = |\sin x| + |\cos x|$ **18.** $\sec^2 x + \csc^2 x = 1$

19. $(1 + \tan \theta)^2 = \sec^2 \theta + 2 \tan \theta$ **20.** $\sqrt{1 + \tan^2 \theta} = \sec \theta$

4.3 SUM AND DIFFERENCE IDENTITIES

In trigonometry we frequently encounter expressions of the type $\sin(\alpha + \beta)$ and we first ask: Is $\sin(\alpha + \beta) = \sin \alpha + \sin \beta$ for all values of α and β? The answer is NO. For instance, if $\alpha = \pi/2$, $\beta = \pi/2$, then $\sin(\pi/2 + \pi/2) = \sin \pi = 0$, while $\sin \pi/2 + \sin \pi/2 = 1 + 1 = 2$, and so the equation is not an identity. The next question is: Can we find a simple formula that gives $\sin(\alpha + \beta)$ in terms of trigonometric functions of α and of β individually? The answer to this is included in the following set of identities called the *sum and difference formulas:*

(I.12)
$$\sin(\alpha + \beta) = \sin \alpha \cos \beta + \cos \alpha \sin \beta$$

(I.13)
$$\sin(\alpha - \beta) = \sin \alpha \cos \beta - \cos \alpha \sin \beta$$

(I.14)
$$\cos(\alpha + \beta) = \cos \alpha \cos \beta - \sin \alpha \sin \beta$$

(I.15)
$$\cos(\alpha - \beta) = \cos \alpha \cos \beta + \sin \alpha \sin \beta$$

(I.16)
$$\tan(\alpha + \beta) = \frac{\tan \alpha + \tan \beta}{1 - \tan \alpha \tan \beta}$$

(I.17)
$$\tan(\alpha - \beta) = \frac{\tan \alpha - \tan \beta}{1 + \tan \alpha \tan \beta}$$

We first prove (I.14) by using the diagrams of Fig. 4.1, where α and β are taken as positive angles and points A and B are on the corresponding terminal sides at a distance of one unit from the origin. From the definitions of trigonometric functions, the coordinates of A and B are:

$$A: (\cos \alpha, \sin \alpha), \qquad B: (\cos(-\beta), \sin(-\beta)) = (\cos \beta, -\sin \beta).$$

Let d be the distance between points A and B and so, by the distance formula, we have:

$$d^2 = (\cos \alpha - \cos \beta)^2 + (\sin \alpha + \sin \beta)^2.$$

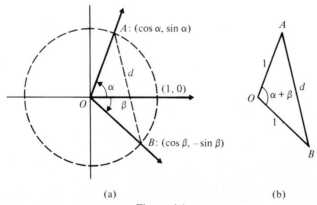

(a)   (b)

Figure 4.1

After applying some simple algebra and using identity (I.9) twice, we get

$$d^2 = 2 - 2(\cos \alpha \, \cos \beta - \sin \alpha \, \sin \beta). \tag{4.1}$$

We now look at triangle AOB of Fig. 4.1(b) where points A, O, B are taken from Fig. 4.1(a). Applying the Law of cosines to triangle AOB, we get:

$$d^2 = 1^2 + 1^2 - 2(1)(1)\cos(\alpha + \beta) = 2 - 2\cos(\alpha + \beta). \tag{4.2}$$

Comparing Eqs. (4.1) and (4.2), we conclude that

$$\cos(\alpha + \beta) = \cos \alpha \, \cos \beta - \sin \alpha \, \sin \beta.$$

This is identity (I.14).

Note. The diagrams of Fig. 4.1 illustrate the case when α and β are positive acute angles. Actually, we could give a similar proof for α and β of any size.

We can now use identities (I.14), (I.4), and (I.5) to prove the remaining identities given above. The following is a proof of (I.15):

$$\cos(\alpha - \beta) = \cos(\alpha + (-\beta)) = \cos \alpha \, \cos(-\beta) - \sin \alpha \, \sin(-\beta)$$
$$= \cos \alpha \, \cos \beta + \sin \alpha \, \sin \beta.$$

Therefore we get identity (I.15):

$$\cos(\alpha - \beta) = \cos \alpha \, \cos \beta + \sin \alpha \, \sin \beta.$$

To prove (I.12) we use identities

$$\sin\left(\frac{\pi}{2} - \theta\right) = \cos \theta \quad \text{and} \quad \cos\left(\frac{\pi}{2} - \theta\right) = \sin \theta,$$

which the student is asked to prove in Problem 1 of Exercise 4.3. Thus,

$$\sin(\alpha + \beta) = \cos\left[\frac{\pi}{2} - (\alpha + \beta)\right] = \cos\left[\left(\frac{\pi}{2} - \alpha\right) - \beta\right]$$
$$= \cos\left(\frac{\pi}{2} - \alpha\right)\cos \beta + \sin\left(\frac{\pi}{2} - \alpha\right)\sin \beta \quad \text{(by (I.15)}$$
$$= \sin \alpha \, \cos \beta + \cos \alpha \, \sin \beta.$$

Therefore, $\sin(\alpha + \beta) = \sin \alpha \, \cos \beta + \cos \alpha \, \sin \beta$ is an identity.

We can now prove (I.16) as follows:

$$\tan(\alpha + \beta) = \frac{\sin(\alpha + \beta)}{\cos(\alpha + \beta)} \quad \text{(by (I.7))}$$
$$= \frac{\sin \alpha \, \cos \beta + \cos \alpha \, \sin \beta}{\cos \alpha \, \cos \beta - \sin \alpha \, \sin \beta} \quad \text{(by (I.14) and (I.15))}$$
$$= \frac{\tan \alpha + \tan \beta}{1 - \tan \alpha \, \tan \beta},$$

where in the last step we divided the numerator and the denominator by $\cos \alpha \, \cos \beta$, and then used (I.7). Therefore,

$$\tan(\alpha + \beta) = \frac{\tan \alpha + \tan \beta}{1 - \tan \alpha \, \tan \beta}$$

is an identity. We leave proofs of (I.13) and (I.17) as Problem 2 in Exercise 4.3.

Examples

⚠️ 1⃝ Prove that $\tan(x - \frac{\pi}{4}) = \dfrac{\sin x - \cos x}{\sin x + \cos x}$ is an identity.

Solution.

$$\text{LHS} = \tan\left(x - \frac{\pi}{4}\right) = \frac{\tan x - \tan (\pi/4)}{1 + \tan x \tan (\pi/4)} \qquad \text{(by (I.17))}$$

$$= \frac{\tan x - 1}{1 + \tan x} \qquad \left(\text{since } \tan \frac{\pi}{4} = 1\right)$$

$$= \frac{(\sin x/\cos x) - 1}{1 + (\sin x/\cos x)} \qquad \text{(by (I.7))}$$

$$= \frac{\sin x - \cos x}{\cos x + \sin x} \qquad \text{(by algebra)}.$$

Therefore LHS = RHS, and so the given equation is an identity. ▮

2⃝ Evaluate $\sin 75°$ and express the answer in exact form.

Solution.

$$\sin 75° = \sin(30° + 45°) = \sin 30° \cos 45° + \cos 30° \sin 45°$$

$$= \frac{1}{2}\frac{\sqrt{2}}{2} + \frac{\sqrt{3}}{2}\frac{\sqrt{2}}{2} = \frac{1}{4}\left(\sqrt{2} + \sqrt{6}\right). \qquad ▮$$

3⃝ Evaluate $\cos (\pi/12)$ and give the answer in exact form.

Solution.

$$\cos \frac{\pi}{12} = \cos\left(\frac{\pi}{4} - \frac{\pi}{6}\right) = \cos \frac{\pi}{4} \cos \frac{\pi}{6} + \sin \frac{\pi}{4} \sin \frac{\pi}{6}$$

$$= \frac{\sqrt{2}}{2}\frac{\sqrt{3}}{2} + \frac{\sqrt{2}}{2}\frac{1}{2} = \frac{1}{4}\left(\sqrt{6} + \sqrt{2}\right). \qquad ▮$$

4⃝ Prove that $\sin x \cos y = \frac{1}{2} [\sin(x + y) + \sin(x - y)]$ is an identity.

Solution. If we add the two equations given in (I.12) and (I.13), we get

$$\sin(x + y) + \sin(x - y) = 2 \sin x \cos y.$$

This is equivalent to the given equation. ▮

EXERCISE 4.3

1. Using definitions of the sine and cosine functions, prove these identities:

$$\cos\left(\frac{\pi}{2} - \theta\right) = \sin \theta \qquad \text{and} \qquad \sin\left(\frac{\pi}{2} - \theta\right) = \cos \theta.$$

2. Prove that the equations given in (I.13) and (I.17) are identities.

3. Establish the following cofunction identities:

a) $\tan\left(\frac{\pi}{2} - \theta\right) = \cot\theta$　　　　　b) $\sin\left(\frac{\pi}{2} + \theta\right) = \cos\theta$

c) $\cos\left(\frac{\pi}{2} + \theta\right) = -\sin\theta$　　　　d) $\tan\left(\frac{\pi}{2} + \theta\right) = -\cot\theta$

e) $\sin\left(\frac{3\pi}{2} - \theta\right) = -\cos\theta$　　　　f) $\cos\left(\frac{3\pi}{2} - \theta\right) = -\sin\theta$

g) $\sin\left(\frac{3\pi}{2} + \theta\right) = -\cos\theta$　　　　h) $\cos\left(\frac{3\pi}{2} + \theta\right) = \sin\theta$

4. Prove that the given equations are identities:

a) $\sin(180° - \theta) = \sin\theta$　　　　　b) $\cos(180° - \theta) = -\cos\theta$

c) $\tan(180° - \theta) = -\tan\theta$　　　　d) $\sin(180° + \theta) = -\sin\theta$

e) $\cos(180° + \theta) = -\cos\theta$　　　　f) $\tan(180° + \theta) = \tan\theta$

5. Evaluate the following. Give answers in exact form.

a) $\cos 75°$　　　　　　b) $\sin 195°$　　　　　　c) $\tan 285°$

d) $\cot 15°$　　　　　　e) $\sec 255°$　　　　　　f) $\csc(-75°)$

6. Evaluate the following. Give answers in exact form, then use your calculator to evaluate the result correct to two decimal places. As a check, evaluate directly by calculator (make certain it is in radian mode).

a) $\tan\dfrac{7\pi}{12}$　　　　　b) $\sec\left(-\dfrac{5\pi}{12}\right)$　　　　　c) $\cos\dfrac{11\pi}{12}$

d) $\sin\dfrac{23\pi}{12}$　　　　e) $\sin\dfrac{13\pi}{12}$　　　　f) $\csc\dfrac{25\pi}{12}$

7. If $\tan\ x = \frac{3}{4}$ and $x + y = \frac{\pi}{4}$, find $\tan y$.

8. If $\tan\alpha = 3$ and $\tan(\alpha + \beta) = -\frac{2}{3}$, find $\tan\beta$.

9. If $x - y = \frac{3\pi}{4}$ and $\tan y = 3$, find $\tan x$.

10. If $\tan(x - y) = -\frac{5}{4}$ and $\tan x = 0.4$, find $\tan y$.

In Problems 11 through 17 determine whether the given equations are identities.

11. $\tan\left(\frac{\pi}{4} + x\right) = \dfrac{1 + \tan\ x}{1 - \tan\ x}$

12. $\sin\left(\frac{\pi}{6} - x\right) = \frac{1}{2}\left(\cos\ x - \sqrt{3}\ \sin\ x\right)$

13. $\dfrac{\cos\ x - \sin\ x}{\cos\ x + \sin\ x} = \tan\left(\frac{\pi}{4} - x\right)$　　　14. $\sec(\alpha + \beta) = \sec\alpha + \sec\beta$

15. $\csc\left(\frac{\pi}{2} - x\right) = \sec\ x$　　　　　　16. $\sin\ x + \sin 2x = \sin 3x$

17. $\cos\left(\frac{5\pi}{2} + x\right) = -\sin\ x$

18. Use $\cos 75° = \cos(30° + 45°)$ to get $\cos 75°$ in exact form. Similarly, express $\sin 75°$ in exact form.

19. Use the result of Problem 31 in Exercise 3.2 to find $\sin 72°$ in exact form.

20. Use Problems 18, 19, and $\cos 3° = \cos(75° - 72°)$ to get $\cos 3°$ in exact form.

21. Prove that each of the following equations is an identity:

a) $\cos x \cos y = \frac{1}{2} [\cos(x + y) + \cos(x - y)]$

b) $\sin x \sin y = \frac{1}{2} [\cos(x - y) - \cos(x + y)]$.

22. Using the results of Example 4 and Problem 21, express each of the following products as a sum or a difference.

a) $(\sin 3\theta)(\cos 5\theta)$ b) $(\cos 3\theta)(\cos 4\theta)$ c) $(\sin 2y)(\sin 4y)$

d) $(\cos 3x)(\sin(-5x))$ e) $(\sin 2y)(\sin(-4y))$ f) $(\sin 3x)(\sin 2x)$

23. In each of the following, write the given expression in equivalent form in terms of $\sin x$ and $\cos x$:

a) $\sin\left(x - \frac{\pi}{4}\right)$ b) $\sin\left(x - \frac{\pi}{2}\right)$ c) $\cos\left(x - \frac{\pi}{4}\right)$

d) $\sin(2x)$ e) $\cos(2x)$ f) $\sin\left(2x - \frac{\pi}{3}\right)$

24. Find the value of each of the following. Express your answer in exact form:

a) $\sin \frac{\pi}{4} \cos \frac{\pi}{12} + \sin \frac{\pi}{12} \cos \frac{\pi}{4}$

b) $\cos 160° \cos 25° + \sin 160° \sin 25°$

c) $\cos^2 47° + \sin^2 47°$

d) $\dfrac{\tan 37° - \tan 67°}{1 + \tan 37° \tan 67°}$

25. If α, β, and γ are three angles of a triangle, prove that

a) $\sin \gamma = \sin \alpha \cos \beta + \cos \alpha \sin \beta$

b) $\cos \gamma = \sin \alpha \sin \beta - \cos \alpha \cos \beta$

4.4 DOUBLE-ANGLE FORMULAS

Useful identities can be derived from the addition formulas given in Section 4.3. The following are called *double-angle identities:*

(I.18)
$$\sin 2\theta = 2 \sin \theta \cos \theta$$

(I.19)
$$\cos 2\theta = \cos^2\theta - \sin^2\theta = 1 - 2 \sin^2\theta = 2 \cos^2\theta - 1$$

(I.20)
$$\tan 2\theta = \frac{2 \tan \theta}{1 - \tan^2\theta}$$

These are special cases of (I.12), (I.14), and (I.16) where we take $\alpha = \theta$ and $\beta = \theta$ (see Problem 1 of Exercise 4.4).

The double-angle identities are useful in simplifying certain trigonometric expressions, and the student should become familiar with them. We consider several examples in which the double-angle identities are used along with identities (I.1) through (I.17) listed on pp. 122 and 129.

Examples

⚠ Prove that $\sin 2x = \dfrac{2 \tan x}{1 + \tan^2 x}$ is an identity.

Solution

$$\text{LHS} = \sin 2x = 2 \sin x \cos x \qquad \text{(by (I.18))}$$

$$\text{RHS} = \frac{2 \tan x}{1 + \tan^2 x} = \frac{2 \tan x}{\sec^2 x} \qquad \text{(by I.10))}$$

$$= \frac{2 \sin x}{\cos x} \div \frac{1}{\cos^2 x} \qquad \text{(by (I.2) and (I.7))}$$

$$= 2 \sin x \cos x \qquad \text{(by algebra)}.$$

Therefore, LHS = RHS and the given equation is an identity. ∎

⚠ If $\sin \theta = 3/5$ and $\cos \theta$ is negative, evaluate the following:

a) $\sin 2\theta$ \qquad\qquad\qquad b) $\cos 2\theta$

Solution. Since $\sin \theta > 0$ and $\cos \theta < 0$, angle θ is in the second quadrant, as shown in Fig. 4.2.

a) To find $\sin 2\theta$ we use (I.18):

$$\sin 2\theta = 2 \sin \theta \cos \theta = 2\left(\frac{3}{5}\right)\left(-\frac{4}{5}\right) = -\frac{24}{25}.$$

b) To find $\cos 2\theta$ we use (I.19):

$$\cos 2\theta = \cos^2\theta - \sin^2\theta = \left(-\frac{4}{5}\right)^2 - \left(\frac{3}{5}\right)^2 = \frac{7}{25}. \qquad \blacksquare$$

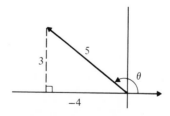

Figure 4.2

⚠️3 Express sin $3x$ as a function of sin x.

Solution.

$$\sin 3x = \sin(2x + x) = \sin(2x) \cos x + \cos(2x) \sin x \quad \text{(by (I.12))}$$
$$= (2\sin x \cos x) \cos x + (\cos^2 x - \sin^2 x) \sin x \quad \text{(by (I.18) and (I.19))}$$
$$= 3 \sin x \cos^2 x - \sin^3 x \quad \text{(by algebra)}$$
$$= 3 \sin x (1 - \sin^2 x) - \sin^3 x \quad \text{(by (I.9))}$$
$$= 3 \sin x - 4 \sin^3 x.$$

Therefore sin $3x = 3 \sin x - 4 \sin^3 x$ is an identity. ∎

⚠️4 Find sin $22°30'$ in exact form. Using your calculator, evaluate the result and give the answer correct to four decimal places.

Solution. We use (I.19) in the form cos $2\theta = 1 - 2 \sin^2\theta$, and take $\theta = 22°30'$ (that is, $2\theta = 45°$):

$$\cos 45° = 1 - 2(\sin 22°30')^2.$$

Solving for $(\sin 22°30')^2$ and using cos $45° = \sqrt{2}/2$, we have

$$(\sin 22°30')^2 = \frac{1 - \sqrt{2}/2}{2} = \frac{2 - \sqrt{2}}{4}.$$

Therefore,

$$\sin 22°30' = \frac{\sqrt{2 - \sqrt{2}}}{2}.$$

Using a calculator, we evaluate the right side and get

$$\sin 22°30' = 0.3827.$$

⚠️5 Prove that sin $4x = 4 \sin x \cos x - 8 \sin^3 x \cos x$ is an identity.

Solution.

$$\text{LHS} = \sin 4x = 2 \sin 2x \cos 2x \quad \text{(by (I.18))}$$
$$= 2(2\sin x \cos x)(1 - 2 \sin^2 x) \quad \text{(by (I.18) and (I.19))}$$
$$= 4 \sin x \cos x - 8 \sin^3 x \cos x \quad \text{(by algebra).}$$

Therefore, LHS = RHS and so the given equation is an identity. ∎

⚠️6 Is $(\sin 6x + \cos 6x)^2 = 1$ an identity?

Solution. We first try a few values of x to see if the equation is satisfied:

if $x = 0$, then LHS $= (\sin 0 + \cos 0)^2 = (0 + 1)^2 = 1$;

if $x = \frac{\pi}{2}$, then LHS $= (\sin 3\pi + \cos 3\pi)^2 = (0 - 1)^2 = 1$;

if $x = \frac{\pi}{4}$, then LHS $= \left(\sin \frac{3\pi}{2} + \cos \frac{3\pi}{2}\right)^2 = (-1 + 0)^2 = 1$.

It appears that the equation may represent an identity. However, if we try $x = 1$, we get

$$\text{LHS} = (\sin 6 + \cos 6)^2 = 0.46 \text{ (to two decimal places)}.$$

Therefore, $(\sin 6 x + \cos 6x)^2 = 1$ is not an identity.   ∎

⚠ Suppose $\sin \theta = 0.3487$ and $0° < \theta < 90°$. Using a calculator, evaluate each of the following to four decimal places:

a) $\sin 2\theta$ b) $\cos 2\theta$ c) $\tan 2\theta$

Solution. Enter 0.3487 into the display. Then with the calculator in either degree or radian mode, press keys (INV) and (sin) (or (sin⁻¹) key) which gives θ in the display, multiply the result by 2, and store it with the (STO) key. Using the (RCL) key as needed, we get:

a) $\sin 2\theta = 0.6536$ b) $\cos 2\theta = 0.7568$ c) $\tan 2\theta = 0.8637$ ∎

Note. On some calculators the store and recall keys may be labeled differently from (STO) and (RCL) .

EXERCISE 4.4

1. Give details of the proof that (I.18), (I.19), and (I.20) are special cases of (I.12), (I.14), and (I.16), respectively.

In Problems 2 through 24, prove that the given equations are identities:

2. $(\sin \theta + \cos \theta)^2 = 1 + \sin 2\theta$

3. $\dfrac{1}{\csc 2\theta} = 2 \sin \theta \cos \theta$

4. $\sin 2\theta \sec \theta = 2 \sin \theta$

5. $(\cos x + \sin x)(\cos x - \sin x) = \cos 2x$

6. $\cos 2x \tan 2x = \sin 2x$

7. $\sin 2x \tan x = 2 \sin^2 x$

8. $(\cos x - \sin x) \sec 2x = \dfrac{1}{\cos x + \sin x}$

9. $(1 + \tan x) \tan 2x = \dfrac{2 \tan x}{1 - \tan x}$

10. $\tan \theta \sin 2\theta = 1 - \cos 2\theta$

11. $\sin 2\theta \sec^2\theta = 2 \tan \theta$

12. $\cot x - \tan x = 2 \cot 2x$

13. $2 \csc 2x = \tan x + \cot x$

14. $\dfrac{2}{1 + \cos 2\theta} = \sec^2\theta$

15. $\cot 2\theta = \dfrac{\cot^2\theta - 1}{2 \cot \theta}$

16. $\cos^4 x - \sin^4 x = \cos 2x$

17. $\dfrac{1 - \tan x}{1 + \tan x} = \sec 2x - \tan 2x$

18. $\dfrac{\sin 2x}{1 + \cos 2x} = \tan x$

19. $(\cot x - \tan x)\tan 2x = 2$

20. $2 \tan \theta \csc 2\theta = 1 + \tan^2\theta$

21. $\dfrac{1 + \tan^2\theta}{\tan \theta} = 2 \csc 2\theta$

22. $\dfrac{1 - \cos 2x}{1 + \cos 2x} = \tan^2 x$　　　　　　　**23.** $\cos 3x = 4 \cos^3 x - 3 \cos x$

24. $\cos 4x = \cos^4 x - 6 \sin^2 x \cos^2 x + \sin^4 x$

25. If $\cos \theta = -12/13$ and θ is in the second quadrant, find in exact form:

　　a) $\sin 2\theta$　　　　　　b) $\cos 2\theta$　　　　　　c) $\tan 2\theta$

26. If $\sin \theta = -5/13$ and $\cos \theta = 12/13$, find in exact form:

　　a) $\sin 2\theta$　　　　　　b) $\cos 2\theta$　　　　　　c) $\tan 2\theta$

27. Suppose $\cos \theta = 0.5873$ and $0° < \theta < 90°$. Using a calculator, evaluate the following to four decimal places:

　　a) $\sin 2\theta$　　　　　　b) $\cos 2\theta$　　　　　　c) $\tan 2\theta$

28. Suppose $\sin \theta = 0.4385$ and $0 < \theta < \pi/2$. Using a calculator, evaluate to four decimal places:

　　a) $\sin 2\theta$　　　　　　b) $\cos 3\theta$　　　　　　c) $\cot 3\theta$

29. Evaluate the following and give answers in exact form:

　　a) $\sin 15° \cos 15°$　　　　b) $\sin^2 105° - \cos^2 105°$　　　c) $1 - 2 \sin^2 \dfrac{5\pi}{12}$

In Problems 30 through 39, determine whether the given equations are identities:

30. $\sec 2x = \dfrac{1}{2 \cos x}$　　　　　　　　　　**31.** $\sin 4x = 2 \sin 2x \cos 2x$

32. $\sin 2x + \sin 3x = \sin 5x$　　　　　　　**33.** $\sin^2 2x = 1 - \cos^2 2x$

34. $2 \cot 2x = \cot x - \tan x$　　　　　　　**35.** $2 \csc 2x = \sec x \csc x$

36. $\sin 3x \sin 2x = \sin 6x$　　　　　　　　**37.** $(\sin 2x + \cos 2x)^2 = 1$

38. $(\sin 4x + \cos 4x)^2 = 1$　　　　　　　**39.** $\sec 2x + \tan 2x = \tan\left(\dfrac{\pi}{4} + x\right)$

40. Triangle ABC is inscribed in a circle, as shown in Fig. 4.3, where Q is the center of the circle, α is one angle and a is the opposite side. Prove that the diameter d of the circle is given by $d = a/\sin \alpha$.

　　Hint. Note that angle BQC is equal to 2α. (Why?) Now use triangle BQC to get the result. This problem also appeared as Problem 23 of Exercise 3.3. However, the solution suggested there is quite different.

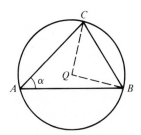

Figure 4.3

41. If α is an acute angle, then the double-angle formulas can be derived by using Fig. 4.4, where triangle ABC is inscribed in a semicircle of unit radius with center Q. Let α be the angle at A and D be the foot of the perpendicular from C. Then

a) show that the labels given to the angles in the diagram are justified and that angle ACB is a right angle;

b) using the triangles shown in the diagram, derive identities (I.18) and (I.19).

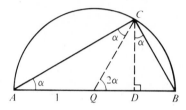

Figure 4.4

4.5 HALF-ANGLE FORMULAS

If we write identity (I.19) in the form $\cos 2x = 1 - 2 \sin^2 x$ and then replace x by $\theta/2$, we get $\cos \theta = 1 - 2 \sin^2 (\theta/2)$. Solving for $\sin (\theta/2)$ gives

$$\sin \frac{\theta}{2} = \sqrt{\frac{1 - \cos \theta}{2}} \quad \text{when } \sin \frac{\theta}{2} \geq 0,$$

$$\sin \frac{\theta}{2} = -\sqrt{\frac{1 - \cos \theta}{2}} \quad \text{when } \sin \frac{\theta}{2} < 0.$$

These two equations are ordinarily written as

(I.21)
$$\sin \frac{\theta}{2} = \pm\sqrt{\frac{1 - \cos \theta}{2}},$$

where the "$\pm$"sign does not mean that we get two values for $\sin (\theta/2)$, but that we select the sign that is consistent with the sign of $\sin (\theta/2)$ (depending upon the quadrant in which $\theta/2$ is located).

In a similar manner, if we replace the angle θ by $\theta/2$ in the form $\cos 2\theta = 2 \cos^2\theta - 1$ of identity (I.19), we get

(I.22)
$$\cos \frac{\theta}{2} = \pm\sqrt{\frac{1 + \cos \theta}{2}},$$

where again we use the sign that agrees with the sign of $\cos (\theta/2)$.

We can now get an identity for $\tan (\theta/2)$ by using (I.21) and (I.22) along with the identity $\tan (\theta/2) = \sin (\theta/2)/\cos (\theta/2)$:

(I.23)

$$\tan \frac{\theta}{2} = \pm \sqrt{\frac{1 - \cos \theta}{1 + \cos \theta}}.$$

Identity (I.23) can be expressed in a more desirable form not involving the "$\pm$" sign. Rather than manipulating (I.23) directly, we can proceed as follows. When θ is replaced by $\theta/2$, identities (I.18) and (I.19) can be written in the form

$$\sin \theta = 2 \sin \frac{\theta}{2} \cos \frac{\theta}{2} \quad \text{and} \quad 1 + \cos \theta = 2 \cos^2 \frac{\theta}{2},$$

respectively. Dividing these two equations, we get

$$\frac{\sin \theta}{1 + \cos \theta} = \frac{2 \sin (\theta/2) \cos (\theta/2)}{2 \cos^2 (\theta/2)} = \frac{\sin (\theta/2)}{\cos (\theta/2)} = \tan \frac{\theta}{2}.$$

Thus,

$$\tan \frac{\theta}{2} = \frac{\sin \theta}{1 + \cos \theta}.$$

An alternative form of this equation is (see Problem 16 of Exercise 4.1):

$$\tan \frac{\theta}{2} = \frac{1 - \cos \theta}{\sin \theta}.$$

Therefore we have the following identities for $\tan (\theta/2)$:

(I.24)

$$\tan \frac{\theta}{2} = \frac{\sin \theta}{1 + \cos \theta} = \frac{1 - \cos \theta}{\sin \theta}.$$

Examples

⚠ Evaluate each of the following and express the answer in exact form:

a) $\sin 22°30'$ b) $\cos 112.5°$ c) $\tan \frac{7\pi}{12}$

Solution.

a) $\sin 22°30' = \sin \left(\frac{45}{2}\right)° = \sqrt{\frac{1 - \cos 45°}{2}} = \frac{1}{2}\sqrt{2 - \sqrt{2}}$;

b) $\cos 112.5° = \cos \left(\frac{225}{2}\right)° = -\sqrt{\frac{1 + \cos 225°}{2}} = -\frac{1}{2}\sqrt{2 - \sqrt{2}}$;

c) $\tan \frac{7\pi}{12} = \tan \frac{7\pi}{2 \cdot 6} = \frac{1 - \cos(7\pi/6)}{\sin (7\pi/6)} = \frac{1 - (-\sqrt{3}/2)}{-1/2} = -(2 + \sqrt{3})$. ∎

2. If $\cos \theta = -3/5$ and $180° < \theta < 270°$ (Fig. 4.5), evaluate the following in exact form:

    a) $\sin \dfrac{\theta}{2}$ b) $\cos \dfrac{\theta}{2}$ c) $\tan \dfrac{\theta}{2}$

Solution. We first note that $90° < \theta/2 < 135°$, and so $\sin (\theta/2)$ is positive and $\cos (\theta/2)$ is negative.

    a) $\sin \dfrac{\theta}{2} = \sqrt{\dfrac{1 - \cos \theta}{2}} = \sqrt{\dfrac{1 - (-3/5)}{2}} = \dfrac{2\sqrt 5}{5}$

    b) $\cos \dfrac{\theta}{2} = -\sqrt{\dfrac{1 + \cos \theta}{2}} = -\sqrt{\dfrac{1 + (-3/5)}{2}} = \dfrac{-\sqrt 5}{5}$

    c) $\tan \dfrac{\theta}{2} = \dfrac{\sin \theta}{1 + \cos \theta} = \dfrac{-4/5}{1 + (-3/5)} = -2$

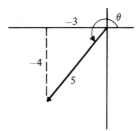

Figure 4.5

3. Evaluate $\sin 15°$ in exact form in two ways:

    a) by using (I.13)   b) by using (I.21)

Solution.

    a) $\sin 15° = \sin(45° - 30°) = \sin 45° \cos 30° - \cos 45° \sin 30°$

$$= \dfrac{\sqrt 6 - \sqrt 2}{4} ;$$

therefore,

$$\sin 15° = \dfrac{\sqrt 6 - \sqrt 2}{4} .$$

    b) $\sin 15° = \sin \left(\dfrac{30}{2}\right)° = \sqrt{\dfrac{1 - \cos 30°}{2}} = \dfrac{1}{2}\sqrt{2 - \sqrt 3};$

therefore,

$$\sin 15° = \dfrac{1}{2}\sqrt{2 - \sqrt 3}.$$

It appears that we get two different answers for $\sin 15°$. We leave it for the student to evaluate each with a calculator to see if they both represent the same number (see Problem 25 of Exercise 4.5). ❚

④   Suppose $\sin (\theta/2) = 0.6843$ and $0° < \theta < 180°$. Use a calculator to evaluate each of the following to four decimal places:

   a) $\sin \theta$ b) $\cos 2\theta$ c) $\tan \dfrac{\theta}{4}$

Solution. Enter 0.6843 into the display. Then with the calculator in either degree or radian mode press (INV) and (sin) keys (or (sin⁻¹) key); then multiply by 2 (this gives θ) and store into memory with the (STO) key. Using the (RCL) key as needed, we get

   a) $\sin \theta = 0.9980$ b) $\cos 2\theta = -0.9919$ c) $\tan \dfrac{\theta}{4} = 0.3957$. ∎

EXERCISE 4.5

In Problems 1 through 4, give answers in exact form; evaluate these results to four decimal places and then check by evaluating directly with a calculator:

1. a) $\sin 67°30'$ b) $\cos(-22.5°)$ c) $\sin 105°$ d) $\cos 105°$

2. a) $\tan 165°$ b) $\cos(247.5°)$ c) $\tan(-195°)$ d) $\cos 285°$

3. a) $\sin \dfrac{\pi}{12}$ b) $\cos \dfrac{5\pi}{8}$ c) $\sin \dfrac{11\pi}{8}$ d) $\tan \dfrac{13\pi}{12}$

4. a) $\cos \dfrac{19\pi}{8}$ b) $\sin\left(-\dfrac{7\pi}{8}\right)$ c) $\sin \dfrac{21\pi}{8}$ d) $\tan\left(-\dfrac{5\pi}{12}\right)$

In Problems 5 through 12 express answers in exact form:

5. If $\cos \theta = -\dfrac{5}{13}$ and $90° < \theta < 180°$, evaluate

   a) $\sin \dfrac{\theta}{2}$ b) $\cos \dfrac{\theta}{2}$ c) $\tan \dfrac{\theta}{2}$ d) $\sec \dfrac{\theta}{2}$

6. If $\tan \theta = -\dfrac{3}{4}$ and $-\dfrac{\pi}{2} < \theta < 0$, find

   a) $\sin \dfrac{\theta}{2}$ b) $\cot \dfrac{\theta}{2}$ c) $\sec \dfrac{\theta}{2}$ d) $\csc \dfrac{\theta}{2}$

7. If $\sin \theta = \dfrac{1}{2}$ and $360° < \theta < 450°$, find $\cos\dfrac{\theta}{2}$ and $\tan\dfrac{\theta}{2}$.

8. If $\cos \theta = -\dfrac{3}{4}$ and $0° < \theta < 180°$, evaluate

   a) $\sin \dfrac{\theta}{2}$ b) $\cos \dfrac{\theta}{2}$ c) $\sin 2\theta$ d) $\cos 2\theta$

9. If $\tan \alpha = 5$ and $\pi < \alpha < \dfrac{3\pi}{2}$, determine

   a) $\sin \alpha$ b) $\sin \dfrac{\alpha}{2}$ c) $\sin 2\alpha$ d) $\tan \dfrac{\alpha}{2}$

10. If $\cos \beta = -\dfrac{1}{\sqrt{2}}$ and $180° < \beta < 360°$, find

   a) $\cos \dfrac{\beta}{2}$ b) $\tan \dfrac{\beta}{2}$ c) $\tan 2\beta$ d) $\cos 2\beta$

11. If $\sin \dfrac{\theta}{2} = -\dfrac{3}{4}$, find $\cos \theta$.

12. If $\cos \dfrac{\theta}{2} = \dfrac{1}{\sqrt{2}}$, find $\cos \theta$.

13. Suppose $\sin \theta = 0.5486$ and $0° < \theta < 90°$. Use a calculator to evaluate each of the following to four decimal places:

a) $\sin \dfrac{\theta}{2}$ b) $\cos \dfrac{\theta}{2}$ c) $\tan \dfrac{\theta}{2}$

14. Suppose $\cos \dfrac{\theta}{2} = 0.6431$ and $0 < \theta < \pi$. Use a calculator to evaluate each of the following to four decimal places:

a) $\sin \theta$ b) $\cos 2\theta$ c) $\tan \dfrac{\theta}{4}$

In Problems 15 through 21, prove that the given equations are identities:

15. $\tan \dfrac{\theta}{2} = \csc \theta - \cot \theta$ 16. $\left(\sin \dfrac{\theta}{2} + \cos \dfrac{\theta}{2} \right)^2 = 1 + \sin \theta$

17. $\cos^2 \dfrac{x}{2} - \sin^2 \dfrac{x}{2} = \cos x$ 18. $2 \sin^2 \dfrac{x}{2} = \dfrac{\sec x - 1}{\sec x}$

19. $\tan \dfrac{x}{2} = \dfrac{\sec x - 1}{\sin x \sec x}$ 20. $2 \sin^2 \dfrac{x}{2} = \sin x \tan \dfrac{x}{2}$

21. $2 \cos^2 \dfrac{x}{2} = \dfrac{\sin x + \tan x}{\tan x}$

22. Follow Example 3 of this section and evaluate $\cos 15°$ by two different methods. Check to see that the two answers actually represent the same number.

23. Follow the instructions of Problem 22 for $\cos 165°$.

24. If $\cos \theta = -\dfrac{3}{5}$ and $90° < \theta < 180°$, find each of the following in exact form:

a) $\cos \dfrac{\theta}{2}$ b) $\cos \dfrac{\theta}{4}$

25. In Example 3 of this section we concluded that the two numbers

$$\dfrac{\sqrt{6} - \sqrt{2}}{4} \quad \text{and} \quad \dfrac{1}{2}\sqrt{2 - \sqrt{3}}$$

are equal. Use your calculator to check this conclusion; then prove that they are equal without using a calculator.

REVIEW EXERCISE

In Problems 1 through 25, prove that the given equations are identities:

1. $\cos x \tan x = \sin x$ 2. $\sec (90° - \theta) \tan \theta = \sec \theta$

3. $\csc \theta \sin 2\theta = 2 \cos \theta$ 4. $\cos(90° - 2\theta) = 2 \sin \theta \cos \theta$

5. $\tan\left(\theta + \dfrac{3\pi}{4} \right) = \dfrac{\cos \theta - \sin \theta}{\cos \theta + \sin \theta}$ 6. $(\sin x + \cos x)^2 = 1 + \sin 2x$

7. $(1 - \sin 2x)(1 + \sin 2x) = \cos^2 2x$ 8. $2 \csc x \sin^2 \dfrac{x}{2} = \dfrac{\sin x}{1 + \cos x}$

9. $\cos\left(\dfrac{\pi}{2} + x \right) \cot(-x) = \cos x$ 10. $\sin \theta \tan \dfrac{\theta}{2} = 1 - \cos \theta$

11. $\left(\sin \dfrac{\theta}{2} - \cos \dfrac{\theta}{2} \right)^2 = 1 - \sin \theta$

12. $\sin^2 \dfrac{\theta}{2} \cos^2 \dfrac{\theta}{2} = \dfrac{\sin^2\theta}{4}$

13. $\csc x \tan x = \sec x$

14. $\cot \dfrac{x}{2} - \tan \dfrac{x}{2} = 2 \cot x$

15. $2 \sin\left(\theta + \dfrac{\pi}{6}\right) = \sqrt{3} \sin \theta + \cos \theta$

16. $\sqrt{2} \cos\left(\theta - \dfrac{3\pi}{4}\right) = \sin \theta - \cos \theta$

17. $\tan 2x \csc 2x = \sec 2x$

18. $\left(1 - \cos \dfrac{x}{2}\right)\left(1 + \cos \dfrac{x}{2}\right) = \sin^2 \dfrac{x}{2}$

19. $\cos^4 \dfrac{x}{2} - \sin^4 \dfrac{x}{2} = \cos x$

20. $\cos 2x \tan 2x = \sin 2x$

21. $(\sec \theta + 1)(\sec \theta - 1) = \tan^2\theta$

22. $(1 + \sin \theta)(1 - \csc \theta) = \sin \theta - \csc \theta$

23. $(1 - \tan \theta) \tan 2\theta = \dfrac{2 \tan \theta}{1 + \tan \theta}$

24. $\cos^2 \dfrac{x}{2} - \sin^2 \dfrac{x}{2} = \cos x$

25. $\cos \theta(1 + \sec \theta) = 2 \cos^2 \dfrac{\theta}{2}$

In Problems 26 through 32, determine whether or not the given equations are identities. Give good reasons for your answers.

26. $\sin x = 2 \sin \dfrac{x}{2} \cos \dfrac{x}{2}$

27. $\tan x \cot x - \sin^2 x = \cos^2 x$

28. $\sqrt{\sec^2\theta - \tan^2\theta} = 1$

29. $(\cos \theta - \sin \theta)^2 = \cos^2\theta - \sin^2\theta$

30. $\sin 2\theta + (\sin \theta - \cos \theta)^2 = 1$

31. $\sin x + \sin 2x = \sin 3x$

32. $\left(\cos \dfrac{x}{2} + \sin \dfrac{x}{2}\right)\left(\cos \dfrac{x}{2} - \sin \dfrac{x}{2}\right) = \cos x$

In Problems 33 through 50, evaluate the given expressions in exact form if angles α, β, and γ satisfy the following conditions:

$$\sin \alpha = \dfrac{3}{5} \quad \text{and} \quad \dfrac{\pi}{2} \leq \alpha \leq \pi,$$

$$\tan \beta = -\dfrac{5}{12} \quad \text{and} \quad -\dfrac{\pi}{2} < \beta < \dfrac{\pi}{2},$$

$$\cos \gamma = \dfrac{4}{5} \quad \text{and} \quad 0 \leq \gamma \leq \pi.$$

33. $\cos \alpha$

34. $\sin 2\alpha$

35. $\sin \dfrac{\gamma}{2}$

36. $\sin(\alpha + \beta)$

37. $\tan(\beta - \gamma)$

38. $\cos \dfrac{\beta}{2}$

39. $\cos 2\beta$

40. $\tan 2\gamma$

41. $\cos(\alpha + 2\beta)$

42. $\tan(2\alpha - \gamma)$

43. $1 - \cos^2\alpha$

44. $\cos^2 \dfrac{\gamma}{2} - \sin^2 \dfrac{\gamma}{2}$

45. $\dfrac{\sin \beta}{\cos \beta}$

46. $\sec^2\beta - \tan^2\beta$

47. $\sin\left(\alpha - \dfrac{3\pi}{2}\right)$

48. $\tan\left(\beta + \dfrac{\pi}{4}\right)$

49. $\sin 2(\alpha + \beta)$

50. $\cos\left(\dfrac{\alpha + \beta}{2}\right)$

CHAPTER FIVE

INVERSE TRIGONOMETRIC FUNCTIONS

5.1 INTRODUCTION

The student has already encountered numerous examples of functions in algebra courses; in Chapter 2 we introduced other functions when we defined the trigonometric (or circular) functions. In each case we start with a set of real numbers, called the *domain* **D** of the function, and we have a *rule of correspondence** according to which each number in **D** is associated with a *unique* real number *y;* this correspondence yields a set of ordered pairs

$$\{(x, y) | x \in D \text{ and } y \text{ is the number associated with } x$$
$$\text{by the given rule of correspondence}\}.$$

In many instances it is convenient to denote the rule of correspondence by a letter such as *f, g, h,* . . ., and we write $y = f(x)$ to mean that *y* is the number associated with *x*. We shall consider a function *f* as either the rule of correspondence or as the resulting set of ordered pairs and write

$$f = \{(x, y) | x \in D, \text{ and } y \text{ corresponds to } x \text{ by the given rule}\}. \quad (5.1)$$

In the set of ordered pairs in (5.1) we call the first member (that is, *x*) the *independent variable* and *y* the *dependent variable* of *f*. The range **R** of *f* is the set of all *y* values that occur in the (*x, y*) ordered pairs; that is,

$$R = \{y | (x, y) \text{ is in } f\}.$$

In some problems we talk about more functions than one and it is necessary to distinguish between their domains and ranges; thus $D(f)$ and $R(f)$ will be used to denote the domain and range of function *f*, respectively.

---

*The rule of correspondence is usually given by an equation, for example, $y = 4x - 3$ or $y = x^3$; however, in some cases it is given by a table listing the ordered pairs, or by a graph, or by a verbal statement. Also, in a more general setting, the concept of function allows the correspondence between elements of sets that need not be real numbers.

The concept of a *relation* is more general than that of a function in that the rule of correspondence allows one or more different numbers y to correspond to each number x in D. Thus every function is a relation but a relation is not necessarily a function. If g denotes a relation that is not a function, then we *do not* write $y = g(x)$ but we denote g by a set of ordered pairs:

$$g = \{(x, y) \mid x \in D \text{ and } y \text{ corresponds to } x \text{ by the given rule}\}.$$

In many situations we are interested in a given function f and we wish to consider the process reverse to the one given by the rule of correspondence defining f. That is, if $y = f(x)$, then for each y in $R(f)$ we ask, "What values of x correspond to it?" This gives us an inverse rule of correspondence which we denote by f^{-1} and which we call the inverse relation* of f. That is,

$$f^{-1} = \{(y, x) \mid y \in R(f) \text{ and } y = f(x)\}. \tag{5.2}$$

Note that in (5.2) we have precisely the same set of ordered pairs as in (5.1) except that the first and second members of each have been interchanged. Thus we have:

$$D(f^{-1}) = R(f) \text{ and } R(f^{-1}) = D(f).$$

If f^{-1} is also a function (that is, for each y in $R(f)$ the corresponding value of x given by the inverse rule of correspondence is *unique*), then f^{-1} is called the *inverse function* of f and we write

$$x = f^{-1}(y). \tag{5.3}$$

Since f^{-1} is a function in its own right and it is customary to use x to represent the independent variable (particularly when we draw graphs) then we can write (5.3) as

$$y = f^{-1}(x). \tag{5.4}$$

As a set of ordered pairs, f^{-1} is given by

$$f^{-1} = \{(x, y) \mid x \in D(f^{-1}) = R(f) \text{ and } x = f(y)\}.$$

To illustrate inverse relations and functions we now consider two examples from algebra. These will lead us to the discussion of inverse trigonometric functions in the remaining sections of this chapter.

Examples

⚠️　An ad for a compact car gives its gas consumption as 16 km per liter. Assuming that it is telling the truth, find:

　　a) The rule of correspondence that gives the distance y (in kilometers) as

---

*The $^{-1}$ in the symbol f^{-1} *is not* to be interpreted as a *negative exponent;* it is merely part of the notation.

a function of the number x of liters of gasoline. How far will the car travel on 24 liters of gasoline?

b) The inverse rule of correspondence that gives x as a function of y. How many liters of gasoline are required to travel 280 km?

c) Draw the graphs describing the two rules of correspondence.

Solution.

a) The phrase "16 km per liter" translates into mathematical language as

$$y = 16x. \tag{5.5}$$

If we denote this by $y = f(x) = 16x$, then the given statement implies that $D(f) = \{x \mid x \geq 0\}$. Also it is clear that $R(f) = \{y \mid y \geq 0\}$. When $x = 24$ liters, then the corresponding value of y is given by

$$y = 16 \times 24 = 384 \text{ km.}$$

b) We can determine the inverse rule of correspondence by solving equation (5.5) for x in terms of y:

$$x = \frac{1}{16} y. \tag{5.6}$$

We see that for each $y \geq 0$ the inverse rule of correspondence given by (5.6) yields a unique value of x; thus it is a function and we can write

$$x = f^{-1}(y) = \frac{1}{16} y.$$

When $y = 280$ km, then the corresponding value of x is given by

$$x = f^{-1}(280) = \frac{1}{16} \times 280 = 17.5 \text{ liters.}$$

c) The graph of (5.5) is shown in Fig. 5.1, a. To draw a graph of function f^{-1} represented by (5.6) we interchange the x and y variables and get

$$y = \frac{1}{16} x.$$

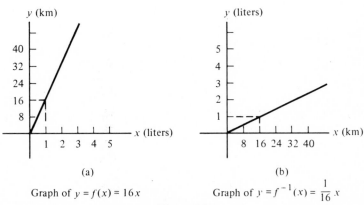

(a)

Graph of $y = f(x) = 16x$

(b)

Graph of $y = f^{-1}(x) = \frac{1}{16} x$

Figure 5.1

In this form x represents the number of kilometers the car travels and y represents the corresponding number of liters of gasoline required. The graph of $y = f^{-1}(x) = (1/16)x$ is shown in Fig. 5.1, b. It should be clear that the graph is the reflection of the graph in Fig. 5.1, a about the line $y = x$. ▮

⚠ The equation $y = x^2$ describes a function where each real number x is associated with a nonnegative number y. Draw graphs to assist in the discussion of the inverse rule of correspondence.

Solution. The graph of $y = f(x) = x^2$ is shown in Fig. 5.2, a; the points on the graph are given by the set of ordered pairs

$$f = \{(x, y) \mid x \in R \text{ and } y = x^2\}.$$

It is clear from the graph that for each real number x_0 there is a unique real number y_0 associated with x_0. Thus, f is a function.

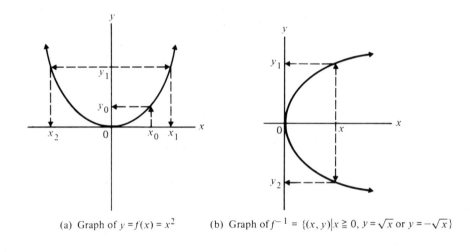

(a) Graph of $y = f(x) = x^2$ (b) Graph of $f^{-1} = \{(x, y) \mid x \geq 0,\ y = \sqrt{x} \text{ or } y = -\sqrt{x}\}$

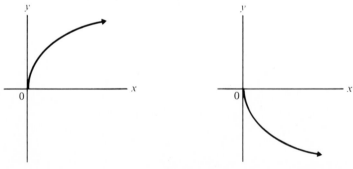

(c) Graph of $f_1^{-1} = \{(x, y) \mid x \geq 0,\ y = \sqrt{x}\}$ (d) Graph of $f_2^{-1} = \{(x, y) \mid x \geq 0,\ y = -\sqrt{x}\}$

Figure 5.2

Now if we reverse the process and look at any given positive number, such as y_1, then there are two corresponding values of x (namely, x_1 and x_2) associated with y_1. These are given by $x_1 = \sqrt{y_1}$ and $x_2 = -\sqrt{y_1}$ and are shown in Fig. 5.2, a. Thus when we solve $y = x^2$ for x in terms of y, we get $x = \sqrt{y}$ or $x = -\sqrt{y}$ for $y \geq 0$, and the inverse relation is given by

$$f^{-1} = \{(y, x) \mid y \geq 0 \text{ and } x = \sqrt{y} \text{ or } x = -\sqrt{y}\}. \qquad (5.7)$$

Thus f^{-1} is a relation that is not a function.

Since we want to draw a graph of f^{-1}, we interchange the x and y variables in (5.7) so that x becomes the independent variable. Thus the set of ordered pairs given by (5.7) can be written as

$$f^{-1} = \{(x, y) \mid x \geq 0 \text{ and } y = \sqrt{x} \text{ or } y = -\sqrt{x}\}. \qquad (5.8)$$

The graph of (5.8) is depicted in Fig. 5.2, b; it shows that for each positive value of x there are two corresponding values of y (illustrated by $y_1 = \sqrt{x}$ and $y_2 = -\sqrt{x}$). It should be clear that this graph is the reflection of the graph in Fig. 5.2, a about the line $y = x$. ∎

In many situations when f^{-1} is not a function, we describe a principal-value inverse function by using only part of the inverse rule of correspondence. In this example we discuss (5.8) in two separate parts:

$$f_1^{-1} = \{(x, y) \mid x \geq 0 \text{ and } y = \sqrt{x}\}, \qquad (5.9)$$
$$f_2^{-1} = \{(x, y) \mid x \geq 0 \text{ and } y = -\sqrt{x}\}. \qquad (5.10)$$

The graphs of the ordered pairs given in (5.9) and in (5.10) are shown in Figs. 5.2, c and 5.2, d respectively. It should be clear that both f_1^{-1} and f_2^{-1} represent functions. It is customary to select one of these two functions and call it the *principal-value inverse function* of f. In this case we take f_1^{-1} and say that the principal-value inverse function is given by F^{-1}, where

$$F^{-1} = \{(x, y) \mid x \geq 0 \text{ and } y = \sqrt{x}\}.$$

In the following three sections we shall discuss the inverse relations for each of the six trigonometric functions. In each case we shall see that we have a situation similar to that encountered in Example 2 where the principal-value inverse function is defined.

EXERCISE 5.1

In the following, assume that the domain of the given function is the largest subset of real numbers, for which the right-hand side of the equation is defined (as a real number).

For the given functions in Problems 1 through 10 determine
a) domain of f b) range of f c) f^{-1}

and state whether or not f^{-1} is a function. If f^{-1} is not a function, define a principal-value inverse function and give the range and domain of this function.

1. $y = f(x) = 3 - 5x$ **2.** $y = f(x) = 4x + 5$

3. $y = f(x) = 4x^2$ **4.** $y = f(x) = 1 - x^2$

5. $y = f(x) = (1 - x)^2$ **6.** $y = f(x) = \dfrac{1}{2x - 1}$

7. $y = f(x) = \dfrac{2 - x}{x}$ **8.** $y = f(x) = \dfrac{x}{x + 4}$

9. $y = f(x) = 4 + \sqrt{x}$ **10.** $y = f(x) = |x|$

In Problems 11 through 14 find a) $f^{-1}(x)$ and b) $f(f^{-1}(x))$ for the given functions:

11. $y = f(x) = 3x - 4$ **12.** $y = f(x) = x + 5$

13. $y = f(x) = \dfrac{2 + x}{x}$ **14.** $y = f(x) = \dfrac{1 - 2x}{x}$

In Problems 15 through 20 find $f^{-1}(x)$; then draw graphs of $y = f(x)$ and $y = f^{-1}(x)$. In each case state whether or not f^{-1} describes a function.

15. $f(x) = 5x + 3$ **16.** $f(x) = \dfrac{3 - x}{4}$ **17.** $f(x) = 9x^2$

18. $f(x) = \sqrt{x + 3}$ **19.** $f(x) = 1 + |x|$ **20.** $f(x) = x - x^2$

5.2 INVERSE SINE AND INVERSE COSINE

1. Inverse Sine Function

We have already encountered the problem of evaluating inverse trigonometric functions when in the process of solving triangles in Chapter 3 we had the value of a trigonometric function and we had to determine the corresponding angle. For instance, in Example 5 of Section 3.1 (p. 67) we were given $\sin \alpha = 0.4835$ and had to determine the corresponding value of α; the [INV] and [sin] (or [sin^{-1}]) calculator keys were used to get $\alpha = 28.91° = 0.5046$ radians. In this section we discuss the problem in general: when $\sin x$ is a given number, determine the corresponding value of x.

    Suppose $f(x) = \sin x$. What can we say about the relation f^{-1}? To answer this question we recall the graph of $y = \sin x$ discussed in Section 2.7 (p. 54) and reproduce it here in Fig. 5.3.

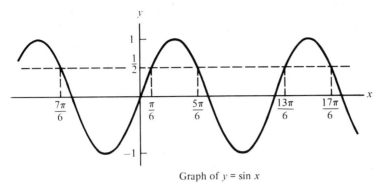

Graph of $y = \sin x$

Figure 5.3

From the graph in Fig. 5.3 we conclude that for each real number x there is a corresponding unique number y; this tells us that $f(x) = \sin x$ represents a function. Now suppose we reverse the process and take any number y, where $-1 \leq y \leq 1$, and see what values of x correspond to it. Looking at the graph we notice that there are infinitely many such values of x; for example if $y = \frac{1}{2}$, then the corresponding values of x are:

$$\frac{\pi}{6}, \frac{5\pi}{6}, \frac{13\pi}{6}, \frac{17\pi}{6}, \ldots, -\frac{7\pi}{6}, \ldots$$

Thus for $f(x) = \sin x$, the inverse relation f^{-1} is not a function. We shall denote f^{-1} by $\sin^{-1}$ and call $\sin^{-1}$ the *inverse sine relation* which is given by

$$\sin^{-1} = \{(y, x) \mid -1 \leq y \leq 1 \text{ and } y = \sin x\}. \qquad (5.11)$$

Since we prefer to denote the independent variable by x, we can write the set of ordered pairs given by (5.11) as

$$\sin^{-1} = \{(x, y) \mid -1 \leq x \leq 1 \text{ and } x = \sin y\}. \qquad (5.12)$$

It should be clear that we interchanged the x and y variables in (5.11) to get (5.12) but in both cases we have precisely the same set of ordered pairs. We use (5.12) to draw a graph of the inverse sine relation. The graph is a sine curve oscillating about the y-axis as shown in Fig. 5.4.

2. Principal-Value Inverse Sine Function

We take a portion of the curve shown in Fig. 5.4 so that for each x in $-1 \leq x \leq 1$ there is a unique value of y corresponding to it. This can be done in any of several ways. For example, we could take the portion between Q and P, or the part between P and M, and so on. It appears that the choice is somewhat arbitrary, but once the choice is made we use it consistently. It is conventional to take the part between Q: $(-1, -\pi/2)$ and P: $(1, \pi/2)$ and call

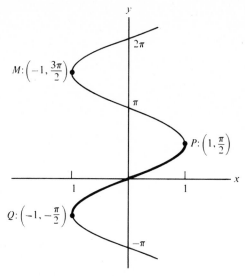

Graph of $\sin^{-1} = \{(x, y) \mid -1 \leqq x \leqq 1 \text{ and } x = \sin y\}$

Figure 5.4

it the *inverse sine function* (sometimes referred to as the *principal-value inverse sine function*). We shall denote this function by Sin^{-1} and write

$$y = \text{Sin}^{-1}x$$

to describe the function given by

$$\text{Sin}^{-1} = \left\{(x,\ y) \mid -1 \leq x \leq 1,\ \ x = \sin y\ \text{ and }\ -\frac{\pi}{2} \leq y \leq \frac{\pi}{2}\right\}.$$

We always use the *capital letter S in* Sin^{-1} *to distinguish the inverse sine function from the inverse sine relation* sin^{-1}. The domain and range of Sin^{-1} are given by

$$D(\text{Sin}^{-1}) = \left\{x \mid -1 \leq x \leq 1\right\},$$
$$R(\text{Sin}^{-1}) = \left\{y \mid -\frac{\pi}{2} \leq y \leq \frac{\pi}{2}\right\}.$$

The graph of $y = \text{Sin}^{-1}x$ is the heavy portion between P and Q of the curve in Fig. 5.4.

Note on Notation. The inverse sine relation is sometimes denoted by arcsin. In this book we shall use sin^{-1} and arcsin interchangeably to denote the inverse sine relation, while either Sin^{-1} or *Arcsin* will be used to denote the inverse sine function.

In summary, we have

a) *Inverse sine relation* is defined by

$$\sin^{-1} = \arcsin = \{(x, \ y)\,|-1 \leq x \leq 1 \quad \text{and} \quad x = \sin \ y\}.$$

b) *Inverse sine function* is defined by

$$y = \text{Sin}^{-1}x = \text{Arcsin } x \text{ is equivalent to } x = \sin \ y \text{ and } -\frac{\pi}{2} \leq y \leq \frac{\pi}{2}.$$

Note. When we write Sin$^{-1}(\frac{1}{2})$ we mean *the angle y* such that $\sin y = \frac{1}{2}$ and $-\pi/2 \leq y \leq \pi/2$; there is only one such value of y and that is $y = \pi/6$. That is, Sin$^{-1}(\frac{1}{2}) = \pi/6$. When we write sin$^{-1}(\frac{1}{2})$ we mean *any angle y* such that $\sin y = \frac{1}{2}$; thus y can be any of the angles $\pi/6$, $5\pi/6$, ..., $-7\pi/6$, $-11\pi/6$, ...

3. Inverse Cosine Function

In discussing the inverse cosine relation and principal-value function we can follow the same procedure as in subsections 1 and 2 above, except we replace the sine function by the cosine function. We omit the details and merely give a summary.

In Fig. 5.5 we have a graph of the *inverse cosine relation* cos^{-1} given by

$$\cos^{-1} = \{(x, \ y)\,|-1 \leq x \leq 1 \quad \text{and} \quad x = \cos \ y\}.$$

We take the portion between points P: $(1, \ 0)$ and Q: $(-1, \ \pi)$ of the curve in Fig. 5.5 to define the *inverse cosine function* Cos^{-1}:

$$y = \text{Cos}^{-1}x = \text{Arccos } x \text{ is equivalent to } x = \cos \ y \text{ and } 0 \leq y \leq \pi.$$

The domain and range of the Cos^{-1} function are given by

$$D(\text{Cos}^{-1}) = \{x\,|-1 \leq x \leq 1\},$$
$$R(\text{Cos}^{-1}) = \{y\,|0 \leq y \leq \pi\}.$$

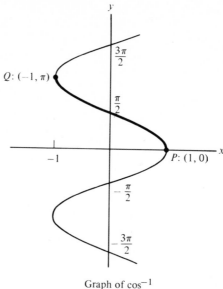

Graph of cos^{-1}

Figure 5.5

Examples

⚠️ Evaluate the following and give answers in exact form in radians and in degrees:

a) $\text{Sin}^{-1} \dfrac{\sqrt{2}}{2}$　　b) $\text{Cos}^{-1}\dfrac{1}{2}$　　c) $\text{Sin}^{-1}\left(-\dfrac{\sqrt{3}}{2}\right)$

d) $\text{Cos}^{-1}\left(-\dfrac{\sqrt{2}}{2}\right)$　　e) $\text{Sin}^{-1}\dfrac{2}{\sqrt{3}}$

Solution.

a) Let $y_1 = \text{Sin}^{-1}(\sqrt{2}/2)$. This is equivalent to $\sin y_1 = \sqrt{2}/2$ and $-\pi/2 \leq y_1 \leq \pi/2$. There is only one value of y_1 that satisfies these conditions: $y_1 = \pi/4$. Therefore, $\text{Sin}^{-1}(\sqrt{2}/2) = \pi/4 = 45°$.

b) Let $y_2 = \text{Cos}^{-1}(1/2)$; then $\cos y_2 = \frac{1}{2}$ and $0 \leq y_2 \leq \pi$, and so $y_2 = \pi/3$. Thus, $\text{Cos}^{-1}(1/2) = \pi/3 = 60°$.

c) Let $y_3 = \text{Sin}^{-1}(-\sqrt{3}/2)$; then $\sin y_3 = -\sqrt{3}/2$ and $-\pi/2 \leq y_3 \leq \pi/2$, and so $y_3 = -\pi/3 = -60°$.

d) Let $y_4 = \text{Cos}^{-1}(-\sqrt{2}/2)$ or equivalently $\cos y_4 = -\sqrt{2}/2$ and $0 \leq y_4 \leq \pi$; so $y_4 = 3\pi/4$. Then $\text{Cos}^{-1}(-\sqrt{2}/2) = 3\pi/4 = 135°$.

e) Since $2/\sqrt{3} > 1$, then $2/\sqrt{3}$ is not in the domain of Sin^{-1}; and so $\text{Sin}^{-1}(2/\sqrt{3})$ is not defined. ∎

⚠️2 Evaluate the following using a calculator. Give answers in radians correct to four decimal places:

a) $\text{Sin}^{-1}(0.346)$ b) $\text{Cos}^{-1}(0.587)$ c) $\text{Sin}^{-1}\left(-\frac{47}{53}\right)$

d) $\text{Cos}^{-1}\left(-\frac{5}{\sqrt{41}}\right)$ e) $\text{Sin}^{-1}\dfrac{5}{1+\sqrt{2}}$

Solution.

> Calculators are programmed to give principal values of the inverse trigonometric relations, that is, inverse-function values.

In this example we want answers in radians, so we place the calculator in radian mode.

a) We enter 0.346 into the display, then press $\boxed{\text{INV}}$ and $\boxed{\text{sin}}$ keys (or $\boxed{\text{sin}^{-1}}$ key on some calculators) and get $\text{Sin}^{-1}(0.346) = 0.3533$.

b) Similar to (a), we get $\text{Cos}^{-1}(0.587) = 0.9434$.

c) We first evaluate $-47/53$ and, with the result in the calculator display, press $\boxed{\text{INV}}$ and $\boxed{\text{sin}}$ keys (or $\boxed{\text{sin}^{-1}}$ key). This gives $\text{Sin}^{-1}(-47/53) = -1.0904$.

d) Similar to (c), we get $\text{Cos}^{-1}(-5/\sqrt{41}) = 2.4669$.

e) Evaluate $5/(1+\sqrt{2})$ and then press the $\boxed{\text{INV}}$ and $\boxed{\text{sin}}$ keys (or $\boxed{\text{sin}^{-1}}$) and the calculator will display "Error" (or a similar notation) to indicate that something is wrong. Of course, the reason is that

$$\frac{5}{1+\sqrt{2}} > 1$$

and so it is not in the domain of Sin^{-1}.   ❚

⚠️3 Same as Example 2 but give answers in degrees to two decimal places.

Solution. Place the calculator in degree mode (most calculators are in degree mode when they are first turned on) and then proceed as in the solution to Example 2.

a) $\text{Sin}^{-1}0.346 = 20.24°$ b) $\text{Cos}^{-1}0.587 = 54.06°$

c) $\text{Sin}^{-1}\left(-\frac{47}{53}\right) = -62.47°$ d) $\text{Cos}^{-1}\left(-\frac{5}{\sqrt{41}}\right) = 141.34°$

e) $\text{Sin}^{-1}\dfrac{5}{1+\sqrt{2}}$ is undefined   ❚

⚠️4 Evaluate the following expressions and give answers in exact form:

a) $\sin\left(\text{Sin}^{-1}\frac{1}{4}\right)$ b) $\sin\left(2\,\text{Sin}^{-1}\frac{1}{4}\right)$

c) $\cos\left(\frac{1}{2}\ \text{Sin}^{-1}\frac{1}{4}\right)$
d) $\cos\left(\text{Sin}^{-1}\frac{2}{3}+\text{Cos}^{-1}\left(\frac{-5}{8}\right)\right)$

e) $\sin\left(\text{Cos}^{-1}\left(\sin\frac{\pi}{6}\right)\right)$
f) $\text{Sin}^{-1}\left(\tan\frac{\pi}{3}\right)$

Solution.

a) Let $\theta = \text{Sin}^{-1}(1/4)$, which is equivalent to

$$\sin\theta = 1/4 \quad \text{and} \quad -\pi/2 \le \theta \le \pi/2.$$

Therefore, θ is in the first quadrant, as shown in Fig. 5.6. Thus,

$$\sin\left(\text{Sin}^{-1}\frac{1}{4}\right)=\sin\ \theta = \frac{1}{4}.*$$

b) Let θ be as in (a) and use the identity $\sin 2\theta = 2\sin\theta\cos\theta$. Thus

$$\sin\left(2\ \text{Sin}^{-1}\frac{1}{4}\right)=\sin\ 2\theta = 2\cdot\frac{1}{4}\cdot\frac{\sqrt{15}}{4}=\frac{\sqrt{15}}{8}.$$

c) Take θ as in (a) and use the identity $\cos\frac{\theta}{2}=\sqrt{\frac{1+\cos\theta}{2}}$:

$$\cos\left(\frac{1}{2}\ \text{Sin}^{-1}\frac{1}{4}\right)=\cos\frac{\theta}{2}=\sqrt{\frac{1+(\sqrt{15}/4)}{2}}=\frac{1}{2}\sqrt{\frac{4+\sqrt{15}}{2}}.$$

d) Let $\alpha = \text{Sin}^{-1}(2/3)$ and $\beta = \text{Cos}^{-1}(-5/8)$; then α and β are as shown in Fig. 5.7. Thus,

$$\cos\left(\text{Sin}^{-1}\frac{2}{3}+\text{Cos}^{-1}\left(-\frac{5}{8}\right)\right)=\cos(\alpha+\beta)=\cos\alpha\cos\beta - \sin\alpha\sin\beta$$
$$=\left(\frac{\sqrt{5}}{3}\right)\left(-\frac{5}{8}\right)-\left(\frac{2}{3}\right)\left(\frac{\sqrt{39}}{8}\right)=-\frac{5\sqrt{5}+2\sqrt{39}}{24}.$$

e) $\sin\left(\text{Cos}^{-1}\left(\sin\frac{\pi}{6}\right)\right)=\sin\left(\text{Cos}^{-1}\frac{1}{2}\right)=\sin\frac{\pi}{3}=\frac{\sqrt{3}}{2}.$

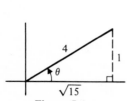

Figure 5.6

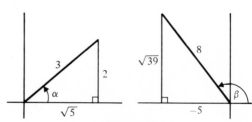

Figure 5.7

*It might be helpful to state a problem such as (a) in words. That is, we want "the sine of an angle whose sine is 1/4." This is not so different from the popular quiz question "Who is buried in Grant's tomb?"

f) Since $\tan(\pi/3) = \sqrt{3}$ and $\sqrt{3}$ is not in the domain of the Sin^{-1} function, $\text{Sin}^{-1}(\tan(\pi/3))$ is not defined.   ∎

△5 Using a calculator, evaluate the expressions given in Example 4. Provide answers correct to four decimal places.

Solution. We could evaluate each of the results found in Example 4. However, we can evaluate directly as follows:

a) First evaluate ¼, then press the (INV), (sin) and (sin) keys in that order. This gives $\sin(\text{Sin}^{-1}(\frac{1}{4})) = 0.2500$.

b) Evaluate ¼, then press (INV), (sin) keys, then multiply this result by 2 and press (sin). This gives $\sin(2\,\text{Sin}^{-1}(\frac{1}{4})) = 0.4841$.

c) Similar to (b), $\cos(\frac{1}{2}\,\text{Sin}^{-1}(\frac{1}{4})) = 0.9920$.

d) Evaluate ⅔, press the (INV) and (sin) keys (this gives $\text{Sin}^{-1}(\frac{2}{3})$), then similarly evaluate $\text{Cos}^{-1}(-\frac{5}{8})$, add the results and finally press (cos). This gives $\cos(\text{Sin}^{-1}(\frac{2}{3}) + \text{Cos}^{-1}(-\frac{5}{8})) = -0.9863$.

Note. In (a) through (d) it does not make any difference whether the calculator is in degree or radian mode. We leave it to the student to explain why this is so.

e) First place the calculator in radian mode (since $\pi/6$ is in radians); then evaluate $\pi/6$ and with this in the display press (sin). This gives $\sin(\pi/6)$ in the display. Now press the (INV) and (cos) keys in that order and the display shows $\text{Cos}^{-1}(\sin(\pi/6))$. Finally press (sin) and get

$$\sin\left(\text{Cos}^{-1}\left(\sin\tfrac{\pi}{6}\right)\right) = 0.8660.$$

f) The student should attempt to evaluate $\text{Sin}^{-1}(\tan(\pi/3))$ with the calculator to see what the response is.   ∎

△6 Is $\text{Sin}^{-1}\frac{3}{5} + \text{Sin}^{-1}\frac{8}{17} = \text{Sin}^{-1}\frac{77}{85}$?

Solution. As a first step we evaluate the left-hand side and the right-hand side by using a calculator:

$$\text{Sin}^{-1}\frac{3}{5} + \text{Sin}^{-1}\frac{8}{17} = 64.94238458°.$$

$$\text{Sin}^{-1}\frac{77}{85} = 64.94238457°.$$

We can be reasonably safe in concluding that the answer to the question is yes. To be absolutely certain we could use the following proof.

Let $\alpha = \text{Sin}^{-1}(3/5)$ and $\beta = \text{Sin}^{-1}(8/17)$. Since $\alpha + \beta$ is approximately $65°$ (from above computations) and $\text{Sin}^{-1}(77/85)$ is between $0°$ and $90°$, we need only show that $\sin(\alpha + \beta) = 77/85$. We can use identity (I.12) of Section 4.2 and get

$$\sin(\alpha + \beta) = \sin\alpha\cos\beta + \cos\alpha\sin\beta = \frac{3}{5}\cdot\frac{15}{17} + \frac{4}{5}\cdot\frac{8}{17} = \frac{77}{85}.$$ ∎

⚠ Find all values of x that satisfy the inequality $5 \text{ Sin}^{-1}x - 4 \leq 0$.

Solution. The given inequality is equivalent to $\text{Sin}^{-1}x \leq 4/5$. To solve this inequality it might be instructive to look at the graph of $y = \text{Sin}^{-1}x$, as shown in Fig. 5.8. We are interested in those values of x that correspond to points on the curve for which $y \leq 4/5 = 0.8$; these points lie between Q and P (inclusive). Thus the solution set is $\{x \,|\, -1 \leq x \leq x_0\}$, where $\text{Sin}^{-1}x_0 = 0.8$. However, if $\text{Sin}^{-1}x_0 = 0.8$, then $x_0 = \sin 0.8$ and so with the calculator in radian mode we find that $x_0 = 0.717$ (to three decimal places). Therefore, the solution set is $S = \{x \,|\, -1 \leq x \leq 0.717\}$. ∎

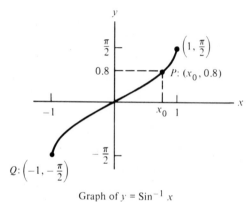

Graph of $y = \text{Sin}^{-1} x$

Figure 5.8

EXERCISE 5.2

In this exercise there may be some problems in which the given expression is not defined. If a calculator is used, the display will show "Error." Explain what part of the problem causes such a response.

1. a) Draw a graph of $y = \text{Sin}^{-1}x$ by first making a table of x, y values.

   b) Make a table of x, y values that satisfy $y = \text{Cos}^{-1}x$ and then draw a graph of $y = \text{Cos}^{-1}x$.

In Problems 2 through 12, evaluate the given expressions and provide answers in radians (real numbers) and in exact form.

2. $\text{Cos}^{-1}1$

3. $\text{Sin}^{-1}\dfrac{\sqrt{2}}{2}$

4. $\text{Cos}^{-1}\left(-\dfrac{2}{\sqrt{3}}\right)$

5. $\text{Sin}^{-1}\left(-\dfrac{1}{2}\right)$

6. $\text{Cos}^{-1}\left(-\dfrac{\sqrt{3}}{2}\right)$

7. $\text{Sin}^{-1}\left(-\dfrac{2}{\sqrt{2}}\right)$

8. $\mathrm{Sin}^{-1}\left(-\dfrac{3}{2\sqrt{3}}\right)$ **9.** $\mathrm{Cos}^{-1}(-1)$ **10.** $\mathrm{Sin}^{-1}(-1)$

11. $\mathrm{Arcsin}\left(-\dfrac{1}{\sqrt{2}}\right)$ **12.** $\mathrm{Arccos}\ \dfrac{1}{2}$

In Problems 13 through 16, find all values of the given expression. Provide answers in exact form in radians and in degrees.

13. $\sin^{-1}\dfrac{\sqrt{2}}{2}$ **14.** $\sin^{-1}\left(-\dfrac{1}{2}\right)$ **15.** $\cos^{-1}(-1)$ **16.** $\cos^{-1}\dfrac{\sqrt{3}}{2}$

In Problems 17 through 30, evaluate the given expression using a calculator and provide results in radians and in degrees correct to two decimal places.

17. $\mathrm{Sin}^{-1}\ 0.3768$ **18.** $\mathrm{Cos}^{-1}\ 0.5732$

19. $\mathrm{Sin}^{-1}\ (-0.537)$ **20.** $\mathrm{Sin}^{-1}\ 2.378$

21. $\mathrm{Arccos}(-1.375)$ **22.** $\mathrm{Arcsin}\ \dfrac{3+\sqrt{5}}{8}$

23. $\mathrm{Cos}^{-1}(\sqrt{17}-5)$ **24.** $\mathrm{Arcsin}\ \dfrac{\sqrt{47}-3}{2}$

25. $\mathrm{Cos}^{-1}\ \dfrac{\pi}{2}$ **26.** $\mathrm{Cos}^{-1}(\sin\ 48°)$

27. $\mathrm{Sin}^{-1}(\sec\ 1.42)$ **28.** $\mathrm{Sin}^{-1}(\tan\ 16°12')$

29. $\mathrm{Cos}^{-1}(\cot\ 112°24')$ **30.** $\mathrm{Sin}^{-1}\left(\cos\ \dfrac{6}{\pi}\right)$

In Problems 31 through 44, evaluate the given expression. Provide answers in exact form.

31. $\sin\left(\mathrm{Sin}^{-1}\ \dfrac{3}{4}\right)$ **32.** $\sin\left(\mathrm{Cos}^{-1}\left(-\dfrac{1}{2}\right)\right)$

33. $\cos\left(2\ \mathrm{Cos}^{-1}\ 0\right)$ **34.** $\cos\left(\mathrm{Sin}^{-1}\ \dfrac{3}{5}-\mathrm{Cos}^{-1}\ \dfrac{4}{5}\right)$

35. $\tan\left(\mathrm{Sin}^{-1}\ \dfrac{3}{2}\right)$ **36.** $\mathrm{Arcsin}(\mathrm{Cos}\ \pi)$

37. $\tan\left(\mathrm{Cos}^{-1}\dfrac{3}{4}+\mathrm{Sin}^{-1}\left(-\dfrac{3}{4}\right)\right)$ **38.** $\sec\left(\mathrm{Cos}^{-1}\left(-\dfrac{3}{5}\right)\right)$

39. $\sin\left(2\ \mathrm{Cos}^{-1}\left(\sin\ \dfrac{\pi}{6}\right)\right)$ **40.** $\cos\left(2\ \mathrm{Cos}^{-1}(-3)+\mathrm{Sin}^{-1}\ \dfrac{2}{5}\right)$

41. $\mathrm{Cos}^{-1}\left(\sin\ \dfrac{3\pi}{2}\right)$ **42.** $\sin\left(\mathrm{Cos}^{-1}(-3)+\mathrm{Sin}^{-1}\ \dfrac{2}{5}\right)$

43. $\cos\left(\mathrm{Sin}^{-1}\left(\cos\ \dfrac{\pi}{3}\right)\right)$ **44.** $\mathrm{Sin}^{-1}\left(\cos\ \dfrac{\pi}{3}\right)$

In Problems 45 through 50, use the calculator to evaluate the given expressions. Provide answers correct to two decimal places. In each problem check whether it makes a difference if the calculator is operating in radian or degree mode.

45. $\sin(\text{Sin}^{-1}0.34 + \text{Cos}^{-1}0.56)$

46. $\tan\left(\text{Cos}^{-1}(-0.37) + \text{Sin}^{-1}(-0.53)\right)$

47. $\cos\left(2 \ \text{Sin}^{-1} \dfrac{\sqrt{5}}{2}\right)$

48. $\sin\left(2 \ \text{Cos}^{-1} \dfrac{1-\sqrt{5}}{2}\right)$

49. $\cos(2 \ \text{Sin}^{-1}0.37 + \text{Cos}^{-1}0.84)$

50. $\sin\left(\text{Sin}^{-1}(-1.24)\right)$

51. Is $\text{Sin}^{-1} \dfrac{3}{5} + \text{Sin}^{-1} \dfrac{5}{13} = \text{Sin}^{-1} \dfrac{56}{65}$?

52. Is $\text{Sin}^{-1} \dfrac{3}{5} + \text{Sin}^{-1} \dfrac{5}{13} = \text{Cos}^{-1} \dfrac{33}{65}$?

53. Is $\text{Sin}^{-1}(-x) = -\text{Sin}^{-1}x$ an identity ?

54. Is $\text{Cos}^{-1}(-x) = \text{Cos}^{-1}x$ an identity ?

55. Is $\text{Cos}^{-1}x = \dfrac{\pi}{2} - \text{Sin}^{-1}x$ an identity ?

In Problems 56 through 60, determine the values of x that satisfy the given equality or inequality.

56. $2 \ \text{Sin}^{-1}x + 1 = 0$

57. $2 \ \text{Cos}^{-1}x - 3 = 0$

58. $3 \ \text{Sin}^{-1}x - 4 \leq 0$

59. $2 \ \text{Cos}^{-1}x + 1 \leq 0$

60. $\text{Sin}^{-1}x - 1 \geq 0$

5.3 INVERSE TANGENT AND INVERSE COTANGENT

In developing the inverse relations and functions associated with the tangent and cotangent functions, we can follow a discussion similar to that on the inverse sine in Section 5.2. However, since there are no new ideas involved, we shall omit the details and merely give a summary of pertinent facts.

1. Inverse Tangent

The *inverse tangent relation* $\tan^{-1}$ is defined by

$$\tan^{-1} = \{(x, \ y) \,|\, x \in R \text{ and } x = \tan y\}.$$

The graph of $\tan^{-1}$ is shown in Fig. 5.9.

For the principal-value inverse tangent function we choose the branch of the curve between $y = -\pi/2$ and $y = \pi/2$, as shown in Fig. 5.9. Thus the definition of the *principal-value inverse tangent function* is:

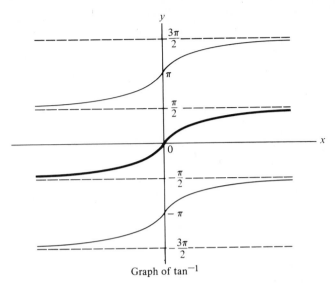

Graph of $\tan^{-1}$

Figure 5.9

$$y = \text{Tan}^{-1}x \text{ is equivalent to } x = \tan y \text{ and } -\frac{\pi}{2} < y < \frac{\pi}{2}$$

The graph of $y = \text{Tan}^{-1}x$ is shown in Fig. 5.9 by the heavy curve. Note that we again use a capital letter to distinguish between the function Tan^{-1} and the relation $\tan^{-1}$. Also, Arctan is used interchangeably with Tan^{-1}.

The domain and range of Tan^{-1} function are given by

$$D(\text{Tan}^{-1}) = \{x \mid x \text{ is any real number}\},$$
$$R(\text{Tan}^{-1}) = \{y \mid -\frac{\pi}{2} < y < \frac{\pi}{2}\}.$$

2. Inverse Cotangent

The *inverse cotangent relation* is defined by

$$\cot^{-1} = \{(x, y) \mid x \in R \text{ and } x = \cot y\}.$$

The graph of this relation is shown in Fig. 5.10. We select the branch between $y = 0$ and $y = \pi$ to define the inverse cotangent function. The *principal-value inverse cotangent function* is defined by

$y = \text{Cot}^{-1}x$ is equivalent to $x = \cot y$ and $0 < y < \pi$.

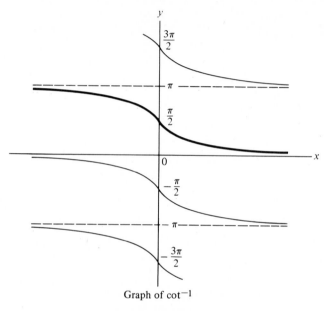

Graph of cot^{-1}

Figure 5.10

The graph of $y = \text{Cot}^{-1}x$ is shown in Fig. 5.10 by the heavy curve. The domain and range of Cot^{-1} (or Arccot) function are given by:

$D(\text{Cot}^{-1}) = \{x \mid x \text{ is any real number}\},$

$R(\text{Cot}^{-1}) = \{y \mid 0 < y < \pi\}.$

Examples

⚠ Evaluate each of the following and give answers in exact form in radians and in degrees.

  a) Tan$^{-1}1$ b) Arctan$(-\sqrt{3})$ c) Cot$^{-1}\left(-\dfrac{1}{\sqrt{3}}\right)$

Solution

a) Let $\theta = \text{Tan}^{-1}1$; then $\tan \theta = 1$ and $-\pi/2 < \theta < \pi/2$. Therefore, $\theta = \pi/4$ and so $\text{Tan}^{-1}1 = \pi/4 = 45°$.

b) Let $\alpha = \text{Arctan}(-\sqrt{3})$; then $\tan \alpha = -\sqrt{3}$ and $-\pi/2 < \alpha < \pi/2$. Thus $\alpha = -\pi/3$ and $\text{Arctan}(-\sqrt{3}) = -\pi/3 = -60°$.

c) Let $\beta = \text{Cot}^{-1}(-1/\sqrt{3})$, then $\cot \beta = -1/\sqrt{3}$ and $0 < \beta < \pi$. Therefore, $\beta = 2\pi/3$ and $\text{Cot}^{-1}(-1/\sqrt{3}) = 2\pi/3 = 120°$. ∎

2 Using a calculator, evaluate each of the following. Give answers in degrees correct to two decimal places.

a) $\text{Tan}^{-1} 2.57$ b) $\text{Tan}^{-1}(-0.478)$

Solution. Place the calculator in degree mode.

a) Enter 2.57, and then press INV and tan keys (or tan⁻¹) and get $\text{Tan}^{-1} 2.57 = 68.74°$.

b) This is similar to (a): $\text{Tan}^{-1}(-0.478) = -25.55°$. ∎

3 Evaluate the following using a calculator. Give answers in radians correct to three decimal places.

a) $\text{Cot}^{-1} 0.5863$ b) $\text{Cot}^{-1}(-2.743)$

Solution. Place the calculator in radian mode.

a) Let $\alpha = \text{Cot}^{-1} 0.5863$; then $\cot \alpha = 0.5863$ and $0 < \alpha < \pi$. Since the calculator does not have a cot key, we use the identity $\cot \alpha = 1/\tan \alpha$. This gives $\tan \alpha = 1/0.58631$ and so $\alpha = \text{Tan}^{-1}(1/0.5063)$. Now we evaluate $1/0.5063$ and, with the result in the calculator display, press the INV and tan keys (or tan⁻¹). This gives $\alpha = 1.041$. Thus $\text{Cot}^{-1} 0.5863 = 1.041$.

b) Let $\theta = \text{Cot}^{-1}(-2.743)$; then $\cot \theta = -2.743$ and $0 < \theta < \pi$. Since the calculator does not have a cot key, we use the identity $\cot \theta = 1/\tan \theta$ and get $\tan \theta = -1/2.743$. Now evaluate $\text{Tan}^{-1}(-1/2.743)$ and remember that the result (angle θ_1) will be between $-\pi/2$ and $\pi/2$. Since the θ we want is between 0 and π, then $\theta = \theta_1 + \pi$, as shown in Fig. 5.11. Therefore $\theta = \pi + \text{Tan}^{-1}(-1/2.743)$. This can be evaluated by the calculator without recording any intermediate steps. Thus $\text{Cot}^{-1}(-2.743) = 2.79$.

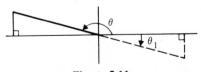

Figure 5.11   ∎

Note. In Example 3 we used the calculator to evaluate $\text{Cot}^{-1}x$ and it was necessary to express $\text{Cot}^{-1}x$ in terms of the Tan^{-1} function, since the calculator does not have a $\boxed{\text{cot}}$ or $\boxed{\text{cot}^{-1}}$ key. In part (b), the final step was slightly different from that of (a) because the value of x was negative. It should be clear from the two cases considered in Example 3 that we have the following situation in general (see Problems 43,b and 44 of this section):

> To evaluate $\text{Cot}^{-1}x$ by calculator use
>
> $\text{Cot}^{-1}x = \text{Tan}^{-1}\dfrac{1}{x}$ if x is positive,
>
> $\text{Cot}^{-1}x = \pi + \text{Tan}^{-1}\dfrac{1}{x}$ if x is negative.

$\boxed{4}$ Find all values of $\tan^{-1}(-1)$ in radian measure and in degree measure.

Solution. Let $\theta = \tan^{-1}(-1)$; then $\tan\theta = -1$ and so angle θ is in the second or fourth quadrant. That is, $\theta_1 = 3\pi/4$ and $\theta_2 = 7\pi/4 = \theta_1 + \pi$. We can get all other solutions by adding (or subtracting) integral multiples of π to (or from) θ_1, since π is the period of the tangent function. Therefore $\tan^{-1}(-1)$ represents any angle in the set

$$\{\theta \mid \theta = \tfrac{3\pi}{4} + k\pi, \text{ where } k \text{ is any integer}\};$$

or in degrees $\{\theta \mid \theta = 135° + k \cdot 180°\}$.   ∎

$\boxed{5}$ Evaluate the following expressions and give answers in exact form:

a) $\tan\left(\text{Cot}^{-1}\dfrac{2}{5}\right)$

b) $\sin\left(\text{Tan}^{-1}\left(-\dfrac{1}{3}\right) + \text{Tan}^{-1}\dfrac{4}{3}\right)$

c) $\cos\left(2\ \text{Tan}^{-1}\left(-\dfrac{3}{4}\right)\right)$

Solution.

a) Let $\theta = \text{Cot}^{-1}(2/5)$; then $\cot\theta = 2/5$ and $0 < \theta < \pi$. We want to find $\tan\theta$, and so $\tan\theta = 1/\cot\theta = 5/2$. That is, $\tan(\text{Cot}^{-1}(2/5)) = 5/2$.

b) Let $\alpha = \text{Tan}^{-1}(-1/3)$ and $\beta = \text{Tan}^{-1}(4/3)$; then α and β are the angles shown in Fig. 5.12. We want $\sin(\alpha + \beta)$. We use identity (I.12) of Section 4.2:

$$\sin(\alpha + \beta) = \sin\alpha\cos\beta + \cos\alpha\sin\beta$$

$$= -\frac{1}{\sqrt{10}}\frac{3}{5} + \frac{3}{\sqrt{10}}\frac{4}{5} = \frac{9}{5\sqrt{10}} = \frac{9\sqrt{10}}{50}.$$

Thus $\sin(\text{Tan}^{-1}(-1/3) + \text{Tan}^{-1}(4/3)) = 9\sqrt{10}/50$.

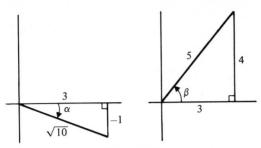

Figure 5.12

c) Let $\theta = \text{Tan}^{-1}(-3/4)$; then θ is the angle shown in Fig. 5.13. We want $\cos 2\theta$. By using identity (I.19) of Section 4.3 we get

$$\cos 2\theta = \cos^2\theta - \sin^2\theta = \left(\frac{4}{5}\right)^2 - \left(-\frac{3}{5}\right)^2 = \frac{7}{25}.$$

Therefore, $\cos(2 \text{ Tan}^{-1}(-3/4)) = 7/25$.   ∎

6 Using a calculator, evaluate $\sec\left(\text{Tan}^{-1}0.348 - 2 \text{ Cos}^{-1}(-0.735)\right)$ correct to four decimal places.

Solution. We can solve this problem with the calculator in either degree or radian mode. First evaluate the angle $\text{Tan}^{-1}0.348 - 2 \text{ Cos}^{-1}(-0.735)$, and, with the result in the calculator display, press the ⌐cos⌐ and ⌐1/x⌐ keys; the answer appears in the display:

$$\sec\left(\text{Tan}^{-1}0.348 - 2 \text{ Cos}^{-1}(-0.735)\right) = -3.9742.$$ ∎

7 a) Prove that $\cos(\text{Tan}^{-1}\sqrt{x^2 - 1}) = 1/x$ for $x \geq 1$ is an identity.

b) Is it an identity if values of $x \leq -1$ are also included?

c) How can the equation be changed to become an identity for all x in $x \leq -1$ or $x \geq 1$?

Solution.

a) Let $\theta = \text{Tan}^{-1}\sqrt{x^2 - 1}$; then $\tan \theta = \sqrt{x^2 - 1}$ and $-\pi/2 < \theta < \pi/2$. Since $\sqrt{x^2 - 1} \geq 0$, angle θ is in the first quadrant for all x. From Fig. 5.14 we see that $\cos (\text{Tan}^{-1}\sqrt{x^2 - 1}) = \cos \theta = 1/x$.

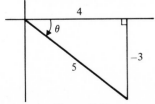

Figure 5.13

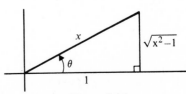

Figure 5.14

b) If we take $x = -\sqrt{2}$, then $\cos\,(\text{Tan}^{-1}\,\sqrt{(-2)^2-1}) = \cos\,(\text{Tan}^{-1}1) = \cos\,\pi/4 = \sqrt{2}/2$. This is not equal to $1/x$ for $x = -\sqrt{2}$. Thus the equation is not an identity if we include $x \le -1$ in the replacement set.

c) $\cos(\text{Tan}^{-1}\sqrt{(x^2-1)}) = 1/|x|$ for $x \le -1$ or $x \ge 1$ is an identity. ▌

⑧ Determine the set of values of x that satisfy the inequality

$$\text{Cot}^{-1}x - 2 \le 0.$$

Solution. The given inequality is equivalent to $\text{Cot}^{-1}x \le 2$. To solve this inequality it may be instructive to look at the graph of $y = \text{Cot}^{-1}x$ shown in Fig. 5.15. We want all values of x that will yield points on the curve to the right of P (such points have $y \le 2$). Thus, our solution set consists of all values of x such that $x \ge x_0$, where $\text{Cot}^{-1}x_0 = 2$. If $\text{Cot}^{-1}x_0 = 2$, then $x_0 = \cot 2$ and with the calculator in radian mode we find that $x_0 = -0.458$ (to three decimal places). Therefore, the solution set is $S = \{x \mid x \ge -0.458\}$.

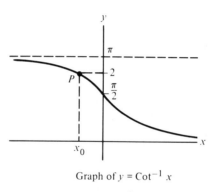

Graph of $y = \text{Cot}^{-1}\,x$

Figure 5.15

▌

EXERCISE 5.3

1. a) Make a table of x, y values that satisfy $y = \text{Tan}^{-1}x$. Then use this table to draw a graph of $y = \text{Tan}^{-1}x$.

   b) Follow instructions similar to those in (a) for $y = \text{Cot}^{-1}x$.

In Problems 2 through 8, evaluate the given expression. State answers in exact form in degree and in radian measure.

2. $\text{Cot}^{-1}(-1)$

3. $\text{Cot}^{-1}\left(\dfrac{1}{\sqrt{3}}\right)$

4. $\text{Tan}^{-1}\left(-\dfrac{\sqrt{3}}{3}\right)$

5. $\text{Arctan}\left(-\sqrt{3}\right)$

6. $\text{Arccot}\left(-\sqrt{3}\right)$

7. $\text{Tan}^{-1}(-1) - \text{Cot}^{-1}(-1)$

8. $\text{Tan}^{-1}\left(\dfrac{1}{\sqrt{3}}\right) + \text{Cot}^{-1}\left(-\sqrt{3}\right)$

In Problems 9 through 12, find all values of the given expression. Provide answers in exact form in degree and in radian measure.

9. $\tan^{-1} \dfrac{1}{\sqrt{3}}$ **10.** $\cot^{-1}(-1)$ **11.** $\cot^{-1}\left(-\sqrt{3}\right)$ **12.** $\tan^{-1}\left(-\dfrac{\sqrt{3}}{3}\right)$

In Problems 13 through 20, evaluate the given expression using a calculator. Provide answers in radian measure (correct to four decimal places) and in degree measure (correct to two decimal places).

13. $\text{Tan}^{-1} 0.738$ **14.** $\text{Arctan}\,(-1.483)$ **15.** $\text{Tan}^{-1} \dfrac{2 + \sqrt{47}}{8}$

16. $\text{Cot}^{-1} 1.532$ **17.** $\text{Arccot}(-2.415)$ **18.** $\text{Arctan}\,\dfrac{\pi}{3}$

19. $\text{Arctan}\left(-\dfrac{3}{5\pi}\right)$ **20.** $\text{Arccot}\left(-\dfrac{4}{3\pi}\right)$

21. Using a calculator, find all values of $\tan^{-1} 2.418$ in radians correct to two decimal places.

22. Find all values of $\cot^{-1}(-0.893)$ in degrees correct to two decimal places.

23. Find all values of $\cot^{-1} \dfrac{4 + \sqrt{5}}{17}$ in degrees correct to two decimal places.

24. Find all values of $\tan^{-1} \dfrac{\sqrt{47} - 8.32}{1 + \sqrt{3}}$ in radians correct to two decimal places.

In Problems 25 through 32 evaluate the expressions and give answers in exact form:

25. $\tan\left(\text{Tan}^{-1} \dfrac{4}{3}\right)$ **26.** $\cot\left(\text{Tan}^{-1}\left(-\dfrac{5}{8}\right)\right)$

27. $\sin\left(2\text{Cot}^{-1}\left(-\dfrac{2}{5}\right)\right)$ **28.** $\cos\left(\dfrac{1}{2}\text{Tan}^{-1}\left(-\dfrac{3}{4}\right)\right)$

29. $\sin\left(\dfrac{\pi}{2} - \text{Tan}^{-1}\left(-\dfrac{4}{3}\right)\right)$ **30.** $\tan(2\,\text{Tan}^{-1} 3)$

31. $\csc\left(\dfrac{1}{2}\text{Tan}^{-1} \dfrac{2}{3}\right)$ **32.** $\tan\left(\text{Cot}^{-1} \dfrac{3}{4} + \text{Tan}^{-1} \dfrac{4}{3}\right)$

33. Show that $2\,\text{Tan}^{-1} \dfrac{1}{3} = \text{Tan}^{-1} \dfrac{3}{4}$.

34. Show that $\text{Tan}^{-1} \dfrac{1}{2} - \text{Tan}^{-1} \dfrac{1}{3} = \text{Tan}^{-1}\dfrac{1}{7}$.

35. Show that $\text{Tan}^{-1}\dfrac{2}{3} + \text{Tan}^{-1}\dfrac{3}{2} = \dfrac{\pi}{2}$.

36. Show that $\text{Cot}^{-1}\left(-\dfrac{3}{4}\right) = \text{Tan}^{-1}\left(-\dfrac{4}{3}\right) + \pi$.

In Problems 37 through 42, you may wish to use the calculator as a first step in answering the question. Note that in Problems 37 and 38 the calculator should be in radian mode.

37. Is $\text{Tan}^{-1} 1 + \text{Tan}^{-1} 2 = \pi + \text{Tan}^{-1}(-3)$?

38. Is $\mathrm{Tan}^{-1}\left(\frac{1}{2}\right) + \mathrm{Tan}^{-1}\left(\frac{1}{3}\right) = \frac{\pi}{4}$?

39. Is $\mathrm{Cot}^{-1}\left(\frac{1}{3}\right) + \mathrm{Cot}^{-1}\left(\frac{1}{4}\right) = \mathrm{Cot}^{-1}\left(-\frac{11}{9}\right)$?

40. Is $\mathrm{Tan}^{-1}\ 4 - \mathrm{Tan}^{-1}\ 3 = \mathrm{Tan}^{-1}\ \frac{1}{13}$?

41. Is $\mathrm{Tan}^{-1}\ \frac{3}{4} + \mathrm{Tan}^{-1}\ \frac{4}{3} = \mathrm{Sin}^{-1}\ 1$?

42. Is $\mathrm{Sin}^{-1}\ \frac{3}{5} - \mathrm{Cos}^{-1}\frac{5}{13} = \mathrm{Tan}^{-1}\left(-\frac{33}{56}\right)$?

In Problems 43 through 45, prove that the given equation is an identity when x is restricted to the values given in each case.

43. a) $\mathrm{Tan}^{-1}x + \mathrm{Tan}^{-1}\frac{1}{x} = \frac{\pi}{2}$ for $x > 0$ b) $\mathrm{Cot}^{-1}x = \mathrm{Tan}^{-1}\frac{1}{x}$ for $x > 0$

44. $\mathrm{Cot}^{-1}x = \pi + \mathrm{Tan}^{-1}\frac{1}{x}$ for $x < 0$

45. a) $\mathrm{Sin}^{-1}\frac{2x}{x^2 + 1} = 2\ \mathrm{Tan}^{-1}x$ for $-1 \le x \le 1$

b) Give an example showing that the equation in (a) is not true when x is any real number.

46. Is $\mathrm{Cot}^{-1}x = \mathrm{Tan}^{-1}(1/x)$ an identity?

47. A movie marquee on Main Street is 1.5 meters wide with its bottom edge 4 meters above the sidewalk, as shown in Fig. 5.16. A person, with eye level h meters above the sidewalk and x meters from point P directly below the edge of the marquee, is walking along Main Street and observes that the marquee (as measured by angle θ) seems small when viewed from far away (when x is large), but upon getting closer angle θ gets larger until it reaches a maximum and then it begins to get smaller again until it becomes $0°$ when seen from directly underneath the edge of the marquee. That is, θ is a function of x. Show that this function is given by

$$\theta = \mathrm{Tan}^{-1}\ \frac{1.5x}{x^2 + (4 - h)(5.5 - h)}.$$

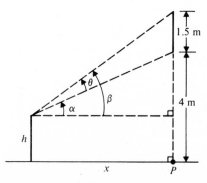

Figure 5.16

Hint. Use the two right triangles involving angles α and β, and the identity

$$\tan \theta = \tan(\beta - \alpha) = \frac{\tan \beta - \tan \alpha}{1 + \tan \beta \, \tan \alpha}.$$

48. Suppose the person in Problem 47 is Janet whose eye level above the sidewalk is 1.5 meters.

a) Show that her view of the marquee is given by the expression

$$\theta = \text{Tan}^{-1} \frac{1.5x}{x^2 + 10}.$$

b) Use your calculator and the result in (a) to complete the following table that gives her view for different values of x in meters. Express angle θ in degrees to two decimal places.

x	40	25	20	10	8	6	5	4	3.5	3.2	3.1	3.0	2.8	2.5	2.0	1.5	1.1	0.5
θ																		

c) Using the results of (b), make a reasonable estimate of how far from point P she should stand to get the best view (that is, the largest value of θ). Refine your estimate by using additional values of x to give an answer correct to two decimal places.

49. Suppose the person in Problem 47 is Preston whose eye level above the sidewalk is 2 meters.

a) Show that his view of the marquee is given by the expression

$$\theta = \text{Tan}^{-1} \frac{1.5x}{x^2 + 7}.$$

b) Compile a table similar to the one in Problem 48.

c) How far from point P should he stand to get the best view?

50. Using the results found in Problems 48 and 49, answer each of the following:

a) If Janet is standing at her spot of maximum view, how far behind her should Preston be to get the same view?

b) When Preston is standing 16 meters from point P, find his view (angle θ) of the marquee from that point.

c) When he is standing 16 meters from P, how far in front of him should Janet be to get the same view he has?

In Problems 51 through 55, find all values of x that satisfy the given equality or inequality.

51. $\text{Tan}^{-1}x = 1$

52. $\tan(\text{Tan}^{-1}x) = x$

53. $\text{Tan}^{-1}(\tan x) = x$

54. $2 \, \text{Cot}^{-1}x + 1 \leq 0$

55. $4 \, \text{Tan}^{-1}x - 3 \geq 0$

5.4 INVERSE SECANT AND INVERSE COSECANT

The inverse secant and cosecant relations are of comparatively little interest in the study of trigonometry, but since they do occur in certain applications in calculus we give the graphs and define the principal values for each.

The graph of the inverse secant relation is depicted in Fig. 5.17 where the heavy part of the curve represents the principal-value inverse secant function $y = \text{Sec}^{-1}x$. Similarly, Fig. 5.18 shows the graph of the inverse cosecant relation with the heavy portion of the curve representing the principal-value inverse cosecant function $y = \text{Csc}^{-1}x$.

Thus we have the following definitions.

The *principal-value inverse secant function* is given by:

$$y = \text{Sec}^{-1}x \text{ is equivalent to } x = \sec y \text{ and}$$
$$0 \leq y < \frac{\pi}{2} \text{ or } \frac{\pi}{2} < y \leq \pi.$$

The *principal-value inverse cosecant function* is given by:

$$y = \text{Csc}^{-1}x \text{ is equivalent to } x = \csc y \text{ and}$$
$$-\frac{\pi}{2} \leq y < 0 \text{ or } 0 < y \leq \frac{\pi}{2}.$$

The domain of both the Sec^{-1} and Csc^{-1} functions is given by $\{x \mid x \leq -1 \text{ or } x \geq 1\}$.

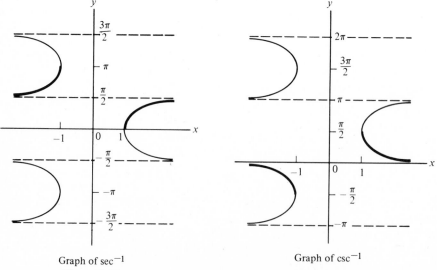

Graph of sec^{-1}

Figure 5.17

Graph of csc^{-1}

Figure 5.18

Note. In Chapter 4 we introduced several identities involving trigonometric functions that are useful in simplifying certain problems. The student should understand that the *corresponding identities do not hold for the inverse trigonometric functions.* For example, csc $x = 1/\sin x$ is an identity but $\text{Csc}^{-1}x$ is not equal to $1/\text{Sin}^{-1}x$; $\text{Tan}^{-1}x$ is not identically equal to $\text{Sin}^{-1}x/\text{Csc}^{-1}x$, and so on. Although we include some identities involving inverse functions in the exercises, they are not used frequently and we do not recommend memorizing them.

Examples

△1 Evaluate in exact form

a) $\cos\left(\text{Sec}^{-1}\left(-\frac{3}{2}\right)\right)$ b) $\tan\left(\text{Sec}^{-1}\left(-\frac{3}{2}\right)\right)$

Solution. Let $\theta = \text{Sec}^{-1}\left(-\frac{3}{2}\right)$; then sec $\theta = -3/2$ and $\pi/2 < \theta \leq \pi$.

That is, θ is the angle shown in Fig. 5.19. Therefore,

a) $\cos\left(\text{Sec}^{-1}\left(-\frac{3}{2}\right)\right) = \cos\theta = -\frac{2}{3}$;

b) $\tan\left(\text{Sec}^{-1}\left(-\frac{3}{2}\right)\right) = \tan\theta = -\frac{\sqrt{5}}{2}$.

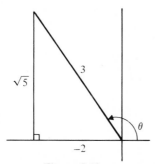

Figure 5.19

△2 Using a calculator, evaluate $\text{Sec}^{-1}(-1.873)$ in degrees correct to two decimal places.

Solution. Let $\alpha = \text{Sec}^{-1}(-1.873)$. Then from the definition of the Sec^{-1} function given in this section, this is equivalent to sec $\alpha = -1.873$ and $90° < \alpha \leq 180°$. Since the calculator does not have a ⌷sec⌷ or ⌷sec⁻¹⌷ key, we use the identity sec $\alpha = 1/\cos\alpha$ to get cos $\alpha = -1/1.873$ and $90° < \alpha \leq 180°$. We can now use the calculator to find α: place it in degree mode, enter $-1/1.873$ into the display, and press the ⌷INV⌷ and ⌷cos⌷ keys (or ⌷cos⁻¹⌷) to get $\alpha = \text{Sec}^{-1}(-1.873) = 122.27°$.

$\triangle$ Using a calculator, evaluate $\text{Csc}^{-1}(-2.478)$ in radians correct to four decimal places.

Solution. This is similar to Example 2 and we include only the essential steps. Let $\theta = \text{Csc}^{-1}(-2.478)$. This is equivalent to $\csc \theta = -2.478$ and $-\pi/2 \leq \theta < 0$. Thus we have $\sin \theta = -1/2.478$ and so $\theta = \text{Sin}^{-1}(-1/2.478)$. Place the calculator in radian mode, enter $-1/2.478$ and then press the $\boxed{\text{INV}}$ and $\boxed{\sin}$ keys (or the $\boxed{\sin^{-1}}$ key). This gives $\theta = \text{Csc}^{-1}(-2.478) = -0.4154$. $\blacksquare$

Note. From Examples 2 and 3 we can conclude the following:

> To evaluate $\text{Sec}^{-1}x$ by calculator, use
> $$\text{Sec}^{-1}x = \text{Cos}^{-1}\frac{1}{x}.$$
> To evaluate $\text{Csc}^{-1}x$ by calculator use
> $$\text{Csc}^{-1}x = \text{Sin}^{-1}\frac{1}{x}.$$

EXERCISE 5.4

In this exercise there may be some problems where the given expression is not defined. If a calculator is used, the display will indicate "Error". Explain what part of the expression is responsible for such an answer.

1. Evaluate the following and give answers in exact form in degrees:

   a) $\text{Sec}^{-1} 2$ b) $\text{Sec}^{-1} \sqrt{2}$ c) $\text{Csc}^{-1}\left(-\dfrac{2}{\sqrt{3}}\right)$

   d) $\text{Sec}^{-1}\left(-\sqrt{2}\right)$ e) $\text{Csc}^{-1}(-1)$

2. Evaluate the following and give answers in exact form in radians:

   a) $\text{Sec}^{-1} \dfrac{2}{\sqrt{3}}$ b) $\text{Sec}\,(-\sqrt{2})$ c) $\text{Csc}^{-1}\sqrt{2}$ d) $\text{Sec}^{-1}(-1)$ e) $\text{Csc}^{-1}(-\sqrt{2})$

3. Evaluate the following and give answers in exact form; then in decimal form correct to four decimal places:

   a) $\sin\left(\text{Sec}^{-1}\dfrac{4}{3}\right)$ b) $\cos\left(\text{Csc}^{-1}\dfrac{4}{3} - \text{Csc}^{-1}\left(-\dfrac{5}{4}\right)\right)$ c) $\text{Sec}^{-1} 3 + \text{Csc}^{-1}\dfrac{1}{3}$

   d) $\text{Sec}^{-1} 4 + \text{Sec}^{-1}\dfrac{4}{\sqrt{15}}$ e) $\sec\left(\text{Sec}^{-1} 3 - \text{Csc}^{-1}(-4)\right)$

4. Evaluate the following. Give answers in exact form.

   a) $\sin\left(2\,\text{Csc}^{-1} 5\right)$ b) $\cos\left(2\,\text{Sec}^{-1}(-3)\right)$

   c) $\sec\left(2\,\text{Sec}^{-1}\dfrac{3}{5}\right)$ d) $\sin\left(\dfrac{1}{2}\,\text{Csc}^{-1}\left(-\dfrac{7}{5}\right)\right)$

   e) $\tan\left(\dfrac{1}{2}\,\text{Sec}^{-1}\left(-\dfrac{5}{2}\right)\right)$

5. Use your calculator to evaluate the following as a real number correct to four decimal places:

   a) $\text{Sec}^{-1}(1.478)$

   b) $\tan(\text{Sec}^{-1} 2.578)$

   c) $\cos\left(\text{Sec}^{-1} \dfrac{1-\sqrt{5}}{3}\right)$

   d) $\text{Csc}^{-1}(-3.478)$

   e) $\sin(2 \text{ Sec}^{-1} 2.576)$

6. Evaluate the given expressions in two forms—exact and correct to two decimal places:

   a) $\sin\left(\text{Sec}^{-1} 2 + \text{Sec}^{-1}(2/\sqrt{3})\right)$

   b) $\cos(\text{Csc}^{-1}(4/3) - \text{Csc}^{-1}(5/4))$

   c) $\cos\left(\text{Sec}^{-1}(-7/4)\right)$

   d) $\tan(\text{Sec}^{-1} 1.2)$

   e) $\sec\left(\text{Csc}^{-1}(-1.5)\right)$

   f) $\text{Sec}^{-1}(2/\sqrt{3}) + \text{Sec}^{-1}(-2/\sqrt{3})$

7. Use your calculator to evaluate the following expressions. Give answers in degrees correct to two decimal places.

   a) $\text{Sec}^{-1}(\tan 74.52°)$

   b) $\text{Csc}^{-1}(\sin 47°)$

   c) $\text{Sec}^{-1}(-3.47)$

   d) $\text{Csc}^{-1}\dfrac{2+\sqrt{5}}{8}$

   e) $\text{Csc}^{-1}(\tan 124°)$

8. Find all values of the given expressions. Provide exact answers in radians.

   a) $\sec^{-1} 2$

   b) $\csc^{-1}(-\sqrt{2})$

9. Find all values of the given expression. Provide exact answers in degrees.

   a) $\sec^{-1}(-2/\sqrt{3})$

   b) $\csc^{-1}(-1)$

10. Prove that $\text{Sec}^{-1}x + \text{Csc}^{-1}x = \dfrac{\pi}{2}$ for $x \geq 1$ is an identity.

11. Prove that $\text{Sec}^{-1}x + \text{Csc}^{-1}x = \dfrac{\pi}{2}$ for $x \leq -1$ is an identity.

    This and Problem 10 prove that $\text{Sec}^{-1}x + \text{Csc}^{-1}x = \dfrac{\pi}{2}$ for $|x| \geq 1$ is an identity.

12. Prove that $\text{Sec}^{-1}\left(\dfrac{1}{x}\right) = \text{Cos}^{-1}x$ for $0 < |x| \leq 1$.

REVIEW EXERCISES

In Problems 1 through 10, evaluate the given expression and state answers in exact form (first in degree measure and then in radian measure).

1. $\text{Sin}^{-1} 1$

2. $\text{Cos}^{-1}\left(-\dfrac{1}{2}\right)$

3. $\text{Tan}^{-1}(-1)$

4. $\text{Sin}^{-1}\left(-\dfrac{\sqrt{3}}{2}\right)$

5. $\text{Cot}^{-1}(-\sqrt{3})$

6. $\text{Sec}^{-1} 2$

7. $\text{Csc}^{-1} 1$

8. $\text{Cos}^{-1}\left(-\dfrac{1}{2}\right) - \text{Sin}^{-1}\left(-\dfrac{1}{2}\right)$

9. $\text{Cos}^{-1}(-1) - \text{Tan}^{-1}(-1)$

10. $\text{Sin}^{-1}\left(\dfrac{1}{\sqrt{2}}\right) - \text{Tan}^{-1}(-1)$

In Problems 11 through 20, evaluate the following expressions in exact form. Angles α, β, and γ are given by:

$$\alpha = \text{Sin}^{-1}\left(-\dfrac{3}{5}\right), \quad \beta = \text{Cos}^{-1}\left(-\dfrac{4}{5}\right), \quad \sin \gamma = -\dfrac{5}{13}, \quad \dfrac{\pi}{2} \leq \gamma \leq \dfrac{3\pi}{2}.$$

11. $\beta - \alpha$

12. $\cos(\alpha + \beta)$

13. $\sin 2\alpha$

14. $\tan (\beta/2)$

15. $\cos (\gamma/2)$

16. $\sin(\alpha - \gamma)$

17. $\tan(\alpha + \gamma)$

18. $1 - \cos^2\beta$

19. $\tan 2\gamma$

20. $\sin\left(\dfrac{\alpha + \gamma}{2} \right)$

In Problems 21 through 45, evaluate the given expression and state answers in exact form (whenever it is reasonable to do so) or as real numbers correct to three decimal places. When a given expression is undefined, tell why.

21. $\sin(\mathrm{Sin}^{-1} 0.436)$

22. $\cos(\mathrm{Cos}^{-1} 1.32)$

23. $\tan(\mathrm{Tan}^{-1} 3)$

24. $\sin(\mathrm{Sin}^{-1} 0.4 + \mathrm{Cos}^{-1} 0.5)$

25. $\cos\left(\dfrac{\pi}{2} - \mathrm{Cos}^{-1} 0.456 \right)$

26. $\tan\left(\dfrac{\pi}{2} + \mathrm{Sin}^{-1} 0.56 \right)$

27. $\sec\left(\mathrm{Cos}^{-1} \dfrac{\pi}{2} \right)$

28. $\sec\left(\mathrm{Sec}^{-1}(-4.73) \right)$

29. $\cos\left(\dfrac{1}{2}\mathrm{Cot}^{-1} 4 \right)$

30. $\mathrm{Sin}^{-1}(\tan 23°)$

31. $\mathrm{Cos}^{-1}(\tan 123°)$

32. $\mathrm{Tan}^{-1}\left(\tan \dfrac{3\pi}{4} \right)$

33. $\tan(2\ \mathrm{Tan}^{-1} 1)$

34. $\tan\left(\dfrac{1}{3}\mathrm{Cos}^{-1} 0.275 \right)$

35. $\sec(\mathrm{Sec}^{-1} 0.52)$

36. $\tan\left(\mathrm{Tan}^{-1} \dfrac{3}{4} - \mathrm{Tan}^{-1} \dfrac{1}{2} \right)$

37. $\tan\left(\mathrm{Sin}^{-1}(1 - \sqrt{3}) \right)$

38. $\sin(2\ \mathrm{Sin}^{-1} 1)$

39. $\cos\left(\dfrac{\pi}{4} - \mathrm{Cos}^{-1} 0.41 \right)$

40. $\cos\left(\mathrm{Sin}^{-1} \dfrac{2}{\pi} \right)$

41. $\sin\left(\cos \dfrac{\pi}{2} \right)$

42. $\mathrm{Tan}^{-1}\left(\sin \dfrac{5\pi}{3} \right)$

43. $\mathrm{Cot}^{-1}(\cos 120°)$

44. $\tan\left(\dfrac{1}{2}\mathrm{Cos}^{-1}(-1) \right)$

45. $\sin\left(\mathrm{Cos}^{-1}\left(\sin \dfrac{\pi}{6} \right) \right)$

In Problems 46 through 55, determine whether the given statement is true or false. Give good reasons for your answers. Recall that $D(f)$ and $R(f)$ denote domain and range of f, respectively.

46. $\sin \dfrac{1 + \sqrt{3}}{2}$ is not defined

47. $\dfrac{\pi}{3}$ is in $D(\mathrm{Sin}^{-1})$

48. $\dfrac{\pi}{3}$ is in $R(\mathrm{Sin}^{-1})$

49. $\tan \dfrac{5\pi}{6}$ is in $D(\mathrm{Sec}^{-1})$

50. $\dfrac{\pi}{2} < \mathrm{Tan}^{-1}(-2) < \pi$

51. $\dfrac{2}{\pi}$ is in $D(\mathrm{Sin}^{-1})$

52. $\dfrac{2}{\pi}$ is in $R(\mathrm{Sin}^{-1})$

53. $\mathrm{Sin}^{-1}\left(\sin \dfrac{\pi}{3} \right) = \sin\left(\mathrm{Sin}^{-1} \dfrac{\pi}{3} \right)$

54. $\mathrm{Sin}^{-1}\left(\sin \dfrac{\pi}{4} \right) = \sin\left(\mathrm{Sin}^{-1} \dfrac{\pi}{4} \right)$

55. $\mathrm{Cos}^{-1}\left(\sin \dfrac{\pi}{6} \right) = \sin\left(\mathrm{Cos}^{-1} \dfrac{\pi}{6} \right)$

CHAPTER SIX

TRIGONOMETRIC EQUATIONS

6.1 CONDITIONAL EQUATIONS

The student already has some experience in solving algebraic equations. For example, equation $x^2 - x - 12 = 0$ is satisfied by $x = 4$ and $x = -3$. That is, if x is replaced in the equation by 4, we get $4^2 - 4 - 12 = 0$, which is a true statement. Similarly, for $x = -3$, we get $(-3)^2 - (-3) - 12 = 0$.

The set of possible replacement values for the variable is called the *replacement set* for that equation. In general, unless otherwise specified, the replacement set will be the largest subset of the set of real numbers, for which the expressions on the two sides of the given equation are defined (as real numbers). The *solution set* for a given equation is a subset of all numbers from the replacement set, each of which satisfies the equation.

We call an equation an *identity* if the solution set is the entire replacement set; otherwise the equation is called a *conditional equation*. In Chapter 4 we have encountered a large number of identity equations involving trigonometric functions. In this chapter we shall consider conditional equations involving trigonometric functions with the primary goal of developing techniques for finding the solution sets for such equations.

Many of our problems will begin with an equation which we will not solve directly in its given form. We shall make use of the identities in Chapter 4 to replace the given equation by an equivalent one that we can solve.

Examples

⚠ Find all solutions of the equation $2 \sin x - 1 = 0$. Express answers in degree measure.

Solution. We have already encountered problems of this type in our discussion of inverse trigonometric relations in Chapter 5. The equation $2 \sin x - 1 = 0$ is equivalent to $\sin x = \frac{1}{2}$ and the solutions to this equation are given by

$\sin^{-1}(\frac{1}{2})$. However, this merely involves notation and does not actually tell us explicitly what numbers belong to the solution set.

Since $\sin x$ is positive, x is an angle in the first or second quadrant, as shown in Fig. 6.1. Two solutions are: $x_1 = 30°$, $x_2 = 150°$. If we add or subtract any integer multiple of $360°$ to either of these, the result will also be a solution, and in this way we get all solutions. Therefore, the solution set is

$$\{x \mid x = 30° + k \cdot 360° \text{ or } x = 150° + k \cdot 360°, \text{ where } k \text{ is any integer}\}.$$

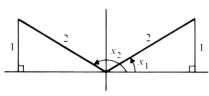

Figure 6.1

2 Solve the equation $\sin(3x - \pi) = 1$, where $-2\pi \le x \le 2\pi$.

Note. $-2\pi \le x \le 2\pi$ implies that the solutions are to be given in radians (real numbers).

Solution. The restriction $-2\pi \le x \le 2\pi$ means that the replacement set for this problem is $\{x \mid -2\pi \le x \le 2\pi\}$. Since $\sin(3x - \pi) = 1$, then $3x - \pi$ must be one of the following:

$$\frac{\pi}{2}, \quad \frac{5\pi}{2}, \quad \frac{9\pi}{2}, \quad \dots, \quad -\frac{3\pi}{2}, \quad -\frac{7\pi}{2}, \quad \dots$$

This set of numbers is given by $(4k + 1)\pi/2$, where k is any integer. Thus, our solutions will be given by

$$3x - \pi = \frac{(4k + 1)\pi}{2}.$$

Solving for x, we get

$$x = \frac{(4k + 3)\pi}{6}.$$

We now select those values of k that will give values of x in the replacement set. We see that if we take k to be $-3, -2, -1, 0, 1, 2$, we get the corresponding values of x:

$$-\frac{3\pi}{2}, \quad -\frac{5\pi}{6}, \quad -\frac{\pi}{6}, \quad \frac{\pi}{2}, \quad \frac{7\pi}{6}, \quad \frac{11\pi}{6}.$$

Therefore, the solution set is

$$\left\{ -\frac{3\pi}{2}, \quad -\frac{5\pi}{6}, \quad -\frac{\pi}{6}, \quad \frac{\pi}{2}, \quad \frac{7\pi}{6}, \quad \frac{11\pi}{6} \right\}.$$

3 Find the solution set for $3 \tan x + 4 = 0$, where $-\pi \le x \le \pi$.

Solution. The given equation is equivalent to tan $x = -4/3$. Since tan x is negative, then x must be in the second or fourth quadrant. The fourth-quadrant angle in the replacement set is $x_1 = \text{Tan}^{-1}(-4/3)$; it can be found by using the calculator. That is, $x_1 = -0.9273$. Since $\tan(\pi + x) = \tan x$ is an identity, the second solution is given by $x_2 = \pi + x_1 = \pi + (-0.9273) = 2.2143$. Since solutions are restricted to the interval $-\pi \le x \le \pi$, the solution set is $\{-0.9273, 2.2143\}$, where the answers are given to four decimal places. ∎

△4 Find the solution set for $\sin(3x - \pi/4) - \sqrt{3} \cos(3x - \pi/4) = 0$.

Solution. In Chapter 4 we indicated that identities are useful in replacing a given problem by an equivalent one that may be easier to solve. Here is a simple example of such a problem.

The given equation can be written as

$$\sin\left(3x - \frac{\pi}{4}\right) = \sqrt{3} \cos\left(3x - \frac{\pi}{4}\right).$$

If we divide both sides by $\cos(3x - \pi/4) \ne 0$, we get

$$\frac{\sin(3x - \pi/4)}{\cos(3x - \pi/4)} = \sqrt{3}.$$

Now we use the identity $\sin \theta / \cos \theta = \tan \theta$ and get

$$\tan\left(3x - \frac{\pi}{4}\right) = \sqrt{3}.$$

Since $\tan(3x - \pi/4)$ is positive, angle $3x - \pi/4$ is in the first or third quadrant, as shown in Fig. 6.2 (where $\theta = 3x - \pi/4$). These angles can be written as $\pi/3 + k\pi$, where k is an integer. Therefore,

$$3x - \frac{\pi}{4} = \frac{\pi}{3} + k\pi,$$

and so $x = (7 + 12k)\pi/36$. These are solutions, provided $\cos(3x - \pi/4) \ne 0$.

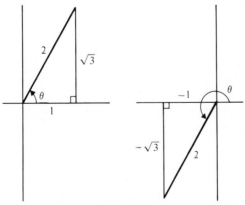

Figure 6.2

The student is urged to show that this indeed is the case. Thus the solution set is

$$\{x \mid x = (7 + 12k)\pi/36, \quad \text{where } k \text{ is any integer}\}. \qquad \blacksquare$$

△5 Find all values of x at which $3 \sin (2x - \pi/12)$ attains a maximum.

Solution. Since the largest value the sine function can have is 1, the maximum value of $3 \sin(2x - \pi/12)$ is 3. Therefore, the problem is equivalent to finding all values of x for which $3 \sin (2x - \pi/12) = 3$, or $\sin (2x - \pi/12) = 1$. All solutions of this equation are given by

$$2x - \frac{\pi}{12} = \frac{\pi}{2} + 2\pi k,$$

where k is an integer. Therefore, the solution set is

$$\{x \mid x = \frac{7\pi}{24} + k\pi, \quad \text{where } k \text{ is any integer}\}. \qquad \blacksquare$$

△6 Find the solution set for the equation $\sqrt{2} \sin x - 3 = 0$.

Solution. The given equation is equivalent to $\sin x = 3/\sqrt{2}$. Since $3/\sqrt{2} > 1$, there are no values of x such that $\sin x = 3/\sqrt{2}$. Therefore, the solution set is the empty set. $\qquad \blacksquare$

EXERCISE 6.1

In each of the following problems express answers in exact form whenever it is reasonable to do so. Otherwise use a calculator and give answers correct to two decimal places. Check your answers when there is a possibility that extraneous solutions may have been introduced.

In Problems 1 through 8 find all solutions of the given equations. Express answers in degree measure.

1. $2 \cos x + 1 = 0$
2. $2 \sin x + \sqrt{3} = 0$
3. $\sqrt{3} \tan x - 1 = 0$

4. $4 \sin x - 3 = 0$
5. $3 \sec x - 7 = 0$
6. $3 \sin x - 5 \cos x = 0$

7. $\sqrt{3} \sin x - 5 = 0$
8. $2 \sin 2x - \sqrt{3} = 0$

In Problems 9 through 20 assume that the replacement set is $\{x \mid 0 \leq x \leq 2\pi\}$ and find the solution set for the given equations.

9. $2 \cos x + \sqrt{3} = 0$
10. $2 \sin x - \sin^2 x = \cos^2 x$

11. $2 \sin\left(3x - \frac{\pi}{4}\right) - 1 = 0$
12. $\sin(2x - 1) + \sqrt{3} \cos(2x - 1) = 0$

13. $\sqrt{3} \sec x - 2 = 0$
14. $3.57 \sin x + 2.16 = 0$

15. $\cot x + \sqrt{3} = 0$ 16. $4 \sec x + \sqrt{7} = 0$

17. $\sin\left(x + \frac{\pi}{3}\right) - 2.4 \cos\left(x + \frac{\pi}{3}\right) = 0$ 18. $3 \sec x + 2 = 0$

19. $5 \cot x + \sqrt{3} = 1$ 20. $\cos(3x - 1.6) + 6.4 \sin(3x - 1.6) = 0$

In Problems 21 through 23, find the solution set for the given equations.

21. $4 \operatorname{Sin}^{-1}x = 3$ 22. $2 \operatorname{Cos}^{-1}x + 1 = 0$ 23. $\sqrt{5} \operatorname{Tan}^{-1}x - 1.6 = 0$

24. Find all real numbers x at which $4 \cos(2x - \pi/3)$ attains a minimum.

25. Find all real numbers x at which $3 \sin(x - \pi/4)$ attains a maximum.

6.2 QUADRATIC EQUATIONS INVOLVING TRIGONOMETRIC FUNCTIONS

In this section we consider problems in which the given equation can be transformed into an equivalent quadratic equation involving one of the trigonometric functions.

Examples

 Solve $2 \sin^2 x - \sin x = 0$, where the replacement set is

$$\{x \mid 0° \le x \le 360°\}.$$

Solution. We first express the given equation in factored form:

$$\sin x (2 \sin x - 1) = 0.$$

We now use the basic property of numbers: If the product of two numbers is zero, then at least one of the numbers must be zero. Therefore, the given equation is equivalent to

$$\sin x = 0 \qquad \text{or} \qquad (2 \sin x - 1) = 0;$$

$\sin x = 0$ gives $x = 0°$, $180°$, $360°$ as solutions, while $2 \sin x - 1 = 0$, or $\sin x = \frac{1}{2}$, gives $x = 30°$, $150°$ as solutions. Thus the solution set is

$$\{0°, 30°, 150°, 180°, 360°\}. \qquad\blacksquare$$

 Find all solutions in degree measure of the equation

$$2 \sin^2 x - \cos^2 x - 5 \sin x - 1 = 0.$$

Solution. The equation can be written as a quadratic equation with regard to $\sin x$ by replacing $\cos^2 x$ with $1 - \sin^2 x$. Therefore,

$$2 \sin^2 x - (1 - \sin^2 x) - 5 \sin x - 1 = 0,$$

or

$$3 \sin^2 x - 5 \sin x - 2 = 0.$$

This can be factored as

$$(3 \sin x + 1)(\sin x - 2) = 0.$$

Thus, the given equation is equivalent to

$$3 \sin x + 1 = 0 \quad \text{or} \quad \sin x - 2 = 0.$$

Therefore,

$$\sin x = -\frac{1}{3} \quad \text{or} \quad \sin x = 2.$$

There is no x satisfying $\sin x = 2$. For $\sin x = -\frac{1}{3}$, the angle x must be in the third or fourth quadrant, as shown in Fig. 6.3. We can use the calculator to find

$$x_1 = \text{Sin}^{-1}(-\frac{1}{3}) = -19.47°$$

and

$$x_2 = 180° + 19.47° = 199.47°.$$

Therefore the solution set is

$$\{x \mid x = -19.47° + k \cdot 360° \quad \text{or} \quad x = 199.47° + k \cdot 360°,$$
$$\text{where } k \text{ is any integer}\}.$$

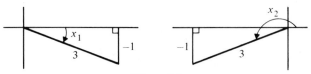

Figure 6.3

⚠ Find the solution set for $2 \cos^2 x - 6 \cos x + 1 = 0$, where $0 \leq x \leq 2\pi$.

Solution. Since the left-hand side of the given equation does not factor in a simple manner, we use the quadratic formula

$$\cos x = \frac{6 \pm \sqrt{36 - 4 \cdot 2 \cdot 1}}{4} = \frac{3 \pm \sqrt{7}}{2}.$$

Therefore, the given equation is equivalent to

$$\cos x = \frac{3 + \sqrt{7}}{2} \quad \text{or} \quad \cos x = \frac{3 - \sqrt{7}}{2}.$$

There is no solution for $\cos x = (3 + \sqrt{7})/2 = 2.8229$. For

$$\cos x = \frac{3 - \sqrt{7}}{2} = 0.1771$$

we see that x is in the first or fourth quadrant, as shown in Fig. 6.4. By using the calculator, we find

$$x_1 = \text{Cos}^{-1} \frac{3 - \sqrt{7}}{2} = 1.3927.$$

The second solution is given by

$$x_2 = 2\pi - x_1 = 2\pi - 1.3927 = 4.8905.$$

Therefore, the solution set is $\{1.3927, 4.8905\}$, where the answers are given to four decimal places.

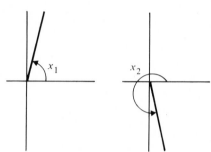

Figure 6.4

⁴⃞ Solve $\sin^2 x - 2 \sin x + 2 = 0$.

Solution. Using the quadratic formula we get

$$\sin x = \frac{2 \pm \sqrt{4 - 8}}{2} = 1 \pm \sqrt{-1}.$$

Since $1 \pm \sqrt{-1}$ are imaginary numbers, there is no value of x that will satisfy the given equation, and so the solution set is the empty set.

EXERCISE 6.2

In the problems of this set, express answers in exact form whenever it is reasonable to do so. Otherwise use a calculator and give answers correct to two decimal places.

In Problems 1 through 8, find all solutions of the given equation and express answers in degree measure.

1. $3 \sin^2 x - \sin x - 2 = 0$

2. $\sin^2 x - \cos^2 x = 0$

3. $\cos^2 x + 2 \cos x + 1 = 0$

4. $\tan^2 x - 1 = 0$

5. $1 - 4 \sin^2 x = 0$

6. $3 \sec^2 x + 2 \sec x - 1 = 0$

7. $\cos^2 x - \sin^2 x + 3 \cos x - 1 = 0$

8. $2 \sin^2 x + 5 \sin x - 3 = 0$

In the following problems, assume that the replacement set is $\{x \mid 0 \leq x \leq 2\pi\}$. Find the solution set for the given equation.

9. $2 \sin^2 x - 5 \sin x - 3 = 0$

10. $\cos^2 x - \sin^2 x = 0$

11. $3 \cos^2 x + \cos x - 2 = 0$

12. $4 - \tan^2 x = 0$

13. $\tan^2 x + 2 \tan x + 1 = 0$

14. $2 \sec^2 x - 3 \sec x - 2 = 0$

15. $3 \sec^2 x - 4 \tan^2 x = 0$

16. $4 \cos^2 x + 3 \cos x - 1 = 0$

17. $4 \sin^2 x + 3 \cos^2 x - 4 = 0$

18. $\cos^2 x - 3 \cos x - 2 = 0$

19. $\sin^2 x + 2 \sin x + 1 = 0$

20. $2 \sec^2 x - \tan^2 x - 3 = 0$

21. $\sin^2 x + 2 \sin x + \cos^2 x = 0$

22. $\sin^2 x = 2 - \cos^2 x$

23. $\sec^2 x - 2 \cos^2 x - \tan^2 x = 0$

24. $2 \cos x \tan^2 x + 2 = 0$

25. $\tan x \cot x + 4 \sin^2 x = 4$

26. $2 \sin^2 x + 2 \sin x - 1 = 0$

27. $\cos^2 x + 3 \cos x - 2 = 0$

28. $2 \tan^2 x - 4 \tan x + 1 = 0$

29. $\sec^2 x + 3 \sec x - 1 = 0$

30. $3 \csc^2 x - 2 \cot^2 x + \cot x - 4 = 0$

31. $\sin^2 x + 4 \cos^2 x + 2 \sin x - 2 = 0$

32. $2 \sec x - \cos x + 5 = 0$

33. $\sin^2 x - \sin x + 2 = 0$

34. $3 \cos^2 x + 4 \cos x + 2 = 0$

35. $25 \sin^2 x - 30 \sin x + 7 = 0$

36. $3.2 \cos^2 x - 1.5 \cos x - 0.48 = 0$

37. $\tan^2 x - 1.48 \tan x - 2.16 = 0$

38. $2.56 \cos^2 x - 1.32 \cos x - 1.21 = 0$

39. $2 \cos^2 x - \cos x - 15 = 0$

40. $9 \sin^2 x - 6 \sin x - 1 = 0$

6.3 EQUATIONS OF THE FORM $a \sin x + b \cos x = c$

An equation of the form $a \sin x + b \cos x = c$ (where a, b, c are given numbers) can be transformed into an equivalent equation of the type already studied in Section 6.1. We do this as follows: divide both sides of the equation by $\sqrt{a^2 + b^2}$ and get

$$\frac{a}{\sqrt{a^2 + b^2}} \sin x + \frac{b}{\sqrt{a^2 + b^2}} \cos x = \frac{c}{\sqrt{a^2 + b^2}}. \tag{6.1}$$

As an illustration, consider Fig. 6.5, where the terminal side of angle α passes through point (a, b) (the diagram shown is for a negative and b positive). Since a and b are given, angle α is determined. We note that

$$\cos \alpha = \frac{a}{\sqrt{a^2 + b^2}} \quad \text{and} \quad \sin \alpha = \frac{b}{\sqrt{a^2 + b^2}}$$

and so Eq. (6.1) can be written as

$$\cos \alpha \sin x + \sin \alpha \cos x = \frac{c}{\sqrt{a^2 + b^2}} \,.$$

The left-hand side of this equation reminds us of the identity for the sine of a sum of two angles, and indeed it can be replaced by $\sin(x + \alpha)$ (see identity I.12 of Section 4.2). Therefore, the given equation can be written in equivalent form

$$\sin(x + \alpha) = \frac{c}{\sqrt{a^2 + b^2}} \,, \tag{6.2}$$

which can be used to find the solution set.

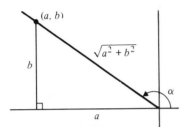

Figure 6.5

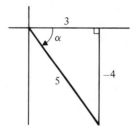

Figure 6.6

Example

⚠ Find all solutions of the equation $3 \sin x - 4 \cos x = 2$. Express answers in radian and in degree measure.

Solution. We first divide both sides of the given equation by $\sqrt{3^2 + (-4)^2} = \sqrt{25} = 5$ and get

$$\tfrac{3}{5} \sin x - \tfrac{4}{5} \cos x = \tfrac{2}{5}. \tag{6.3}$$

Plot the point $(3, -4)$ and let α be the angle, as shown in Fig. 6.6. We see that $\cos \alpha = 3/5$ and $\sin \alpha = -4/5$; substituting these into Eq. (6.3) gives

$$\sin x \cos \alpha + \cos x \sin \alpha = \tfrac{2}{5}.$$

This can be written as

$$\sin(x + \alpha) = \tfrac{2}{5}. \tag{6.4}$$

Angle α can be found by using a calculator: $\alpha = \mathrm{Sin}^{-1}(-4/5) = -0.9273$. Hence Eq. (6.4) becomes $\sin(x - 0.9273) = 2/5$. Thus $x = \sin^{-1}(2/5) + 0.9273$.

Let $\theta = \sin^{-1} 2/5$; then angle θ is in the first or second quadrant, as shown in Fig. 6.7. Therefore

$$\theta_1 = \mathrm{Sin}^{-1} \tfrac{2}{5} = 0.4115 \qquad \text{and} \qquad \theta_2 = \pi - 0.4115 = 2.7301.$$

This gives us two solutions,

$$x_1 = 0.4115 + 0.9273 = 1.3388,$$
$$x_2 = 2.7301 + 0.9273 = 3.6574.$$

The solution set is

$\{x \mid x = 1.3388 + 2\pi k$ or $x = 3.6574 + 2\pi k$, where k is any integer$\}$.

In degree measure the solution set is

$\{x \mid x = 76.71° + k \cdot 360°$ or $x = 209.55° + k \cdot 360°\}$.

Note. In the above solution we transformed the given equation into an equivalent equation $\sin(x + \alpha) = 2/5$, where α was determined by plotting the point $(3, -4)$. We could just as well have started by plotting the point, say $(4, 3)$ that determines angle β, as shown in Fig. 6.8. That is, $\sin \beta = 3/5$, $\cos \beta = 4/5$, and so Eq. (6.3) can be written as

$$\sin x \sin \beta - \cos x \cos \beta = \frac{2}{5} \text{ or } \cos x \cos \beta - \sin x \sin \beta = -\frac{2}{5}.$$

This reminds us of the identity for the cosine of the sum of two angles, and so the given equation is equivalent to $\cos(x + \beta) = -2/5$, where $\beta = \text{Sin}^{-1}(3/5)$. The student should solve the equation and see if the results agree with the solution set given above.

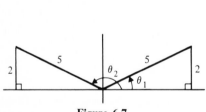

Figure 6.7

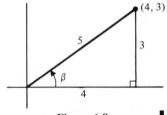

Figure 6.8

EXERCISE 6.3

In Problems 1 through 10 assume that the replacement set is $\{x \mid 0 \leq x \leq 2\pi\}$. Find the solution set for the given equations; provide answers correct to two decimals.

1. $4 \sin x + 3 \cos x = 1$

2. $2 \sin x - 3 \cos x = \sqrt{17}$

3. $\cos x - 2 \sin x = 2$

4. $\sin x + 2 \cos x + 1 = 0$

5. $2 \sin x - 5 \cos x = 8$

6. $\sin^2 x - 2 \sin x \cos x = 0$

7. $3 \cos x + 4 \sin x = 2$

8. $\sin x + \cos x = 1$

9. $\sin x + \cos x = \sqrt{2}$

10. $\sin x + \sqrt{3} \cos x = 1$

In Problems 11 through 20 assume that the replacement set is $\{x \mid 0° \leq x \leq 360°\}$. Find the solution set for the given equations; provide answers correct to the nearest minute.

11. $\sin x - \cos x = 1$ **12.** $\sqrt{2} \sin x + \sqrt{3} \cos x = 2$

13. $3 \cos x + 4 \sin x = 1$ **14.** $\sin x - 3 \cos x = 4$

15. $2 \cos^2 x - \sin x \cos x = 0$ **16.** $1.3 \sin x - 1.8 \cos x = 2.5$

17. $2 \cos^2 x - \sin x \cos x + \cos x = 0$ **18.** $3 \sin^2 x - 2 \sin x \cos x + 3 \sin x = 0$

19. $3 \sin 2x - 4 \cos 2x = 3$ **20.** $\sin 2x + 2 \cos 2x = 1$

6.4 EQUATIONS INVOLVING FUNCTIONS OF MULTIPLE ANGLES

In this section we make use of the double-angle identities I.18 through I.20 (p. 133) to help us solve certain trigonometric equations.

Examples

⚠ Solve the equation $\sin 2x - \sin x = 0$.

Solution. Using I.18 we can replace $\sin 2x$ by $2 \sin x \cos x$ and get

$$2 \sin x \cos x - \sin x = 0.$$

This can be written as

$$(\sin x)(2 \cos x - 1) = 0.$$

Therefore, the given equation is equivalent to

$$\sin x = 0 \quad \text{or} \quad \cos x = \tfrac{1}{2}.$$

We have solved several problems of this type before and so we merely give the final result. The solution set is

$$\{x \mid x = k\pi \quad \text{or} \quad x = \tfrac{\pi}{3} + 2k\pi \quad \text{or} \quad x = -\tfrac{\pi}{3} + 2k\pi, \text{ where } k \text{ is any integer}\}.$$

In degree measure the solution set is

$$\{x \mid x = k \cdot 180° \quad \text{or} \quad x = 60° + k \cdot 360° \quad \text{or} \quad x = -60° + k \cdot 360°\}. \quad \blacksquare$$

⚠ Find the solution set for the equation $\cos 4x + 3 \sin 2x + 4 = 0$, where the replacement set is $\{x \mid 0° \leq x \leq 360°\}$.

Solution. We use identity I.19 to replace $\cos 4x$ by $1 - 2 \sin^2 2x$, and so the given equation becomes

$$1 - 2 \sin^2 2x + 3 \sin 2x + 4 = 0.$$

This can be written as

$$2 \sin^2 2x - 3 \sin 2x - 5 = 0 \quad \text{or} \quad (2 \sin 2x - 5)(\sin 2x + 1) = 0.$$

Therefore, the given equation is equivalent to $\sin 2x = 5/2$ or $\sin 2x = -1$; the first of these gives no solutions and the second gives

$$2x = 270° + k \cdot 360° \qquad \text{or} \qquad x = 135° + k \cdot 180°.$$

The solutions that are in the replacement set are $x = 135°$ and $x = 315°$. Thus the solution set is $\{135°, 315°\}$. ∎

△3 Solve the equation $2 \sin^2 2x - 7 \sin x \cos x + 1 = 0$, where $0 \le x \le 2\pi$.

Solution. We observe that $\sin x \cos x$ can be replaced by $\frac{1}{2} \sin 2x$, according to identity I.18, and so the given equation is equivalent to

$$4 \sin^2 2x - 7 \sin 2x + 2 = 0.$$

We can solve for $\sin 2x$ by using the quadratic formula

$$\sin 2x = \frac{7 \pm \sqrt{49 - 32}}{8} = \frac{7 \pm \sqrt{17}}{8}.$$

Since $(7 + \sqrt{17})/8 > 1$, there are no values of x that satisfy

$$\sin 2x = \frac{7 + \sqrt{17}}{8}$$

For $\sin 2x = (7 - \sqrt{17})/8$ we see that since $(7 - \sqrt{17})/8 > 0$, angle $2x$ must be in the first or second quadrant, as shown in Fig. 6.9. Using a calculator, we find

$$2x_1 = \operatorname{Sin}^{-1} \frac{7 - \sqrt{17}}{8} = 0.3678 \qquad \text{and} \qquad 2x_2 = \pi - 2x_1 = 2.7738.$$

We can get two other solutions that are in the replacement set, from

$$2x_3 = 2x_1 + 2\pi = 6.6510 \qquad \text{and} \qquad 2x_4 = 2x_2 + 2\pi = 9.0570.$$

Thus all the solutions of the given problem are

$$x_1 = 0.1839, \qquad x_2 = 1.3869, \qquad x_3 = 3.3255, \qquad x_4 = 4.5285.$$

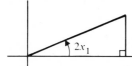 

Figure 6.9 ∎

△4 Find all the solutions of equation $\sin 2x + \cos 2x = 0$. Express answers as real numbers.

Solution. The given equation is equivalent to each of the following

$$\sin 2x = - \cos 2x, \qquad \frac{\sin 2x}{\cos 2x} = -1, \qquad \tan 2x = -1.$$

Therefore, $2x$ is an angle in the second or fourth quadrant, and the general solution is given by

$$2x = \text{Tan}^{-1}(-1) + k\pi = -\frac{\pi}{4} + k\pi,$$

where k is any integer. The solution set for the given equation is

$$\left\{x \,\middle|\, x = -\frac{\pi}{8} + \frac{k\pi}{2}\right\}.$$

Note. Since our solution involved a step in which both sides of an equation were divided by an expression containing x, it is possible that extraneous solutions may have been introduced. We urge the student to check whether the given equation is actually satisfied by

$$x = -\frac{\pi}{8} + \frac{k\pi}{2}.$$

■

EXERCISE 6.4

In Problems 1 through 16, the replacement set is $\{x \,|\, 0 \le x \le 2\pi\}$. Solve the given equations. Provide answers in exact form if possible; otherwise round off to two decimal places. Check for possible extraneous solutions when necessary.

1. $2 \sin 2x - \cos 2x = 0$

2. $\sin 3x + \cos 3x = 0$

3. $\sin 2x = 3 \cos x$

4. $\cos 2x + \cos x + 1 = 0$

5. $\cos 2x + \cos x = 0$

6. $\sin 2x = \cos\left(x - \frac{\pi}{2}\right)$

7. $\cos 2x + 4 \cos x - 5 = 0$

8. $\cos 4x + 4 = 3 \sin 2x$

9. $(1 - \tan^2 x)\tan 2x + 2 \sin x = 0$

10. $(1 + \tan^2 x)\cos^2 x + 2 \sin 2x = 0$

11. $\sin^2 2x + 4 \sin x \cos x + 1 = 0$

12. $4 \sin^2 x + 3 \cos 2x - 1 = 0$

13. $(\sin x - \cos x)^2 - 0.5 = 0$

14. $\sin^2 x - 3 \sin 2x = \cos^2 x$

15. $4 \sin 2x \cos 2x + \tan^2 x = \sec^2 x$

16. $3 \sin 2x = 4 \cos 2x$

In Problems 17 through 30, find the solution sets of the given equations, where the replacement is $\{x \,|\, 0° \le x \le 360°\}$. Give answers in exact form if possible; otherwise round off to two decimal places.

17. $\cos 2x + 3 \sin x + 1 = 0$

18. $4 \cos 2x - 3 \sin 2x = 0$

19. $2 \sin 2x = \cos x$

20. $\cos 4x + 3 \sin 2x + 4 = 0$

21. $\sin 2x = \cos(x + 90°)$

22. $\cos 2x + \cos^2 x = \sin^2 x$

23. $2(\sin x + \cos x)^2 + 1 = 0$ **24.** $(\sin 2x - \cos 2x)^2 - 1 = 0$

25. $\sin^2 x - \cos 2x = 1$ **26.** $\sqrt{2 \cos^2 x - 1} = -0.5$

27. $(1 - \tan^2 x)\cos x \tan 2x = 4 \sin^3 x$ **28.** $\sin 4x = \sin 2x$

29. $\sin 6x = \sin 3x$ **30.** $2 \sin x \csc 2x - \cos x = 0$

6.5   EQUATIONS INVOLVING TRIGONOMETRIC AND ALGEBRAIC FUNCTIONS

In the preceding sections of this chapter all the equations considered involved only trigonometric functions. Similarly in algebra courses, all the equations studied involve only algebraic expressions (such as $x^2 - 2x + 1 = 0$ or $x + \sqrt{3x - 1} = 5$). In this section we consider equations involving both algebraic and trigonometric functions. These are somewhat more difficult to solve but we shall see that the calculator will help considerably.

Examples

⚠ Solve the equation $\sin x + x = 0$.

Solution. In problems of this type we shall rely on graphs to give us some insight into possible solutions. We first write the given equation as $\sin x = -x$ and draw graphs of $y = \sin x$ and $y = -x$ on the same system of coordinates. Solutions to our problem will be given by the x-coordinates of the points of intersection of the two curves. We see from the diagram in Fig. 6.10 that there is only one point of intersection—the origin—and so the solution set for $\sin x + x = 0$ is $\{0\}$.

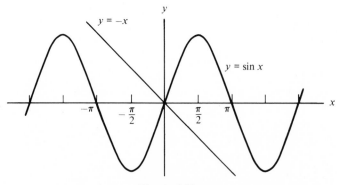

Figure 6.10

2 Find the solution set for the equation $\cos x - x = 0$.

Solution. We first write the given equation in the form $\cos x = x$, and then draw the graphs of $y = \cos x$ and $y = x$ on the same system of coordinates, as shown in Fig. 6.11. We see that there is only one point of intersection, so our problem is to find the x-coordinate of that point; we shall denote it by x_0.

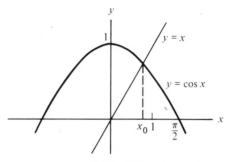

Figure 6.11

There are systematic techniques for finding x_0 to any desired number of decimal places, but these require the study of calculus. The present approach makes use of the calculator and common sense.

Set the calculator in radian mode and then make a reasonable estimate of the value of x_0 from the diagram; call it x_1 and then evaluate $\cos x_1 - x_1$. If this number is positive, then x_1 is to the left of x_0, that is $x_1 < x_0$ (look at the graph); if it is negative, $x_1 > x_0$. Of course, our goal is to find x_0 such that $\cos x_0 - x_0 = 0$. It so happens that there is no finite decimal that has this property, and so we shall be satisfied with an approximate answer, say, correct to three decimal places. We compile a table containing our estimated values of x and the corresponding values of $\cos x - x$, and at each step our estimated x will be based on the previous values of x and $\cos x - x$.

From the diagram, a reasonable first guess at x_0 is 0.7.

Estimated x	0.7	0.72	0.74	0.735	0.736	0.739	0.7395
$(\cos x) - x$	0.065	0.032	−0.0015	0.0068	0.0052	0.00014	−0.0007

We see that 0.7395 is to the right of x_0 and 0.739 is slightly to the left of x_0, and so $x = 0.739$ is an approximation of x_0 that is correct to three decimal places. *Note.* An interesting approach to solving this problem is discussed in Problem 12 of Exercise 6.5.   ▌

EXERCISE 6.5

In Problems 1 through 10, solve the given equation and give the answers correct to two decimal places. If a problem has more than one solution, find the nonzero solution nearest to $x = 0$ (if there are two such solutions, find the positive one).

Note. In each of the problems, x is necessarily a real number. For example, it does not make sense to solve $\sin x = x$ with x in degrees since $\sin x$ is always a real number and cannot be equal to x-degrees. Therefore be certain that your calculator is in radian mode when you solve these problems.

1. $\sin x + 2x = 0$

2. $\sin x - \dfrac{x}{2} = 0$

3. $\cos x + x = 0$

4. $\cos x = x^2$

5. $\cos x = \dfrac{x}{3}$

6. $\tan x = x$

7. $\tan x + 3x = 0$

8. $\sin x + x^2 = 0$

9. $\cos x + 1 = x^2$

10. $\sin x - 3x^2 = 0$

11. Find the smallest positive solution of $x \sin x - 1 = 0$. *Hint.* You may wish to write this as $\sin x = 1/x$.

12. In Example 2 of this section we used a guess approach to find the solution of $\cos x - x = 0$ to three decimal places. Now consider the same problem but try the following approach.

Set your calculator in radian mode and start with *any number* in the display (this is the feature that makes this approach interesting), then press ⌐cos⌐. A new number appears in the display; press ⌐cos⌐ again, and again a new number appears in the display. Continue doing this (that is, press the ⌐cos⌐ key repeatedly) and watch the display to see what happens. If you eventually get a number in the display (call it x_0) that is not changing, then the calculator is telling you that $\cos x_0 = x_0$. This is precisely the solution of $\cos x - x = 0$ to the digit capacity of your calculator. Draw graphs of $y = \cos x$ and $y = x$ on the same set of coordinates and see if you can analyze why this technique works.

The student is urged to try the technique described in Problem 12 on other problems. The idea is to write your problem in the form $f(x) = x$ and then start with a guess (say x_1), evaluate $f(x_1)$, then evaluate f of this number (that is $f(f(x_1))$), and continue this. If your calculator display eventually does not change (call the number in the display x_0), then you have $f(x_0) = x_0$, which is the solution of the given equation. As an example, try this approach to find the solution of $\sin x - x^2 = 0$ by considering $\sqrt{\sin x} = x$. Take $0 < x < \pi$, since we want $\sin x > 0$ for $\sqrt{\sin x}$.

6.6 USING IDENTITIES IN SOLVING EQUATIONS

In this section we consider various types of equations; the identities of Chapter 4 are used to transform the given equation into an equivalent equation that we can solve.

⚠️ Find the solution set for $2(\sin x + \cos x)^2 = 1$, where $0 \le x \le 2\pi$.

Solution. Each of the following equations is equivalent to the given equation:

$$2(\sin^2 x + 2 \sin x \cos x + \cos^2 x) = 1 \qquad \text{(by algebra)},$$
$$2(1 + 2 \sin x \cos x) = 1 \qquad \text{(by (I.9))},$$
$$2(1 + \sin 2x) = 1 \qquad \text{(by (I.18))},$$
$$\sin 2x = -\frac{1}{2} \qquad \text{(by algebra)}.$$

Therefore,

$$2x = -\frac{\pi}{6} + k \cdot 2\pi \qquad \text{or} \qquad 2x = -\frac{5\pi}{6} + k \cdot 2\pi$$

where k is any integer. Then

$$x = -\frac{\pi}{12} + k\pi \qquad \text{or} \qquad x = -\frac{5\pi}{12} + k\pi.$$

We select those values of k that give values of x in the replacement set. In both cases we use $k = 1$ or 2. Thus the solution set is

$$\left\{ \frac{11\pi}{12}, \frac{23\pi}{12}, \frac{7\pi}{12}, \frac{19\pi}{12} \right\} \qquad\qquad \blacksquare$$

⚠️ Find the solution set for $\cos x - \sin (x/2) = 1$, where $-180° \le x \le 180°$.

Solution. We use the double-angle identity $\cos 2\theta = 1 - 2 \sin^2\theta$ to replace $\cos x = \cos[2(x/2)]$ by $1 - 2 \sin^2(x/2)$. Then the given equation is equivalent to

$$1 - 2 \sin^2\frac{x}{2} - \sin \frac{x}{2} = 1.$$

Simplifying and factoring, we get

$$\left(\sin \frac{x}{2}\right)\left(2 \sin \frac{x}{2} + 1\right) = 0.$$

That is,

$$\sin \frac{x}{2} = 0 \qquad \text{or} \qquad \sin \frac{x}{2} = -\frac{1}{2}.$$

From $\sin (x/2) = 0$ we get $x/2 = 0°$ as the only solution that gives x in the interval $-180° \le x \le 180°$. Thus $x = 0°$. From $\sin (x/2) = -\frac{1}{2}$, we see that angle $x/2$ is in the third or fourth quadrant, and so the only angle that gives x in the interval $-180° \le x \le 180°$, is $x/2 = -30°$. That is, $x = -60°$. Therefore, the solution set is $\{0°, -60°\}$. $\qquad \blacksquare$

⚠️ Find the solution set for $\sin 3x - \sin x = 0$, where the replacement set is $\{x \mid 0 \le x \le \pi\}$.

Solution. In problems involving equations of the type $f(x) = 0$, we attempt to express $f(x)$ as a product (that is, to factor $f(x)$). We begin with identities I.12 and I.13:

$$\sin(\alpha + \beta) = \sin \alpha \cos \beta + \cos \alpha \sin \beta,$$

$$\sin(\alpha - \beta) = \sin \alpha \cos \beta - \cos \alpha \sin \beta.$$

Subtracting these two, we get the identity

$$\sin(\alpha + \beta) - \sin(\alpha - \beta) = 2 \cos \alpha \sin \beta.$$

To make this fit our problem, let $\alpha + \beta = 3x$ and $\alpha - \beta = x$. Solving for α and β, we get $\alpha = 2x$ and $\beta = x$. Thus we have the identity

$$\sin 3x - \sin x = 2 \cos 2x \sin x.$$

That is, we have factored the left-hand side of the given equation and so we have $2 \cos 2x \sin x = 0$. This is equivalent to $\cos 2x = 0$ or $\sin x = 0$. Solutions of these equations that are in the replacement set are: $x = \pi/4$ or $3\pi/4$ for $\cos 2x = 0$, and $x = 0$ or π for $\sin x = 0$. Therefore the solution set is $\{0, \pi/4, 3\pi/4, \pi\}$.   ∎

△4   Find the solution set for the equation

$$\cos^3 x + \sin^2 x \cos x - \cos x = 0, \quad \text{where } 0 \leq x \leq 2\pi.$$

Solution. The given equation is equivalent to each of the following:

$$\cos x(\cos^2 x + \sin^2 x) - \cos x = 0,$$
$$\cos x - \cos x = 0.$$

In this form we have an equation that is satisfied by all values of x. Therefore the solution set is equal to the replacement set $\{x \mid 0 \leq x \leq 2\pi\}$. Thus the given equation is an identity.   ∎

△5   Find the solution set for the equation

$$(1 - \tan^2 x)\csc x \tan 2x - 4 \cos x = 0, \quad \text{where } 0 \leq x \leq 2\pi.$$

Solution. Using identity I.20 of Section 4.4, we can replace $\tan 2x$ by $2 \tan x/(1 - \tan^2 x)$ and transform the given equation into

$$2 \csc x \tan x - 4 \cos x = 0.$$

In the process, we cancelled $1 - \tan^2 x$, and so the resulting equation may not be equivalent to the given equation; we may have introduced extraneous values that might be roots of the second equation but not of the first. Therefore, it will be necessary to check the final answers.

Replacing $\csc x$ by $1/\sin x$ and $\tan x$ by $\sin x/\cos x$, we get

$$\frac{2}{\cos x} - 4 \cos x = 0.$$

This can be written as $\cos^2 x = \frac{1}{2}$ or $\cos x = \pm 1/\sqrt{2}$. Therefore, the possible solutions of the given equation are:

$$x = \frac{\pi}{4}, \qquad x = \frac{3\pi}{4}, \qquad x = \frac{5\pi}{4}, \qquad x = \frac{7\pi}{4}.$$

If we check each one of these in the original equation, we see that none is a solution. Therefore, the solution set is the empty set. Check to see that the expression involved in cancellation, $1 - \tan^2 x$, is equal to zero for each of these values of x.   ∎

EXERCISE 6.6

In Problems 1 through 5, assume that the replacement set is $\{x \mid 0° \le x \le 360°\}$. Find the solution sets for the given equations. Provide answers in exact form. Check for possible extraneous solutions when necessary.

1. $2(\sin x - \cos x)^2 = 1$ **2.** $\sin 2x - 2 \cos x = 0$ **3.** $\sin x - \cos \frac{x}{2} = 0$

4. $\sin 3x + \sin x = 0$ **5.** $\cos 3x - \cos x = 0$

In Problems 6 through 16, use the replacement set $\{x \mid 0 \le x \le 2\pi\}$. Find the solution sets of the given equations. Express answers in exact form if it is reasonable to do so; otherwise, give answers to two decimal places.

6. $4(\sin x + \cos x)^2 = 3$ **7.** $\cos x \tan x + \sin 2x = 0$

8. $\cos^3 x + \sin^2 x \cos x + 3 \cos x + 1 = 0$ **9.** $\cos x + \cos x \tan^2 x - 2 \sin x = 0$

10. $\sin^2 \frac{x}{2} + 2 \cos x = 1$ **11.** $\tan x + \cot x = 3$

12. $\cos 3x + \cos x = 0$ **13.** $\cos x + \sin \frac{x}{2} = 1$

14. $\sin x \cot x - \cos 2x = 0$ **15.** $2 \sin^2 x = \cos^2 x$

16. $\sin^3 x + \sin x \cos^2 x - \sin x = 0$

REVIEW EXERCISE

In Problems 1 through 45, find all values of x that satisfy the given equations and $0 \le x \le 2\pi$. Express answers in exact form whenever it is reasonable to do so; otherwise, give answers correct to three decimal places. Check answers when there is a possibility that extraneous solutions may have been introduced.

1. $2 \cos x - 1 = 0$ **2.** $2 \sin x + \sqrt{3} = 0$

3. $2 \sin \frac{x}{2} + 1 = 0$ **4.** $1 + \sqrt{3} \tan x = 0$

5. $3 \sin x - 4 \cos x = 0$ **6.** $2 \tan x - 5 \cot x = 0$

7. $6 \sin^2 x + 5 \sin x - 4 = 0$ **8.** $\sin^2 x + 2 \cos^2 x = 2$

9. $3 \sin x - 4 \cos x = 5$ **10.** $1 - \tan^2 x = 4$

11. $2 \cos^2 x - 3 \cos x = 0$ **12.** $2 \sin x + \cos x + \sqrt{5} = 0$

13. $\sin^2 x - 2 \sin x + 3 = 0$ **14.** $\sin^2 x - \cos^2 x + 1 = 0$

15. $3 \cos^2 x + \cos x - 1 = 0$ **16.** $2 \sin x = \sqrt{3} \sin x + 1$

17. $2 \sin^2 \frac{x}{2} + \cos x - 1 = 0$ **18.** $\sin 2x = 2 \sin x$

19. $\cos 2x = 2 \cos x$

20. $\sin\left(\frac{\pi}{2} + x\right) = \sin x$

21. $\tan\left(\frac{3\pi}{2} - x\right) = \tan(-x)$

22. $\cos^2 x - \sin 2x = 0$

23. $\sin^2 x - \cos^2 x = 0$

24. $\sin(\text{Sin}^{-1}x) = 1$

25. $\sin(\text{Sin}^{-1}x) = x$

26. $\text{Sin}^{-1}(\sin x) = x$

27. $3 \text{ Cos}^{-1}x + 2 = 0$

28. $2 \cos 2x + 1 = 0$

29. $\sin\left(\frac{3\pi}{2} + x\right) + \cos x = 0$

30. $\tan(\pi + x) - \sin x = 0$

31. $\sqrt{3} \sin x - 2 = 0$

32. $\tan^2 x - \sqrt{3} \tan x = 0$

33. $3 \cos x - x = 0$

34. $1 + \sin x = x$

35. $\cos x = x - 1$

36. $\sin^2 2x - 4 \sin x \cos x + 1 = 0$

37. $2 \sin^2 \frac{x}{2} = 1 + \cos x$

38. $1.42 \sin^2 x - \sin x = 0$

39. $3.42 \cos^2 2x - \cos x = 0$

40. $2 \sin^4 x - 2 \cos^4 x + 1 = 0$

41. $\sin^2 x = 2 - \cos^2 x$

42. $1 + \text{Cos}^{-1}x = 0$

43. $1 + \text{Sin}^{-1}x = 0$

44. $\sin x \tan x + \cos x = 1$

45. $\cos x \tan x + \sin x = 1$

In Problems 46 through 50, find all values of x that satisfy the given inequality.

46. $\text{Tan}^{-1}x \geq 1$

47. $2 \text{ Sin}^{-1}x \leq 1$

48. $\tan x \geq 1$ and $-\pi < x < \pi$

49. $1 + \cos x \leq 0$

50. $2 \text{ Cos}^{-1}x \geq 1$

CHAPTER SEVEN

GRAPHS OF TRIGONOMETRIC FUNCTIONS

7.1 GRAPHS OF GENERAL SINE AND COSINE FUNCTIONS

In Section 2.7 we discussed graphs of the six basic trigonometric functions. We saw that the sine and cosine functions have period 2π. Thus, in graphing $y = \sin x$ or $y = \cos x$, it is sufficient to draw the graph for the interval $0 \leq x \leq 2\pi$, and the remainder of the graph will be a cyclic repetition of that portion.

In applications, one frequently encounters the problem of graphing more general functions, such as

$$y = 3 \sin\left(2x - \frac{\pi}{4}\right) \qquad \text{or} \qquad y = -2 \cos\left(\pi x + \frac{\pi}{2}\right).$$

These are particular examples of a general class of functions described by the equations

$$\boxed{\begin{aligned} y &= a \sin(bx + c), \\ y &= a \cos(bx + c), \end{aligned}} \qquad (7.1)$$

where a, b, and c are called *parameters;* that is, they are given real numbers in any particular case. We make the obvious exceptions that $a \neq 0$ and $b \neq 0$.

In this section we are interested in exploring the graphs of the functions described by Eqs. (7.1). We shall do this by considering a sequence of special cases to determine the role played by each of the parameters in the process of drawing such graphs.

1. Functions of the Form $y = a \sin x$

We first consider three particular examples and from these we shall make some general observations concerning the role of parameter a.

Examples

⚠ Draw the graph of $y = 3 \sin x$.

Solution. In order to discuss the graph of $y = 3 \sin x$, we first draw the graph of $y = \sin x$ shown by the broken curve in Fig. 7.1 (see Section 2.7).

It is clear that for a given value of x, the value of y in $y = 3 \sin x$ is three times the corresponding value of y in $y = \sin x$. Thus we get the solid curve shown in Fig. 7.1.

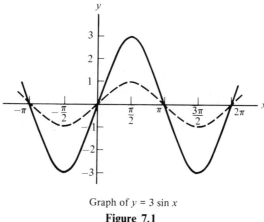

Graph of $y = 3 \sin x$

Figure 7.1

⚠ Draw the graphs of $y = \frac{1}{2} \sin x$ and $y = -2 \sin x$.

Solution. To draw the graphs of these two equations, we can follow a pattern similar to that used in the preceding example. They are shown in Figs. 7.2 and 7.3, where again the broken curve represents $y = \sin x$ and the solid curve corresponds to the given equation. *Note.* For $y = -2 \sin x$, the values of y are

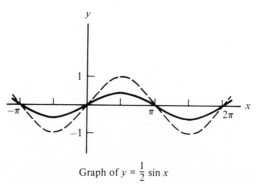

Graph of $y = \frac{1}{2} \sin x$

Figure 7.2

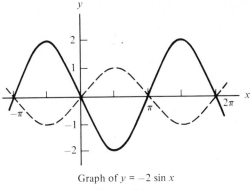

Graph of $y = -2 \sin x$

Figure 7.3

obtained from the corresponding values of $y = \sin x$ by multiplying them by -2. The negative sign has the effect of reflecting the $y = 2 \sin x$ curve about the x-axis.   ∎

In these examples we make the following observations: Each curve is periodic and has the same period of 2π as $y = \sin x$. Each curve oscillates about the x-axis in a similar fashion reaching its highest and lowest points at fixed distances from the x-axis. We describe this feature by introducing the word *amplitude* to represent the maximum distance of the curve from the axis about which it oscillates. We say that the amplitudes of $y = \sin x$, $y = 3 \sin x$, $y = \frac{1}{2} \sin x$, and $y = -2 \sin x$ are 1, 3, $\frac{1}{2}$, and 2, respectively.

The properties observed in the above examples hold for all equations of the type $y = a \sin x$. That is, the graph of $y = a \sin x$ oscillates about the x-axis with a period of 2π and an *amplitude* of $|a|$. Thus the parameter a determines the amplitude.

2. Functions of the Form $y = \sin bx$

Again we consider special cases that will give us some insight into the role of parameter b.

Examples

△1 Graph of $y = \sin 2x$.

We first recall that $\sin(\theta + 2\pi) = \sin \theta$ for every value of θ. If we replace θ by $2x$, we have $\sin(2x + 2\pi) = \sin 2x$. That is, $\sin(2(x + \pi)) = \sin 2x$ for each value of x. This means that the curve $y = \sin 2x$ will repeat itself every π units on the x-axis. Therefore, it is sufficient to draw the graph for the interval $0 \le x \le \pi$ and the remainder of the curve will be a cyclic repetition of this portion. We can get a reasonably accurate graph by using the equally spaced values of x, as given in the accompanying table:

x	0	$\dfrac{\pi}{8}$	$\dfrac{\pi}{4}$	$\dfrac{3\pi}{8}$	$\dfrac{\pi}{2}$	$\dfrac{5\pi}{8}$	$\dfrac{3\pi}{4}$	$\dfrac{7\pi}{8}$	π
y	0	$\dfrac{\sqrt{2}}{2}$	1	$\dfrac{\sqrt{2}}{2}$	0	$-\dfrac{\sqrt{2}}{2}$	-1	$-\dfrac{\sqrt{2}}{2}$	0

These are plotted in Fig. 7.4, and the graph of $y = \sin 2x$ is drawn.

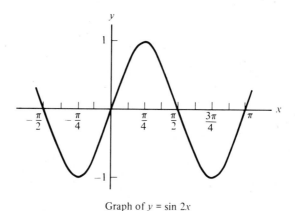

Graph of $y = \sin 2x$

Figure 7.4

We see that the graph of $y = \sin 2x$ is equivalent to the graph of $y = \sin \theta$, where $\theta = 2x$. That is, the graph of $y = \sin 2x$ is a sine curve with period π and amplitude 1. ∎

② Graph of $y = \sin(-3x)$.

We first use identity I.4 of Section 4.1, which allows us to replace $\sin(-3x)$ by $-\sin 3x$, and so our equation is equivalent to

$$y = -\sin 3x.$$

Next we observe that

$$\sin 3\left(x + \frac{2\pi}{3}\right) = \sin(3x + 2\pi) = \sin 3x$$

for each value of x. This means that the curve $y = -\sin 3x$ will repeat itself on consecutive intervals of $2\pi/3$ units on the x-axis. Therefore, it is sufficient to draw the graph for the interval $0 \le x \le 2\pi/3$. We use the set of points given in the accompanying table to draw the graph shown in Fig. 7.5:

x	0	$\dfrac{\pi}{12}$	$\dfrac{\pi}{6}$	$\dfrac{\pi}{4}$	$\dfrac{\pi}{3}$	$\dfrac{5\pi}{12}$	$\dfrac{\pi}{2}$	$\dfrac{7\pi}{12}$	$\dfrac{2\pi}{3}$
y	0	$-\dfrac{\sqrt{2}}{2}$	-1	$-\dfrac{\sqrt{2}}{2}$	0	$\dfrac{\sqrt{2}}{2}$	1	$\dfrac{\sqrt{2}}{2}$	0

Thus the graph of $y = \sin(-3x)$ is a sine curve with amplitude 1 and period $2\pi/3$.

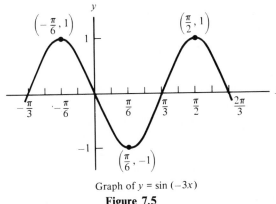

Graph of $y = \sin(-3x)$

Figure 7.5

From the above two examples we can draw the following conclusions concerning the general case. The graph of $y = \sin bx$ is a sine curve with period $2\pi/|b|$ and amplitude 1. Thus parameter b determines the period of the function described by $y = \sin bx$.

3. Functions of the Form $y = \sin(bx + c)$.

We consider two examples from which we shall get some insight concerning the role of parameter c.

Examples

⚠ Graph of $y = \sin\!\left(x + \dfrac{\pi}{4}\right)$.

Suppose $\theta = x + \pi/4$; first draw the graph of $y = \sin\theta$. This is a standard sine curve with period 2π and amplitude 1, as shown in Fig. 7.6(a). We can now use this curve to draw the graph of $y = \sin(x + \pi/4)$ by noting that for each point (θ, y) on the $y = \sin\theta$ curve, we have a corresponding point

$(x, y) = (\theta - \pi/4, y)$ on the graph of $y = \sin(x + \pi/4)$. That is,

$$y = \sin\left(x + \frac{\pi}{4}\right) = \sin\left(\left(\theta - \frac{\pi}{4}\right) + \frac{\pi}{4}\right) = \sin\theta.$$

This is shown in the accompanying table, which gives the value of y for each of the corresponding values of θ and x:

θ	0	$\dfrac{\pi}{4}$	$\dfrac{\pi}{2}$	$\dfrac{3\pi}{4}$	π	$\dfrac{5\pi}{4}$	$\dfrac{3\pi}{2}$	$\dfrac{7\pi}{4}$	2π
x	$-\dfrac{\pi}{4}$	0	$\dfrac{\pi}{4}$	$\dfrac{\pi}{2}$	$\dfrac{3\pi}{4}$	π	$\dfrac{5\pi}{4}$	$\dfrac{3\pi}{2}$	$\dfrac{7\pi}{4}$
y	0	$\dfrac{\sqrt{2}}{2}$	1	$\dfrac{\sqrt{2}}{2}$	0	$-\dfrac{\sqrt{2}}{2}$	-1	$-\dfrac{\sqrt{2}}{2}$	0

We can now plot the (x, y) points from this table and draw the graph of $y = \sin(x + \pi/4)$ as shown in Fig. 7.6(b). The solid portions of the curves shown in Fig. 7.6 correspond to the points given in the table.

We observe that in this example we can draw the graph of $y = \sin(x + \pi/4)$ by taking the standard sine curve $y = \sin x$ and moving it $\pi/4$ units horizontally to the left. This type of horizontal translation of the standard curve is called a *phase shift*. We say that the graph of $y = \sin(x + \pi/4)$ has a phase shift of $\pi/4$ units to the left.

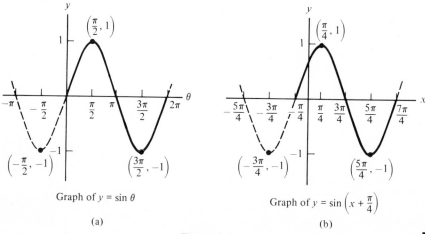

Graph of $y = \sin\theta$

(a)

Graph of $y = \sin\left(x + \dfrac{\pi}{4}\right)$

(b)

Figure 7.6

<u>2</u>   Graph of $y = \sin(2x - \pi)$.

We first write the equation in the form $y = \sin 2(x - \pi/2)$ and then assume $\theta = x - \pi/2$. From our observations concerning Fig. 7.6(b), we conclude that the graph of $y = \sin 2\theta$ is a sine curve of period $2\pi/2 = \pi$ and amplitude 1; it is shown in Fig. 7.7(a). Following a procedure similar to that of the preceding example, we can draw the graph of $y = \sin 2(x - \pi/2)$ as shown in Fig. 7.7(b). The solid parts of the curves in Fig. 7.7 correspond to the points given in the table:

θ	0	$\dfrac{\pi}{8}$	$\dfrac{\pi}{4}$	$\dfrac{3\pi}{8}$	$\dfrac{\pi}{2}$	$\dfrac{5\pi}{8}$	$\dfrac{3\pi}{4}$	$\dfrac{7\pi}{8}$	π
x	$\dfrac{\pi}{2}$	$\dfrac{5\pi}{8}$	$\dfrac{3\pi}{4}$	$\dfrac{7\pi}{8}$	π	$\dfrac{9\pi}{8}$	$\dfrac{5\pi}{4}$	$\dfrac{11\pi}{8}$	$\dfrac{3\pi}{2}$
y	0	$\dfrac{\sqrt{2}}{2}$	1	$\dfrac{\sqrt{2}}{2}$	0	$-\dfrac{\sqrt{2}}{2}$	-1	$-\dfrac{\sqrt{2}}{2}$	0

We note that the graph of $y = \sin(2x - \pi) = \sin 2(x - \pi/2)$ is a sine curve with period π and phase shift $\pi/2$ to the right.

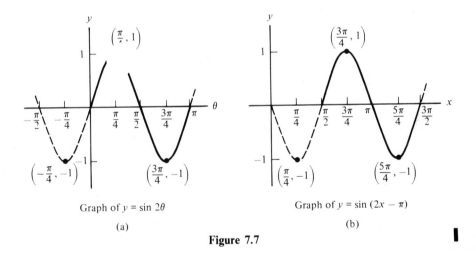

Graph of $y = \sin 2\theta$

(a)

Graph of $y = \sin (2x - \pi)$

(b)

Figure 7.7

From the preceding two examples we conclude the following: The graph of $y = \sin(bx + c)$ is a sine curve with period $2\pi/|b|$, amplitude 1, and phase shift $|c/b|$. Thus the parameter c (along with b) determines the magnitude of the phase shift.

If the sine function were replaced by the cosine function in each of the above cases, we would arrive at similar conclusions. We are now in a position to summarize the properties of graphs of the general sine and cosine curves $y = a \sin(bx + c)$ and $y = a \cos(bx + c)$.

A. The graph of $y = a \sin(bx + c)$ is a sine curve with period $2\pi/|b|$, amplitude $|a|$, and phase shift $|c/b|$ (that is, the curve $y = a \sin bx$ is moved $|c/b|$ units to the right if $c/b < 0$, and to the left if $c/b > 0$).

B. The graph of $y = a \cos(bx + c)$ is a cosine curve with period $2\pi/|b|$, amplitude $|a|$, and phase shift $|c/b|$.

Example

a) Draw the graph of $y = -4 \sin(\pi/2 - 2x)$.

b) Find the domain and range of the function defined by
$$f(x) = -4 \sin\left(\frac{\pi}{2} - 2x\right).$$

Solution.

a) We first write the given equation as $y = -4 \sin[-2(x - \pi/4)]$ and then use identity (I.4) of Section 4.1, that is, $\sin(-\theta) = -\sin \theta$; we get

$$y = 4 \sin 2\left(x - \frac{\pi}{4}\right).$$

This equation is equivalent to the given equation and this is the form we use to draw the graph. From (A) we see that the graph is a sine curve with period $2\pi/2 = \pi$, amplitude 4, and phase shift $\pi/4$. Thus, we first draw the graph of $y = 4 \sin 2x$ (the broken curve shown in Fig. 7.8) and translate it $\pi/4$ units to the right to get the curve we want (shown as the solid curve).

As a check we suggest locating a few "key points" on our graph by finding pairs of numbers (x, y) that satisfy the given equation. Such points are the

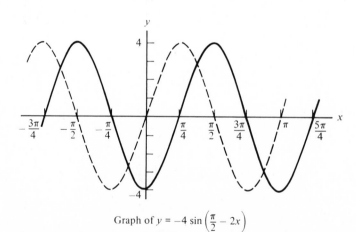

Graph of $y = -4 \sin\left(\frac{\pi}{2} - 2x\right)$

Figure 7.8

x-intercepts given by $y = 0$, that is, $\sin(\pi/2 - 2x) = 0$, and the highest or lowest points given by $y = \pm 4$, that is, $\sin(\pi/2 - 2x) = \pm 1$. These are given in the following table and we see that they are points on the solid curve of Fig. 7.8:

x	$\dfrac{\pi}{4}$	$\dfrac{\pi}{2}$	$\dfrac{3\pi}{4}$	π	$\dfrac{5\pi}{4}$
y	0	4	0	-4	0

Note. Since $\sin(\pi/2 - 2x) = \cos 2x$ is an identity, we could have written the given equation as $y = -4 \cos 2x$ and used this equation to draw the graph.

  b) From the graph in Fig. 7.8 we see that

$$D(f) = \{x \mid x \text{ is any real number}\},$$
$$R(f) = \{y \mid -4 \le y \le 4\}.$$ ∎

EXERCISE 7.1

In the following problems, give the period and amplitude of the functions defined by the given equations. Then draw a graph of one complete cycle of the curve.

1. $y = 2 \sin x$

2. $y = -3 \sin x$

3. $y = -4 \cos x$

4. $y = 2 \cos x$

5. $y = \dfrac{1}{2} \sin x$

6. $y = \dfrac{2}{3} \cos x$

7. $y = \sin 3x$

8. $y = \sin \dfrac{x}{2}$

9. $y = -2 \cos 3x$

10. $y = 3 \sin(-2x)$

11. $y = -4 \sin(-x)$

12. $y = 3 \sin(\pi x)$

13. $y = -3 \cos\left(\dfrac{\pi}{2} x\right)$

14. $y = \sin(-3\pi x)$

15. $y = -2 \cos(-\pi x)$

16. $y = -2 \sin 4x$

17. $y = \sin\left(x + \dfrac{\pi}{2}\right)$

18. $y = \sin(2x + \pi)$

19. $y = \cos(3x - \pi)$

20. $y = -\cos(\pi - 2x)$

21. $y = 4 \sin(3x - \pi)$

22. $y = -3 \sin(\pi - 2x)$

23. $y = 2 \sin\left(2x + \dfrac{\pi}{2}\right)$

24. $y = \dfrac{3}{2} \cos\left(-3x + \dfrac{3\pi}{2}\right)$

25. $y = -3 \sin(2\pi x + \pi)$

26. $y = \dfrac{1}{2} \sin\left(\dfrac{\pi}{2} - \pi x\right)$

27. $y = -3 \cos \pi(2x + 1)$

28. $y = \dfrac{1}{2} \sin \pi\left(3 - \dfrac{x}{2}\right)$

29. $y = -3 \cos\left(2\pi x - \dfrac{\pi}{2}\right)$

30. $y = \sqrt{2} \sin\left(\dfrac{x}{2} + \dfrac{\pi}{4}\right)$

7.2 GRAPHS OF TANGENT AND COTANGENT FUNCTIONS

In Section 7.1 we discussed in some detail the graphs of the sine and cosine functions. In this section we treat the tangent and cotangent functions in an analogous fashion but omit the details and merely give the following summary.

In Section 2.7 we discussed the graphs of the equations $y = \tan x$ and $y = \cot x$, and we suggest that the student review them at this point. We noted that the graph of each has a period π.

We now give a summary for the general case and then include two examples to illustrate how such graphs can be drawn.

A. The graph of $y = a \tan(bx + c)$ is a tangent curve with period $\pi/|b|$.

B. The graph of $y = a \cot(bx + c)$ is a cotangent curve with period $\pi/|b|$.

Note. There is no amplitude associated with any of these curves. Also, the phase shift of each is $|c/b|$, although it is not common practice to talk about phase shift for these curves.

Examples

⚠ Draw the graph of $y = 3 \tan(2x - \pi/2)$.

Solution. From (A) we conclude that the graph of this equation is a tangent curve with period $\pi/2$. We first locate a few key points that will allow us to draw the essential features of the graph. The tangent function has no maximum or minimum values; therefore we do not look for highest or lowest points. However, $\tan \theta$ is not defined for certain values of θ; these values determine vertical lines called *asymptotes* to the curve.*

Therefore, the key values of x that will help us draw the graph are:

a) *x-intercepts:* These are the values of x for which $\tan(2x - \pi/2) = 0$; and so $2x - \pi/2 = 0,\ \pi,\ 2\pi, \ldots,\ -\pi,\ -2\pi, \ldots$ That is, the intercepts are $x = \pi/4,\ 3\pi/4,\ 5\pi/4, \ldots,\ -\pi/4,\ -3\pi/4, \ldots$

b) *Asymptotes:* These are given by the values of x for which $\tan(2x - \pi/2)$ is not defined: that is, $2x - \pi/2 = \pi/2,\ 3\pi/2, \ldots,\ -\pi/2,\ -3\pi/2, \ldots$; and so $x = \pi/2,\ \pi, \ldots,\ 0,\ -\pi/2, \ldots$

We include these key values of x along with a few intermediate values in the following table. Since the curve has a period $\pi/2$, the table includes intermediate values only in the interval $0 < x < \pi/2$ (the U indicates that the y-value is undefined):

x	$-\dfrac{\pi}{2}$	$-\dfrac{\pi}{4}$	0	$\dfrac{\pi}{16}$	$\dfrac{\pi}{8}$	$\dfrac{3\pi}{16}$	$\dfrac{\pi}{4}$	$\dfrac{5\pi}{16}$	$\dfrac{3\pi}{8}$	$\dfrac{7\pi}{16}$	$\dfrac{\pi}{2}$	$\dfrac{3\pi}{4}$	π
y	U	0	U	−7.24	−3	−1.24	0	1.24	3	7.24	U	0	U

---

* We say that a line is an asymptote to a curve if its points get closer and closer to the points of the curve. For example, from Fig. 7.9 we see that the line $x = \pi/2$ is an asymptote to the given curve. Similarly, $x = 3\pi/2,\ x = 5\pi/2, \ldots,\ x = 0,\ x = -\pi/2, \ldots$ are all asymptotes to the given curve.

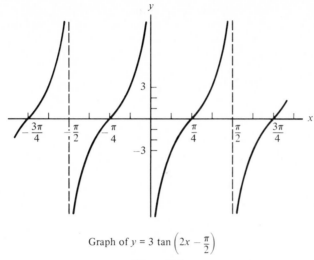

Graph of $y = 3 \tan\left(2x - \dfrac{\pi}{2}\right)$

Figure 7.9

We now plot these points and draw the graph shown in Fig. 7.9.
Note. Since $\tan(2x - \pi/2) = -\cot 2x$ is an identity, then the given equation is equivalent to $y = -3 \cot 2x$ and we could have used this equation to draw the graph. ∎

△2 Draw a graph of $y = 2 \cot\left(\dfrac{x}{2}\right)$.

Solution. Following a pattern similar to that of the previous example, we first locate some key points.

a) *x-intercepts:* These are the values of x for which $\cot (x/2) = 0$; that is, $x/2 = \pi/2, 3\pi/2, \ldots, -\pi/2, -3\pi/2, \ldots$ Thus $x = \pi, 3\pi, \ldots, -\pi, -3\pi, \ldots$

b) *Asymptotes:* These are given by values for x for which $\cot (x/2)$ is undefined; that is, $x/2 = 0, \pi, 2\pi, \ldots, -\pi, -2\pi, \ldots$ Thus $x = 0, 2\pi, 4\pi, \ldots,$ $-2\pi, -4\pi, \ldots$

From (B) we find that our curve is a cotangent curve with period $\pi \div \frac{1}{2} = 2\pi$. Next we make a table of (x, y) values that includes key points and some intermediate points for $0 < x < 2\pi$. Then these are plotted and the curve is drawn, as shown in Fig. 7.10 (here again, U indicates that the y-value is undefined):

x	-2π	$-\pi$	0	$\dfrac{\pi}{4}$	$\dfrac{\pi}{2}$	$\dfrac{3\pi}{4}$	π	$\dfrac{5\pi}{4}$	$\dfrac{3\pi}{2}$	$\dfrac{7\pi}{4}$	2π	3π	4π
y	U	0	U	4.83	2	0.83	0	-0.83	-2	-4.83	U	0	U

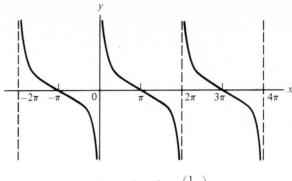

Graph of $y = 2 \cot \left(\frac{1}{2} x \right)$

Figure 7.10

EXERCISE 7.2

In the following problems: a) determine the period of the given function; b) make a table of x, y values of the function using selected key values of x; c) draw a graph of the given function.

1. $y = 3 \tan x$ 　　　　　　 2. $y = -3 \tan 2x$ 　　　　　　 3. $y = -2 \cot x$

4. $y = 3 \cot \frac{x}{2}$ 　　　　　 5. $y = 2 \tan\left(-\frac{x}{2}\right)$ 　　　　 6. $y = -3 \tan\left(\frac{\pi}{2} x\right)$

7. $y = -4 \tan\left(2x + \frac{\pi}{2}\right)$ 　　　　　　　　 8. $y = -3 \cot\left(2x - \frac{\pi}{2}\right)$

9. $y = 2 \tan\left(\pi x - \frac{\pi}{2}\right)$ 　　　　　　　 10. $y = \frac{1}{2} \cot\left(\frac{\pi}{2} x - \pi\right)$

11. $y = \sqrt{3} \tan \pi\left(x + \frac{3}{2}\right)$ 　　　　　　 12. $y = 3 \tan\left(2x + 1\right)$

7.3 GRAPHS OF SECANT AND COSECANT FUNCTIONS

In this section we consider the graphs of functions of the type described by $y = a \sec (bx + c)$ and $y = a \csc (bx + c)$. The graphs of $y = \sec x$ and $y = \csc x$ were discussed in Section 2.7; we suggest that the student review them at this point. Repeating the pattern of Section 7.2, we state the following conclusions:

A. The graph of $y = a \sec(bx + c)$ is a secant curve with period $2\pi / |b|$.

B. The graph of $y = a \csc(bx + c)$ is a cosecant curve with period $2\pi / |b|$.

Note. We do not associate amplitude with these curves. Also in each case we can use $|c/b|$ to describe a horizontal translation of a secant or cosecant curve, but it is not common practice to talk about phase shift for these curves.

Examples

 a) Draw a graph of $y = 2 \sec(\pi x - \pi/2)$.

b) Determine the domain and range of the function described by

$$f(x) = 2 \sec(\pi x - \pi/2).$$

Solution.

a) The graph of this equation is a secant curve with period $2\pi/\pi = 2$. Therefore, it is sufficient to draw the graph corresponding to the interval $0 \leq x \leq 2$. We first determine some key values of x that will give the essential features of the graph, that is, the x-values for which $\sec(\pi x - \pi/2) = \pm 1$ or is undefined (U). We include these and a few intermediate values in the following table:

x	0	$\frac{1}{4}$	$\frac{1}{2}$	$\frac{3}{4}$	1	$\frac{5}{4}$	$\frac{3}{2}$	$\frac{7}{4}$	2
y	U	$2\sqrt{2}$	2	$2\sqrt{2}$	U	$-2\sqrt{2}$	-2	$-2\sqrt{2}$	U

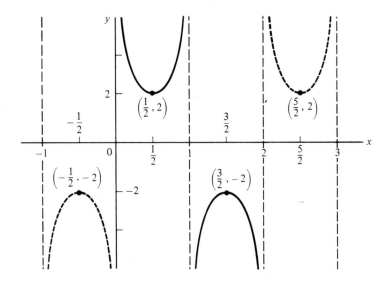

Graph of $y = 2 \sec\left(\pi x - \frac{\pi}{2}\right)$

Figure 7.11

It is clear that for each x, the corresponding value of y is the sum of y_1 and y_2 for that value of x. And so we geometrically add the corresponding ordinates of C_1 and C_2 to get the ordinates of the graph for the given equation. This is illustrated in Fig. 7.13 for $x = x_0$; the corresponding value of $y = y_0$ is obtained by adding a and b. We also make an observation concerning the key points labeled A, B, C, D, and E in Fig. 7.13. If we take the values $x = -\pi$, $\quad$ 0, π, $\quad 2\pi$, $\quad 3\pi$, then in each case the corresponding value of $y_2 = \sin x$ is zero, so the value of y is $y_1 = x/3$. Thus the curve passes through points on the line $y_1 = x/3$ given by $(k\pi, k\pi/3)$, where k is any integer. That is, the graph of $y = x/3 + \sin x$ is a curve winding around the line $y = x/3$, as shown in Fig. 7.13. $\blacksquare$

3. *Multiplying ordinates.* Draw the graph of $y = x \cos x$.

Solution. In a manner similar to that of Example 2 we first draw the graphs of $y_1 = x$ and $y_2 = \cos x$ on the same system of coordinates, as shown by the broken curves in Fig. 7.14.

We see that for each x, the corresponding value of y is the product of y_1 and y_2 for that value of x. We can locate some key points on the curve by noting that:

1. Whenever the curve $y_2 = \cos x$ crosses the x-axis, the corresponding value of y_2 is zero; therefore $y = y_1 \cdot y_2 = 0$. Thus points given by $x = (2k - 1)\pi/2$ (where k is any integer) and $y = 0$ will be on the desired curve, as shown in Fig. 7.14.

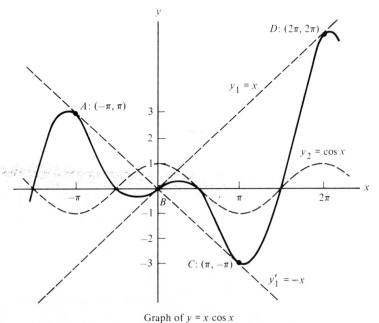

Graph of $y = x \cos x$

Figure 7.14

2. For values of x such as $-\pi$, 0, π, 2π, the corresponding values of $y_2 = \cos x$ are 1 or -1, and so the corresponding points on our curve will be on the line $y_1 = x$ or $y'_1 = -x$. These points are indicated by A, B, C, D in Fig. 7.14. Thus the graph of the given equation oscillates between the lines $y_1 = x$ and $y'_1 = -x$, as shown in Fig. 7.14.

EXERCISE 7.4

In the following problems, draw the graph of the given equation.

1. $y = 1 + \sin x$ 2. $y = 2 - \cos x$ 3. $y = \frac{x}{2} + 2 \sin x$

4. $y = 2x + \sin x$ 5. $y = 2x + \cos x$ 6. $y = x - 2 \cos x$

7. $y = \sin x - 1$ 8. $y = 2 \cos x - 3$ 9. $y = x \sin x$

10. $y = 2x \cos x$ 11. $y = -x \cos 2x$ 12. $y = x \sin(-2x)$

13. $y = \sqrt{x} \sin x$ 14. $y = \sqrt{x} + \sin x$ 15. $y = \sqrt{x} + \sin(-x)$

16. $y = \sqrt{x} \cdot \cos 2x$

7.5 THE USE OF IDENTITIES IN GRAPHING

There have been several instances in this textbook where our approach to solving problems involved a sequence of steps in which the given problem was transformed into an equivalent one with a known solution. In this section we discuss the problems of drawing graphs of equations in which trigonometric identities are used to transform the given equation to an equivalent one whose graph may be familiar to us.

Examples

⚠ Draw the graph of $y = (\sin x + \cos x)^2$.

Solution. We first write the given equation in the following equivalent forms:

$$y = \sin^2 x + 2 \sin x \cos x + \cos^2 x \quad \text{(by algebra)}$$
$$= 1 + 2 \sin x \cos x \quad \text{(by (I.9))}$$
$$= 1 + \sin 2x. \quad \text{(by (I.18))}.$$

We recognize the final form as an equation of the type discussed in the preceding section. It is a sine curve (of period $2\pi/2 = \pi$) that winds about the line $y = 1$, as shown in Fig. 7.15. ∎

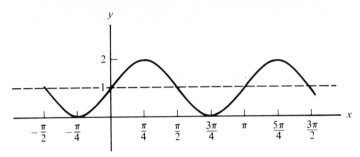

Graph of $y = (\sin x + \cos x)^2$

Figure 7.15

2. Draw the graph of $y = 3^{\cos 2x} \cdot 3^{\sin^2 x - \cos^2 x}$.

Solution. The given equation can be written in the following equivalent forms:

$$y = 3^{\cos 2x + (\sin^2 x - \cos^2 x)} \qquad \text{(by algebra)},$$
$$= 3^{\cos 2x - \cos 2x} \qquad \text{(by (I.19))}.$$

Therefore, the given equation is equivalent to $y = 3^0 = 1$ and its graph is the line $y = 1$, as shown in Fig. 7.16.

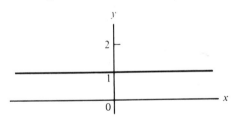

Graph of $y = 3^{\cos 2x} \cdot 3^{(\sin^2 x - \cos^2 x)}$

Figure 7.16

3. Draw the graph of $y = \sin x + \sqrt{3} \cos x$.

Solution. In this problem we follow a procedure similar to that used in Section 6.3. That is, we factor from the right-hand side,

$$\sqrt{1^2 + (\sqrt{3})^2} = \sqrt{4} = 2.$$

and so

$$y = 2\left(\frac{1}{2} \sin x + \frac{\sqrt{3}}{2} \cos x\right).$$

We now replace $1/2$ by $\cos(\pi/3)$ and $\sqrt{3}/2$ by $\sin(\pi/3)$ and get

$$y = 2(\sin x \cos \frac{\pi}{3} + \cos x \sin \frac{\pi}{3}).$$

By identity (I.12) we have

$$y = 2 \sin\left(x + \frac{\pi}{3}\right).$$

We recognize this as a type of equation discussed in Section 7.1. Thus the graph of the given equation is a sine curve with period 2π, amplitude 2, and phase shift $\pi/3$. This is shown in Fig. 7.17.

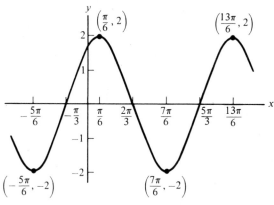

Graph of $y = \sin x + \sqrt{3} \cos x$

Figure 7.17

$\blacksquare$

$\boxed{4}$ Draw the graph of $y = \cot\left(\mathrm{Cos}^{-1} \dfrac{x}{\sqrt{1 + x^2}}\right)$.

Solution. Let

$$\theta = \mathrm{Cos}^{-1} \frac{x}{\sqrt{1 + x^2}}, \qquad \text{then} \qquad \cos\theta = \frac{x}{\sqrt{1 + x^2}}.$$

Since Cos^{-1} is the principal-value inverse cosine function, the angle θ must lie within $0 \le \theta \le \pi$; so we draw θ in the first quadrant (if $x > 0$) or in the second quadrant (if $x < 0$) (see Fig. 7.18). In either case, $\cot\theta = x$; therefore the given equation is equivalent to $y = x$. Thus the graph is the straight line shown in Fig. 7.19.

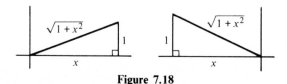

Figure 7.18

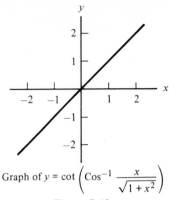

Graph of $y = \cot\left(\cos^{-1}\dfrac{x}{\sqrt{1+x^2}}\right)$

Figure 7.19

EXERCISE 7.5

In the following problems: a) determine the domain of the given function; b) draw a graph; c) state the range of the function.

1. $y = (\cos x - \sin x)^2$

2. $y = \cos^4 x - \sin^4 x$

3. $y = 2 \cos x \tan x$

4. $y = \sin x \cos x$

5. $y = 2 \sin^2 x \cot x$

6. $y = \sqrt{3} \sin x - \cos x$

7. $y = \sin x + \cos x$

8. $y = \sin x - \sqrt{3} \cos x$

9. $y = \cos x - \sin x$

10. $y = (1 - \tan x) \tan 2x$

11. $y = (1 - 2 \sin^2 x) \sec 2x$

12. $y = 3^{\cos^2 x} \cdot 3^{\sin^2 x}$

13. $y = \cos 2x - \sqrt{3} \sin 2x$

14. $y = \cos^2 x + \cos^2 x \tan^2 x$

15. $y = \cos(\cos^{-1}x)$

16. $y = \sin(\sin^{-1}x)$

17. $y = 4^{\sin x \cos x} \cdot 2^{-\sin 2x}$

18. $y = 2 \cos^2 \dfrac{x}{2}$

19. $y = \tan\left(\sin^{-1}\dfrac{x}{\sqrt{1+x^2}}\right)$

20. $y = \cos\left(\sin^{-1}\dfrac{\sqrt{x^2-1}}{x}\right)$

REVIEW EXERCISE

In the following problems, the given equation defines a function. a) Is this function periodic? If it is, find the period; b) state the domain of the function; c) draw a graph; d) use the graph to give the range of the function.

1. $y = 2 \cos x$

2. $y = 3 \sin(-x)$

3. $y = 1 + \tan x$

4. $y = 4 \sin 2x$

5. $y = 1 - \cos x$

6. $y = \sin\left(x + \dfrac{\pi}{3}\right)$

7. $y = 3 \cot x$

8. $y = |\sin x|$

9. $y = 6 \sin x \cos x$

10. $y = -2 \sec x$

11. $y = -2 \sin 2x$

12. $y = \cos^2 x - \sin^2 x$

13. $y = x + \cos x$

14. $y = 2x \cdot \sin x$

15. $y = \sqrt{\sin x - 1}$

16. $y = \sin x + \cos x$

17. $y = \sin 2\left(x - \dfrac{\pi}{4}\right)$

18. $y = \tan(2x + \pi)$

19. $y = \sin\left(\text{Sin}^{-1} x\right)$

20. $y = \text{Sin}^{-1}(\sin x)$

CHAPTER EIGHT

COMPLEX NUMBERS

8.1 INTRODUCTION

The system of *real numbers* is essential in the development of pure mathematics as well as applications of mathematics. However, even a simple problem, such as finding the roots of the equation $x^2 + 1 = 0$, has no solution in the set of real numbers. To remedy this, we complement real numbers by adding the so-called *imaginary numbers*. The union of the real numbers and imaginary numbers is called the set of *complex numbers*. The system of complex numbers is of great importance in physics, engineering and abstract mathematics. In this chapter we shall use trigonometric functions to aid us in dealing with complex numbers.

In algebra courses the student has studied the basic properties of real numbers relating to the four binary operations $(+, -, \times, \div)$ and to the order relations $(<)$ and $(>)$. When the imaginary numbers are introduced into the system, it is necessary to investigate the properties of addition, subtraction, multiplication, and division as they apply to complex numbers. In the system of complex numbers it is not possible to define an order relation similar to that of the real numbers; that is, we do not talk about one imaginary number being smaller or greater than the other.

In this chapter we discuss some of the elementary properties of complex numbers and focus most of our attention on operations with imaginary numbers since everything we have already learned about real numbers will still be true within the system of complex numbers.

We define imaginary numbers in terms of real numbers as follows:

If a and b are real numbers $(b \neq 0)$ and i is a new symbol defined by the property $i^2 = -1$, then $a + bi$ is called an *imaginary number*.

We call a the *real part* and b the *imaginary part* of $a + bi$. If $a = 0$, then we say that bi is a *pure imaginary number.* We write $i = \sqrt{-1}$ and apply ordinary rules of algebra in working with complex numbers. Examples of imaginary numbers are: $3 + 4i$, $5 - 2i$, $\sqrt{3} + i$, $-17i$, $-2i$, $1/\pi - ((1 + \sqrt{5})/2)i$.

We can think of the set of complex numbers as all numbers of the form $a + bi$, where a and b are any real numbers; $a + bi$ is called *standard form of a complex number.* If $b = 0$, we have real numbers, while if $b \neq 0$ we have imaginary numbers. Suppose a, b, c, d are real numbers. We state the following definitions related to two complex numbers $a + bi$ and $c + di$:

Equality: $\qquad\quad a + bi = c + di$ if and only if $a = c$ and $b = d$.

Addition: $\qquad\quad (a + bi) + (c + di) = (a + c) + (b + d)i$.

Subtraction: $\qquad (a + bi) - (c + di) = (a - c) + (b - d)i$.

Multiplication: $\quad (a + bi) \cdot (c + di) = (ac - bd) + (ad + bc)i$.

Division: $\qquad\quad (a + bi) \div (c + di) = \dfrac{ac + bd}{c^2 + d^2} + \dfrac{bc - ad}{c^2 + d^2}i,$

where c and d are not both zero.

The definitions of equality, addition, and subtraction appear to be natural, while the last two need some explanation. They can be deduced by thinking of $a + bi$ and $c + di$ as algebraic expressions and applying the familiar rules of algebra, except that we replace i^2 by -1. For example, the definition of division comes from the following:

$$\frac{a + bi}{c + di} = \frac{(a + bi)(c - di)}{(c + di)(c - di)} = \frac{ac + bci - adi - bdi^2}{c^2 - d^2i^2}$$

$$= \frac{ac + bci - adi + bd}{c^2 + d^2} = \frac{(ac + bd) + (bc - ad)i}{c^2 + d^2}$$

$$= \frac{ac + bd}{c^2 + d^2} + \frac{bc - ad}{c^2 + d^2}i.$$

Actually this is the pattern we shall use in dividing two complex numbers, rather than substituting directly into the above definition.

In the above division process the first step involved multiplication of numerator and denominator by $c - di$. We call $c - di$ the *complex conjugate* of the number $c + di$. We shall use the following notation:

> If $z = x + iy$, where x and y are real numbers, then the *conjugate of z*
> is denoted by $\bar{z}$; that is $\bar{z} = x - iy$.

1. Square Root of a Complex Number

The square root of a nonnegative real number b is defined as a number x that
satisfies $x^2 = b$. For example, for $\sqrt{4}$ we solve $x^2 = 4$; there are two numbers
($x = 2$ and $x = -2$) that satisfy this equation. We choose 2 as the principal
square root and write $\sqrt{4} = 2$. In a similar fashion we can talk about the
square root of any negative number. For example, if $\sqrt{-4} = z$,
then $z^2 = -4$. There are two complex numbers that satisfy this equation:
$z = 2i$ and $z = -2i$. We choose $z = 2i$ as the principal value and write
$\sqrt{-4} = 2i$.

   This leads us to the definition:

> The square root of a real number is given by:
> 1) if $a \geq 0$, then $\sqrt{a}$ is a nonnegative number whose square is a;
> 2) if $a < 0$, say $a = -b$, where $b > 0$, then $\sqrt{a} = \sqrt{-b} = \sqrt{b}\, i$.

   As illustrations we have: $\sqrt{9} = 3$; $\sqrt{-16} = \sqrt{16}\, i = 4i$; $\sqrt{-2} = \sqrt{2}\, i$.
   In Section 8.5 we shall describe a technique that can be used to evaluate
square roots of complex numbers. In this text we are not interested in defining
principal-value square roots of imaginary numbers; this is a topic of study in
a course on complex variables. However, as one more example we consider the
problem of expressing $\sqrt{i}$ in standard form as a complex number.

   Let $z = \sqrt{i}$ and so $z^2 = i$. Suppose $z = x + iy$, where x and y are real
numbers. We want x, y such that

$$(x + iy)^2 = i.$$

This is equivalent to

$$x^2 - y^2 + 2xyi = i.$$

From our definition of equality of two complex numbers we have

$$x^2 - y^2 = 0 \quad \text{and} \quad 2xy = 1.$$

Solving these two equations simultaneously we find $x = 1/\sqrt{2}$, $y = 1/\sqrt{2}$ or
$x = -1/\sqrt{2}$, $y = -1/\sqrt{2}$.   Thus

$$z = \frac{1}{\sqrt{2}} + \frac{1}{\sqrt{2}}i \quad \text{and} \quad z = -\frac{1}{\sqrt{2}} - \frac{1}{\sqrt{2}}i$$

are possible values of $\sqrt{i}$. We can take the first answer as the principal value and write

$$\sqrt{i} = \frac{1}{\sqrt{2}} + \frac{1}{\sqrt{2}} i.$$

2. Quadratic Formula

In algebra the student learns that if a, b, c are real numbers and $a \neq 0$, then the quadratic equation $ax^2 + bx + c = 0$ has two roots given by

$$x = \frac{-b \pm \sqrt{b^2 - 4ac}}{2a}.$$

It is possible to show that this result can be extended to allow a, b, c to be any complex numbers. If $b^2 - 4ac$ is an imaginary number, then we encounter the problem of determining the square root of such a number. We shall see how this can be done in Section 8.5.

Examples

⚠ Write the following expressions as complex numbers in standard form:
a) $(3 + 4i) + (5 - 8i)$ b) $(2 - 3i) - (-4 + i)$
c) $(3 - 4i)(2 + i)$ d) $(1 - 3i) \div (3 + 4i)$

Solution
a) $(3 + 4i) + (5 - 8i) = (3 + 5) + (4 - 8)i = 8 - 4i$
b) $(2 - 3i) - (-4 + i) = (2 + 4) + (-3 - 1)i = 6 - 4i$
c) $(3 - 4i)(2 + i) = 6 + 3i - 8i - 4i^2 = 6 - 5i + 4 = 10 - 5i$
d) $(1 - 3i) \div (3 + 4i) = \dfrac{1 - 3i}{3 + 4i} = \dfrac{(1 - 3i)(3 - 4i)}{(3 + 4i)(3 - 4i)} = \dfrac{3 - 13i + 12i^2}{9 - 16i^2}$

$$= \frac{3 - 13i - 12}{9 + 16} = \frac{-9 - 13i}{25} = -\frac{9}{25} - \frac{13}{25}i.$$ ∎

② If $f(z) = z^3 + 2z^2 - 3$, find $f(1 + i)$.

Solution
$f(1 + i) = (1 + i)^3 + 2(1 + i)^2 - 3 = 1 + 3i + 3i^2 + i^3 + 2(1 + 2i + i^2) - 3$
           $= 1 + 3i - 3 - i + 2 + 4i - 2 - 3 = -5 + 6i.$

Note that we used the familiar rules of algebra, treating i as though it were a variable and replacing i^2 by -1. ∎

③ If $z = 2 - i$, find
a) $\bar{z}$ b) $z \cdot \bar{z}$ c) $\bar{z}/z$

Solution

a) $\bar{z} = 2 + i$

b) $z \cdot \bar{z} = (2 - i)(2 + i) = 4 - i^2 = 4 + 1 = 5$

c) $\dfrac{\bar{z}}{z} = \dfrac{2 + i}{2 - i} = \dfrac{(2 + i)(2 + i)}{(2 - i)(2 + i)} = \dfrac{4 + 4i + i^2}{4 - i^2} = \dfrac{4 + 4i - 1}{4 + 1} = \dfrac{3}{5} + \dfrac{4}{5}i$ ∎

4. Find the roots of $2z^2 + 2iz - 1 = 0$.

Solution. We apply the quadratic formula and get

$$z = \frac{-2i \pm \sqrt{(2i)^2 - 4 \cdot 2 \cdot (-1)}}{2 \cdot 2} = \frac{-2i \pm \sqrt{-4 + 8}}{4} = -\frac{1}{2}i \pm \frac{1}{2}.$$

Therefore the roots are: $z = \dfrac{1}{2} - \dfrac{1}{2}i$ and $z = -\dfrac{1}{2} - \dfrac{1}{2}i.$ ∎

5. Evaluate $(2 + \sqrt{-3})(2 - \sqrt{-3})$.

Solution

$$(2 + \sqrt{-3})(2 - \sqrt{-3}) = (2 + \sqrt{3}\, i)(2 - \sqrt{3}\, i)$$
$$= 2^2 - (\sqrt{3}\, i)^2 = 4 - 3i^2 = 4 + 3 = 7.$$ ∎

6. Is $z = 1 + \sqrt{3}\, i$ a zero of the polynomial $P(z) = z^2 - 2z + 4$?

Solution. To say that a number is a *zero of the function P(z)* is equivalent to saying that it is *a root of the equation* $P(z) = 0$. Thus, we are asking "Is $z = 1 + \sqrt{3}\, i$ a root of the equation $z^2 - 2z + 4 = 0$?" To answer this, we evaluate

$$P(1 + \sqrt{3}\, i) = (1 + \sqrt{3}\, i)^2 - 2(1 + \sqrt{3}\, i) + 4$$

and see whether the result is equal to zero:

$$\begin{aligned}
P(1 + \sqrt{3}\, i) &= (1 + \sqrt{3}\, i)^2 - 2(1 + \sqrt{3}\, i) + 4 \\
&= (1 + 2\sqrt{3}\, i + 3i^2) - 2 - 2\sqrt{3}\, i + 4 \\
&= 1 + 2\sqrt{3}\, i - 3 - 2 - 2\sqrt{3}\, i + 4 \\
&= (1 - 3 - 2 + 4) + (2\sqrt{3} - 2\sqrt{3})i \\
&= 0 + 0i = 0.
\end{aligned}$$

Therefore, the answer to the given question is YES. ∎

EXERCISE 8.1

In the following problems express answers in the form $a + bi$, where a and b are real numbers.

1. Evaluate the following:

   a) i^3
   b) i^6
   c) i^{32}
   d) i^{17}
   e) $(-i)^3$
   f) $(-i)^5$
   g) $(-i)^8$
   h) $(-i)^{17}$

2. Evaluate the following:

   a) $\dfrac{1}{i^4}$
   b) $\dfrac{3+i}{i^3}$
   c) $2i^4 - 3i^{20}$
   d) $\dfrac{1}{i^2 - i}$

3. Evaluate the following:

   a) $\sqrt{9} \cdot \sqrt{16}$
   b) $\sqrt{9}\,\sqrt{-16}$
   c) $\sqrt{-9}\,\sqrt{-16}$
   d) $\dfrac{\sqrt{9}}{\sqrt{-16}}$
   e) $\dfrac{\sqrt{-9}}{\sqrt{16}}$
   f) $\dfrac{\sqrt{-9}}{\sqrt{-16}}$

4. If $z = 1 - i$, evaluate the following:

   a) z^2
   b) $\dfrac{1}{z^2}$
   c) $3z^2 - 2z^3$
   d) $z \cdot \bar{z}$
   e) $(\bar{z})^3$
   f) $z \div \bar{z}$

5. If $f(z) = 2 - 3z - z^2$, determine the following:

   a) $f(-2)$
   b) $f(1 + i)$
   c) $f\left(\dfrac{1}{\sqrt{2}} + \dfrac{1}{\sqrt{2}}i\right)$

6. Show that

   a) $\left(\dfrac{1}{\sqrt{2}} + \dfrac{1}{\sqrt{2}}i\right)^2 = i$
   b) $\left(\dfrac{1}{\sqrt{2}} - \dfrac{1}{\sqrt{2}}i\right)^2 = -i$

7. Show that

   a) $\left(\dfrac{\sqrt{3}}{2} + \dfrac{1}{2}i\right)^3 = i$
   b) $\left(\dfrac{1}{2} + \dfrac{\sqrt{3}}{2}i\right)^3 = -1$

8. Find the complex numbers that might possibly be used for $\sqrt{-i}$. That is, find the complex numbers z such that $z^2 = -i$.

9. Express the following in standard form $a + bi$:

   a) $\sqrt{-4} + \left(3 - 5\sqrt{-4}\right)$
   b) $\left(\sqrt{-48} + 2\right) - \sqrt{-27}$
   c) $\sqrt{-8}\left(2 + \sqrt{-2}\right)$
   d) $\left(1 + \sqrt{-8}\right)\left(1 - \sqrt{-8}\right)$
   e) $\dfrac{1}{1 - \sqrt{-9}}$
   f) $\dfrac{\sqrt{-2}}{3 + \sqrt{-8}}$

10. Determine the roots of the given equations:

    a) $z^2 - 3z + 4 = 0$
    b) $3z^2 + z - 1 = 0$
    c) $z^2 + 16 = 0$

11. Determine the roots of the given equations:

    a) $2z^2 - 3iz + 2 = 0$
    b) $z^2 + 2iz + 3 = 0$
    c) $iz^2 - 3z + i = 0$
    d) $2iz^2 + z + i = 0$

12. If $z = x + iy$ (where x and y are real numbers), prove that
    a) the real part of z is equal to $(z + \bar{z})/2$
    b) the imaginary part of z is equal to $(z - \bar{z})/2$

13. Determine real numbers x and y that satisfy the equation

$$x - 3y - (3x + y)i = -7 + i.$$

14. Solve the equation $z - 3\bar{z} = 1 + i$ for z. (Let $z = x + iy$, then find x and y.)

15. Determine all pairs of real numbers x, y such that:

$$x^2 + 2x + yi = 2 + y + (8 - x)i.$$

16. a) Is $1 + i$ a root of the equation $z^2 - z + 1 - i = 0$?
    b) Is $1 - i$ a root of the equation given in (a)?

17. Is $-3i$ a root of the equation $2z^3 - z^2 + 18z - 9 = 0$?

18. Is $1 - \sqrt{5}i$ a zero of the polynomial $z^3 - z^2 + 4z + 6$?

19. a) Is $1 - i$ a root of the equation $z^3 - 3z^2 + 2z - 1 - i = 0$?
    b) Is $1 + i$ a root of the equation given in (a)?

20. a) Is $1 + \sqrt{3}i$ a root of the equation $z^3 - 3z^2 + 6z - 4 = 0$?
    b) Is $1 - \sqrt{3}i$ a root of the equation given in (a)?

8.2 GEOMETRIC REPRESENTATION OF COMPLEX NUMBERS

The set of complex numbers C is given by

$$C = \{x + iy \mid x \text{ and } y \text{ are real numbers and } i^2 = -1\}.$$

We can establish a correspondence between C and the set of points in the plane in a natural way: Each complex number $x + iy$ we associate with a point (x, y) in the plane and vice versa; we denote this correspondence by $x + iy \leftrightarrow (x, y)$.

In this setting we refer to the plane as the *complex plane* and label points in it either by (x, y) or by $x + iy$. The real numbers correspond to points on the x-axis ($x \leftrightarrow (x, 0)$), while the purely imaginary numbers correspond to points on the y-axis ($yi \leftrightarrow (0, y)$). Thus, the x-axis is called the *real axis*, while the y-axis is referred to as the *imaginary axis*. Some examples of this correspondence are given in Fig. 8.1.

In some problems it is useful to associate each complex number with a *geometric vector*, as shown in Fig. 8.2(a) where the vector has the origin as its initial point and $x + iy$ as its terminal point. Other examples of this correspondence are illustrated by Fig. 8.2(b).

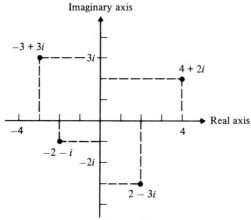

Figure 8.1

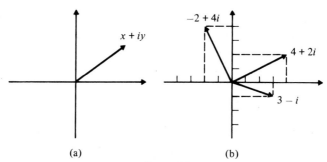

Figure 8.2

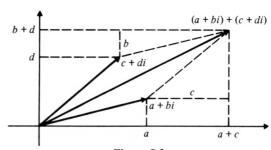

Figure 8.3

Representation of complex numbers by geometric vectors provides us with a convenient geometric interpretation of the sum of complex numbers. The sum $(a + bi) + (c + di)$ is associated with the diagonal vector of the parallelogram depicted in Fig. 8.3.

Examples

⚠ For each of the given complex numbers show the corresponding point (x, y) in the complex plane. Also, draw the corresponding geometric vector.

   a) $5 + 3i$ b) $-\frac{5}{2} + 3i$ c) $\pi - 2i$ d) $3i$

Solution (See Fig. 8.4)

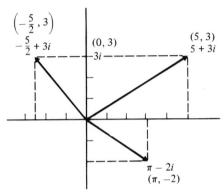

Figure 8.4

⚠ Illustrate each of the following by a diagram using geometric vectors:

   a) $(4 + 2i) + (1 + 3i)$ b) $(1 - 4i) + (-2 + i)$ c) $(3 + i) - (1 + 3i)$

Solution. These vectors are shown in the diagrams of Fig. 8.5, where in (c) we use

$$(3 + i) - (1 + 3i) = (3 + i) + (-1 - 3i).$$

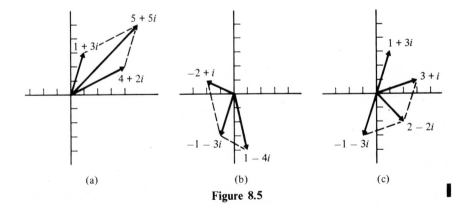

        (a)   (b)   (c)

Figure 8.5

EXERCISE 8.2

In Problems 1 through 8 give the ordered pair of real numbers associated with the given complex number:

1. $3 + 5i$ **2.** $-3 + i$ **3.** $4i$ **4.** $\sqrt{5}$

5. $-\sqrt{3} + 2i$ **6.** $1 - \pi i$ **7.** 0 **8.** $\dfrac{1}{1 - i}$

In Problems 9 through 12 give the complex number associated with the given ordered pair:

9. $(0, -4)$ **10.** $(5, 2)$ **11.** $(-4, -3)$ **12.** $(\sqrt{2}, -\sqrt{3})$

In Problems 13 through 16 illustrate the given complex number by drawing the associated geometric vector:

13. $-1 + 3i$ **14.** $-4 - 5i$ **15.** $-\sqrt{2} + \pi i$ **16.** $\dfrac{1}{1 - 2i}$

In Problems 17 through 20 illustrate geometrically the given sum or difference:

17. $(2 + 3i) + (5 + i)$ **18.** $(1 - 3i) + (4 + 2i)$

19. $(4 - i) - (3 + 5i)$ **20.** $(2 - 3i) - (5 + 2i)$

21. If $z = 3 - 4i$, on the same set of axes show the points associated with the following expressions:

     a) z b) $-z$ c) $\bar{z}$

     d) $\dfrac{z + \bar{z}}{2}$ e) $\dfrac{z - \bar{z}}{2}$ f) $\sqrt{z \cdot \bar{z}}$

22. If $z = -1 + i$, give the ordered pairs corresponding to

     a) z^2 b) $\left(\bar{z}\right)^2$ c) $\dfrac{1}{z}$ d) $z^2 + z + 1$

23. If $z = -1/2 + \left(\sqrt{3}/2\right)i$, draw the geometric vector associated with

     a) z b) z^2 c) $\dfrac{1}{\left(\bar{z}\right)^2}$ d) $\sqrt{z \cdot \bar{z}}$

24. If point $P(x, y)$ is associated with the complex number $x + iy$, then state the conditions on x and y to describe the following:

     a) P is on the positive real axis   b) P is on the imaginary axis
     c) P is in the first quadrant   d) P is to the right of the imaginary axis
     e) P is below the real axis

8.3 TRIGONOMETRIC FORM OF COMPLEX NUMBERS

We continue the development of the preceding section where complex numbers were represented as points in the complex plane or as geometric vectors. Suppose $x + iy$ corresponds to point P: (x, y) in the complex plane, as shown

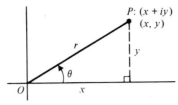

Figure 8.6

in Fig. 8.6. Let r be the distance from the origin O to P and θ be the directed angle between the positive real axis and $\overline{OP}$. We see that

$$x = r \cos \theta \quad \text{and} \quad y = r \sin \theta;$$

therefore

$$x + iy = r(\cos \theta + i \sin \theta).$$

We call $r(\cos \theta + i \sin \theta)$ the *trigonometric*, or the *polar form* of a complex number z whose rectangular form is $z = x + iy$. The real number r is given by

$$r = \sqrt{x^2 + y^2} \, ;$$

it is called the *absolute value*, or the *modulus*, of z and is frequently denoted by $r = |z|$. Since r is the length of the geometric vector associated with z, it is sometimes referred to as the *length* of z.

The angle θ is called the *argument* of z and is denoted by $\theta = \arg z$. It is determined by the two equations

$$\sin \theta = \frac{y}{\sqrt{x^2 + y^2}} \quad \text{and} \quad \cos \theta = \frac{x}{\sqrt{x^2 + y^2}}.$$

Note that angle θ is not unique, since we can add or subtract any integral multiple of 2π (or $360°$) to or from the given θ and use the resulting angle in place of θ. The smallest nonnegative angle that can be used for θ is sometimes called the *principal argument* of z. Also note that

$$z \cdot \bar{z} = (x + iy)(x - iy) = x^2 - i^2 y^2 = x^2 + y^2 = r^2,$$

and so

$$r = \sqrt{z \cdot \bar{z}}.$$

In the *special case* where P is the origin $(0, 0)$, we take $r = 0$ and do not specify any particular corresponding value of θ.

Representing complex numbers in trigonometric form is particularly useful in problems involving multiplication or division.

1. Multiplication of Complex Numbers in Polar Form

Let $z_1 = r_1(\cos \theta_1 + i \sin \theta_1)$ and $z_2 = r_2(\cos \theta_2 + i \sin \theta_2)$ be complex numbers in polar form. We now consider the product $z_1 \cdot z_2$:

$$z_1 \cdot z_2 = r_1(\cos \theta_1 + i \sin \theta_1) \cdot r_2(\cos \theta_2 + i \sin \theta_2)$$
$$= r_1 r_2[(\cos \theta_1 \cos \theta_2 - \sin \theta_1 \sin \theta_2) + i(\sin \theta_1 \cos \theta_2 + \cos \theta_1 \sin \theta_2)]$$
$$= r_1 r_2[\cos(\theta_1 + \theta_2) + i \sin(\theta_1 + \theta_2)],$$

where in the last step we used identities I.12 and I.14 of Chapter 4. Therefore,

$$z_1 \cdot z_2 = r_1 r_2[\cos(\theta_1 + \theta_2) + i \sin(\theta_1 + \theta_2)]. \tag{8.1}$$

Using Eq. (8.1), we can give a geometric interpretation of the product of two complex numbers: $z_1 \cdot z_2$ is a complex number of length $r_1 r_2$ and argument $\theta_1 + \theta_2$. We can state this as follows:

$$|z_1 z_2| = |z_1| \cdot |z_2| \quad \text{and} \quad \arg(z_1 z_2) = \arg z_1 + \arg z_2. \tag{8.2}$$

Note. The fact that we add arguments when we multiply complex numbers suggests that a complex number can be expressed in exponential form. This is indeed the case. In advanced mathematics courses one learns that z can be expressed as $z = r \cdot e^{i\theta}$, where e is a special irrational number $e = 2.71828\ldots$ (see Chapter 10, p. 277).

2. Division of Complex Numbers in Polar Form

Let z_1 and z_2 be complex numbers expressed in polar form as above (and $z_2 \neq 0$). Then

$$\frac{z_1}{z_2} = \frac{r_1}{r_2} [\cos(\theta_1 - \theta_2) + i \sin(\theta_1 - \theta_2)]. \tag{8.3}$$

The proof of Eq. (8.3) is similar to that of Eq. (8.1) and is left to the student as Problem 1 of Exercise 8.3.

From Eq. (8.3) we see that the modulus and argument of z_1/z_2 are given by:

$$\left| \frac{z_1}{z_2} \right| = \frac{|z_1|}{|z_2|} \quad \text{and} \quad \arg\left(\frac{z_1}{z_2}\right) = \arg z_1 - \arg z_2. \tag{8.4}$$

Examples

In the following examples let

$$z_1 = 1 + i, \quad z_2 = \sqrt{3} - i, \quad z_3 = -2 - 2\sqrt{3}i, \quad z_4 = -3 + 4i.$$

⚠ Express in polar form:

    a) z_1 b) z_2 c) z_3 d) z_4

Solution

  a) $r_1 = |z_1| = \sqrt{1^2 + 1^2} = \sqrt{2}$ and $\theta_1 = \pi/4 = 45°$ (see Fig. 8.7,a).
    Therefore,

$$z_1 = \sqrt{2}\left(\cos \tfrac{\pi}{4} + i \sin \tfrac{\pi}{4}\right) \quad \text{or} \quad z_1 = \sqrt{2}\,(\cos 45° + i \sin 45°).$$

  b) $r_2 = |z_2| = \sqrt{(\sqrt{3})^2 + (-1)^2} = \sqrt{4} = 2$ and $\theta_2 = 11\pi/6 = 330°$ (see
    Fig. 8.7(b)). Thus

$$z_2 = 2\left(\cos \tfrac{11\pi}{6} + i \sin \tfrac{11\pi}{6}\right) \quad \text{or} \quad z_2 = 2(\cos 330° + i \sin 330°).$$

  c) From Fig. 8.7(c) we see that

$$z_3 = 4\left(\cos \tfrac{4\pi}{3} + i \sin \tfrac{4\pi}{3}\right) \quad \text{or} \quad z_3 = 4(\cos 240° + i \sin 240°).$$

  d) From Fig. 8.7(d) we see that

$$\theta_4 = \text{Cos}^{-1}\left(-\tfrac{3}{5}\right) = 2.2143 = 126.87°.$$

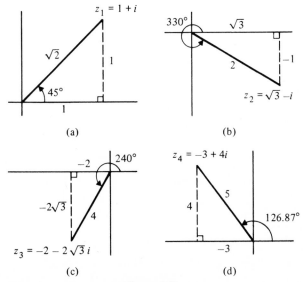

(a)   (b)

(c)   (d)

Figure 8.7

Therefore,

$$z_4 = 5(\cos\ 2.2143 + i\ \sin\ 2.2143)$$

or

$$z_4 = 5(\cos\ 126.87° + i\ \sin\ 126.87°).$$ ∎

2̸ Find these expressions in polar and rectangular form:
  a) $z_1 \cdot z_2$ b) $z_3 \cdot z_4$ c) $z_1 \cdot z_2 \cdot z_3$

Solution. In each case we use Eq. (8.1).

  a) $z_1 \cdot z_2$ $= (\sqrt{2})(2)[\cos(45° + 330°) + i\ \sin(45° + 330°)]$
        $= 2\sqrt{2}[\cos\ 375° + i\ \sin\ 375°]$
        $= 2\sqrt{2}\ (\cos\ 15° + i\ \sin\ 15°)$ (polar form)
        $= 2.73 + 0.73\ i$ (rectangular form).

  b) $z_3 \cdot z_4$ $= (4)(5)[\cos(240° + 126.87°) + i\ \sin(240° + 126.87°)]$
        $= 20(\cos\ 366.87° + i\ \sin\ 366.87°)$
        $= 20(\cos\ 6.87° + i\ \sin\ 6.87°)$ (polar form)
        $= 19.86 + 2.39\ i$ (rectangular form).

  c) $z_1 \cdot z_2 \cdot z_3 = (\sqrt{2})(2)(4)\left[\cos\left(\frac{\pi}{4} + \frac{11\pi}{6} + \frac{4\pi}{3}\right) + i\ \sin\left(\frac{\pi}{4} + \frac{11\pi}{6} + \frac{4\pi}{3}\right)\right]$
        $= 8\sqrt{2}\left(\cos\frac{41\pi}{12} + i\ \sin\frac{41\pi}{12}\right)$
        $= 8\sqrt{2}\left(\cos\frac{17\pi}{12} + i\ \sin\frac{17\pi}{12}\right)$ (polar form)
        $= -2.93 - 10.93\ i$ (rectangular form). ∎

3̸ Evaluate these expressions in polar and rectangular form:
  a) $\frac{z_1}{z_2}$ b) $\frac{z_3}{z_4}$

Solution. In each case we use Eq. (8.3).

  a) $\frac{z_1}{z_2} = \frac{\sqrt{2}}{2}\ [\cos(45° - 330°) + i\ \sin(45° - 330°)]$

      $= \frac{\sqrt{2}}{2}\ [\cos(-285°) + i\ \sin(-285°)]$ (polar form)

      $= \frac{\sqrt{2}}{2}\ [\cos\ 285° - i\ \sin\ 285°]$

      $= 0.18 + 0.68i$ (rectangular form).

  b) $\frac{z_3}{z_4} = \frac{4}{5}\left[\cos\left(\frac{4\pi}{3} - 2.2143\right) + i\ \sin\left(\frac{4\pi}{3} - 2.2143\right)\right]$

      $= \frac{4}{5}[\cos(1.9745) + i\ \sin(1.9745)]$ (polar form)

      $= -0.31 + 0.74i$ (rectangular form). ∎

4 Express $3(\cos\ 60° - i\ \sin\ 60°)$ in polar form.

Solution. The polar form of a complex number is $r(\cos\ \theta + i\ \sin\ \theta)$, where $r \geq 0$. The given number is not in polar form because of the minus sign. However, since $\cos(-60°) = \cos\ 60°$ and $\sin(-60°) = -\sin\ 60°$, we can write

$$3(\cos\ 60° - i\ \sin\ 60°) = 3[\cos(-60°) + i\ \sin(-60°)].$$

We can also write this as $3(\cos\ 300° + i\ \sin\ 300°)$.

5 Express $-4(\cos\ 120° + i\ \sin\ 120°)$ in polar form.

Solution. The given number is not in polar form because the factor -4 is not an acceptable value for r $(r \geq 0)$. We can use identities

$$\cos(180° + \theta) = -\cos\ \theta \quad \text{and} \quad \sin(180° + \theta) = -\sin\ \theta,$$

and so for $\theta = 120°$ we get

$$-\cos\ 120° = \cos\ 300° \quad \text{and} \quad -\sin\ 120° = \sin\ 300°.$$

Thus

$$-4(\cos\ 120° + i\ \sin\ 120°) = 4(\cos\ 300° + i\ \sin\ 300°).$$

6 Express $3(\sin\ 60° - i\ \cos\ 60°)$ in polar form.

Solution. Using

$$\cos(270° + \theta) = \sin\ \theta \quad \text{and} \quad \sin(270° + \theta) = -\cos\ \theta,$$

we get for $\theta = 60°$:

$$\sin\ 60° = \cos(270° + 60°) = \cos\ 330°$$

and

$$-\cos\ 60° = \sin(270° + 60°) = \sin\ 330°.$$

Thus

$$3(\sin\ 60° - i\ \cos\ 60°) = 3(\cos\ 330° + i\ \sin\ 330°),$$

and this is in polar form.

EXERCISE 8.3

In problems of this exercise give answers in exact form whenever possible; a calculator and state the results in decimals (two places for degree measu for radian measure).

1. If z_1 and z_2 are complex numbers expressed in polar form, prove that

$$\frac{z_1}{z_2} = \frac{r_1}{r_2}[\cos(\theta_1 - \theta_2) + i \sin(\theta_1 - \theta_2)].$$

2. Express the given numbers in polar form:

    a) -3 b) $1 - i$ c) $-i$ d) $1 + \sqrt{3}i$

3. Express in polar form

    a) π b) $3 - 4i$ c) $i^5 - i^4$ d) $12 - 5i$

4. Express in polar form

    a) $-3 - 3i$ b) $5i^2 - 2i - 3$ c) $\dfrac{1}{i}$ d) $\dfrac{1}{i - i^2}$

5. Express in rectangular form

    a) $3(\cos 45° + i \sin 45°)$ b) $5(\cos 180° + i \sin 180°)$ c) $\cos \dfrac{4\pi}{3} + i \sin \dfrac{4\pi}{3}$

6. Express in rectangular form:

    a) $\cos\left(-\dfrac{7\pi}{6}\right) + i \sin\left(-\dfrac{7\pi}{6}\right)$ b) $\cos 450° + i \sin 450°$

    c) $3(\cos 137° + i \sin 137°)$

7. Determine why the given number is not in polar form. Then express it in polar form:

    a) $4(\cos 45° - i \sin 45°)$ b) $-3(\cos 300° + i \sin 300°)$

    c) $-\cos \dfrac{5\pi}{6} + i \sin \dfrac{5\pi}{6}$

8. Express in polar form:

    a) $3\left(-\cos \dfrac{\pi}{6} + i \sin \dfrac{\pi}{6}\right)$ b) $-5(\cos 40° - i \sin 40°)$

    c) $-\cos 120° - i \sin 120°$

Problems 9 through 12 express answers in:

    a) polar form   b) rectangular form

$(\cos 15° + i \sin 15°) \cdot (\cos 30° + i \sin 30°)$

$4(\cos 47° - i \sin 47°) \cdot (\cos 43° - i \sin 43°)$
Hint. Write each factor in polar form first and then use Eq. (8.1).

$$\frac{8(\cos 150° + i \sin 150°)}{4(\cos 30° + i \sin 30°)} \qquad\qquad 12. \frac{\cos 50° + i \sin 50°}{\cos 80° - i \sin 80°}$$

roblems 13 through 15, let

    $z_1 = 3(\cos 210° - i \sin 210°)$ and $z_2 = 6(\sin 60° + i \cos 60°)$;

ate the given expressions by using Eq. (8.1) or Eq. (8.3):

    $\cdot z_2$ 14. $z_2 \div z_1$ 15. $\dfrac{1}{z_2}$

roblems 16 through 20, let $z_1 = \sqrt{3} + i$ and $z_2 = -2 + 2i$; write the given ers in polar form:

16. a) z_1 b) z_2 **17.** a) $\bar{z}_1$ b) $\bar{z}_2$

18. a) $z_1 \cdot z_2$ b) $\bar{z}_1 \cdot \bar{z}_2$ **19.** a) $z_1 \div z_2$ b) $\bar{z}_1 \div \bar{z}_2$

20. a) $\dfrac{1}{z_1}$ b) $\dfrac{1}{z_2}$

21. If $z = r(\cos \theta + i \sin \theta)$ represents a complex number in polar form, show that
a) $z^2 = r^2(\cos 2\theta + i \sin 2\theta)$ b) $z^3 = r^3(\cos 3\theta + i \sin 3\theta)$

22. If $z = r(\cos \theta + i \sin \theta)$ represents a complex number in polar form and $r \neq 0$, show that
a) $\dfrac{1}{z} = \dfrac{1}{r} [\cos(-\theta) + i \sin(-\theta)]$ b) $\dfrac{1}{z^2} = \dfrac{1}{r^2} [\cos(-2\theta) + i \sin(-2\theta)]$

23. Use Problem 21 to evaluate: **24.** Use Problem 22 to evaluate:
a) $\left(\sqrt{2} - \sqrt{2}i\right)^2$ b) $\left(1 + \sqrt{3}i\right)^3$ a) $\dfrac{1}{1+i}$ b) $\dfrac{1}{\left(\sqrt{3} - i\right)^2}$

8.4 DE MOIVRE'S THEOREM

Suppose $z = r(\cos \theta + i \sin \theta)$ represents a complex number in polar form. If we apply Eq. (8.1) to the special case where $z_1 = z_2 = z$, we get
$$z \cdot z = r \cdot r[\cos(\theta + \theta) + i \sin (\theta + \theta)],$$
that is
$$z^2 = r^2(\cos 2\theta + i \sin 2\theta).$$
If we again apply Eq. (8.1) to $z_1 = z$ and $z_2 = z^2$, we get
$$z^3 = r^3(\cos 3\theta + i \sin 3\theta).$$
This suggests that for each positive integer n,

$$z^n = r^n(\cos n\theta + i \sin n\theta). \qquad (8.5)$$

This is known as *DeMoivre's theorem* named after the French mathematician Abraham DeMoivre (1667–1754). The student is asked to give a formal proof in Problem 16 of Exercise 8.4.

If we take $r = 1$ in Eq.(8.5), then for each positive integer n we have the special case:

$$(\cos \theta + i \sin \theta)^n = \cos n\theta + i \sin n\theta.$$

Equation (8.5) is stated for the case when n is a positive integer. For exponents that are not positive integers, we follow a pattern similar to that encountered in algebra. We first define z^k when k is zero, then when k is a negative integer. In Section 8.5 we consider the case when k is a rational number.

We state the following definitions.

Zero exponent: if $z \neq 0$, then $z^0 = 1$.

Negative-integer exponent: if n is any positive integer and $z \neq 0$, then $z^{-n} = 1/z^n$.

We now investigate z^{-n} when n is a positive integer. Let

$$z = r(\cos\theta + i\sin\theta);$$

then

$$z^{-n} = \frac{1}{z^n} = \frac{1}{r^n(\cos n\theta + i\sin n\theta)} \qquad \text{(by Eq. (8.5))}$$

$$= \frac{1}{r^n} \cdot \frac{\cos 0 + i\sin 0}{\cos n\theta + i\sin n\theta} \qquad \text{(since } 1 = \cos 0 + i\sin 0)$$

$$= r^{-n}[\cos(-n\theta) + i\sin(-n\theta)] \qquad \text{(by Eq. (8.3))}.$$

Thus we have

$$z^{-n} = r^{-n}[\cos(-n\theta) + i\sin(-n\theta)].$$

This is precisely Eq. (8.5) for negative integers.

Equation (8.5) also holds for $n = 0$, since $z^0 = 1$, and

$$r^0[\cos(0 \cdot \theta) + i\sin(0 \cdot \theta)] = 1 \cdot (\cos 0 + i\sin 0) = 1.$$

Therefore, we can generalize Eq. (8.5) and say:

> If $z = r(\cos\theta + i\sin\theta)$ and n is *any integer,*
> then $z^n = r^n(\cos n\theta + i\sin n\theta)$. $\qquad$ (8.6)

Examples

⚠ Express the following as a complex number in polar form and rectangular form:

a) $(1 + i)^6$ $\qquad\qquad$ b) $(-1 + \sqrt{3}i)^8$ $\qquad\qquad$ c) $(3 - 4i)^4$

Solution

a) We first express $1 + i$ in polar form and then use the result given in Eq. (8.6):

$$(1 + i)^6 = \left[\sqrt{2}(\cos 45° + i\sin 45°)\right]^6$$

$$= \left(\sqrt{2}\right)^6[\cos(6 \cdot 45°) + i\sin(6 \cdot 45°)] \qquad \text{(by (8.6))*}$$

$$= 8(\cos 270° + i\sin 270°) \qquad \text{(polar form)}$$

$$= 8[0 + i(-1)] = -8i \qquad \text{(rectangular form)}.$$

---

*To appreciate this step (DeMoivre's theorem), we suggest that the student evaluates $(1 + i)^6$ by multiplying six factors, each $(1 + i)$, or by using the binomial theorem.

b) $(-1 + \sqrt{3}i)^8 = \left[2\left(\cos \frac{2\pi}{3} + i \sin \frac{2\pi}{3}\right)\right]^8$

$= 2^8\left[\cos\left(8 \cdot \frac{2\pi}{3}\right) + i \sin\left(8 \cdot \frac{2\pi}{3}\right)\right]$

$= 256\left[\cos \frac{16\pi}{3} + i \sin \frac{16\pi}{3}\right]$

$= 256\left[\cos\left(4\pi + \frac{4\pi}{3}\right) + i \sin\left(4\pi + \frac{4\pi}{3}\right)\right]$

$= 256\left[\cos \frac{4\pi}{3} + i \sin \frac{4\pi}{3}\right]$ (polar form)

$= 256\left[-\frac{1}{2} + i\left(-\frac{\sqrt{3}}{2}\right)\right]$

$= -128 - 128\sqrt{3}i$ (rectangular form).

c) $(3 - 4i)^4 = \left[r(\cos \theta + i \sin \theta)\right]^4 = r^4(\cos 4\theta + i \sin 4\theta)$,

where $r = 5$ and $\theta = \text{Sin}^{-1}(-4/5)$ (see Fig. 8.8). Using a calculator, we evaluate

$$4\theta = 4 \; \text{Sin}^{-1}\left(-\frac{4}{5}\right) = -212.52°.$$

Therefore

$(3 - 4i)^4 = 625[\cos(-212.52°) + i \sin(-212.52°)]$ (polar form)

$= -527 + 336i$ (rectangular form).

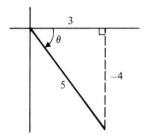

Figure 8.8

2⃝ Evaluate the following and express answers in polar form and rectangular form:

a) $[2(\cos 22°30' + i \sin 22° 30']^4$ b) $(\cos 45° - i \sin 45°)^5$

Solution

a) Using Eq. (8.6) we get

$[2(\cos 22°30' + i \sin 22°30']^4 = 2^4[\cos 4(22°30') + i \sin 4(20°30')]$

$= 16(\cos 90° + i \sin 90°)$ (polar form)

$= 16 \; i$ (rectangular form).

b) We first express $\cos 45° - i \sin 45°$ in polar form as

$$\cos 45° - i \sin 45° = \cos(-45°) + i \sin(-45°).$$

Then by using Eq. (8.6) we get

$$\begin{aligned}(\cos 45° - i \sin 45°)^5 &= [\cos(-45°) + i \sin(-45°)]^5 \\ &= \cos 5(-45°) + i \sin 5(-45°) \\ &= \cos(-225°) + i \sin(-225°) \quad \text{(polar form)} \\ &= -\frac{\sqrt{2}}{2} + \frac{\sqrt{2}}{2}i \quad \text{(rectangular form).}\end{aligned}$$ ▮

△3 Express $\sin 4\theta$ and $\cos 4\theta$ as identities in terms of $\sin \theta$ and $\cos \theta$.

Solution. Substituting $n = 4$ and $z = \cos \theta + i \sin \theta$ into Eq. (8.6) gives

$$(\cos \theta + i \sin \theta)^4 = \cos 4\theta + i \sin 4\theta.$$

Applying the binomial expansion

$$(a + b)^4 = a^4 + 4a^3b + 6a^2b^2 + 4ab^3 + b^4$$

to the left-hand side of this equation, we get

$$\cos^4\theta + (4 \cos^3\theta \sin \theta)i + 6(\cos^2\theta \sin^2\theta)i^2 + (4 \cos \theta \sin^3\theta)i^3 + (\sin^4\theta)i^4$$
$$= \cos 4\theta + i \sin 4\theta.$$

Now replace i^2 by -1, i^3 by $-i$, and i^4 by 1, and collect real and imaginary terms:

$$[\cos^4\theta - 6 \cos^2\theta \sin^2\theta + \sin^4\theta] + [4 \cos^3\theta \sin \theta - 4 \cos \theta \sin^3\theta]i$$
$$= \cos 4\theta + i \sin 4\theta.$$

Using the definition of equality of two complex numbers (given in Section 8.1), we get

$$\boxed{\begin{aligned} \sin 4\theta &= 4 \cos^3\theta \sin \theta - 4 \cos \theta \sin^3\theta, \\ \cos 4\theta &= \cos^4\theta - 6 \cos^2\theta \sin^2\theta + \sin^4\theta. \end{aligned}}$$ ▮

These are identities.

By using the technique illustrated in Example 3, we can solve the general problem of determining identities in which $\sin n\theta$ and $\cos n\theta$ are expressed in terms of $\sin \theta$ and $\cos \theta$.

EXERCISE 8.4

In this exercise give answers in exact form whenever it is reasonable; otherwise give results in decimal form (two places for degree measure, four places for radian measure). Express answers in polar form and rectangular form.

1. Evaluate:
   a) $(\cos 30° + i \sin 30°)^5$
   c) $(\cos 40° + i \sin 40°)^{-3}$

   b) $\{2[\cos(-45°) + i\sin(-45°)]\}^4$

2. Evaluate:
   a) $(\cos 47° + i \sin 47°)^6$
   c) $[\cos(-20°) + i\sin(-20°)]^{-6}$

   b) $\left[3\left(\cos\frac{\pi}{3} + i \sin\frac{\pi}{3}\right)\right]^4$

3. Evaluate:
   a) $[2(\cos 150° - i \sin 150°)]^3$

   b) $\dfrac{16}{[2(\cos 45° - i \sin 45°)]^4}$

4. Evaluate:
   a) $[-3(\cos 20° + i \sin 20°)]^4$

   b) $\dfrac{81}{\{-3[\cos(\pi/12) + i \sin(\pi/12)]\}^4}$

5. Evaluate:
   a) $(-1 + i)^8$
   b) $(\sqrt{3} - i)^4$
   c) $(1 + i)^{-3}$

6. Evaluate:
   a) $\left(\sqrt{2} + \sqrt{2}\,i\right)^4$
   b) $\dfrac{1}{\left(1 - \sqrt{3}\,i\right)^6}$
   c) $(2 + i)^6$

7. Evaluate:
   a) $(-1 + i)^4 \cdot \left(1 + \sqrt{3}\,i\right)^6$
   b) $\dfrac{(2 + 2i)^4}{\left(\sqrt{3} + i\right)^3}$

8. Evaluate:
   a) $(1 - i)^{-3} \cdot (1 + i)^4$
   b) $(2 - 3i)^2 \cdot (4 + 3i)^4$

In Problems 9 through 12, let $z = 1 - i$ and $w = -\sqrt{3} + i$. Evaluate the given expressions:

9. $z^4 - z$

10. $z^3 \cdot w^4$

11. $z^4 - w^4$

12. $z^4 + z^3 + z^2 + z + 1$ *Hint*. The identity $(z - 1)(z^4 + z^3 + z^2 + z + 1) = z^5 - 1$ may be useful.

13. If $f(z) = z^4 - 2z^3 + z$, find:
    a) $f(i)$
    b) $f(-1 + i)$

14. In Eq. (8.6) take $n = 2$, $r = 1$, and get identities (I.18) and (I.19) of Chapter 4.

15. Express $\sin 3\theta$ and $\cos 3\theta$ as identities in terms of $\sin \theta$ and $\cos \theta$.

16. Prove that for each positive integer n:

$$z^n = [r(\cos \theta + i \sin \theta)]^n = r^n(\cos n\theta + i \sin n\theta).$$

Hint. Use mathematical induction. That is, let $E(n)$ represent the equation $z^n = r^n(\cos n\theta + i \sin n\theta)$, where n can be replaced by any positive integer. This gives us an infinite number of statements $E(1)$, $E(2)$, $E(3)$, ... and our claim is that each one is true. For example,

$$\text{when } n = 1, \quad E(1) \text{ represents } z = r(\cos\ \theta + i\ \sin\ \theta);$$
$$\text{when } n = 2, \quad E(2) \text{ represents } z^2 = r^2(\cos\ 2\theta + i\ \sin\ 2\theta);$$
$$\text{when } n = 3, \quad E(3) \text{ represents } z^3 = r^3(\cos\ 3\theta + i\ \sin\ 3\theta);$$
$$\vdots \qquad\qquad \vdots \qquad\qquad \vdots$$

Obviously it is impossible to verify the truth of each of these statements individually (there are too many of them). The *principle of mathematical induction* comes to our rescue; it states:

If $E(1)$ is true and the truth of $E(k)$ implies the truth of $E(k + 1)$, where k is any given (but unspecified) positive integer, then $E(n)$ is true for each positive integer n.

Therefore, you must show that $E(1)$ is true (this should be obvious) and that from $z^k = r^k(\cos\ k\theta + i\ \sin\ k\theta)$ it follows that

$$z^{k+1} = r^{k+1}[\cos(k+1)\theta + i\ \sin(k+1)\theta].$$

8.5 RATIONAL-NUMBER EXPONENTS AND ROOTS OF COMPLEX NUMBERS

1. Rational-Number Exponents

In Section 8.4 we arrived at Eq. (8.6), which is valid for any integer n. We now consider the problem of defining $z^{m/n}$, where m/n is any rational number.* In a manner similar to that used in algebra for real numbers, we define $z^{m/n}$ as a complex number w that satisfies the equation $w^n = z^m$. In general, this involves a problem of multiple values of w. We shall consider the special case of $z^{1/n}$ (the general case can be reduced to this, since $z^{m/n} = (z^m)^{1/n}$). Complex number $z^{m/n}$ is also written as $\sqrt[n]{z^m}$ for $n > 2$ and as $\sqrt{z^m}$ for $n = 2$.

2. Roots of Complex Numbers

If n is a positive integer, then the nth root of a complex number z is denoted by $\sqrt[n]{z}$ or by $z^{1/n}$. Let $z^{1/n} = w$; then using the definition given above, we get $w^n = z$. Suppose z and w are expressed in the polar form as

$$z = r(\cos\ \theta + i\ \sin\ \theta), \qquad w = R(\cos\ \alpha + i\ \sin\ \alpha).$$

Then $w^n = z$ becomes

$$[R(\cos\ \alpha + i\ \sin\ \alpha)]^n = r(\cos\ \theta + i\ \sin\ \theta).$$

---

* Here we are assuming that m and n are integers ($n > 1$) and m/n is in lowest terms. The reason for the last requirement is to avoid situations illustrated by

$$(-1)^{1/2} = \sqrt{-1} = i, \qquad \text{while} \qquad (-1)^{2/4} = \sqrt[4]{(-1)^2} = \sqrt[4]{1} = 1.$$

Using Eq. (8.2), we get

$$R^n (\cos \; n\alpha + i \; \sin \; n\alpha) = r (\cos \; \theta + i \; \sin \; \theta).$$

From the definition of equality of two complex numbers, it follows that

$$R^n \cos(n\alpha) = r \; \cos \; \theta \qquad \text{and} \qquad R^n \sin(n\alpha) = r \; \sin \; \theta.$$

Solving these two equations for R and α gives

$$R = r^{1/n} = \sqrt[n]{r} \qquad \text{and} \qquad \alpha = \frac{\theta + k \cdot 2\pi}{n} \; ,$$

where k is any integer (see Problem 21 of Exercise 8.5). Therefore, all nth roots of z are given by

$$w_k = r^{1/n} \left[\cos\left(\frac{\theta}{n} + \frac{2\pi k}{n}\right) + i \; \sin\left(\frac{\theta}{n} + \frac{2\pi k}{n}\right) \right]. \tag{8.7}$$

If we let k take on various integral values, we see that $w_0, w_1, w_2, \ldots, w_{n-1}$ are distinct complex numbers:

$$
\begin{aligned}
w_0 &= r^{1/n} \left[\cos \frac{\theta}{n} + i \; \sin \frac{\theta}{n} \right], \\
w_1 &= r^{1/n} \left[\cos\left(\frac{\theta}{n} + \frac{2\pi}{n}\right) + i \; \sin \left(\frac{\theta}{n} + \frac{2\pi}{n}\right) \right], \\
w_2 &= r^{1/n} \left[\cos\left(\frac{\theta}{n} + \frac{4\pi}{n}\right) + i \; \sin \left(\frac{\theta}{n} + \frac{4\pi}{n}\right) \right], \\
&\;\;\vdots \qquad\qquad \vdots \\
w_{n-1} &= r^{1/n} \left[\cos\left(\frac{\theta}{n} + \frac{2(n-1)\pi}{n}\right) + i \; \sin\left(\frac{\theta}{n} + \frac{2(n-1)\pi}{n}\right) \right].
\end{aligned}
\tag{8.8}
$$

If we evaluate w_n by replacing k with n in (8.7), we get

$$
\begin{aligned}
w_n &= r^{1/n} \left[\cos\left(\frac{\theta}{n} + \frac{2\pi n}{n}\right) + i \; \sin \left(\frac{\theta}{n} + \frac{2\pi n}{n}\right) \right] \\
&= r^{1/n} \left[\cos\left(\frac{\theta}{n} + 2\pi \right) + i \; \sin\left(\frac{\theta}{n} + 2\pi \right) \right] \\
&= r^{1/n} \left[\cos \frac{\theta}{n} + i \; \sin \frac{\theta}{n} \right] = w_0.
\end{aligned}
$$

In a similar manner we can show that each $k \geq n$ or $k < 0$ will give a w_k that is included in (8.8).

Therefore, $\sqrt[n]{z}$ will have n distinct values given by (8.8). These are called the *n*th roots of *z*. The *principal* nth root is given by

$$w_0 = r^{1/n}\left(\cos \frac{\theta}{n} + i \; \sin \frac{\theta}{n}\right),$$

where θ is the smallest positive angle used in expressing z in polar form.

Geometrically, all nth roots of z are located on the circle with center at the origin and radius $\sqrt[n]{r}$; they are equally spaced along the circle with the angle between any two consecutive roots being $2\pi/n$ (as given in (8.8)). These are shown in Fig. 8.9.

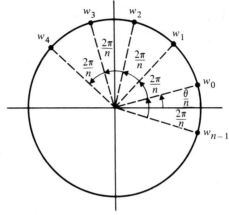

Figure 8.9

Examples

1. Find the fourth roots of -1.

Solution. We wish to find the roots of the equation $z^4 = -1$. First express -1 in polar form:

$$-1 = \cos \pi + i \sin \pi.$$

Substituting into the formulas given in (8.8) we get:

$$w_0 = \cos \tfrac{\pi}{4} + i \sin \tfrac{\pi}{4} = \frac{\sqrt{2}}{2} + i \frac{\sqrt{2}}{2},$$

$$w_1 = \cos \tfrac{3\pi}{4} + i \sin \tfrac{3\pi}{4} = -\frac{\sqrt{2}}{2} + i \frac{\sqrt{2}}{2},$$

$$w_2 = \cos \tfrac{5\pi}{4} + i \sin \tfrac{5\pi}{4} = -\frac{\sqrt{2}}{2} - i \frac{\sqrt{2}}{2},$$

$$w_3 = \cos \tfrac{7\pi}{4} + i \sin \tfrac{7\pi}{4} = \frac{\sqrt{2}}{2} - i \frac{\sqrt{2}}{2}.$$

2. Find the roots of $z^4 - 2z^2 + 2 = 0$.

Solution. The given equation is quadratic with regard to z^2. Solving for z^2 by using the quadratic formula, we get:

$$z^2 = \frac{-(-2) \pm \sqrt{(-2)^2 - 4(1)(2)}}{2(1)} = \frac{2 \pm \sqrt{-4}}{2} = 1 \pm i.$$

Therefore, $z^2 = 1 + i$ or $z^2 = 1 - i$, and the roots of the given equation will be square roots of $1 + i$ and of $1 - i$. We first express $1 + i$ and $1 - i$ in polar form:

$$1 + i = \sqrt{2}(\cos\ 45° + i\ \sin\ 45°),$$
$$1 - i = \sqrt{2}(\cos\ 315° + i\ \sin\ 315°).$$

Using (8.8) with $n = 2$, we get the following solutions:
$z^2 = 1 + i$ gives:

$$w_0 = \left(\sqrt{2}\right)^{1/2}\left[\cos\ \frac{45°}{2} + i\ \sin\frac{45°}{2}\right] = \sqrt[4]{2}\ (\cos\ 22.5° + i\ \sin\ 22.5°)$$

$$= 1.10 + 0.46i;$$

$$w_1 = \left(\sqrt{2}\right)^{1/2}\left[\cos\left(\frac{45°}{2} + \frac{360°}{2}\right) + i\ \sin\left(\frac{45°}{2} + \frac{360°}{2}\right)\right]$$

$$= \sqrt[4]{2}\ (\cos\ 202.5° + i\ \sin\ 202.5°) = -1.10 - 0.46i.$$

$z^2 = 1 - i$ gives:

$$w_0' = \left(\sqrt{2}\right)^{1/2}\left[\cos\frac{315°}{2} + i\ \sin\frac{315°}{2}\right]$$

$$= \sqrt[4]{2}\ [\cos\ 157.5° + i\ \sin\ 157.5°] = -1.10 + 0.46i;$$

$$w_1' = \left(\sqrt{2}\right)^{1/2}\left[\cos\left(\frac{315°}{2} + \frac{360°}{2}\right) + i\ \sin\left(\frac{315°}{2} + \frac{360°}{2}\right)\right]$$

$$= \sqrt[4]{2}\ (\cos\ 337.5° + i\ \sin\ 337.5°) = 1.10 - 0.46i.$$

Therefore, the solution set for the given equation is

$$\{1.10 + 0.46i, \quad -1.10 + 0.46i, \quad 1.10 - 0.46i, \quad -1.10 - 0.46i\},$$

where the numbers are given to two decimal places. The numbers in the solution set are shown in Fig. 8.10, where the radius of the circle is $\sqrt[4]{2}$.

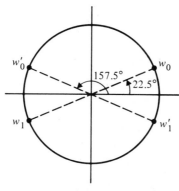

Figure 8.10

$\triangle{3}$ Evaluate $(1 - i)^{4/3}$.

Solution. Since $(1 - i)^{4/3} = [(1 - i)^4]^{1/3}$, we first determine $(1 - i)^4$ in polar form and then apply (8.8) to find the three cube roots of the result:

$$(1 - i)^4 = \left[\sqrt{2}(\cos\ 315° + i\ \sin\ 315°)\right]^4$$

$$= \left(\sqrt{2}\right)^4[\cos(4 \cdot 315°) + i\ \sin(4 \cdot 315°)]$$

$$= 4(\cos\ 1260° + i\ \sin\ 1260°)$$

$$= 4(\cos\ 180° + i\ \sin\ 180°).$$

The cube roots of this number are:

$$w_0 = 4^{1/3}\left(\cos\ \frac{180°}{3} + i\ \sin\frac{180°}{3}\right) = \sqrt[3]{4}\ (\cos\ 60° + i\ \sin\ 60°)$$
$$= 0.79 + 1.37i;$$

$$w_1 = 4^{1/3}\left[\cos\left(\frac{180°}{3} + \frac{360°}{3}\right) + i\ \sin\left(\frac{180°}{3} + \frac{360°}{3}\right)\right]$$
$$= \sqrt[3]{4}[\cos\ 180° + i\ \sin\ 180°] = -1.59;$$

$$w_2 = 4^{1/3}\left[\cos\left(\frac{180°}{3} + \frac{2 \cdot 360°}{3}\right) + i\ \sin\left(\frac{180°}{3} + \frac{2 \cdot 360°}{3}\right)\right]$$
$$= \sqrt[3]{4}[\cos\ 300° + i\ \sin\ 300°] = 0.79 - 1.37i.$$

Therefore, w_0, w_1, w_2 are the three complex values of $(1 - i)^{4/3}$. ∎

$\triangle{4}$ Find the square roots of $-3 - 4i$.

Solution. We want to evaluate $(-3 - 4i)^{1/2}$. We first express $-3 - 4i$ in polar form:

$$-3 - 4i = 5(\cos\ \theta + i\ \sin\ \theta),$$

where θ is the angle shown in Fig. 8.11. Therefore,

$$(-3 - 4i)^{1/2} = [5(\cos\ \theta + i\ \sin\ \theta)]^{1/2}.$$

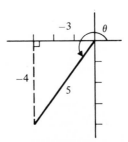

Figure 8.11

Using the results given by (8.8), where $n = 2$, we get

$$w_0 = 5^{1/2} \left(\cos \frac{\theta}{2} + i \sin \frac{\theta}{2} \right),$$

$$w_1 = 5^{1/2} \left[\cos\left(\frac{\theta}{2} + \frac{2\pi}{2} \right) + i \sin \left(\frac{\theta}{2} + \frac{2\pi}{2} \right) \right]$$

$$= 5^{1/2} \left[\cos\left(\frac{\theta}{2} + \pi \right) + i \sin \left(\frac{\theta}{2} + \pi \right) \right]$$

$$= 5^{1/2} \left[- \cos \frac{\theta}{2} - i \sin \frac{\theta}{2} \right] = -5^{1/2} \left(\cos \frac{\theta}{2} + i \sin \frac{\theta}{2} \right) = -w_0.$$

We can write w_0 in better form by using the half-angle identities. Since $\pi < \theta < 3\pi/2$, then $\pi/2 < \theta/2 < 3\pi/4$ and so angle $\theta/2$ is in the second quadrant. Therefore, $\cos (\theta/2)$ is negative and $\sin (\theta/2)$ is positive. Since $\cos \theta = -3/5$ (see Fig. 8.11), then

$$\cos \frac{\theta}{2} = -\sqrt{\frac{1 + \cos \theta}{2}} = -\sqrt{\frac{1 + (-3/5)}{2}} = -\frac{1}{\sqrt{5}},$$

$$\sin \frac{\theta}{2} = +\sqrt{\frac{1 - \cos \theta}{2}} = +\sqrt{\frac{1 - (-3/5)}{2}} = \frac{2}{\sqrt{5}}.$$

Thus we have

$$w_0 = \sqrt{5} \left(\cos \frac{\theta}{2} + i \sin \frac{\theta}{2} \right) = \sqrt{5} \left(-\frac{1}{\sqrt{5}} + \frac{2i}{\sqrt{5}} \right) = -1 + 2i,$$

$$w_1 = -w_0 = 1 - 2i.$$

Therefore the square roots of $-3 - 4i$ are $-1 + 2i$ and $1 - 2i$.   ∎

EXERCISE 8.5

In the problems of this exercise, express answers in polar form. Then give answers in rectangular form as exact numbers (when possible) or to two decimal places.

1. Find the cube roots of 1.   **2.** Determine the fourth roots of i.

3. Find the fifth roots of $1 - \sqrt{3}\, i$.

4. Determine the roots of the equation $z^4 + 1 - i = 0$.

5. Find the sixth roots of -1 and show the results in a diagram.

6. Determine the sixth roots of $64(\cos 126° + i \sin 126°)$.

7. Find the fourth roots of $16 \left(\sqrt{3} + i \right)$.

8. Determine the values of $\left(\sqrt{3} - i \right)^{3/4}$.

9. Determine the values of $\left(\dfrac{1 - i}{\sqrt{2}} \right)^{-2/3}$.

In Problems 10 through 13 solve the given quadratic equations:

10. $z^2 - (2 + 3i)z - 1 + 3i = 0$ **11.** $z^2 - 3z + 3 - i = 0$

12. $2z^2 + 2\sqrt{2}(-1 + i)z - 1 - 2i = 0$ **13.** $z^2 + z + 1 - i = 0$

14. Find the roots of the equation $z^4 + 1 = 0$.

15. Find the roots of the equation $z^3 + z^2 + iz + i = 0$.

16. Find the roots of the equation $z^5 + 2z^3 - z^2 - 2 = 0$.

17. Find the square roots of $3 - 4i$.   **18.** Find the square roots of $3 + 4i$.

19. Find the square roots of $-5 + 12i$.   **20.** Find the roots of $z^2 - iz - 1 + i = 0$.

21. In the derivation of Eq. (8.7) we encountered the problem of solving the following two equations simultaneously for R and α in terms of r and θ:

$$R^n \cos(n\alpha) = r \cos \theta,$$
$$R^n \sin(n\alpha) = r \sin \theta.$$

Carry out the solution and show that $R = r^{1/n}$ and $\alpha = (\theta + k \cdot 2\pi)/n$. *Hint.* First eliminate α by squaring each of the given equations and then adding the resulting equations. Use identity (I.9) (p. 122). After you get R, substitute the result in either of the given equations and then solve for α.

REVIEW EXERCISE

In Problems 1 through 12 evaluate the given expression and present the result in the form $a + bi$, where a and b are real numbers. Give answers in exact form whenever it is reasonable to do so; otherwise give a and b correct to two decimal places.

1. $(1 + i)^3$ **2.** $(3 - 2i)^2$ **3.** $(1 + 2i)^4$

4. $(\sqrt{3} + i)^6$ **5.** $(1 + i)^{-2}$ **6.** $625(3 + 4i)^{-4}$

7. $(1 + i)\left(\sqrt{3} - i\right)^{-4}$ **8.** $\dfrac{(3 + 4i)^5}{(4 + 3i)^4}$ **9.** $\dfrac{(1 + 2i)(3 + 4i)^3}{(1 - i)^4}$

10. $\left(\dfrac{\sqrt{3}}{2} - \dfrac{1}{2}i\right)^6$ **11.** $(1 + i)^3 - (1 - i)^5$ **12.** $\left(\dfrac{1}{2} + \dfrac{\sqrt{3}}{2}i\right)^{12}$

In Problems 12 through 15, the function f is defined on the set of complex numbers and is given by $f(z) = 3 - 4i + z^2$, where z is any complex number. Evaluate the given expressions and provide exact answers in form $a + bi$, where a and b are real numbers:

13. $f(-3)$ **14.** $f(2 - 2i)$ **15.** $f\left(1 - \sqrt{3}i\right)$

In Problems 16 through 20, give answers in form $a + bi$, where a and b are real numbers:

16. Solve the quadratic equation $z^2 + (2 - i)z - i = 0$.

17. Find the cube roots of $\left(\sqrt{3} - i\right)/2$.

18. Find the fourth roots of $\dfrac{3}{5} - \dfrac{4}{5}i$.

19. Solve the equation $z^4 + (1 + i)z^2 + i = 0$.

20. Solve the equation $z^2 - 2iz - 2 = 0$.

CHAPTER NINE

POLAR COORDINATES

9.1 INTRODUCTION

Many problems involve equations containing two variables. We have found it helpful to have geometric representations of such relationships, since these can frequently provide insights that are not readily apparent from the equation itself. In some problems the situation is reversed, in that we have a problem described geometrically and it becomes useful to consider it in an algebraic setting, which usually involves an equation containing two variables. The form of the equation we get will depend to a large degree upon the reference (or coordinate) system we decide to use. So far, all of our geometric representations have been in a rectangular (or cartesian) system of coordinates. This has served us well for most problems. However, there are situations where a given geometrical problem translates into a cumbersome equation if rectangular coordinates are used as the reference system. In this chapter we introduce a system of coordinates known as *polar coordinates* that is particularly useful in many situations.

As indicated at the beginning of this book, our geometric objects are restricted to a given plane (in future courses the student will encounter problems requiring three-dimensional geometry). A rectangular system of coordinates begins with two perpendicular lines. It is customary to take these lines as horizontal and vertical and call them the x-axis and the y-axis, respectively. On each axis we have a one-to-one correspondence between points and real numbers.* This provides us with a system that has a one-to-one correspondence between pairs of real numbers (x, y) and points P in the plane.

---

* That is, we assume that each point of a given line can be associated with a unique real number, and vice versa; this same correspondence associates each real number with a unique point on the line.

The *system of polar coordinates* begins with a ray (half-line) called the *polar axis;* its initial point is called the *polar origin* (point O), as shown in Fig. 9.1.

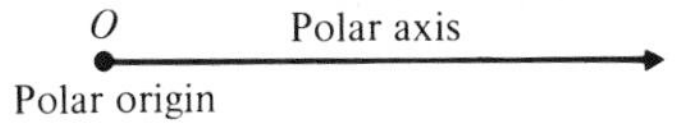

$$O \qquad \text{Polar axis}$$
$$\text{Polar origin}$$

Figure 9.1

Let point P be any point (other than O) in the plane (Fig. 9.2). Let the ray $\overrightarrow{OP}$ be the terminal side of the directed angle θ obtained by rotating the polar axis about point O through the angle of measure θ (which can be of any size and positive or negative). We call $\overrightarrow{OP}$ the θ-*ray*.

If the distance from O to P is denoted by r, where r is a positive number, then the polar coordinates of P will be an ordered pair of r and θ values denoted by $[r, \theta]$.*

In many problems it is convenient to allow the first member of the ordered pair $[r, \theta]$ to be a negative number. This can be done by considering the ordered pair $[-r, \theta + \pi]$, where r is a positive number. Then $[-r, \theta + \pi]$ represents point Q that is at a directed distance of $-r$ along the $(\theta + \pi)$-ray; this means a distance of r in the opposite direction, which puts Q on the θ-ray. That is, point Q is the same as point P. Therefore, both $[r, \theta]$ and $[-r, \theta + \pi]$ are names of the same point P in polar coordinates, as shown in Fig. 9.2.

It is clear that the θ-ray and the $(\theta + 2\pi)$-ray are the same; so $[r, \theta]$ and $[r, \theta + 2\pi]$ represent the same point. In fact, point P shown in Fig. 9.2 can be represented by any of the ordered pairs:

$$[r, \theta + 2k\pi] \quad \text{or} \quad [-r, \theta + (2k + 1)\pi], \text{ where } k \text{ is any integer.}$$

The above discussion indicates how to name any point P in the plane in terms of polar coordinates. The special case where P is the polar origin is denoted by $[0, \theta]$, where angle θ can have any value.

Note that in polar coordinates we do not enjoy the luxury we have in rectangular coordinates where there is a one-to-one correspondence between

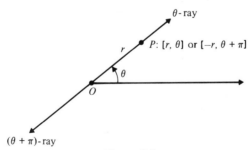

Figure 9.2

---

* We use the bracket notation $[r, \theta]$ to distinguish the name of a point in polar coordinates from its corresponding name (x, y) in rectangular coordinates.

points in the plane and ordered pairs of real numbers. In polar coordinates each point P can be represented by infinitely many ordered pairs; however, a given ordered pair is associated with exactly one point. Although the lack of a one-to-one correspondence is an undesirable feature of polar coordinates, it does not create a serious problem.

We remind the student that in algebra the definition of *equality of ordered pairs* is given by:

$$(a, b) = (c, d) \quad \text{if and only if} \quad a = c \quad \text{and} \quad b = d.$$

We retain this definition of ordered pairs $[r, \theta]$ and *we do not say that* $[r, \theta]$ *equals* $[-r, \theta + \pi]$ even though they both represent the same point.

Examples

 For each of the following, draw a diagram to illustrate the given ray:

a) 30°-ray   b) 480°-ray   c) − 150°-ray   d) $\frac{5\pi}{4}$-ray

Solution. (See Fig. 9.3.)

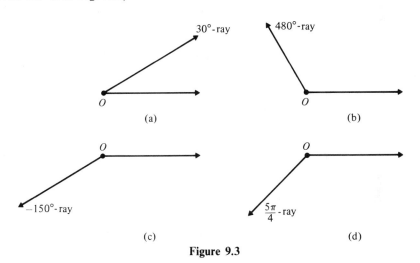

30°-ray   480°-ray

O O

(a)   (b)

O O

−150°-ray $\frac{5\pi}{4}$-ray

(c)   (d)

Figure 9.3

 In each of the following give two other names for the given ray:
a) 45°-ray   b) π-ray   c) 2.5-ray   d) − 2.5-ray

Solution.
    a) 405°-ray; − 315°-ray   b) 3π-ray; − 3π-ray
    c) $(2.5 + 2\pi)$-ray = 8.78-ray; $(2.5 − 2\pi)$-ray = − 3.78-ray.
    d) $(− 2.5 + 2\pi)$-ray = 3.78-ray; $(− 2.5 + 4\pi)$-ray = 10.07-ray.

⚠️3 Point P shown in Fig. 9.4 is on the 30°-ray at a distance 2 from the polar origin. Give four different names for P in polar coordinates.

Solution. Any of the following pairs can be used as the name of point P:

$$[2, 30°]; \qquad [2, 30° + 360°] = [2, 390°];$$
$$[2, 30° - 360°] = [2, -330°]; \qquad [-2, 30° + 180°] = [-2, 210°].$$

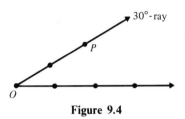

Figure 9.4

⚠️4 Suppose point P is at a distance of 3 from the polar origin on the $7\pi/6$-ray. Let Q be the point obtained by reflecting P about the line ℓ perpendicular to the polar axis and passing through the polar origin (Fig. 9.5). Give four different names for Q in polar coordinates.

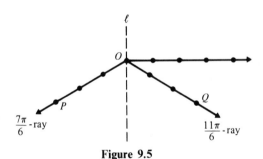

Figure 9.5

Solution. From the diagram we see that point Q is on the $11\pi/6$-ray and 3 units from O. Therefore, Q can be represented by any of the following ordered pairs:

$$[3, \tfrac{11\pi}{6}]; \qquad [3, -\tfrac{\pi}{6}]; \qquad [-3, \tfrac{5\pi}{6}]; \qquad [3, -\tfrac{13\pi}{6}].$$

⚠️5 Draw sketches to illustrate the points corresponding to the given ordered pairs in polar coordinates:

a) $[2, 40°]$ \qquad b) $[-3, 580°]$ \qquad c) $[3, \tfrac{3\pi}{4}]$ \qquad d) $[-4, -3\pi]$

Solution. (See Fig. 9.6.)

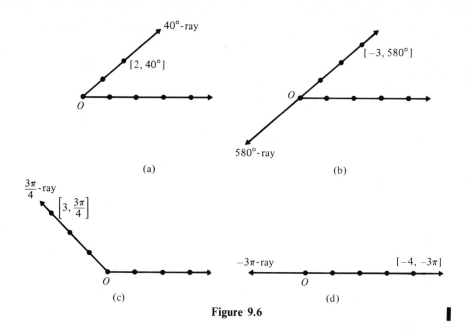

Figure 9.6

EXERCISE 9.1

1. In the following cases, a point is described relative to the polar axis with polar origin O. Draw a diagram showing the given point and name four different ordered pairs $[r, \theta]$ that describe the point in polar coordinates:
   a) P is 3 units from O on the 50°-ray
   b) Q is 4 units from O on the -60°-ray
   c) T is 2 units from O on the 540°-ray

2. Suppose that points P, Q, and T of Problem 1 are reflected about the polar origin O to get new points P_1, Q_1 and T_1, respectively. For each of these points give an ordered pair $[r, \theta]$ that can be used to represent the point in polar coordinates.

3. Suppose that points P, Q, and T of Problem 1 are reflected about the polar axis to get new points P_2, Q_2, T_2, respectively. For each of these points give an ordered pair $[r, \theta]$ corresponding to the point in polar coordinates.

4. In each of the following, a point is described relative to the polar axis with polar origin O. Draw a diagram showing the given point and then write four different ordered pairs of real numbers $[r, \theta]$ that can be used to name the point in polar coordinates:
   a) P is 2 units from O on the $2\pi/3$-ray
   b) Q is 3 units from O on the $-11\pi/12$-ray
   c) T is 4 units from O on the $17\pi/6$-ray

5. Suppose that points P, Q, and T of Problem 4 are reflected about the polar origin to get points P_1, Q_1, and T_1, respectively. For each of these points give an ordered pair $[r, \theta]$ of real numbers to name the points in polar coordinates.

6. Suppose that points P_1, Q_1, and T_1 of Problem 5 are reflected about the line through O perpendicular to the polar axis to get points P_2, Q_2, and T_2, respectively. For each of these points give an ordered pair $[r, \theta]$ of real numbers that can be used to represent the point in polar coordinates. How are P_2, Q_2, T_2 geometrically related to P, Q, T of Problem 4?

7. Draw a diagram that illustrates the points corresponding to the given ordered pairs:
   a) $[3, 60°]$ b) $[-4, 45°]$ c) $[-2, 180°]$ d) $[-3, -450°]$

8. Draw a diagram showing the points that correspond to the given ordered pairs:
   a) $[4, \frac{4\pi}{3}]$ b) $[-3, \frac{5\pi}{12}]$ c) $[2, 17\pi]$ d) $[-2, -2.36]$

9. The points given in Problem 7 are reflected about the polar origin. Give ordered pairs $[r, \theta]$ of real numbers representing the new points in polar coordinates.

10. The points given in Problem 8 are reflected about the polar axis. Give ordered pairs $[r, \theta]$ of real numbers that can be used to represent the new points.

9.2 GRAPHS IN POLAR COORDINATES

In algebra and in earlier parts of this book we encountered a variety of problems in which the equation was given in the form $y = f(x)$ and then a graph (curve) corresponding to the given equation was drawn, using a system of rectangular coordinates. In this section we consider a similar problem: Given $r = f(\theta)$, draw the curve corresponding to this equation in polar coordinates.

Examples

⚠ Sketch the curve whose equation in polar coordinates is $r = 2 \sin \theta$.

Solution. We first determine several ordered pairs $[r, \theta]$ that satisfy the given equation. These are shown in the following table:

θ	0	$\frac{\pi}{6}$	$\frac{\pi}{4}$	$\frac{\pi}{3}$	$\frac{\pi}{2}$	$\frac{2\pi}{3}$	$\frac{3\pi}{4}$	$\frac{5\pi}{6}$	π
r	0	1	$\sqrt{2}$	$\sqrt{3}$	2	$\sqrt{3}$	$\sqrt{2}$	1	0

Note that it is not necessary to continue with larger values of θ since $\sin(\theta + \pi) = -\sin \theta$ is an identity, and so

$$[r, \theta + \pi] = [2 \sin(\theta + \pi), \theta + \pi] = [-2 \sin \theta, \theta + \pi].$$

Therefore,

$$[r, \theta + \pi] = [-2 \sin \theta, \theta + \pi] \quad \text{and} \quad [r, \theta] = [2 \sin \theta, \theta]$$

represent the same point.

In a similar manner we can show that negative values of θ produce no points that are not already included in the points given by $0 \leq \theta \leq \pi$.

We now plot the points given in the table and then draw the curve shown in Fig. 9.7. Thus $r = 2 \sin \theta$ appears to be an equation of a circle, and indeed it is. ▮

 Sketch the curve whose equation in polar coordinates is $r = 1 + \cos \theta$.

Solution. As in Example 1, we first make a table giving ordered pairs $[r, \theta]$ that satisfy the given equation (the r-values are given in decimal form to two places):

θ	0°	45°	90°	135°	180°	225°	270°	315°	360°
r	2	1.71	1	0.29	0	0.29	1	1.71	2

Since $\cos(\theta + 2\pi) = \cos \theta$ is an identity, it is clear that we would get no new points by considering values of θ that lie outside the interval $0° \leq \theta \leq 360°$. We plot these points and draw the curve, as shown in Fig. 9.8. The curve is called a *cardioid* for obvious reasons.

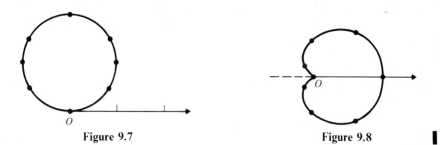

Figure 9.7   Figure 9.8   ▮

 Sketch the curve whose equation in polar coordinates is $r = 3$.

Solution. As in the preceding two examples, we first make a table of ordered pairs $[r, \theta]$. The variable θ does not appear explicitly in the given equation; if this causes any problems, we can write the equation in equivalent form as $r = 3 + 0 \cdot \theta$. We see that no matter what value of θ we use, r will always be equal to 3. Thus the corresponding points are on a circle of radius 3 with center at the polar origin, as shown in Fig. 9.9. ▮

 Sketch the curve whose equation in polar coordinates is $r = \sin 3\theta$.

Solution. We first note that sin $3(\theta + \pi) = -\sin 3\theta$ is an identity. Thus the point given by

$$[r, \theta + \pi] = [\sin 3(\theta + \pi), \theta + \pi] = [-3 \sin \theta, \theta + \pi]$$

is the same as the point given by $[r, \theta] = [3 \sin \theta, \theta]$. Therefore, it is sufficient to use values of θ in the interval $0 \leq \theta \leq \pi$, as shown in the following table:

θ	$\frac{\pi}{12}$	$\frac{\pi}{6}$	$\frac{\pi}{4}$	$\frac{\pi}{3}$	$\frac{5\pi}{12}$	$\frac{\pi}{2}$	$\frac{7\pi}{12}$	$\frac{2\pi}{3}$	$\frac{3\pi}{4}$	$\frac{5\pi}{6}$	$\frac{11\pi}{12}$	π
r	0.71	1	0.71	0	-0.71	-1	-0.71	0	0.71	1	0.71	0

Plotting the points given in this table and connecting them in an obvious manner gives the *three-leaf rose* shown in Fig. 9.10. ▌

5\ Sketch the curve whose equation in polar coordinates is given by $r = -\theta$, where $\theta \geq 0$.

Solution. Note that the given equation implies that radian measure is to be used for θ. We first make a table of ordered pairs $[r, \theta]$ that satisfy the equation:

θ	0	$\frac{\pi}{4}$	$\frac{\pi}{2}$	$\frac{3\pi}{4}$	π	$\frac{5\pi}{4}$	$\frac{3\pi}{2}$	$\frac{7\pi}{4}$	2π
r	0	-0.79	-1.57	-2.36	-3.14	-3.93	-4.71	-5.50	-6.28

Plotting these points and drawing a curve through them gives a *spiral*, as shown in Fig. 9.11. The curve begins at the polar origin and (as θ increases) winds around in the counterclockwise direction, as illustrated in Fig. 9.11. ▌

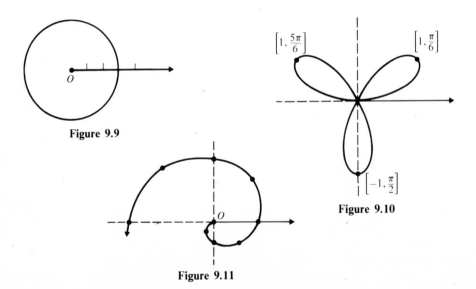

Figure 9.9

$\left[1, \frac{5\pi}{6}\right]$ $\left[1, \frac{\pi}{6}\right]$

$\left[-1, \frac{\pi}{2}\right]$

Figure 9.10

Figure 9.11

EXERCISE 9.2

Sketch the curves corresponding to the equations given in polar coordinates:

1. $r = \cos\theta$ 2. $r = 3\cos\theta$

3. $r = 2$ 4. $r = -2\sin\theta$

5. $r = 1 + \sin\theta$ 6. $r = 1 - \sin\theta$

7. $r = 1 - \cos\theta$ 8. $r = 3 + \sin^2\theta + \cos^2\theta$

9. $r = \sin 2\theta$ 10. $r = \cos 3\theta$

11. $r = \cos^2\theta - \sin^2\theta$ 12. $r^2 = 4$

13. $r = \cos\theta \tan\theta$ 14. $r = \sin^2\theta$

15. $r = \sin\left(\theta + \dfrac{\pi}{4}\right)$ 16. $r = \cos(\theta + \pi)$

17. $r = 1 + 2\cos\theta$ 18. $r = 2 - \sin\theta$

19. $r = \theta$, where $\theta \geq 0$ 20. $r = \dfrac{3}{\theta}$, where $\theta \geq 1$

9.3 RELATIONSHIP BETWEEN POLAR AND RECTANGULAR COORDINATES

Suppose the polar axis coincides with the positive x-axis, as shown in Fig. 9.12, and suppose P is any point in the plane. The name of point P is (x, y) relative to the x, y-axes, and $[r, \theta]$ relative to the polar axis. The following equations give the relationship between rectangular and polar coordinates:

$$\boxed{\begin{aligned} x &= r\cos\theta, \\ y &= r\sin\theta; \end{aligned}} \qquad (9.1)$$

$$\boxed{\begin{aligned} r^2 &= x^2 + y^2, \\ \tan\theta &= \frac{y}{x}. \end{aligned}} \qquad (9.2)$$

The equations given in (9.1) are *transformation equations from polar to rectangular coordinates*. For each pair $[r, \theta]$ there is precisely one pair (x, y) corresponding to it.

The equations given in (9.2) are known as the *transformation equations from rectangular to polar coordinates*. Note that for a given pair (x, y) we can get multiple pairs $[r, \theta]$ representing the same point. Since r can be taken as

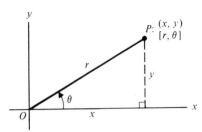

Figure 9.12

$\sqrt{x^2 + y^2}$ or as $-\sqrt{x^2 + y^2}$, and $\theta = \tan^{-1}(y/x)$ is multiple-valued, we must be careful to match appropriate values of r and θ. This is illustrated by the following examples.

Examples

⚠ Find all ordered pairs $[r, \theta]$ associated with the points given in rectangular coordinates:

    a) $(3, 4)$ b) $(-2, -1)$

Solution.

    a) We use Eq. (9.2) as follows. First find r, θ, where $r > 0$:

$$r = \sqrt{3^2 + 4^2} = 5 \qquad \text{and} \qquad \theta = \tan \frac{4}{3};$$

θ is in the first quadrant (Fig. 9.13). This gives the set of ordered pairs:

$$A = \{[5,\ 53.13° + k \cdot 360°] \mid k \text{ is any integer}\}.$$

    Now find r, θ, where $r < 0$:

$$r = -\sqrt{3^2 + 4^2} = -5 \qquad \text{and} \qquad \theta = \tan \frac{4}{3};$$

θ is in the third quadrant. This gives the set of ordered pairs:

$$B = \{[-5,\ 233.13° + k \cdot 360°] \mid k \text{ is any integer}\}.$$

Therefore, the name of the point associated with $(3, 4)$ is given in polar coordinates by any one of the ordered pairs in the union of sets A and B; that is $A \cup B$.

    b) In a manner similar to (a) we can write the following. For $r > 0$:

$$r = \sqrt{(-2)^2 + (-1)^2} = \sqrt{5} \qquad \text{and} \qquad \tan \theta = \frac{-1}{-2} = \frac{1}{2},$$

where θ is in the third quadrant (Fig. 9.14). That is,

$$r = \sqrt{5} \qquad \text{and} \qquad \theta = 3.61 + k \cdot 2\pi.$$

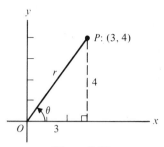

Figure 9.13

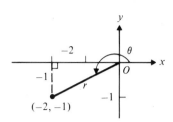

Figure 9.14

For $r < 0$,

$$r = -\sqrt{5} \qquad \text{and} \qquad \tan \theta = \frac{1}{2},$$

where θ is in the first quadrant. That is, $r = -\sqrt{5}$ and $\theta = 0.46 + k \cdot 2\pi$.

Therefore, point $(-2, -1)$ is represented in polar coordinates by any of the ordered pairs in the set:

$$\{[\sqrt{5}, \; 3.61 + k \cdot 2\pi] \mid k \text{ any integer}\} \cup \{[-\sqrt{5}, \; 0.46 + k \cdot 2\pi] \mid k \text{ any integer}\}. \quad \blacksquare$$

◢2◣ The given ordered pairs name points in polar coordinates. Find the names of the same points in rectangular coordinates:

a) $[4, 60°]$ b) $[-3, 180°]$ c) $[4, -3\pi/4]$ d) $[-2, 2.48]$

Solution. We use the formulas of Eq. (9.1), which are valid even when r is negative.

a) $x = 4 \cos 60° = 4 \cdot \frac{1}{2} = 2; \quad y = 4 \sin 60° = 4 \cdot \sqrt{3}/2 = 2\sqrt{3}.$
Therefore, the point in rectangular coordinates is given by $(2, 2\sqrt{3})$.

b) $x = -3 \cos 180° = -3(-1) = 3; \quad y = -3 \sin 180° = -3 \cdot 0 = 0.$
Therefore, the given point is $(3, 0)$ in rectangular coordinates.

c) $x = 4 \cos (-3\pi/4) = -2\sqrt{2}; \quad y = 4 \sin (-3\pi/4) = -2\sqrt{2}.$
Thus, the given point is denoted by $(-2\sqrt{2}, -2\sqrt{2})$ in rectangular coordinates.

d) $x = -2 \cos 2.48 = 1.58; \quad y = -2 \sin 2.48 = -1.23.$
Therefore, $[-2, 2.48]$ is represented by $(1.58, -1.23)$ in rectangular coordinates. $\blacksquare$

◢3◣ Find an equation in polar coordinates that describes the same set of points (same curve) as $x^2 + y^2 - 2x = 0$ in rectangular coordinates.

Solution. Substituting $x = r \cos \theta$ and $y = r \sin \theta$ into the given equation, we get

$$(r \cos \theta)^2 + (r \sin \theta)^2 - 2(r \cos \theta) = 0.$$

This is equivalent to $r^2 - 2r \cos \theta = 0$; and so $r = 0$ or $r = 2 \cos \theta$. Since $r = 0$ gives only the polar origin as a point and from $r = 2 \cos \theta$ we get the point $[0, \pi/2]$, which is also the polar origin, we can neglect $r = 0$ in our solution. That is, $r = 2 \cos \theta$ will describe the same set of points as $x^2 + y^2 - 2x = 0$.   ∎

4. Find an equation in rectangular coordinates that describes the same set of points as $r = 2 \sin \theta + \cos \theta$ in polar coordinates.

Solution. Since a direct substitution for r and θ from Eq. (9.2) would involve $\sqrt{x^2 + y^2}$, it is simpler to first multiply both sides of the given equation by r:

$$r^2 = 2r \sin \theta + r \cos \theta.$$

Now, replacing r^2 by $x^2 + y^2$, $r \sin \theta$ by y, and $r \cos \theta$ by x, we get

$$x^2 + y^2 = 2y + x.$$

Note. In this example we should check the possibility that we may have introduced some extraneous points by multiplying both sides of the given equation by r. This can occur only if we had multiplied by the value $r = 0$. Since $r = 0$ represents the origin, the only possible extraneous point is the origin. Thus we must check whether the origin is also a point on the curve represented by the polar equation. We see that $2 \sin \theta + \cos \theta = 0$ for $\theta = \text{Tan}^{-1}(-\frac{1}{2}) = -0.46$; that is, $[0, -0.46]$ satisfies the given equation, and so the origin is on the given curve.   ∎

5. Draw a graph of the equation $\theta = 2$ in polar coordinates. Then find an equivalent equation in rectangular coordinates.

Solution. The graph of $\theta = 2$ is a line through the origin, as shown in Fig. 9.15. Since $\tan \theta = y/x$, the corresponding equation in rectangular coordinates is $y/x = \tan 2$ or $y = x(\tan 2)$. In decimal form this is $y = -2.19\ x$.   ∎

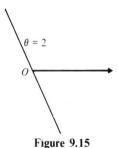

$\theta = 2$

O

Figure 9.15

EXERCISE 9.3

In each case, when the answer is expressed in decimal form, give the result correct to two decimal places.

1. In the following, points are given in rectangular coordinates. Find the names of the points in polar coordinates:
   a) $(-1, 1)$ b) $(-1, -\sqrt{3})$ c) $(\pi, 4)$ d) $(-1.57, 2.43)$

2. For each of the points in Problem 1, find the set of all possible ordered pairs $[r, \theta]$ that can be used as polar coordinates for the given points.

3. Express the following points in polar coordinates with $r \geq 0$ and $0 \leq \theta \leq 2\pi$:

   a) $(-3, 3)$ b) $(1, -3)$ c) $\left(\pi, \dfrac{1 + \sqrt{5}}{2}\right)$

4. Express the following points in polar coordinates using the least positive angle and $r < 0$:
   a) $(4, -3)$ b) $(-\sqrt{3}, \sqrt{3})$ c) $(2.52, -2\pi)$

5. Express the following points in rectangular coordinates:

   a) $[2, \dfrac{\pi}{2}]$ b) $[-3, -\dfrac{3\pi}{4}]$ c) $[2.24, -0.37]$

6. Express the following points in rectangular coordinates:
   a) $[0, 30°]$ b) $[4, -630°]$ c) $[-2, 47°37']$

7. Determine whether the given pair satisfies the equation $r^2 \sin \theta = 1$:
   a) $[1, \dfrac{\pi}{2}]$ b) $[-1, -\dfrac{\pi}{2}]$ c) $[\sqrt{2}, \dfrac{5\pi}{6}]$ d) $[0, 0]$ e) $[1, \dfrac{3\pi}{2}]$

8. The position of point P is given in rectangular coordinates. Determine whether P lies on the curve whose equation in polar coordinates is $r = 1 + \cos \theta$:

   a) $(0, 0)$ b) $(0, 1)$ c) $(2, 0)$ d) $\left(\dfrac{1 + \sqrt{2}}{2}, \dfrac{1 + \sqrt{2}}{2}\right)$.

9. Let $[r_1, \theta_1]$ be polar coordinates of point P and $[r_2, \theta_2]$ be polar coordinates of point Q. If d represents the distance between P and Q, show that d is given by
$$d = \sqrt{r_1^2 + r_2^2 - 2r_1 r_2 \cos(\theta_1 - \theta_2)}.$$

10. Use the result of Problem 9 to find the distance between each of the given pairs of points:
    a) $[3, 0], [\pi, \pi]$ b) $[1, \dfrac{\pi}{3}], [-2, \dfrac{3\pi}{4}]$
    c) $[-3.4, 32°], [1.6, 1.47]$ d) $[-2.4, 3.2], [3.7, -0.64]$

In Problems 11 through 14, find an equation in rectangular coordinates that describes the same set of points (same curve) as the given equation in polar coordinates:

11. $r \cos \theta = 3$

12. $3\theta = 4$

13. $r(1 - \sin \theta) = 2$

14. $r = 2 \cos(\theta + \pi)$

In Problems 15 through 18, find an equation in polar coordinates that describes the same set of points (same curve) as the given equation in rectangular coordinates. Then sketch the curve using either of the equations.

15. $x^2 + y^2 = 1$

16. $2xy = 3$

17. $3x - y = 0$ **18.** $x^2 + y^2 + x = \sqrt{x^2 + y^2}$

19. Are all points of the curve whose equation is $r = \sin \theta$ also on the curve with equation $r \csc \theta = 1$? Substantiate your answer.

20. Express $r = \sin 2\theta$ as an equation in rectangular coordinates.

REVIEW EXERCISE

In any problem where both rectangular and polar coordinates are used, it is assumed that the positive x-axis coincides with the polar axis.

1. The name of a point is given in rectangular coordinates; give a name of the point in polar coordinates:

   a) $(1, 0)$ b) $(-3, 0)$ c) $(4, 4)$ d) $(-2, 2)$

   e) $(-\sqrt{3}, -1)$ f) $(\sqrt{2}, -\sqrt{2})$ g) $(0, 4)$ h) $(0, -3)$

2. As in Problem 1, find a name of the given point in polar coordinates. Find r and θ (in radians) to two decimal places:

   a) $(3, 4)$ b) $(-5, 1)$ c) $(3, -5)$ d) $(-2, -1)$

3. The name of a point is given in polar coordinates. Draw a diagram illustrating the point and then write its name in rectangular coordinates:

   a) $[4, \frac{\pi}{3}]$ b) $[-2, \frac{5\pi}{6}]$ c) $[4, \pi]$

   d) $[-1, \frac{9\pi}{4}]$ e) $[-3, -\frac{3\pi}{4}]$

4. Follow the instructions of Problem 3. Give answers to two decimal places:

   a) $[1, \frac{5\pi}{7}]$ b) $[-4, 3.47]$ c) $[2.3, 1.35]$

   d) $[-2, \frac{17\pi}{5}]$ e) $[3, -4.32]$

In Problems 5 through 12, an equation is given in polar coordinates. Draw a graph of the corresponding curve:

5. $r = \sin \theta$ **6.** $r^2 = 16$ **7.** $r = 2 \sin(-\theta)$

8. $r = \cos \theta - 1$ **9.** $r = 3 \sec \theta$ **10.** $r = \cos 2\theta$

11. $2r = \theta$, where $\theta \geq 0$ **12.** $r = \sin\left(\theta + \frac{\pi}{2}\right)$

13. Find an equation in polar coordinates that describes the same curve as $x^2 + y^2 = 4$. Draw a graph of the curve.

14. Find an equation in polar coordinates that describes the same curve as $x^2 + y^2 + y = \sqrt{x^2 + y^2}$. Draw a graph of the curve.

15. Draw a graph of $r(1 + \cos \theta) = 1$. Then find an equation in rectangular coordinates that describes the same curve.

16. Draw a graph of $r \sin \theta = 3$. Then find an equation in rectangular coordinates that describes the same curve.

CHAPTER TEN

LOGARITHMS

In the past, one of the important uses of logarithms has been as an aid in computational problems, particularly in those that involve only multiplication, division, raising to powers, or extracting roots of numbers. With the introduction of hand-held calculators, the use of logarithms for computational purposes has been practically abandoned. However, logarithmic functions occur in many applications as well as in theoretical mathematics, and so they still present an important topic for study. In this chapter our discussion will be primarily directed toward the study of basic *properties of logarithms* rather than their use for computation.

We introduce logarithmic functions as inverses of exponential functions. Therefore, it may be helpful to first review the properties of exponents that the student has already encountered in algebra.

10.1 EXPONENTS

The exponential functions that are of interest can be described by

$$f(x) = b^x,$$

where b is a given *positive* number and $b \neq 1$, while x is any real number.* Each such b yields an *exponential function; b* is called the *base* of b^x.

The following *rules of exponents* are basic in working with exponents: if u and v are any real numbers and a and b are positive numbers, then:

(E.1) $$b^u \cdot b^v = b^{u+v}$$

$$b^u / b^v = b^{u-v}$$ (E.2)

---

* If b is a *negative* number, it is possible to define b^x but in general this involves a discussion of complex numbers. This is reserved for later courses in complex variables. Also, we make the restriction that $b \neq 1$ because for $b = 1$, the function $f(x) = 1^x$ is equal to 1 for all x; that is, it is a constant function and we prefer not to call it an exponential function.

(E.3) $$(b^u)^v = b^{uv}$$

(E.4) $$(ab)^u = a^u \cdot b^u$$

(E.5) $$(a/b)^u = a^u/b^u$$

Note that (E.4) and (E.5) are formulas for raising products and quotients to powers. We do not have analogous simple results for raising sums and differences to powers, that is, $(a + b)^n$ is not identically equal to $a^n + b^n$; similarly for $(a - b)^n$. These operations involve the binomial expansion formula.

In addition to the above rules we need the following definitions:
Zero exponent:

$$b^0 = 1 \quad \text{for any } b > 0; \tag{10.1}$$

Negative exponent:

$$b^{-u} = \frac{1}{b^u} \quad \text{for } b > 0 \text{ and any real number } u; \tag{10.2}$$

Radical notation. Radicals are frequently used to denote expressions involving a rational-number exponent. If m and n are integers (with $n > 1$) and $b > 0$, then $b^{m/n}$ is written in radical form as $\sqrt[n]{b^m}$. That is,

$$b^{m/n} = \sqrt[n]{b^m}. \tag{10.3}$$

Note. When $n = 2$, we make a special case and write $b^{m/2} = \sqrt{b^m}$ (not $\sqrt[2]{b^m}$).

If formulas (E.4) and (E.5) are written in radical form for the special case of $u = 1/n$, we get

(E.6) $$\sqrt[n]{ab} = \sqrt[n]{a}\,\sqrt[n]{b}$$

(E.7) $$\sqrt[n]{\frac{a}{b}} = \sqrt[n]{a}/\sqrt[n]{b}$$

Examples

⚠ Evaluate the following and express answers in exact form:

a) $4^3 \cdot 4^2$ b) $4^3 \div 4^5$ c) $2^3 \div 2^{-5}$

d) $64^{3/2}$ e) $(16^{3/4})^2$ f) $(25^{-3})^{-1/2}$

Solution

a) $4^3 \cdot 4^2 = 4^{3+2} = 4^5 = 1024$

b) $4^3 \div 4^5 = 4^{3-5} = 4^{-2} = \dfrac{1}{4^2} = \dfrac{1}{16}$

c) $2^3 \div 2^{-5} = 2^{3-(-5)} = 2^{3+5} = 2^8 = 256$

d) $64^{3/2} = (8^2)^{3/2} = 8^3 = 512$

e) $(16^{3/4})^2 = 16^{(3/4)\,(2)} = 16^{3/2} = (4^2)^{3/2} = 4^3 = 64$

f) $(25^{-3})^{-1/2} = 25^{(-3)\,(-1/2)} = 25^{3/2} = (5^2)^{3/2} = 5^3 = 125$ ∎

⚠️ 2 In Example 1, all of the problems were selected so that the answers can be expressed in simple rational-number form. In this example we consider problems where this is not possible, so we get approximate decimal answers using the calculator.

Find the decimal approximation (rounded off to four places) of the following:

a) $7^{1/2} = \sqrt{7}$ b) $7^{3/4}$ c) $3\sqrt{17^4}$

d) $3^{-\sqrt{2}}$ e) $\left(\dfrac{1+\sqrt{5}}{2}\right)^{\sqrt{3}}$ f) $\left(\dfrac{1-\sqrt{3}}{2}\right)^{\sqrt{2}}$

Solution

a) To evaluate $\sqrt{7}$, we can use the ⟨√x⟩ key; pressing 7 aı⎺⎺ ⟨√x⟩ , we get the answer directly in the display: $\sqrt{7} = 2.6458$. We could also use the ⟨yˣ⟩ key to evaluate $7^{1/2}$.

b) To evaluate $7^{3/4}$ we use the ⟨yˣ⟩ key and press the following sequence of keys:
For algebraic calculators:

         7   ⟨yˣ⟩   ⟨(⟩   3   ⟨÷⟩   4   ⟨)⟩   ⟨=⟩

For RPN calculators:

         7   ⟨ENT⟩   3   ⟨ENT⟩   4   ⟨÷⟩   ⟨yˣ⟩

The display shows $7^{3/4} = 4.3035$.

c) Using the definition given by (10.3), we can write $\sqrt[3]{17^4}$ as $17^{4/3}$. Following a sequence of key strokes similar to those of (b), we get $\sqrt[3]{17^4} = 43.7118$.

d) We evaluate $3^{-\sqrt{2}}$ by pressing the following sequence of keys:
Algebraic calculators:

         3   ⟨yˣ⟩   2   ⟨√x⟩   ⟨+/−⟩   ⟨=⟩

RPN calculators:

         3   ⟨ENT⟩   2   ⟨√x⟩   ⟨CHS⟩   ⟨yˣ⟩

The display shows: $3^{-\sqrt{2}} = 0.2115$.

e) To find $\left((1+\sqrt{5})/2\right)^{\sqrt{3}}$ we first evaluate $(1+\sqrt{5})/2$ and then, with the result in the display, stroke a sequence of keys similar to that in (d). This gives $\left((1+\sqrt{5})/2\right)^{\sqrt{3}} = 2.3013$.

f) This case is similar to (e). However, the calculator indicates "Error" for the final result. The difficulty is that $(1-\sqrt{3})/2$ is a negative number.

On most calculators the $\boxed{y^x}$ *key can be used to evaluate exponentials only when the base is positive.* This is consistent with our requirement that $b > 0$ in $f(x) = b^x$. Thus $\left((1 - \sqrt{3})/2\right)^{\sqrt{2}}$ is undefined within the context of our discussion of exponential functions. ∎

/3\ a) Rationalize the denominator in $4/(\sqrt{5} - 1)$ and then use a calculator to check the result.

b) Similarly, rationalize the numerator of $(\sqrt{17} + 1)/8$.

Solution

a) Our goal is to express $4/(\sqrt{5} - 1)$ as a fraction without a radical in the denominator. This can be done by multiplying the numerator and denominator by $\sqrt{5} + 1$, as follows:

$$\frac{4}{\sqrt{5} - 1} = \frac{4(\sqrt{5} + 1)}{(\sqrt{5} - 1)(\sqrt{5} + 1)} = \frac{4(\sqrt{5} + 1)}{5 - 1} = \frac{4(\sqrt{5} + 1)}{4} = \sqrt{5} + 1.$$

As a check, we use a calculator to evaluate $4/(\sqrt{5} - 1)$ and $\sqrt{5} + 1$:

$$\frac{4}{\sqrt{5} - 1} = 3.236067979, \ \sqrt{5} + 1 = 3.236067977 \text{ (to nine decimal places)}.$$

The disagreement in the final decimal digit is due to the round-off error in the calculator.

b) $$\frac{\sqrt{17} + 1}{8} = \frac{(\sqrt{17} + 1)(\sqrt{17} - 1)}{8(\sqrt{17} - 1)} = \frac{17 - 1}{8(\sqrt{17} - 1)} = \frac{16}{8(\sqrt{17} - 1)}$$
$$= \frac{2}{\sqrt{17} - 1}.$$

As a check,

$$\frac{\sqrt{17} + 1}{8} = 0.640388203, \qquad \frac{2}{\sqrt{17} - 1} \doteq 0.640388203. \quad ∎$$

/4\ When a principal of P dollars is invested at compound interest, the amount A accumulated at the end of n years is given by the formula

$$A = P\left(1 + \frac{r}{m}\right)^{mn},$$

where r is the interest rate and m is the number of times per year the interest is compounded.

If \$1250 is invested at a bank that pays 7.75% interest compounded twice a year, what is the value of the investment at the end of 8 years?

Solution
$$A = 1250\left(1 + \frac{0.0775}{2}\right)^{2 \cdot 8} \text{ dollars} = 1250\left(1 + \frac{0.0775}{2}\right)^{16} \text{ dollars}.$$

Using a calculator to evaluate this, we get $A = \$2296.61$. ∎

⑤ Evaluate the product $y = (0.00000048763) \cdot (5347000000)$ and give the answer rounded off to four significant digits.

Solution Since the number of digits in each of the given numbers is greater than the digit capacity of the calculator, we first express the numbers in scientific notation (see Appendix B). Thus, we have

$$y = (4.8763 \times 10^{-7}) \cdot (5.347 \times 10^9) = (4.8763) \cdot (5.347) \times 10^2$$

$$= 2607 \text{ (to four significant digits).} \qquad\blacksquare$$

⑥ Suppose f is a function given by $f(x) = (1 + x)^{1/x}$, where $x > -1$ and $x \neq 0$. Evaluate $f(x)$ for several values of x near zero; then make a reasonable guess about what value is approached by $(1 + x)^{1/x}$ as x approaches zero.

Solution We use a calculator to complete the following table of $f(x)$ values for the given values of x:

x	$f(x)$	x	$f(x)$
1	2	-0.8	7.47674
0.5	2.25	-0.5	4
0.2	2.48832	-0.2	3.05176
0.1	2.59374	-0.1	2.86797
0.01	2.70481	-0.01	2.73200
0.001	2.71692	-0.001	2.71964
0.0001	2.71815	-0.0001	2.71842

From the values of $f(x)$ in the above table we conclude that $(1 + x)^{1/x}$ is approaching a limit that lies between 2.71815 and 2.71842 (as x approaches 0). $\qquad\blacksquare$

The number e

In Example 6, we observed that as x approaches zero, $(1 + x)^{1/x}$ seems to approach 2.718. . . as a limit. This is actually the case (as the student will see in calculus) and the limiting value is a transcendental number denoted by e:

$$e = 2.718281828. . .$$

The number e is an important number that occurs frequently in applied as well as theoretical problems in mathematics.*

---

⑦ Simplify $\dfrac{(1 + x^{-1})^2}{(1 + x)^2}$.

---

* The letter e is used in honor of the Swiss mathematician Leonhard Euler (1707–1783), one of the greatest mathematicians of all time.

Solution

$$\frac{(1 + x^{-1})^2}{(1 + x)^2} = \frac{(1 + 1/x)^2}{(1 + x)^2} = \frac{[(x + 1)/x]^2}{(1 + x)^2} = \frac{(x + 1)^2/x^2}{(1 + x)^2}$$

$$= \frac{(x + 1)^2}{x^2} \cdot \frac{1}{(1 + x)^2} = \frac{(x + 1)^2}{x^2(1 + x)^2} = \frac{1}{x^2}. \qquad \blacksquare$$

EXERCISE 10.1

In Problems 1 through 25, evaluate the given expression and give answers in simplified exact form:

1. $3^4 \cdot 3^2$

2. $6^5 \cdot 6^{-3}$

3. $4^{-1/2} \cdot 4^{5/2}$

4. $5^{2/3} \cdot 5^{-8/3}$

5. $(3^4)^{-3/2}$

6. $8 \cdot (16^{-3/4})$

7. $(25)^{3/4}(5)^{-5/2}$

8. $36^{5/4} \, 6^{-3/2}$

9. $(9^{2/3}) \div (3^{7/3})$

10. $\dfrac{4(2^{-7/4})}{2^{1/4}}$

11. $\dfrac{3^4(5^{-2})}{3^5(5^{-4})}$

12. $\left(\dfrac{2^{-4} \cdot 8^{-3}}{16^{-5}} \right)^2$

13. $21^{-1/2} \div (3^{1/2} \cdot 7^{-3/2})$

14. $(2^2)^3$

15. $2^{(2^3)}$

16. $\dfrac{\sqrt[3]{27}}{\sqrt[4]{256}}$

17. $\left(\sqrt{2} + \sqrt{8} \right)^2$

18. $\left(\dfrac{1 + \sqrt{5}}{2} \right)^2 - \left(\dfrac{1 + \sqrt{5}}{2} \right)$

19. $\sqrt{5^2 + 12^2}$

20. $\left(\sqrt{3} - \sqrt{8} \right)^2$

21. $\left(\dfrac{1 - \sqrt{5}}{2} \right) - \left(\dfrac{1 - \sqrt{5}}{2} \right)^2$

22. $\sqrt{1007^2 + 1224^2}$

23. $\sqrt{1097^2 - 585^2}$

24. $\left(\dfrac{\sqrt[3]{2} \cdot \sqrt[4]{3}}{\sqrt[6]{6}} \right)^{12}$

25. $\dfrac{7^{5/2} - 63^{3/2}}{\sqrt{7}}$

In Problems 26 through 43 use a calculator to evaluate the given expression and round off answers to two decimal places. If your calculator indicates "Error" for any problem, explain the response. For problems involving the number e, use $e = 2.718281828$ (correct to nine decimal places).

26. $5^{3/4}$

27. $7 \cdot 3^{-3/4}$

28. $4^{2/3} - 3^{5/4}$

29. $\sqrt[3]{5} - \sqrt{3}$

30. $\dfrac{\sqrt{5} + \sqrt{3}}{\sqrt{5} - \sqrt{3}}$

31. $\left(\dfrac{1 - \sqrt{5}}{2} \right)^{1/2}$

32. $\sqrt[5]{7^2 + 17^3}$

33. $\dfrac{4\sqrt{3} + \sqrt[3]{10}}{\sqrt{3} + \sqrt{2}}$

34. $\left(\dfrac{5}{2 - \sqrt{5}}\right)^{1/4}$

35. $\left(\dfrac{2}{1 + \sqrt{5}}\right)^{1/4}$

36. $(0.0000004385) \cdot (6534200000)$

37. $(3.74 \times 10^{-8})(5.43 \times 10^7)$

38. $\dfrac{(2.47 \times 10^{-4})(3.42 \times 10^2)}{4.36 \times 10^{-3}}$

39. e^2

40. $e^{-1/2}$

41. $\sqrt{e}$

42. $e^{-\sqrt{3}}$

43. $\sqrt[3]{e - 1}$

44. Rationalize the denominator; then use a calculator to check your answers:

a) $\dfrac{8}{\sqrt{5} + 1}$

b) $\dfrac{27}{\sqrt{10} - 1}$

c) $\dfrac{\sqrt{3}}{\sqrt{2} - 1}$

45. Rationalize the numerator; then use a calculator to check your answers:

a) $\dfrac{\sqrt{3} + 1}{4}$

b) $\dfrac{(1 + \sqrt{5})^2}{2}$

c) $\dfrac{1 - \sqrt{17}}{4}$

In Problems 46 through 56, simplify the given expression; provide answers without negative exponents. Assume that x and y represent positive numbers.

46. $x^2 \cdot x^3$

47. $\dfrac{y^2 \cdot y^{-3}}{y^{-1}}$

48. $3^{x^2} \cdot 3^{2 - x^2}$

49. $\left(\dfrac{x^3 \cdot x^{-2}}{x^4}\right)^{-1}$

50. $\dfrac{(x^3 + x^2)^2}{x^4}$

51. $\left(\dfrac{x^{-3/4} \cdot x^2}{x^3}\right)^{-4}$

52. $\dfrac{x^{-1} + x}{x + x^2}$

53. $\sqrt{x}/\sqrt{x^3}$

54. $(e^x - e^{-x})^2 - (e^{2x} + e^{-2x})$

55. $\dfrac{x - x^{-1}}{x + 1}$

56. $\dfrac{x^{-1} + 1}{x^{-2} - x^{-1} - 2}$

In Problems 57 through 65, evaluate the indicated expression and round off results to two decimal places:

57. If $f(x) = 2^x$, evaluate
   a) $f(-2/3)$

   b) $f(5/3)$

   c) $f(-2/3) \cdot f(5/3)$

58. If $g(x) = 5^{-2x}$, evaluate:

   a) $g\left(\dfrac{1}{3}\right)$

   b) $g\left(-\dfrac{2}{5}\right)$

   c) $g\left(\dfrac{1}{3}\right) \div g\left(-\dfrac{2}{3}\right)$

59. If $f(x) = 3^{(-x^2 + 2x)}$, evaluate:

a) $f\left(\frac{1}{3}\right)$ b) $f\left(\frac{\sqrt{2}}{2}\right)$ c) $f\left(-\frac{1}{2}\right)$

60. If $g(x) = 2^x + 2^{-x}$, evaluate:

a) $g(1)$ b) $g(-3)$ c) $g\left(1 - \sqrt{3}\right)$

61. If $g(x) = 3^{4x}/3^{x^2}$, find:

a) $g(1)$ b) $g\left(\frac{1}{2}\right)$

62. If $f(x) = 4^{x^2} \cdot 1^{-2x^2}$, find:

a) $f(\sqrt{2})$ b) $f\left(\frac{1}{\sqrt{3}}\right)$ c) $f(-3.478)$

63. If $g(x) = \dfrac{x^4 - 1}{x^3 + x^2 + x + 1}$, find:

a) $g(2)$ b) $g(\sqrt{3})$ c) $g(-1)$

64. If $f(x) = x^{5/2} + x^{3/2}$, find:
a) $f(4)$ b) $f(-2)$

65. If $f(x) = 2.48(1.08)^x$, find:
a) $f(3)$ b) $f(-0.25)$

In Problems 66 through 70, determine whether the given statement is true or false:

66. $\sqrt{9 + 4\sqrt{5}} = 2 + \sqrt{5}$ **67.** $\dfrac{\sqrt{6} - \sqrt{2}}{4} = \dfrac{1}{2}\sqrt{2 - \sqrt{3}}$

68. $\sqrt{a^2 + b^2} = a + b$ for all real numbers a and b

69. $\dfrac{1}{\sqrt{2} - 1} = \sqrt{2} + 1$

70. $(e^x + e^{-x})^2 - (e^x - e^{-x})^2 = 4$,   where x is any real number.

10.2 GRAPHS OF EXPONENTIAL FUNCTIONS

In this section we are interested in exploring properties of exponential functions by drawing graphs of $y = b^x$, where b is a given positive number and $b \neq 1$. As an illustration, consider the following examples, where different values of b are used.

Examples

⚠ Draw a graph of $y = 3^x$.

Solution. We first compile the following table, then plot the corresponding points and draw a graph, as shown in Fig. 10.1. The values of y are determined by calculator to two decimal places:

x	-3	-2	-1	-0.5	0	0.5	1	1.5	2	3
y	0.04	0.11	0.33	0.58	1	1.73	3	5.20	9	27

We see that the graph of $y = 3^x$ is an increasing curve (that is, y increases as x increases) and the values of y run through all positive numbers. Thus we say that $f(x) = 3^x$ is an *increasing function* with domain $D(f)$ and range $R(f)$ given by

$$D(f) = \{x \mid x \text{ is any real number}\},$$
$$R(f) = \{y \mid y > 0\}.$$

 Draw a graph of $y = \left(\frac{1}{3}\right)^x = 3^{-x}$.

Solution Following the pattern of Example 1, we first make a table of x, y values, plot these points, and draw the curve, as shown in Fig. 10.2. It is instructive to compare the x, y values of this table with those in the table of Example 1:

x	-3	-2	-1.5	-1	-0.5	0	0.5	1	2	3
y	27	9	5.20	3	1.73	1	0.58	0.33	0.11	0.04

From the curve shown in Fig. 10.2 we can conclude the following: $g(x) = (1/3)^x$ is a *decreasing function* (that is, y decreases as x increases) with domain and range given by

$$D(g) = \{x \mid x \text{ is any real number}\},$$
$$R(g) = \{y \mid y > 0\}.$$

Note. The curve in this example is a reflection of the curve in Example 1 about the y-axis.

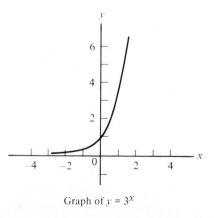

Graph of $y = 3^x$

Figure 10.1

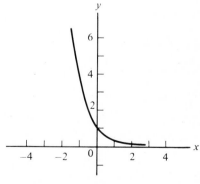

Graph of $y = \left(\frac{1}{3}\right)^x = 3^{-x}$

Figure 10.2

⚠️3 Draw a graph of $y = e^x$.

The number $e = 2.71828182\ldots$ was introduced in Example 6 of Section 10.1.

Solution We first make a table of x, y values, plot the corresponding points, and then draw a curve through these points, as shown in Fig. 10.3. Some calculators have an ⌐eˣ⌐ key, so the y value can be determined directly by pressing the ⌐eˣ⌐ key after x is entered in the display. For calculators that do not have the ⌐eˣ⌐ key, we suggest that 2.718281828 (round off to calculator capacity) be stored with the ⌐STO⌐ key and recalled with the ⌐RCL⌐ key when needed. In Section 10.4 we shall see how we can evaluate e^x for a given x without storing e.

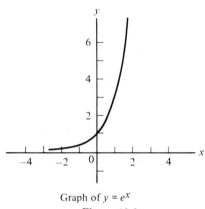

Graph of $y = e^x$

Figure 10.3

In the following table we give the y values to two decimal places:

x	-3	-2.5	-2	-1.5	-1	-0.5	0	0.5	1	1.5	2	2.5	3
y	0.05	0.08	0.14	0.22	0.37	0.61	1	1.65	2.72	4.48	7.39	12.18	20.09

From the curve in Fig. 10.3 we conclude that $F(x) = e^x$ is an increasing function with domain and range given by

$$D(F) = \{x \mid x \text{ is any real number}\},$$
$$R(F) = \{y \mid y > 0\}.$$

∎

The above examples lead us to the following general conclusions concerning the functions given by $G(x) = b^x$:

1. The domain and range of G are given by:

$$D(G) = \{x \mid x \text{ is any real number}\},$$
$$R(G) = \{y \mid y > 0\}.$$

2. If $0 < b < 1$, then G is a decreasing function, while if $b > 1$, G is an increasing function.

EXERCISE 10.2

In Problems 1 through 15 make a table of several x, y values that satisfy the given equation (provide y to two decimal places), plot the corresponding (x, y) points, and then draw the curve.

1. $y = 2^x$

2. $y = (\frac{1}{2})^x$

3. $y = (1.53)^x$

4. $y = (1.53)^{-x}$

5. $y = e^{-x}$

6. $y = 2e^x$

7. $y = (e - 1)^x$

8. $y = \left(\dfrac{e - 1}{2}\right)^x$

9. $y = \left(\dfrac{1 + \sqrt{5}}{2}\right)^x$

10. $y = \dfrac{1}{2}(e^x + e^{-x})$

11. $y = 1 + e^x$

12. $y = -3^x$

13. $y = -3^{-x}$

14. $y = 3^{-x/2}$

15. $y = \frac{1}{2}(e^x - e^{-x})$

Note. -3^x means $-(3^x)$ and not $(-3)^x$. Similarly, -3^{-x} means $-(3^{-x})$.

16. If $f(x) = 1 - 5^{-x}$, evaluate the following to two decimal places:

a) $f(0)$ b) $f(1)$ c) $f(\frac{1}{2})$ d) $f(-2)$ e) $f(-0.24)$

17. If $g(x) = 1/(1 + e^x)$, evaluate the following to two decimal places:

a) $g(0)$ b) $g(1)$ c) $g(2)$ d) $g(-3)$ e) $g(-0.64)$

18. The predicted population P of a certain city is given by the formula:

$$P = 450\,000 \cdot 1.08^{n/12},$$

where n is the number of years after 1980. Find the predicted population for each of the years (round off answers to the nearest thousand):

a) 1985   b) 1990   c) 1995   d) 2000

19. A function that occurs frequently in the study of probability and statistics is given by

$$f(x) = \frac{1}{\sqrt{2\pi}} \, e^{-x^2/2},$$

where x is any real number. Compute the corresponding values of $f(x)$ to two decimal places for x equal to 0, 0.2, 0.4, 0.6, 0.8, 1.0, 1.2, 1.4, 1.6, 1.8, 2.0. Plot a graph of $y = f(x)$. Note that $f(-x) = f(x)$ and use this to draw the graph for negative values of x.

20. Follow the instructions of Problem 19 to plot a graph of

$$g(x) = \frac{1}{\sqrt{2\pi}}\, e^{-(x+1)^2/2},$$

where x is any real number. Use values of x beginning with -1.0 up to $x = 3.0$ with increments of 0.2.

10.3 LOGARITHMS: DEFINITION AND BASIC PROPERTIES

1. Example of a Logarithmic Function

At the beginning of this chapter we indicated that logarithmic functions would be defined as inverses of exponential functions. This can be illustrated by considering $f(x) = 3^x$. A graph of $y = f(x)$ is shown in Fig. 10.1 reproduced in Fig. 10.4.

Geometrically, we can see that for each real number x_0 there is a unique positive number y_0 corresponding to it (point (x_0, y_0) on the curve). We describe this by saying that the function f maps each real number into a positive real number, for example: $-1 \to \frac{1}{3}$, $0 \to 1$, $1 \to 3$, $1.5 \to 5.196$, $2 \to 9$, and so on.

If we reverse the above mapping process, it is clear (from the graph) that for each positive real number y there is exactly one corresponding real number x. In other words, $f(x) = 3^x$ has an inverse function that maps the positive real numbers into the real numbers; for example, $\frac{1}{3} \to -1$, $1 \to 0$, $3 \to 1$, $5.196 \to 1.5$, $9 \to 2$, and so on. It is customary to denote this function by $\log_3$ and call it the

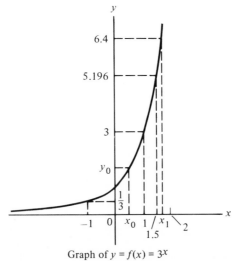

Graph of $y = f(x) = 3^x$

Figure 10.4

logarithmic function with base 3. That is, $y = 3^x$ and $x = \log_3 y$ describe the same set of points (x, y) and so we have:

$$x = \log_3 y \text{ is equivalent to } y = 3^x.$$

In other words, if we solve $y = 3^x$ for x in terms of y, the result is expressed by $x = \log_3 y$.

The above correspondences could be written as

$$\log_3 \tfrac{1}{3} = -1; \quad \log_3 1 = 0; \quad \log_3 3 = 1; \quad \log_3 5.196 = 1.5; \quad \log_3 9 = 2.$$

If we wish to evaluate, say, $\log_3 6.4$, we see from the graph that the answer is the number x_1 that lies between 1.5 and 2.0. We could make a crude estimate of x_1 from the graph but we shall see later that a calculator can be used to find x_1 correct to several decimal places.

2. Graph of $y = \log_3 x$

The graph of $y = 3^x$ or $x = \log_3 y$ is shown in Fig. 10.1. However, since $\log_3$ is a function in its own right and since it is customary to use x as the independent variable, we would like to draw a graph of $y = \log_3 x$. Since this is equivalent to $x = 3^y$, it should be clear that if we interchange the x and y values in the table preceding Fig. 10.1, we shall have points satisfying $y = \log_3 x$. Thus we get the following table:

x	0.04	0.11	0.33	0.58	1	1.73	3	5.20	9	27
y	-3	-2	-1	-0.5	0	0.5	1	1.5	2	3

Plotting the corresponding points and drawing the curve, we get the graph shown in Fig. 10.5. This is equivalent to reflecting the curve in Fig. 10.1 about the line $y = x$.

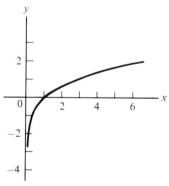

Graph of $y = \log_3 x$

Figure 10.5

3. Definition of Logarithmic Functions in General

In the above example we introduced the $\log_3$ function. This leads us to the following definition of logarithmic functions in general:

    If b is any given *positive number and $b \neq 1$*, then we define the $\log_b$ function as the inverse of the exponential function with base b. That is,

$$\log_b x = y \text{ is equivalent to } x = b^y, \qquad (\textbf{L.1})$$

where the domain of $\log_b$ is $\{x \mid x > 0\}$ and the range is $\{y \mid y$ is any real number$\}$. The expression $\log_b x$ is read as "the logarithm of x to the base b."

4. Properties of Logarithmic Functions

Suppose we wish to evaluate $\log_b 1$ and $\log_b b$. Let $\log_b 1 = a$, then from (L.1) this is equivalent to $b^a = 1$. Since $b^0 = 1$, then a must be zero. That is $\log_b 1 = 0$. Similarly, let $\log_b b = c$, then $b^c = b$, and we see that $c = 1$.

    These two special cases of $\log_b x$ for any base b are worth noting:

$$\log_b 1 = 0 \qquad \text{and} \qquad \log_b b = 1. \qquad (\textbf{L.2})$$

Three important properties of logarithms are given by the following formulas. If u and v are any positive numbers and t is any real number, then

$$\log_b(uv) = \log_b u + \log_b v, \qquad (\textbf{L.3})$$

$$\log_b\left(\frac{u}{v}\right) = \log_b u - \log_b v, \qquad (\textbf{L.4})$$

$$\log_b(u^t) = t(\log_b u). \qquad (\textbf{L.5})$$

    To prove the result given by (L.3), let $\log_b u = h$ and $\log_b v = k$. Using the definition given in (L.1), we have $u = b^h$ and $v = b^k$. Since formula (L.3) involves $u \cdot v$, we multiply these two equations to get

$$u \cdot v = b^h \cdot b^k = b^{h+k}.$$

But using (L.1) again we see that $uv = b^{h+k}$ is equivalent to $\log_b(uv) = h + k$. Replacing h by $\log_b u$ and k by $\log_b v$, we get Eq. (L.3).

    Proofs of (L.4) and (L.5) are similar. The three properties given here are essentially restatements of the corresponding properties of exponents (E.1), (E.2), and (E.3) stated in Section 10.1.

    Note. Equations (L.3), (L.4), and (L.5) involve logarithms of products, quotients, and powers. We do not give formulas for sums and differences; the reason is that there are no simple results for $\log_b(u + v)$ and $\log_b(u - v)$.

Examples

 Evaluate the following and give answers in exact form:

a) $\log_2 8$ b) $\log_{1/2} 4$ c) $\log_3 \dfrac{\sqrt{27}}{3\sqrt{3}}$

d) $\log_{1/4}\left(16\sqrt[3]{4}\right)$ e) $\log_{10} 1000$ f) $\log_{10} 0.0001$

Solution

a) Let $\log_2 8 = r$. Then by (L.1), $2^r = 8 = 2^3$. Thus $r = 3$ and so $\log_2 8 = 3$.

b) Let $\log_{1/2} 4 = s$. Then by (L.1), $(\frac{1}{2})^s = 4 = 2^2$. That is, $2^{-s} = 2^2$ and so $s = -2$. Thus $\log_{1/2} 4 = -2$.

c) Since $\dfrac{\sqrt{27}}{3\sqrt{3}} = \dfrac{\sqrt{9 \cdot 3}}{3\sqrt{3}} = \dfrac{3\sqrt{3}}{3\sqrt{3}} = 1$, then using (L.2) we get

$$\log_3 \frac{\sqrt{27}}{3\sqrt{3}} = \log_3 1 = 0.$$

d) Let $\log_{1/4}(16\sqrt[3]{4}) = m$. Then by (L.1), $(1/4)^m = 16\sqrt[3]{4}$. This is equivalent to $4^{-m} = 4^2 \cdot 4^{1/3} = 4^{7/3}$, so $m = -7/3$. That is, $\log_{1/4}(16\sqrt[3]{4}) = -7/3$.

e) Let $\log_{10} 1000 = p$. Then by (L.1), $10^p = 1000 = 10^3$. Thus, $p = 3$ and so $\log_{10} 1000 = 3$.

f) Let $\log_{10}(0.0001) = q$. Then by (L.1), $10^q = 0.0001 = 10^{-4}$ and so $q = -4$. Thus $\log_{10}(0.0001) = -4$.   ∎

$\triangle\!\!2$ Given that $\log_5 3 = 0.6826$ and $\log_5 6 = 1.1133$, evaluate the following and provide answers to four decimal places:

a) $\log_5 2$ b) $\log_5(\log_2 8)$ c) $(\log_5 12) \div (\log_5 3)$

Solution

a) $\log_5 2 = \log_5(6/3) = \log_5 6 - \log_5 3 = 1.1133 - 0.6826 = 0.4307$ (by (L.4)).

b) We first evaluate $\log_2 8$; from (L.1) it should be clear that $\log_2 8 = 3$. Therefore, $\log_5(\log_2 8) = \log_5 3 = 0.6826$.

c) We first evaluate $\log_5 12$:

$$\log_5 12 = \log_5(2^2 \cdot 3) = \log_5 2^2 + \log_5 3 = 2\,\log_5 2 + \log_5 3 \text{ (by (L.3), (L.5))}.$$

Using $\log_5 2 = 0.4307$ (from part (a)) and $\log_5 3 = 0.6826$, we get

$$\log_5 12 = 2(0.4307) + 0.6826 = 1.5440.$$

Thus, $(\log_5 12) \div (\log_5 3) = (1.5440) \div (0.6826) = 2.2619.$ ∎

$\triangle\!\!3$ Write $3\log_5 2 + \dfrac{3}{2}\log_5 8 - \dfrac{1}{2}\log_5 32$ as $\log_5$ of a number.

Solution

$3 \log_5 2 + \dfrac{3}{2} \log_5 8 - \dfrac{1}{2} \log_5 32 = \log_5 2^3 + \log_5 8^{3/2} - \log_5 32^{1/2}$ (by (L.5))

$\quad = \log_5\left(\dfrac{2^3 \cdot 8^{3/2}}{32^{1/2}}\right)$ (by (L.3), (L.4))

$\quad = \log_5\left(\dfrac{2^3 \cdot 2^{9/2}}{2^{5/2}}\right)$ (by (E.3))

$\quad = \log_5(2^5)$ (by (E.1), (E.2))

$\quad = \log_5 32.$ ▮

④ If p and q are positive numbers, write each of the following in terms of $\log_b p$ and $\log_b q$:

  a) $\log_b(p \cdot q^3)$ b) $\log_b\left(\dfrac{p^{3/4}\sqrt{q}}{\sqrt[3]{p}\, q^2}\right)$

Solution

  a) $\log_b(p \cdot q^3) = \log_b p + \log_b q^3$ (by (L.3))

  $\quad = \log_b p + 3\,\log_b q$ (by (L.5)).

  b) $\log_b\left(\dfrac{p^{3/4}\sqrt{q}}{\sqrt[3]{p}\, q^2}\right) = \log_b\left(\dfrac{p^{3/4}q^{1/2}}{p^{1/3}q^2}\right) = \log_b\left(\dfrac{p^{5/12}}{q^{3/2}}\right)$ (by (E.5))

  $\quad = \log_b p^{5/12} - \log_b q^{3/2}$ (by (L.4))

  $\quad = \dfrac{5}{12}\log_b p - \dfrac{3}{2}\log_b q$ (by (L.5)) ▮

⑤ Solve for x:

  a) $\log_3(2x + 1) - \log_3(4x) = 1$ b) $\log_3(2x - 1) - \log_3(4x) = 1$
  c) $\log_{10}x + \log_{10}(x + 48) = 2$

Solution

  a) Applying the formula in (L.4) to the given equation we get $\log_3[(2x + 1)/4x] = 1$. According to the definition stated in (L.1), this can be written as $(2x + 1)/4x = 3$. Thus, $2x + 1 = 12x$ and so $x = 1/10$. We wish to see if $x = 1/10$ actually satisfies the given equation. Substituting $x = 1/10$ into the left-hand side gives

  $\text{LHS} = \log_3\left(\dfrac{2}{10} + 1\right) - \log_3\left(\dfrac{4}{10}\right) = \log_3\dfrac{6}{5} - \log_3\dfrac{2}{5}$

  $\quad = \log_3\left(\dfrac{6}{5} \div \dfrac{2}{5}\right)$ (by (L.4))

  $\quad = \log_3 3.$

Since $\log_3 3 = 1$ (as can be seen from (L.2)), then $x = 1/10$ is a solution of the given equation.

  b) Following a pattern similar to that in (a), we get $x = -1/10$. Substituting $-1/10$ for x in the left-hand side of the given equation, we get

$$\text{LHS} = \log_3\left(-\tfrac{2}{10} - 1\right) - \log_3\left(-\tfrac{4}{10}\right) = \log_3\left(-\tfrac{6}{5}\right) - \log_3\left(-\tfrac{2}{5}\right).$$

Since $-6/5$ and $-2/5$ are not in the domain of the $\log_3$ function (that is, $\log_3(-6/5)$ and $\log_3(-2/5)$ are not defined), we see that $x = -1/10$ is not a solution of the given equation. Thus, there is no real number x that satisfies the given equation.

c) Using Eq. (L.3), we can write the given equation as $\log_{10}[x(x + 48)] = 2$. By (L.1), this is equivalent to $x(x + 48) = 10^2 = 100$. Thus we have the quadratic equation $x^2 + 48x - 100 = 0$ to solve. This can be done by factoring: $(x + 50)(x - 2) = 0$. Thus $x = -50$ and $x = 2$ are solutions of the quadratic equation. Substituing $x = -50$ into the left-hand side of the given equation, we get $\text{LHS} = \log_{10}(-50) + \log_{10}(-50 + 2)$. This is undefined and so $x = -50$ is not a solution. Substituting $x = 2$ into the given equation, we see that it is a solution. Thus, the given equation has one solution: $x = 2$. ∎

EXERCISE 10.3

In Problems 1 through 15, evaluate the given expressions and give the answers in exact form. If the given expression is not defined, tell why.

1. $\log_2 32$

2. $\log_3 \dfrac{1}{27}$

3. $\log_5 \dfrac{125}{\sqrt{5}}$

4. $\log_7 \dfrac{49\sqrt{7}}{7^{5/2}}$

5. $\log_{10} 100$

6. $\log_{10}\sqrt{1000}$

7. $\log_{10} \dfrac{0.0001}{\sqrt[3]{0.0001}}$

8. $\log_e \dfrac{\sqrt{e}}{\sqrt[4]{e}}$

9. $\log_{0.5} 2$

10. $\log_5(\log_5 5)$

11. $\log_7(\log_7 1)$

12. $\log_8(\log_3 3)$

13. $\log_3\left(\log_5 \dfrac{1}{5}\right)$

14. $\log_{10}\left(\log_{10} \dfrac{\sqrt{10}}{10}\right)$

15. $\log_2(4\sqrt{2})$

In Problems 16 through 24, p and q are positive numbers. Write the given expressions in terms of $\log_b p$ and $\log_b q$:

16. $\log_b(p^4 q^5)$

17. $\log_b(p^{3/2} \div q^2)$

18. $\log_b \dfrac{\sqrt{p}\, q^2}{p^3 \sqrt{q}}$

19. $\log_b \dfrac{p^{3/2} q^{4/3}}{p^{-3/4} q^{5/6}}$

20. $\log_b \dfrac{p + q}{p^{-1} + q^{-1}}$

21. $\log_b \dfrac{p - q}{pq(q^{-1} - p^{-1})}, \; p > q$

22. $\log_b\left(b\sqrt{pq}\right)$

23. $\log_b \dfrac{pq}{b}$

24. $\log_b \dfrac{b^2}{pq}$

In Problems 25 through 40, use the following to evaluate the given expression and provide answers to four decimal places:

$$\log_5 2 = 0.43068, \qquad \log_5 3 = 0.68261, \qquad \log_5 7 = 1.20906,$$
$$\log_3 11 = 2.18266, \qquad \log_3 22 = 2.81359.$$

25. $\log_5 6$ **26.** $\log_5 63$ **27.** $\log_5 75$

28. $\log_3 2$ **29.** $\log_3 66$ **30.** $\log_3 \sqrt{44}$

31. $\log_3 \sqrt{54}$ **32.** $\log_5(\log_3 9)$ **33.** $\log_5 \sqrt[4]{21}$

34. $\log_3 99$ **35.** $\log_5 10.5$ **36.** $\log_5 \dfrac{\sqrt{14}}{5}$

37. $\log_5(\log_5 25)$ **38.** $(\log_3 9)(\log_5 42)$ **39.** $(\log_3 33) \div (\log_5 81)$

40. $\log_5 70 - \log_3 4$

In Problems 41 through 45, write each of the given expressions as $\log_b$ of a number (for the given b):

41. $\log_3 5 + \log_3 20$ **42.** $2\log_3 5 - \log_3 4$

43. $\frac{1}{2}\log_7 4 + \frac{2}{3}\log_7 27 - \frac{1}{6}\log_7 64$ **44.** $3\log_2 3 - 2\log_2 9 + 2\log_2 5$

45. $\frac{1}{3}\log_2 5 - \frac{1}{2}\log_2 20 + \frac{1}{4}\log_2 81$

In Problems 46 through 55 solve for the indicated letter. When necessary, be certain to check whether your solution satisfies the given equation:

46. If $\log_3 x = 4$, then $x =$ _____.   **47.** If $\log_b 16 = 2$, then $b =$ _____.

48. If $\log_5(1/25) = y$, then $y =$ _____.   **49.** If $\log_5(3x - 1) = 1$, then $x =$ _____.

50. If $\log_5(4x) - \log_5(2x - 1) = 2$, then $x =$ _____.

51. If $\log_3(2x) + \log_3(5x) = \log_3 10$, then $x =$ _____.

52. If $\log_b \dfrac{1}{27} = -3$, then $b =$ _____.

53. If $\log_5 25 + \log_3 27 = 2x + 1$, then $x =$ _____.

54. a) If $\log_7 x^2 - \log_7(x + 6) = 0$, then $x =$ _____.

    b) If $2\log_7 x - \log_7(x + 6) = 0$, then $x =$ _____.

55. If $\log_{10} x + \log_{10}(x + 3) = 1$, then $x =$ _____.

In Problems 56 through 64, determine whether the given statement is true, false, or meaningless. A statement is meaningless if any part of it is undefined. Substantiate your answers.

56. $\log_3 9 - \log_3 2 = \log_3(4.5)$ **57.** $\log_5\left(\dfrac{3}{2}\right) + \log_5 2 = \log_5 3$

58. $\log_7(3^2 + 4^2) = 2\log_7 3 + 2\log_7 4$ **59.** $\log_3 \dfrac{1 - \sqrt{3}}{2} = \log_3(1 - \sqrt{3}) - \log_3 2$

60. $\log_{10} 100 - \log_{10} 0.01 = 4$ **61.** $\log_5 \dfrac{3}{2} = \dfrac{\log_5 3}{\log_5 2}$

62. $\log_5 \dfrac{2}{\sqrt{5} + 1} = \log_5\left(\sqrt{5} - 1\right) - \log_5 2$

63. $\log_2(\log_2 \frac{1}{2}) = -1$ **64.** $\log_3(1 + \log_2 4) = 1$

10.4 USING A CALCULATOR TO EVALUATE LOGARITHMS

In the preceding section we encountered several instances where we were able to evaluate logarithms by converting to exponential form. For example, to evaluate $\log_3 \sqrt{27}$ we let $\log_3 \sqrt{27} = y$, which is equivalent to $3^y = \sqrt{27} = 3^{3/2}$. Thus $y = 3/2$ and we have $\log_3 \sqrt{27} = 3/2$. However, a similar procedure to evaluate $\log_3 6.4 = z$ leads to $3^z = 6.4$. Since 6.4 cannot be expressed as a simple power of 3, we are unable to complete the solution as we did in the first example. In this section we discuss techniques for solving such problems by using a calculator.

1. Common and Natural Logarithms

For computational purposes the frequently used base of logarithms is $b = 10$. Since it is cumbersome to write the subscript 10 in $\log_{10}$ each time, we shall write "log" and it is understood that the base is 10. It is an interesting fact that the transcendental number $e = 2.718281828 \ldots$ occurs naturally as a base of logarithms for theoretical (as well as computational) purposes in the study of calculus (see Example 6 of Section 10.1). Since the notation $\log_e$ is awkward, we replace it by ln. Thus we have the following notation:

$$\begin{array}{l} \log_{10} x \text{ is written as log } x, \\ \log_e x \text{ is written as ln } x. \end{array}$$

Logarithms with base 10 are called *common logarithms*, while those with base e are called *natural logarithms*.

2. Logarithms with Calculators

Most scientific calculators have both ⌊log⌋ and ⌊ln⌋ keys. We shall consider several examples to illustrate the use of these keys. Some calculators have the ⌊ln⌋ key but not the ⌊log⌋ key; we shall see that this is sufficient for our purposes.

The ⌊log⌋ and ⌊ln⌋ keys represent functions of one variable. If a number x is entered into the display of the calculator and then the ⌊ln⌋ key is pressed, the result $\ln x$ will appear immediately in the display (it is not necessary to press the ⌊=⌋ key on algebraic calculators).

Examples

⚠ Evaluate the following correct to four decimal places:

a) $\ln 2$ b) $\log 0.0037$ c) $\ln \dfrac{1 + \sqrt{5}}{2}$ d) $\ln \dfrac{2 - \sqrt{17}}{3}$

Solution

a) Pressing the keys 2   and $\boxed{\text{ln}}$ gives ln $2 = 0.6931$.

b) If the calculator has a $\boxed{\text{log}}$ key, then entering 0.0037 into the display and pressing $\boxed{\text{log}}$ gives log $0.0037 = -2.4318$. If there is no $\boxed{\text{log}}$ key, we can use the $\boxed{\text{ln}}$ key as follows: Let log $0.0037 = y$; this is equivalent to $10^y = 0.0037$. Now take ln of both sides of this equation: ln $10^y =$ ln 0.0037, which is equivalent to y ln $10 =$ ln 0.0037. Thus $y =$ ln $0.0037/$ln 10, and this can be evaluated by using the $\boxed{\text{ln}}$ and $\boxed{\div}$ keys.

c) To evaluate ln$[(1 + \sqrt{5})/2]$, we first compute $\left(1 + \sqrt{5}\right)/2$ and, with the result in the calculator display, press the $\boxed{\text{ln}}$ key. This gives $\ln\left[\left(1 + \sqrt{5}\right)/2\right] = 0.4812$.

d) To evaluate $\ln\left[\left(2 - \sqrt{17}\right)/3\right]$, we follow a procedure similar to that in (c). In this case the calculator indicates "Error" and the reason is that $(2 - \sqrt{17})/3$ is a negative number and so is not in the domain of the ln function. That is, $\ln\left[\left(2 - \sqrt{17}\right)/3\right]$ is undefined. ∎

3. Change of Base

In using a calculator to evaluate $\log_b u$, where b is a positive number different from e or 10 (and $b \neq 1$), it is necessary to convert to logarithms with base e or base 10. We do so as follows.

Let $\log_b u = t$, which is equivalent to $b^t = u$. Taking ln of both sides of this equation gives ln $b^t =$ ln u, which is equivalent to t ln $b =$ ln u. Thus we get $t =$ ln $u/$ln b. Therefore, we have the following formula that expresses $\log_b u$ in terms of ln u and ln b:

$$\boxed{\log_b u = \frac{\ln u}{\ln b}.}$$
(10.4)

Similarly, if we used log in place of ln in the above discussion, we would get

$$\boxed{\log_b u = \frac{\log u}{\log b}.}$$
(10.5)

We continue with more examples.

⚠ Evaluate the following and give answers rounded off to four decimal places:

a) $\log_3 7.5$ b) $\log_5 0.0348$ c) $\log_7 \dfrac{1 + \sqrt{5}}{2}$ d) $\log_8(3 - \sqrt{10})$

Solution In each of these problems, either Eq. (10.4) or Eq. (10.5) can be used. We choose Eq. (10.4) since some calculators have a ⬚ln key but not a ⬚log key.

a) $\log_3 7.5 = \dfrac{\ln 7.5}{\ln 3} = 1.8340$

b) $\log_5 0.0348 = \dfrac{\ln\ 0.0348}{\ln\ 5} = -2.0865$

c) $\log_7 \dfrac{1 + \sqrt{5}}{2} = \dfrac{\ln[(1 + \sqrt{5})/2]}{\ln\ 7} = 0.2473$

d) $\log_8(3 - \sqrt{10}) = \dfrac{\ln(3 - \sqrt{10})}{\ln\ 8}$.

When we attempt to evaluate $\ln(3 - \sqrt{10})$, we get an indication of "Error." The reason is that $3 - \sqrt{10}$ is a negative number and it is not in the domain of the ln function. Thus $\log_8(3 - \sqrt{10})$ is not defined.   ▌

4. Inverse Logarithms

In the above examples all of the problems were of the following type: Given a positive number u, find $\log u$ or $\ln u$. We are now interested in the reverse problem: Given the value of $\log u$ or $\ln u$, determine u. For example, given $\log\ u = 0.4735$, we wish to find u. The notation that has been traditionally used is $u = $ Antilog 0.4735. However, since this really involves the inverse of the log function, we shall denote it by $u = $ Inv log 0.4735. This is read "u is the inverse log of 0.4735." The notation adopted here is also consistent with that used on many calculators with an ⬚INV key. As another example of notation, if $\ln\ v = 1.2654$, then we write $v = $ Inv ln 1.2654. We say "v is the inverse ln of 1.2654."

So far, in the two examples being considered here we merely introduced a certain notation. Now we proceed to actually determine u and v. Since the log function is defined as the inverse of the 10^x function, then the inverse of the log function must be this exponential function. Therefore,

$$u = \text{Inv log } 0.4735 = 10^{0.4735}.$$

(This is precisely what the definition in (L.1) of Section 10.3 tells us.) Now u can be determined by using a calculator as follows:

If the calculator has an $\boxed{\text{INV}}$ key, then, with 0.4735 in the display, pressing the $\boxed{\text{INV}}$ and $\boxed{\text{log}}$ keys gives $u = 2.9751$ (to four decimal places).

If the calculator has a $\boxed{10^x}$ key, then evaluate $u = 10^{0.4735}$ directly by pressing $\boxed{10^x}$ after 0.4735 has been entered into the display.*

Similarly, the ln function and the e^x function† are inverses of each other, so the solution of ln $v = 1.2654$ is $v = \text{Inv ln } 1.2654 = e^{1.2654}$. Thus v can be found by pressing the $\boxed{\text{INV}}$ and $\boxed{\text{ln}}$ keys or by using the $\boxed{e^x}$ key after 1.2654 has been entered. Therefore, $v = 3.5445$ (to four decimal places).

The above discussion illustrates the following:

> $\boxed{10^x}$ and $\boxed{\text{log}}$ keys are inverses of each other;
> $\boxed{e^x}$ and $\boxed{\text{ln}}$ keys are inverses of each other.

Thus,

$$10^{\log x} = x \text{ for all } x > 0 \text{ and } \log(10^x) = x \text{ for } x \in R,$$
$$e^{\ln x} = x \text{ for all } x > 0 \text{ and } \ln(e^x) = x \text{ for } x \in R.$$

> Therefore,
> to find 10^u, enter u and press $\boxed{10^x}$ or $\boxed{\text{INV}}$ and $\boxed{\text{log}}$;   (10.6)
> to find e^u, enter u and press $\boxed{e^x}$ or $\boxed{\text{INV}}$ and $\boxed{\text{ln}}$ (10.7)

---

3. Solve the following for v correct to four decimal places:
   a) $v = \text{Inv log } 0.243$ b) ln $v = 1.345$ c) log $v = -1.4382$
   d) $e^v = 0.456$ e) $10^v = 1.4837$ f) $\ln(2v + 1) - \ln 3 = 1.48$

Solution

   a) Following the instructions stated in (10.6), we get $v = 1.7498$.

   b) ln $v = 1.345$ is equivalent to $v = \text{Inv ln } 1.345$ or $v = e^{1.345}$.
      Following procedure (10.7), we get $v = 3.8382$.

   c) log $v = -1.4382$ is equivalent to $v = \text{Inv log}(-1.4382)$ or $v = 10^{-1.4382}$.
      Using (10.6), we get $v = 0.0365$.

   d) $e^v = 0.456$ is equivalent to $v = \text{ln } 0.456$. Enter 0.456 and press the $\boxed{\text{ln}}$
      key; this gives $v = -0.7853$.

---

* If your calculator has neither the $\boxed{\text{log}}$ nor the $\boxed{10^x}$ keys but has $\boxed{\text{ln}}$ and $\boxed{e^x}$ keys, proceed as follows: Express the original problem, log $u = 0.4735$, in equivalent ln form by using the change-of-base formula given by Eq. (10.4). That is, ln $u = \ln 10 \cdot \log u$ (with $b = 10$). Therefore,

$$\ln u = \ln 10 \cdot \log u = 2.30259 \log u = 2.30259 \cdot 0.4735 = 1.0903.$$

Thus, $u = e^{1.0903}$, which can be evaluated by using the $\boxed{e^x}$ key.

† When we say "the e^x function" we mean the function f determined by $f(x) = e^x$.

e) $10^v = 1.4837$ is equivalent to $v = \log 1.4837$. This can be evaluated by using the ⬚log⬚ key to get $v = 0.1713$.

If the calculator does not have a ⬚log⬚ key, then take ln of both sides of the given equation to get $v \ln 10 = \ln 1.4837$. Therefore, $v = \ln 1.4837/\ln 10$, which can be evaluated by using the ⬚ln⬚ and ⬚÷⬚ keys.

f) The given equation is equivalent to $\ln[(2v + 1)/3] = 1.48$. Thus $(2v + 1)/3 = e^{1.48}$ and so $v = (3e^{1.48} - 1)/2$. We can now use (10.7) to find $e^{1.48}$ and then continue with the remaining arithmetic operations. This gives $v = 6.0894$. ∎

 Evaluate the following expressions:

   a) $e^{\ln 5}$ b) $10^{-\log 5}$ c) $\log(10^{-4.5})$ d) $\ln(e^{-0.47})$

Solution

a) Since the e^x and the ln functions are inverses of each other, ln takes 5 into some number and then e^x function reverses this process and gives 5 as the result. Thus $e^{\ln 5} = 5$.

An alternative way of saying essentially the same thing is to let $y = e^{\ln 5}$. Taking ln of both sides of this equation and using (L.5) and (L.2) of Section 10.3, we get

$$\ln y = \ln(e^{\ln 5}) = \ln 5 \cdot \ln e = \ln 5.$$

Thus $\ln y = \ln 5$ and so $y = 5$.

b) To evaluate $10^{-\log 5}$ we first note that $10^{-\log 5} = 10^{\log(5^{-1})}$. Thus, as in (a), we get

$$10^{\log(5^{-1})} = 5^{-1} = \frac{1}{5},$$

and so $10^{-\log 5} = 1/5$.

c) The 10^x function takes -4.5 into a number, and then the log function reverses this process giving -4.5 as the result. Thus, $\log(10^{-4.5}) = -4.5$.

d) This is similar to (c), and so $\ln(e^{-0.47}) = -0.47$. ∎

 Solve $2 \ln(2v - 1) + 2 \ln v = 1$ for v.

Solution Dividing both sides of the given equation by 2 and using property (L.3) we get $\ln[v(2v - 1)] = \frac{1}{2}$. This is equivalent to $v(2v - 1) = e^{1/2}$. Thus we have to solve the quadratic equation $2v^2 - v - \sqrt{e} = 0$. Applying the quadratic formula, we get

$$v = \frac{1 \pm \sqrt{1 + 8\sqrt{e}}}{4}.$$

Thus $v_1 = 1.917$, $v_2 = -0.6917$. When we substitute these into the original equation, we see that v_2 is not a solution. Therefore, there is only one solution: $v = 1.1917$. ∎

EXERCISE 10.4

If your calculator should indicate "Error" while solving any problem in this set, determine the reason for such a response.

In Problems 1 through 26, evaluate the given expression and give answers rounded off to four decimal places:

1. $\ln 5$

2. $\ln 0.47$

3. $\log 1.87$

4. $\log 0.0435$

5. $\ln(1.56^2 + 2.73^2)$

6. $\log(2.43\sqrt{5.75})$

7. $\ln(2 - \sqrt{5.43})$

8. $\log\left(\dfrac{1 + \sqrt{3}}{8}\right)$

9. $\log\left(\dfrac{2 - \sqrt{6}}{5}\right)$

10. $\ln \dfrac{\sqrt[3]{1.24}}{\sqrt[5]{0.43}}$

11. $\log_3 6$

12. $\log_5 3.47$

13. $\log_7(\sqrt{3} - 1)$

14. $\log_{15}\left(\dfrac{5 - \sqrt{7}}{8}\right)$

15. $\log_5\left(\sqrt{3.4} + \sqrt{5.6}\right)$

16. $\log_{0.3}(2.47)$

17. $\log_8 \dfrac{\sqrt{1.37} + 3}{\sqrt{2.41}}$

18. $\ln\left[\left(\dfrac{1 + \sqrt{5}}{2}\right)^2 - \left(\dfrac{1 + \sqrt{5}}{2}\right)\right]$

19. $\log\left[\left(\dfrac{2}{\sqrt{5} - 1}\right)^2 - \left(\dfrac{2}{\sqrt{5} - 1}\right)\right]$

20. $\ln(\sqrt{2} + 1) + \ln(\sqrt{2} - 1)$

21. $e^{\ln 1.43}$

22. $10^{\log 2.54}$

23. $\log(10^{-0.42})$

24. $\ln(e^{3.2})$

25. $e^{-\ln 2}$

26. $e^{-3\ln 2}$

In problems 27 through 64 determine the value of v correct to four decimal places:

27. $v = \text{Inv} \log 0.478$

28. $v = \text{Inv} \log(-0.587)$

29. $\ln v = 1.532$

30. $v = \text{Inv} \ln(-1.378)$

31. $\log v = -0.372$

32. $v = \text{Inv} \log(1 - \sqrt{3})$

33. $\ln v = 1 - \sqrt{3}$

34. $10^v = 0.573$

35. $10^v = -0.473$

36. $e^v = 0.875$

37. $e^{-v} = 1.238$

38. $e^{-v} = -0.471$

39. $10^{-v} = 1.378$

40. $e^{2v} = 0.431$

41. $e^v = \dfrac{3 + \sqrt{7}}{4}$

42. $e^{(-3v + 1)} = 0.475$

43. $v = 10^{-0.47}$

44. $v = 10^{\sqrt{3}}$

45. $v = e^{1.43}$

46. $v = e^{-0.71}$

47. $v = 10^{1.36}$

48. $e^{v + 1} = 3e^{2v - 1}$

49. $e^{2v - 1} = 1.362$

50. $10^{-(2v + 3)} = 1.57$

51. $10^{-(4v + 1)} = -3.473$

52. $\log(3v + 4) = \log 2 + \log(v^2 + 1)$

53. $\ln(2v - 5) - \ln 7 = 2.43$

54. $\ln(v - 5) + \ln 2.43 = 1.56$

55. $\ln \ v + e^{-2.4} = 3.45$ **56.** $\ln(e^{v-1}) = e^{-1.6}$ **57.** $\log(10^{v+3}) = 5$

58. $\ln(e^{1-3v}) = 4$ **59.** $1 + \log(10^{2-v}) = 0$ **60.** $2 \ln v + e^{-1.2} = e^{1.2}$

61. $\ln(2v + 1) + \ln v = 1$ **62.** $\log(3v - 1) + \log \ v = 1$

63. $\ln(v + 1) + \ln(v - 3) = 1$ **64.** $2 \ln(3v) = 1 - 2 \ln(1 - v)$

In Problems 65 through 72, determine whether the given statement is true, false, or meaningless (a statement is meaningless if any part of it is undefined). Substantiate your answers.

65. $10^{\log \ 8} = 8$ **66.** $e^{-\ln 3} = \frac{1}{3}$ **67.** $e^{\ln(-3)} = \frac{1}{3}$

68. $\log[\text{Inv} \ \log(-4)] = -4$ **69.** Inv $\ln(\ln 3) = 3$

70. $e^{(\ln 6 - \ln 2)} = 3$ **71.** $e^{\ln 2 \cdot \ln 3} = 6$ **72.** $\ln(e^2 + e^3) = 5$

10.5 SOLVING EXPONENTIAL AND LOGARITHMIC EQUATIONS

Solving an equation in which the unknown appears in the exponent, usually involves the use of logarithms. We encountered some examples of such problems in the preceding section, where the base of the exponential was either 10 or e. We are now interested in the more general problem where the exponential base is any positive number. In the following examples several such problems are illustrated. Also included are examples in which the unknown appears as part of a logarithmic expression.

Examples

⚠️ Solve the following for x and give the answer rounded off to four decimal places:

    a) $3^x = 5$ b) $1.47^{-2x} = 2.53$ c) $5^{-x} = 3 \cdot 4^{2x+1}$

Solution

    a) Taking ln of both sides of the equation gives $\ln \ 3^x = \ln \ 5$. This is equivalent to $x(\ln \ 3) = \ln \ 5$, and so $x = \ln \ 5/\ln \ 3$. To evaluate with an algebraic calculator press 5 ,⌐ln⌐ ,⌐÷⌐ , 3 ,⌐ln⌐ ,⌐=⌐ ; this gives $x = 1.4650$.

    With an RPN calculator, press 5 ,⌐ln⌐ , 3 ,⌐ln⌐ ,⌐÷⌐ and the result appears in the display. Substituting $x = 1.4650$ into the given equation as a check, we see that this is the desired solution.

    Note. We could have taken the log of both sides of the given equation as the first step. The resulting solution is $x = \log \ 5/\log \ 3 = 1.4650$. Also, note that $\log \ 5/\log \ 3$ is not the same as $\log(5/3)$.

b) This is similar to (a). The solution is

$$x = \frac{\ln 2.53}{-2 \ln 1.47} \quad \text{or} \quad x = \frac{\log 2.53}{-2 \log 1.47}.$$

Using a calculator to evaluate this expression, we get $x = -1.2047$. As a check, we can now substitute this value of x into the given equation to see that this is the desired solution.

c) Taking ln of both sides of the given equation, we get

$$\ln 5^{-x} = \ln(3 \cdot 4^{2x+1}).$$

We now proceed by using properties of the ln function and some algebra:

$$-x(\ln 5) = \ln 3 + (2x + 1)(\ln 4), \quad \text{(by (L.3), (L.5))}$$
$$x(-\ln 5 - 2 \ln 4) = \ln 3 + \ln 4, \quad \text{(by algebra)}$$
$$x = -\frac{\ln 3 + \ln 4}{\ln 5 + 2 \ln 4}. \quad \text{(by algebra)}$$

Evaluating by calculator gives $x = -0.5671$. Checking this value of x in the given equation we see that it is the desired solution. Note that the final expression for x could have been simplified before the evaluation as follows:

$$x = -\frac{\ln 3 + \ln 4}{\ln 5 + 2 \ln 4} = -\frac{\ln(3 \cdot 4)}{\ln(5 \cdot 4^2)} = -\frac{\ln 12}{\ln 80}.$$ ∎

⚠️2 Find the roots of the equation $e^{-x} - x = 0$ correct to two decimal places.

Solution In this example, x appears in a linear term as well as in the exponent. Such equations are more difficult to solve than those considered in Example 1. If we write the problem as $e^{-x} = x$ and take ln of both sides, as we did in Example 1, the resulting equation is $-x = \ln x$. This does not help in solving for x. Therefore, we use a different approach and solve by a process of estimation.

We can get information about the number of roots and their approximate values by drawing graphs. Suppose we draw the graphs of $y = e^{-x}$ and $y = x$ on the same set of coordinates. Our problem then is to find the x-values of the points of intersection of the two curves depicted in Fig. 10.6. The diagram shows that there is only one root; call it x_0. From the graph, a reasonable estimate of x_0 is 0.6. Evaluating e^{-x} for $x = 0.6$ gives $e^{-0.6} = 0.55$, and so it is clear from the graph that x_0 is to the left of 0.6. We now try $x = 0.5$, and so $e^{-0.5} = 0.61$. Thus, from the graph we see that x_0 is to the right of 0.5. Trying 0.57 gives $e^{-0.57} = 0.57$. This tells us that $x = 0.57$ is the desired solution (to two decimal places).

For another interesting way of solving this problem see Problem 31 of Exercise 10.5.

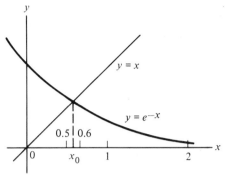

Figure 10.6

⬛

△3 Solve the system of equations and give answers correct to three decimal places:

$$8^x \cdot 5^y = 7,$$
$$4^x \cdot 3^{-y} = 16.$$

Solution The problem is to find a pair of numbers x, y that will satisfy both given equations. Taking ln of both sides of each of the equations and using properties (L.3) and (L.5) of the ln function we obtain

$$x(\ln 8) + y(\ln 5) = \ln 7$$
$$x(\ln 4) - y(\ln 3) = \ln 16.$$

We now have a system of two linear equations that can be solved by usual techniques. For example, we can eliminate y by multiplying the first equation by ln 3 and the second by ln 5 and then adding the resulting equations. This gives

$$x(\ln 8 \ \ln 3 + \ln 4 \ \ln 5) = \ln 7 \ \ln 3 + \ln 16 \ \ln 5.$$

Solving for x and evaluating the result by calculator, we get

$$x = \frac{\ln 7 \ \ln 3 + \ln 16 \ \ln 5}{\ln 8 \ \ln 3 + \ln 4 \ \ln 5} = 1.462 \text{ (to three decimal places)}.$$

To determine y, substitute $x = 1.4616$ (use an extra decimal place) into any of the above equations, say, in $x \ln 8 + y \ln 5 = \ln 7$, and then solve for y. This gives

$$y = \frac{\ln 7 - 1.4616 \ln 8}{\ln 5} = -0.679.$$

As a check, it is easy to substitute these values of x and y into the two given equations and see that we have the desired solution.   ⬛

⚠️4 Find the roots of the equation log x + log($3x$ − 1) = log 4.

Solution Using (L.3) of Section 10.3, we can write the given equation as log[$x(3x − 1)$] = log 4. Thus $x(3x − 1) = 4$, and so we have to solve the quadratic equation $3x^2 − x − 4 = 0$. This can be done by factoring the left side: $(3x − 4)(x + 1) = 0$. Thus we have two possible solutions: $x_1 = 4/3$, $x_2 = −1$.

Since we are looking for solutions to the given equation, we check by substituting each of these into that equation. As a check on $x_1 = 4/3$, we have

$$\text{LHS} = \log \tfrac{4}{3} + \log\left[3 \cdot \tfrac{4}{3} − 1\right] = \log \tfrac{4}{3} + \log 3$$
$$= (\log 4 − \log 3) + \log 3 = \log 4.$$

Thus $x = 4/3$ is a solution.

When we substitute $x = −1$ into the given equation, we get, for the left-hand side, log(−1) + log(−4). Since neither log(−1) nor log(−4) is defined, we conclude that $x = −1$ is not a solution. Therefore, the given equation has only one solution: $x = 4/3$. ∎

⚠️5 Find the roots of ln($2x$ + 1) = 1.56 + ln(x − 4). Give answers correct to three decimal places.

Solution We write the given equation as ln($2x$ + 1) − ln(x − 4) = 1.56; applying (L.4) of Section 10.3 we have

$$\ln \frac{2x + 1}{x − 4} = 1.56 \quad \text{or} \quad \frac{2x + 1}{x − 4} = e^{1.56}.$$

Using algebra we solve for x as follows:

$$2x + 1 = e^{1.56}(x − 4), \quad 4e^{1.56} + 1 = (e^{1.56} − 2)x, \quad x = \frac{4e^{1.56} + 1}{e^{1.56} − 2}.$$

This can be evaluated by a calculator to get $x = 7.262$. As a check, we substitute $x = 7.262$ into the given equation and see that it is a solution. ∎

EXERCISE 10.5

In Problems 1 through 25, find the roots of the given equation. Give answers in exact form whenever it is reasonable to do so; otherwise, correct to two decimal places. Check answers when there is a possibility of having extraneous solutions.

1. $5^x = 8$

2. $7^{-x} = 4$

3. $10^{-x} = 5.46$

4. $e^{3x−1} = 2.47$

5. $3.56^{-x} = 0.435$

6. $1.08^x = 2.563$

7. $248 \cdot 1.08^{16x} = 327$

8. $250 \cdot 1.13^{-x} = 124$

9. $250\left(1 + \frac{x}{3}\right)^{12} = 321$

10. $453\left(1 + \frac{x}{4}\right)^{6} = 485$

11. $5^x = 17^{x-1}$

12. $7^{2x+1} = 12^{-x}$

13. $8^x = 2.43 \cdot 5^x$

14. $6^{4x+3} = 1.5 \cdot 3^x$

15. $\log x + \log(5x - 6) = \log 8$

16. $2 \ln(2x - 1) - \ln 9 = \ln 4$

17. $2 \ln(x - 2) = \ln x$

18. $2 \log(2x - 3) = \log x + \log 12$

19. $\ln(3x - 5) - \ln(x + 1) = 1$

20. $\log(3x) = \log(6 - x) - 2$

21. $\log 3^x = 5x + 1$

22. $\frac{1}{\sqrt{2\pi}} e^{-x^2/2} = 0.25$

23. $e^{-x} - 2x = 0$

24. $e^{1-x} - ex = 0$

25. $10^{1-x} - 20x = 0$

In Problems 26 through 30, solve the given system of equations. Give answers in exact form if it is reasonable to do so; otherwise, to three decimal places.

26. $10^x \cdot 10^y = 1000$
   $10^x \cdot 10^{-3y} = 100$

27. $3^x \cdot 3^{-2y} = 27$
   $5^x \cdot 5^{1-y} = 625$

28. $2^x \cdot 4^y = \frac{1}{16}$
   $3^x \cdot 9^{-y} = \frac{1}{27}$

29. $3^x \cdot 5^y = 8$
   $2^x \cdot 4^{-y} = 7$

30. $7^{3x-1} \cdot 5^{2y} = 1$
   $3^{2x} \cdot 4^{-y} = 1$

31. In Example 2 of this section we found the root of $e^{-x} - x = 0$ by an estimation process. Try the following with your calculator. Enter *any number* into the display of your calculator, then press the keys in the given sequence:

   a) If your calculator has an $\boxed{e^x}$ key, press $\boxed{+/-}$ $\boxed{e^x}$ $\boxed{+/-}$ $\boxed{e^x}$, and so on. That is, press the change-sign key and the $\boxed{e^x}$ key repeatedly. After each $\boxed{e^x}$ look at the display. Continue until you see something interesting and then give an intuitive explanation of what is happening by using graphs similar to the one in Example 2.

   b) If your calculator does not have an $\boxed{e^x}$ key, then carry out the instructions of (a), except replace the $\boxed{e^x}$ key by $\boxed{INV}$ and $\boxed{\ln}$ keys (this is equivalent to $\boxed{e^x}$, as we saw in (10.7)).

32. Following instructions similar to those in Problem 31, solve the equations:

   a) $2^{-x} - x = 0$

   b) $e^{-x} - 4x = 0$

   Hint. Write the equation in the form $f(x) = x$. Then take any real number (call it x_0) and successively evaluate $f(x_0)$, $f(f(x_0))$, $f(f(f(x_0)))$, etc.

REVIEW EXERCISE

Give answers to the problems in exact form whenever it is reasonable to do so. Otherwise express results in decimal form rounded off to three decimal places. In problems involving undefined quantities, explain why the answer is undefined.

In Problems 1 through 15, evaluate the given expressions:

1. $\log 8$

2. $\log \sqrt{43}$

3. $\ln 23$

4. $\log(\sqrt{2} + \sqrt{3})$

5. $\ln(36^3)$

6. $\log(\ln 48)$

7. $\ln(\log 48)$

8. $\ln\left(\dfrac{\sqrt{2} + \sqrt{6}}{3}\right)$

9. $\log_5 8$

10. $\log_3(\sqrt{5} + \sqrt{12})$

11. $\log_7(\log 24)$

12. $\log_8(e^3)$

13. $\log(\ln 0.6)$

14. $\log_5(1 - \sqrt{2})$

15. $\log_3(27\sqrt{3})$

In Problems 16 through 24, functions f and g are defined by $f(x) = e^x + e^{-x}$ and $g(x) = 3\ln(2x - 1)$. Evaluate the given expressions.

16. $f(0)$

17. $g(0)$

18. $f(\sqrt{2})$

19. $f\left(-\dfrac{5}{2}\right)$

20. $g(4)$

21. $f(2) \cdot g(2)$

22. $f(3) \div g(5)$

23. $f(\sqrt{2}) + g(\sqrt{2})$

24. $(f(\sqrt{3}))^2$

In Problems 25 through 36, solve the given equations:

25. $\ln e^x = 3$

26. $\log e^x = 3$

27. $1 - \ln(2x + 1) = 3$

28. $\log(\ln x) = 1$

29. $\ln(\log x) = 1$

30. $e^{2x-1} = 4$

31. $e^{3x} = 10^{1-x}$

32. $\log 10^{4-3x} = 1$

33. $3^{x-1} = 4$

34. $5^x = 3(7^x)$

35. $2e^x + 1 = 0$

36. $3e^x - 1 = 0$

37. Plot a graph of $y = e^{-x}$.

38. Plot a graph of $y = -4^x$.

39. Plot a graph of $y = 1 - 3^x$.

40. If $y = x \cdot 2^{-x}$ and $x \geq 0$, make a table of x, y values that satisfy the equation; use values of x beginning with $x = 0$ at 0.2 units apart until you reach 3.0. Plot these points and make a reasonable estimate of the value of x at which y attains a maximum. Refine your estimate by more computations and then find the maximum value of y.

INTRODUCTION TO THE CALCULATOR

INTRODUCTION TO
THE CALCULATOR

There are two types of scientific calculators suitable for studying a trigonometry course. One type involves algebraic entry while the other is based on the Reverse Polish Notation (RPN). The entry system depends upon the electronic circuitry installed in the calculator during its manufacture. The basic difference between using the algebraic entry and RPN is the order of pressing the four arithmetic-function keys. Calculators with algebraic entry place the binary operation between the two numbers, such as 2 $\boxed{+}$ 3 $\boxed{=}$, while in the RPN machines, the arithmetic operation follows both numbers after they are entered into the calculator; for instance, 2 $\boxed{\text{ENT}}$ 3 $\boxed{+}$ is the sequence that evaluates the sum of 2 and 3.

One basic feature common to both entry systems is the use of real numbers in decimal form. Calculators operate with rational approximations of all real numbers correct to the capacity of the particular machine. Calculators cannot handle imaginary numbers directly. When an attempt is made to find $\sqrt{-4}$, the calculator will display *Error* in some way. In this case the error indication tells us that $\sqrt{-4}$ is not a real number. Another instance when the calculator indicates error occurs during an attempt to divide by zero. A good way to find the type of error indication a calculator displays is to press the keys 0 and $\boxed{1/x}$. Whenever the error symbol is displayed, the user should be alerted to the fact that the calculator is being asked to perform an unacceptable operation.

Each entry system has its advantages and disadvantages. The student is urged to evaluate each system and choose the calculator that fits his interests and needs best. Appendix A is devoted to helping the student become proficient in using the calculator. We discuss separately algebraic calculators (Section A.1) and RPN calculators (Section A.2).

A.1 ALGEBRAIC CALCULATORS

Algebraic calculators can easily be identified by the presence of an $\boxed{=}$ key on the keyboard. Some calculators with algebraic entry are preprogrammed to follow the conventional hierarchy of arithmetic operations, while others perform operations sequentially as entered into the calculator. To determine whether a calculator uses hierarchy of arithmetic, calculate $2 + 3 \cdot 5$ by pressing 2 [+] 3 [×] 5 [=] . If the display shows 17, the calculator is accepting the entire sequence of instructions and then performing the multiplication before the addition. In this case we say that addition is a *pending* operation. It is performed only after the entire sequence is entered and the machine can then respond according the to conventional priority of multiplication and division over addition and subtraction. On the other hand, if the display shows 25, the machine is performing the operations in the order in which they are entered. That is, it is performing the calculation $(2 + 3) \cdot 5$.

Texas Instruments is a major manufacturer of calculators with algebraic entry. Some of their less sophisticated models do not follow arithmetical hierarchy; however, most of their scientific calculators use the so-called *algebraic operating system* (AOS) and are preprogrammed to follow the hierarchy of arithmetic in calculations. *In the instructions given here we assume that all algebraic calculators have AOS.* If this is not the case, the order of entry can be adjusted as necessary. For example, $2 + 3 \cdot 5$ can be calculated by pressing 3 [×] 5 [+] 2 [=] .

1. Using the Keys [+] [−] [×] [÷] [=] [+/−] [(] [)] [x²]

In order to use the calculator efficiently, it is helpful to know something about the operation of the machine. The series of examples given below is designed to help the reader make some important observations involving the order in which pending operations are carried out in an AOS calculator.

Examples

△ Calculate $5 - 7 + 4$.

Solution. Press the calculator keys corresponding to the numbers and operations, as written from left to right, carefully watching the display to see when a given command is executed:

$$\text{Press } 5 \; [-] \; 7 \; [+] \; 4 \; [=] .$$ ∎

△ Calculate $5 - 7 + 4 \cdot 3$.

Solution

$$\text{Press } 5 \; [-] \; 7 \; [+] \; 4 \; [×] \; 3 \; [=] .$$

Observe how all pending operations are executed when the [=] key is pressed. ∎

△3 Calculate $\dfrac{5-7+4}{3}$.

Solution

$$\text{Press } \boxed{(} \; 5 \; \boxed{-} \; 7 \; \boxed{+} \; 4 \; \boxed{)} \; \boxed{\div} \; 3 \; \boxed{=} \; .$$

Note that the numerator is evaluated after the right-parenthesis key $\boxed{)}$ is pressed. As an alternative solution, press $5 \; \boxed{-} \; 7 \; \boxed{+} \; 4 \; \boxed{=} \; \boxed{\div} \; 3 \; \boxed{=}$. Thus, when the left-parenthesis key $\boxed{(}$ is not entered, one can use the $\boxed{=}$ key to compute the numerator before dividing by 3. ▌

△4 Calculate $5 - 7 + 4 \cdot 3^2$.

Solution

$$\text{Press } 5 \; \boxed{-} \; 7 \; \boxed{+} \; 4 \; \boxed{\times} \; 3 \; \boxed{x^2} \; \boxed{=} \; .$$

Note that pressing $\boxed{x^2}$ squares only the contents of the display. Pressing $\boxed{=}$ executes all pending operations. ▌

△5 Calculate $5 - 7 + (4 \cdot 3)^2$.

Solution

$$\text{Press } 5 \; \boxed{-} \; 7 \; \boxed{+} \; \boxed{(} \; 4 \; \boxed{\times} \; 3 \; \boxed{)} \; \boxed{x^2} \; \boxed{=} \; .$$

The problem requires that $4 \cdot 3$ be multiplied before squaring. Parentheses keys are used here to accomplish this. ▌

△6 Calculate $5 \div (-7 + 4 \cdot 3)$.

Solution

$$\text{Press } 5 \; \boxed{\div} \; \boxed{(} \; 7 \; \boxed{+/-} \; \boxed{+} \; 4 \; \boxed{\times} \; 3 \; \boxed{)} \; \boxed{=} \; .$$

The parentheses serve to compute the divisor before the division is carried out. Special note should be taken of the use of the change-sign key $\boxed{+/-}$. This key changes the sign of the number in the display. The calculator will not accept the sequence $5 \; \boxed{\div} \; \boxed{(} \; \boxed{-} \; 7 \ldots$ Such a sequence treats the $\boxed{-} \; 7$ command as subtraction rather than a negative number, but the algebraic calculator cannot accept two operation commands in sequence (such as $\boxed{\div}$ and $\boxed{-}$). ▌

2.   Clearing the Calculator

If the last key pressed is $\boxed{=}$, all pending operations have been executed and the calculator is ready for a new problem without pressing the clear key. Some calculators have a clear-entry key that clears only the number in the display, while a separate key is used to clear all pending operations. Other calculators have a key labeled $\boxed{\text{ON/C}}$ that serves three purposes. It is used to turn the calculator on; then, during computations, if it is pressed once, the number in the display *only* will be cleared while, if it is pressed twice in succession, all pending operations are also cleared.

The clear-entry feature is especially useful since one of the most frequent mistakes is to key in an incorrect number after the calculator already has several pending operations. We illustrate this in the following example where a 7 rather than an 8 was entered and this mistake is corrected by using the clear-entry key.

⚠️ Evaluate $2 + 3 \cdot 5 - 24 \div 6 + 8$.

Solution

Press 2 ⊞ 3 ⊠ 5 ⊟ 24 ⊡ 6 ⊞ 7 ON/C 8 ⊜.   ▌

EXERCISE A.1

Calculations in Problems 1 through 15 involve integers only. This is intended to allow the student to mentally follow the arithmetic and observe when the pending operations are performed by the calculator. Some important features of the calculator are illustrated in these problems; therefore, the student is encouraged to consider each calculation carefully.

1. $5 + 3 \cdot 7$

2. $(5 + 3) \cdot 7$

3. $(5 + 3) - 7$

4. $(5 + 3)(-7)$

5. $2 + 12 \div 3 - 7$

6. $2 + 12 \div (3 - 7)$

7. $\dfrac{(15 - 4) \cdot 5}{2} + 3 \cdot 5 - 7$

8. $\dfrac{(15 - 4) \cdot 5}{2 + 3 \cdot 5 - 7}$

9. $\dfrac{(1/2) - 3}{4}$

10. $(1/2) - (3/4)$

11. $2 \cdot 3^2 + 4 \cdot 5^2$

12. $(2 \cdot 3)^2 + (4 \cdot 5)^2$

13. $(2 \cdot 3 + 4 \cdot 5)^2$

14. $\left(\dfrac{3 \cdot 4^2}{2} \right) \cdot 5^2$

15. $(3 \cdot 4^2) \div (2 \cdot 5^2)$

Use your calculator to solve Problems 16 through 30. Answers correct to three decimal places are provided for a quick check.

Answers

16. $(1.87)(34.61) + 3.872$ 68.593

17. $(45.9 - 29.76)^2 + 52.86$ 313.360

18. $45.9 - 29.76^2 + 52.86$ $- 786.898$

19. $\dfrac{563 + 284}{18.7}$ 45.294

Answers

20. $563 + \dfrac{284}{18.7}$ 578.187

21. $\dfrac{52.9 \cdot 0.3876}{21.3}$ 0.963

22. $12^2 + 5^2 - 2 \cdot 5 \cdot 12 \cdot 0.9848$ 50.824

23. $(12^2 + 5^2 - 2 \cdot 5 \cdot 12)(0.9848)$ 48.255

24. $(-37.48 + 59.32)^2 - 31.97$ 445.016

25. $(37.48 - 59.32)^2 - 31.97$ 445.016

26. $\dfrac{(15.39 - 4.72) \cdot 5}{2.3} + 3.78 \cdot 5.43$ 43.721

27. $\dfrac{(15.39 - 4.72) \cdot 5}{2.3 + 3.78 \cdot 5.43}$ 2.337

28. $\dfrac{21.8 + 4.32^2}{5.12} 5.39^2$ 229.593

29. $\dfrac{2}{3} + \dfrac{3}{4} - \dfrac{7}{8}$ 0.542

30. $\dfrac{(2/7) + (3/8)}{(1/6) + (1/7)}$ 2.135

3. Using the Keys $\boxed{1/x}$ $\boxed{\sqrt{x}}$ $\boxed{y^x}$ $\boxed{\text{STO}}$ $\boxed{\text{RCL}}$.

Scientific calculators have several keys in addition to the basic keys described in the preceding section. Here we shall consider the use of five more keys and defer discussion of others until the appropriate places in the text. The $\boxed{1/x}$ and $\boxed{\sqrt{x}}$ keys give the reciprocal and the square root, respectively, of the number in the display. The $\boxed{y^x}$ key operates by entering a positive number y, followed by $\boxed{y^x}$, then the number x, followed by $\boxed{=}$. For example, to evaluate 7^3, keys are pressed in the following order: $7 \boxed{y^x} 3 \boxed{=}$ and the result 343 appears in the display. Similarly, to find $\sqrt[3]{7}$, we evaluate $7^{1/3}$ by pressing the following keys: $7 \boxed{y^x} 3 \boxed{1/x} \boxed{=}$, which gives $\sqrt[3]{7} = 1.9129$ (to four decimal places).

A lengthy computation frequently involves the evaluation of intermediate numbers that must be recorded and used later to complete the calculation.

Scientific calculators allow the user to store a number with the $\boxed{\text{STO}}$ key* and recall it when needed with the $\boxed{\text{RCL}}$ key, thus avoiding the necessity of recording intermediate steps. This feature will be illustrated in examples given in this section.

Examples

$\triangle$ Calculate $\sqrt{3.9^2 + 7.3^2}$

Solution

$$\text{Press } \boxed{(} \; 3.9 \; \boxed{x^2} \; \boxed{+} \; 7.3 \; \boxed{x^2} \; \boxed{)} \; \boxed{\sqrt{x}} \; .$$

The display shows 8.2764727. Alternative solution:

$$\text{Press } 3.9 \; \boxed{x^2} \; \boxed{+} \; 7.3 \; \boxed{x^2} \; \boxed{=} \; \boxed{\sqrt{x}} \; .$$

This method uses the $\boxed{=}$ key to calculate the radicand before taking the square root. ∎

$\triangle$ Calculate $12^3 - 4^5$.

Solution

Press $12 \; \boxed{y^x} \; 3 \; \boxed{-} \; 4 \; \boxed{y^x} \; 5 \; \boxed{=} \; .$

The display shows 704. ∎

$\triangle$ Calculate $\sqrt[3]{24.3} \cdot \sqrt[5]{32.7}$

Solution   The problem can be rewritten as $(24.3^{1/3}) \cdot (32.7^{1/5})$; then press

$$24.3 \; \boxed{y^x} \; 3 \; \boxed{1/x} \; \boxed{\times} \; 32.7 \; \boxed{y^x} \; 5 \; \boxed{1/x} \; \boxed{=} \; .$$

The displays shows 5.8180615. Note that when the $\boxed{\times}$ key is pressed in this sequence, at that point the calculator evaluates $(24.3)^{1/3}$; in this computation it is not necessary to press the $\boxed{=}$ key before the $\boxed{\times}$ key. ∎

$\triangle$ Calculate $\sqrt{1.3^2 + 2.8^2 - 2(1.3)(2.8)(0.3215)}$

Solution Press

$$1.3 \; \boxed{x^2} \; \boxed{+} \; 2.8 \; \boxed{x^2} \; \boxed{-} \; 2 \; \boxed{\times} \; 1.3 \; \boxed{\times} \; 2.8 \; \boxed{\times} \; 0.3215 \; \boxed{=} \; \boxed{\sqrt{x}} \; .$$

The display shows 2.6813206. ∎

$\triangle$ Calculate $\dfrac{1}{\sqrt{5.61 + 24.93}}$.

---

*Some calculators have multiple storage capacity and require a number address to follow the $\boxed{\text{STO}}$ key. The owner's manual that accompanies such a calculator gives details.

Solution

Press $\boxed{(}$ 5.61 $\boxed{+}$ 24.93 $\boxed{)}$ $\boxed{\sqrt{x}}$ $\boxed{1/x}$.

The display shows 0.18095287.   ∎

/6\ Calculate $\dfrac{1}{5.2^3 + 3.8^4} + \sqrt{4.2^2 + 3.97}$.

Solution Press

5.2 $\boxed{y^x}$ 3 $\boxed{+}$ 3.8 $\boxed{y^x}$ 4 $\boxed{=}$ $\boxed{1/x}$ $\boxed{STO}$ 4.2 $\boxed{x^2}$ $\boxed{+}$ 3.97 $\boxed{=}$ $\boxed{\sqrt{x}}$
$\boxed{+}$ $\boxed{RCL}$ $\boxed{=}$

The display shows 4.6515201. Storage is used to store the first part while the
second part is being calculated.   ∎

/7\ Calculate $(5.873)^3 + 3(5.873)^2 - 9(5.873) + 4$.

Solution Press

5.873 $\boxed{STO}$ $\boxed{y^x}$ 3 $\boxed{+}$ 3 $\boxed{\times}$ $\boxed{RCL}$ $\boxed{x^2}$ $\boxed{-}$ 9 $\boxed{\times}$ $\boxed{RCL}$ $\boxed{+}$ 4 $\boxed{=}$.

The display shows 257.19166. Use of the $\boxed{STO}$ key eliminates the need to key in
the four-digit number 5.873 three separate times.

Note. The $\boxed{y^x}$ key will function only when the base is positive. The calculator
will indicate an *Error* if the base is negative.

/8\ Use the calculator to evaluate the following:

a) $\sqrt{5.3 - 9.7}$ b) $\sqrt[3]{-12.97}$ c) $(-3.1)^4$ d) $(-3.1)^5$

Solution

a) Press $\boxed{(}$ 5.3 $\boxed{-}$ 9.7 $\boxed{)}$ $\boxed{\sqrt{x}}$. The display will indicate an *Error*.
   This is predictable since $5.3 - 9.7 = -4.3$ and the square root of a
   negative number is not a real number.

b) Rewrite $\sqrt[3]{-12.97}$ as $(-12.97)^{1/3}$ and press
   12.97 $\boxed{+/-}$ $\boxed{y^x}$ 3 $\boxed{1/x}$ $\boxed{=}$;
   the result indicates an *Error*. This is because the calculator will not
   accept a negative base y when the $\boxed{y^x}$ key is used. However $\sqrt[3]{-12.97}$
   is a real number equal to $-\sqrt[3]{12.97}$. We therefore calculate $\sqrt[3]{12.97}$ by
   pressing 12.97 $\boxed{y^x}$ 3 $\boxed{1/x}$ $\boxed{=}$. The display shows 2.3495. Therefore
   we have $\sqrt[3]{-12.97} = -2.3495$.

c) When evaluating $(-3.1)^4$, the calculator will indicate an *Error* if we
   press 3.1 $\boxed{+/-}$ $\boxed{y^x}$ 4 $\boxed{=}$, but we know that $(-3.1)^4 = (3.1)^4$, and this
   can be calculated by using the $\boxed{y^x}$ key. Press 3.1 $\boxed{y^x}$ 4 $\boxed{=}$. The
   display shows 92.3521. Thus $(-3.1)^4 = 92.3521$.

d) Since $(-3.1)^5 = -(3.1)^5$, we first evaluate $(3.1)^5$ by pressing 3.1 $\boxed{y^x}$ 5 $\boxed{=}$. The display shows 286.2915, so we conclude that $(-3.1)^5 = -286.2915$. ∎

EXERCISE A.1 (Continued)

Use a calculator to solve the following problems. Answers rounded off to three decimal places are given as a check.

Answers

1. $\sqrt{47.23 + 52.18}$ 9.970

2. $\sqrt{39.4 + (5.8)(7.3)}$ 9.041

3. $\sqrt{54.6 - 31.93}$ 4.761

4. $\sqrt{(9.1)(3.6) - (7.28)(5.97)}$ Imaginary number

5. $\sqrt{9.2^2 + 4.1^2}$ 10.072

6. $\sqrt{(3.87 + 9.4) \cdot 4.83^2}$ 17.595

7. $\sqrt[3]{12.96}$ 2.349

8. $\sqrt[3]{-243.78}$ -6.247

9. $\sqrt[5]{32.786}$ 2.010

10. $\sqrt[4]{17.39}$ 2.042

11. $\dfrac{1}{2} + \dfrac{1}{3} + \dfrac{1}{4} + \dfrac{1}{5}$ 1.283

12. $\dfrac{2}{3} + \dfrac{3}{4} + \dfrac{5}{6}$ 2.250

13. $\dfrac{1}{\sqrt{2}} + \dfrac{1}{\sqrt{3}} + \dfrac{1}{\sqrt{4}}$ 1.784

14. $\dfrac{5}{\sqrt{12}} + \dfrac{7}{\sqrt{3}}$ 5.485

15. $\sqrt[3]{3.47^5 + 29.3^3}$ 29.494

16. $(-4.3)^2 + (-5.9)^3$ -186.889

17. $(-4.1)^3 + (-5.9)^4$ 1142.815

18. $\sqrt{11.9^2 + 13.2^2 - 2(11.9)(13.2)(0.4937)}$ 12.679

19. $\sqrt{[11.9^2 + 13.2^2 - 2(11.9)(13.2)](0.4937)}$ 0.913

20. $\sqrt{4 - \sqrt{2}}$ 1.608

The problems given in Exercises A.2 (pp. 309–310) provide opportunity for additional practice in using AOS calculators. The student is urged to do most of them.

A.2 RPN CALCULATORS

Calculators using Reverse Polish Notation (RPN) can easily be identified by the presence of the ⎡ENT⎤ key (and the absence of the ⎡=⎤ key). A major manufacturer of RPN calculators is Hewlett–Packard (HP). In the following discussion we shall describe the operation of RPN calculators consistent with HP scientific calculators. The student should be able to adapt the treatment found here to other brands quite easily by referring to the owner's manual.

1. Registers and Use of Stack

The only external means of communication between the calculator and its user is through the keyboard and the numbers appearing in the display. At any time there is only one number in the display; however, the calculator accepts several numbers and stores them for recall on keyboard command. The places used to store the numbers are called registers and may be thought of as physical places inside the machine where a number is kept until needed. HP machines have four such registers. The content of one register is displayed by the machine. This is called the X register. Registers not visible to the user are called Y, Z, and T. These four registers form the *stack* or *automatic memory* of the machine. In order to use RPN calculators efficiently, it is essential to understand the operation of the stack.

If we represent the stack as a mailbox-like set of compartments ⎡X | Y | Z | T⎤, where X, Y, Z, and T are the addresses for the boxes, then we can visualize what is happening inside the calculator. When a sequence of digit keys is pressed, the corresponding number appears in the X register. Pressing the ⎡ENT⎤ key shifts the number into the Y register, and the machine is ready to accept a second number. For example, pressing 2 gives ⎡2 | Y | Z | T⎤ ; when we follow this with ⎡ENT⎤ we get ⎡2 | 2 | Z | T⎤ . If we now press 3, the 2 in the X register is replaced by 3 and the 2 in the Y register remains. Pressing ⎡ENT⎤ shifts the contents as shown: $X{\rightarrow}Y{\rightarrow}Z{\rightarrow}T{\rightarrow}$lost, retaining the number entered in the X register as well as in the Y register. The series of key strokes

$$2 \text{ ⎡ENT⎤ } 3 \text{ ⎡ENT⎤ } 1 \; 5 \text{ ⎡ENT⎤ } 4$$

provides us with this arrangement of numbers in the stack: ⎡4 | 15 | 3 | 2⎤ .

Observe that the 15 in the Y register was accomplished without pressing key ⎡ENT⎤ between 1 and 5. This feature best describes the purpose of the ⎡ENT⎤ key; that is, to separate the numbers entered into the machine. Pressing the ⎡ENT⎤ key after 4 will give ⎡4 | 4 | 15 | 3⎤ , losing the 2 (and the calculator is now ready to accept a new number in the X register). It may appear that having only a four-stack capacity is a serious limitation; but this is not the case, since we can perform most of our computations without any additional registers, as will be demonstrated in the following examples. In fact, some RPN calculators have only three register stacks and they perform adequately in most problems.

For arithmetic operations only the numbers in the X and Y registers are used directly. If x is in X and y is in Y, then pressing any one of the keys $\boxed{+}$ $\boxed{-}$ $\boxed{\times}$ or $\boxed{\div}$ gives the corresponding result $y + x$, $y - x$, $y \times x$ or $y \div x$ in the display.

For example, to evaluate $2 + 3$ press 2 $\boxed{\text{ENT}}$ 3 to get $\boxed{3 \mid 2 \qquad}$; then pressing the $\boxed{+}$ key gives $\boxed{5 \qquad}$. To evaluate $15 - 4$, press 1 5 $\boxed{\text{ENT}}$ 4 $\boxed{-}$; the result will show 11 in the display. Similar steps are followed in the operations of multiplication and division.

Examples

In the following examples the grids indicate the content of each register after the key shown in the left column has been pressed. A blank register does not necessarily mean an empty register (contains 0), but rather that we are not concerned with its content in our computation.

Note. Two solutions are given for some of the following problems. It is important for the reader to understand that there are several methods for solving a given problem. After some practice with the calculator the user will discover efficient keying patterns.

⚠ Calculate $7 + 6 \cdot 4$.

Solution 1   *Solution 2* We evaluate $6 \cdot 4 + 7$
Press 7 $\boxed{\text{ENT}}$ 6 $\boxed{\text{ENT}}$ 4 $\boxed{\times}$ $\boxed{+}$ by pressing 6 $\boxed{\text{ENT}}$ 4 $\boxed{\times}$ 7 $\boxed{+}$

Key	X	Y	Z	T
7	7			
ENT	7	7		
6	6	7		
ENT	6	6	7	
4	4	6	7	
×	24	7		
+	31			

Key	X	Y	Z	T
6	6			
ENT	6	6		
4	4	6		
×	24			
7	7	24		
+	31			

Note. In Solution 2, the $\boxed{\text{ENT}}$ key was not pressed before the 7. The machine knows it is receiving a new number after any operation and, in this example, it is not tempted to write 247. Solution 1 is a less natural way to perform the computation, but it illustrates how helpful it is to know the contents of the registers.   ▮

Calculate $5 \cdot 3 - 4$.

Solution

Key	X	Y	Z	T
5	5			
ENT	5	5		
3	3	5		
×	15			
4	4	15		
−	11			

 Calculate $7 + 3(4 + 6)$.

Solution 1

Key	X	Y	X	T
7	7			
ENT	7	7		
3	3	7		
ENT	3	3	7	
4	4	3	7	
ENT	4	4	3	7
6	6	4	3	7
+	10	3	7	
×	30	7		
+	37			

Solution 2 Evaluate $(4 + 6) \cdot 3 + 7$.

Key	X	Y	X	T
4	4			
ENT	4	4		
6	6	4		
+	10			
3	3	10		
×	30			
7	7	30		
+	37			

Note. In Solution 1, all of the numbers are entered into the stack and then the operations are performed in the appropriate order. In Solution 2, operations are performed sequentially according to the conventional principle of beginning within the parentheses. This is a more efficient method in terms of number of steps.

△4 Calculate $(15 - 4) \cdot 3 + 2$.

Solution 1 (Key 15 means we press
the digit keys 1 and 5 in that order.)

Solution 2

$$2 + 3(15 - 4)$$

Key	X	Y	Z	T
15	15			
ENT	15	15		
4	4	15		
−	11			
3	3	11		
×	33			
2	2	33		
+	35			

Key	X	Y	Z	T
2	2			
ENT	2	2		
3	3	2		
ENT	3	3	2	
15	15	3	2	
ENT	15	15	3	2
4	4	15	3	2
−	11	3	2	2
×	33	2	2	2
+	35	2	2	2

Note. Solution 2 is given to illustrate the contents of the registers when the *T* register is used. Once a number (2, in this case) is entered into the *T* register, it remains there and shifts into the *Z* and then the *Y* register as the content of the *Y* register is being used in an operation. This property of the stack is useful in performing some computations (see Example 2 on p. 302).

The contents of the *Y*, *Z*, and *T* registers can be displayed by using the roll key R↓ . For example, continuation of Solution 2 by pressing the R↓ key four times would give the results shown below:

	X	Y	Z	T
	35	2	2	2
R↓	2	2	2	35
R↓	2	2	35	2
R↓	2	35	2	2
R↓	35	2	2	2

∎

⑤ If $f(x) = 5x^2 - 4x + 1$, evaluate $f(3)$.

Solution

To evaluate $f(3) = 5 \cdot 3^2 - 4 \cdot 3 + 1$, we proceed in the following way:

Key	X	Y	Z	T
3	3			
ENT	3	3		
x	9			
5	5	9		
x	45			

4	4	45		
ENT	4	4	45	
3	3	4	45	
x	12	45		
−	33			
1	1	33		
+	34			

2. The CHS and x↔y Keys

The CHS key changes the sign of the contents of the X register *only* and must be used to enter a negative number into the machine. The CHS key does not shift the content of the X register to Y; hence, it is necessary to use the ENT key to separate numbers after the CHS key is pressed and before a new number is entered. The x↔y key interchanges the contents of the X and Y registers and leaves the contents of Z and T undisturbed. This key is frequently used when performing lengthy calculations involving subtraction and/or division.

Examples

① Calculate $-3 + 4 \cdot 5$.

Solution 1

Key	X	Y	Z	T
3	3			
CHS	− 3			
ENT	− 3	− 3		
4	4	− 3		
ENT	4	4	− 3	
5	5	4	− 3	
x	20	− 3		
+	17			

Solution 2 Treat it as a subtraction.

Key	X	Y	Z	T
3	3			
ENT	3	3		
4	4	3		
ENT	4	4	3	
5	5	4	3	
x	20	3		
x↔y	3	20		
−	17			

Note. Solution 2 is given to illustrate the use of the ⌈x↔y⌉ key. It should be clear that a more efficient sequence of keys is possible by first evaluating $4 \cdot 5$ and then subtracting 3 from the result.   ∎

2. If $f(x) = 4x^4 + 5x^2$, find $f(-3)$.

Solution We wish to evaluate $4(-3)^4 + 5(-3)^2$.

Key	X	Y	Z	T
3	3			
CHS	− 3			
ENT	− 3	− 3		
ENT	− 3	− 3	− 3	
ENT	− 3	− 3	− 3	− 3
x	9	− 3	− 3	− 3
x	− 27	− 3	− 3	− 3
x	81	− 3	− 3	− 3

4	4	81	− 3	− 3
x	324	− 3	− 3	− 3
x↔y	− 3	324	− 3	− 3
ENT	− 3	− 3	324	− 3
x	9	324	− 3	− 3
5	5	9	324	− 3
x	45	324	− 3	− 3
+	369	− 3	− 3	− 3

Thus, $f(-3) = 369$.   ∎

3. Overflowing the Stack

Occasionally it happens that a given sequence of keying instructions results in overflowing the stack and an alternative method must be devised to perform the calculations. Obviously with the numbers used in these examples, one would simply do some of the calculations mentally; however, if the numbers involved happen to be, say, four-digit numbers, it is helpful to be able to do all of the arithmetic with the calculator.

Example   Calculate $\dfrac{25}{2 + 3(4 + 2)}$.

Solution

At this point the numerator is lost. However, we can continue to evaluate the denominator, reenter the numerator, and then use the $\boxed{\text{x}\leftrightarrow\text{y}}$ key as follows:

Key	X	Y	Z	T
25	25			
ENT	25	25		
2	2	25		
ENT	2	2	25	
3	3	2	25	
ENT	3	3	2	25
4	4	3	2	25
ENT	4	4	3	2

	X	Y	Z	T
2	2	4	3	2
+	6	3	2	
x	18	2		
+	20			
25	25	20		
x↔y	20	25		
÷	1.25			

A more judicious choice of keying the denominator would avoid the overflow problem encountered in the above example. Also, storage registers are available that would alleviate the problem. We shall discuss the use of storage keys later.

4. Clearing the Calculator

Calculators have various keys for clearing parts of the machine. One key that clears the display only (that is, the X register) is generally labeled $\boxed{\text{CLX}}$ and is especially useful in correcting an error when a wrong number is entered into the display. Some of the more sophisticated calculators have special keys for clearing only the storage registers, or the prefix, or the program in programmable calculators. The owner's manual explains how these keys operate in a particular calculator. In fact, the reader is urged to consult the owner's manual whenever there is a question concerning the operation of any key.

If one wishes to clear the entire machine, turning the calculator off and then on will do it, except for the sophisticated calculators with a continuous memory. It is not always necessary to clear the stack (or even the display) before beginning a new computation, since only the numbers entered for a given calculation are used and the content of the other registers is irrelevant.

EXERCISE A.2

The problems in this exercise can be solved by using the keys ⟨ + ⟩ ⟨ − ⟩ ⟨ x ⟩ ⟨ ÷ ⟩ ⟨ CHS ⟩ ⟨ x↔y ⟩; however the more experienced student may prefer other keys, such as ⟨ 1/x ⟩ and ⟨ x² ⟩.

1. For each indicated calculation two keying methods are given. In each key sequence, fill in a grid giving the content of the X, Y, Z, and T registers after each command has been executed by the calculator. Determine which method evaluates the given calculation correctly.

a)

$8 \cdot 4 - 5$	
Key	Key
8	8
ENT	ENT
4	4
ENT	x
5	5
−	−
x	

b)

$(7 + 4) \cdot 8$	
Key	Key
7	7
ENT	ENT
4	4
+	ENT
8	8
x	x
	+

c)

$(9 \cdot 6) \div (4 \cdot 7)$	
Key	Key
9	9
ENT	ENT
6	6
x	x
4	4
ENT	÷
7	7
x	÷
÷	

d)

$10 - 5(7 + 3)$	
Key	Key
10	7
ENT	ENT
5	3
ENT	+
7	5
ENT	x
3	10
+	−
x	
−	

2. Determine what numerical expression is being evaluated by each given sequence of keystrokes.

a)

Key
2
ENT
4
ENT
1
−
x
3
+

b)

Key
5
ENT
4
x
2
−
3
+

c)

Key
5
ENT
4
+
3
÷
2
−

d)

Key
5
ENT
4
+
3
÷
2
x↔y
−

e)

Key
4
ENT
6
x
3
ENT
6
x
+
7
÷

f)

Key
1
ENT
4
4
÷
1
ENT
5
÷
+

3. Give a sequence of keys that will correctly evaluate each of the given expressions. In each case make a grid showing the content of all stack registers after each key has been pressed:

a) $2 + 3 + 4 - 6$ b) $2 - 4 + 5 \cdot 7$ c) $4 \div 2 + 6 \div 3$

d) $\dfrac{4 + 6}{2 + 3}$ e) $3(2 - 6) + 4(5 - 2)$

In the following problems, evaluate the given expression using a calculator. Make a grid whenever necessary to get a sequence of keys giving the correct answer. Your computations can be checked with the answers given to four decimal places.

Answers

4. $(1.4 + 3.6)(2.1)$ 10.5000

5. $(3.8 - 4.3)(6.3)$ $- 3.1500$

6. $2.9 + 1.6 \div 3$ 3.4333

7. $\dfrac{1.96 + 2.3}{4.2 - 3.1}$ 3.8727

8. $14.98 - \dfrac{4.3 + 2.6}{5.7}$ 13.7695

9. $\dfrac{5.4(6.9 - 1.2) + 4}{7 + 4.3}$ 3.0779

10. $\dfrac{1}{4} + \dfrac{1}{5} + \dfrac{1}{7}$ 0.5929

11. $\dfrac{3}{4} + \dfrac{4}{5} + \dfrac{2}{7}$ 1.8357

12. $5^2 + 7 \cdot 5 - 3$ 57

13. $\dfrac{2 \cdot 4^2 - 5 \cdot 4 - 3}{2 \cdot 4 + 1}$ 1

14. $\left(\dfrac{3.8}{5.1} \right)^2 + \dfrac{9.6}{4.3}$ 2.7877

15. $5(-1.32)^4 + 4(-1.32)^3$ 5.9799

16. $\dfrac{3.48 - (1.23)(4.75)}{8.41 - 2.54(3.57 - 6.75)}$ $- 0.1433$

17. If $f(x) = 1.47x - 5.36$, find $f(3.4)$ $- 0.3620$

18. If $f(x) = \dfrac{1.56 - 2.36x}{1.57x}$, find $f(-5.7)$ $- 1.6775$

19. If $f(x) = 7.3x^2 - 4.1x + 3.5$, find $f(3.78)$ 92.3073

20. If $f(x) = \dfrac{2.4x^2 - 3.5x - 1.8}{3.2 - 1.5x}$, find $f(-4.3)$.   5.9716

5. The Keys $\boxed{x^2}$ $\boxed{1/x}$ $\boxed{\text{STO}}$ $\boxed{\text{RCL}}$ $\boxed{y^x}$ $\boxed{\sqrt{x}}$

There is no *one* correct way to perform a given calculation although some methods of key entry may be more efficient than others. In the preceding section we considered an example in which we evaluated $f(x) = 5x^2 - 4x + 1$ at $x = 3$. A more efficient sequence of keys would include the use of the $\boxed{x^2}$ key. Pressing the $\boxed{x^2}$ key squares the content of the X register, while the content of the other registers remains unchanged. This is illustrated in the following grid where we evaluate $f(3)$ if $f(x) = 5x^2 - 4x + 1$.

Key	X	Y	Z	T	Remarks
5	5				
$\boxed{\text{ENT}}$	5	5			
3	3	5			
$\boxed{x^2}$	9	5			3^2 is evaluated
$\boxed{\text{x}}$	45				$5 \cdot 3^2$ in X
4	4	45			
$\boxed{\text{ENT}}$	4	4	45		
3	3	4	45		
$\boxed{\text{x}}$	12	45			$3 \cdot 4$ in X
$\boxed{-}$	33				$5 \cdot 3^2 - 4 \cdot 3$ in X
1	1	33			
$\boxed{+}$	34				$5 \cdot 3^2 - 4 \cdot 3 + 1$ in X

The $\boxed{\sqrt{x}}$ and $\boxed{1/x}$ keys operate in a manner similar to that of $\boxed{x^2}$; pressing $\boxed{\sqrt{x}}$ takes the square root of the number in the X register and displays the result, while $\boxed{1/x}$ takes the reciprocal of the number appearing in the X register and displays it. Each of these keys leaves the content of the Y, Z, and T registers unchanged.

All scientific calculators have at least one memory storage and some have several. When the $\boxed{\text{STO}}$ key is pressed, the content of the X register is placed in a memory storage separate from any of the stack registers. Pressing the recall key $\boxed{\text{RCL}}$ will return that number to the X register whenever it is needed and also retain the number in the memory.

If a calculator has more than one memory storage, it is necessary to tell the machine the address of the particular memory to be used. For instance, if the calculator has eight memories numbered 0 through 7, the storage command consists of $\boxed{\text{STO}}$ followed by one of the numbers 0 through 7. Similarly for recall, press $\boxed{\text{RCL}}$ followed by the number 0 through 7 corresponding to the address where the number is stored.

Examples

⚠️1 If $f(x) = \dfrac{7x^2}{3x-4}$, find $f\left(\dfrac{1+\sqrt{5}}{2}\right)$ correct to four decimal places.

Solution We wish to evaluate

$$7\left(\frac{1+\sqrt{5}}{2}\right)^2 \div [3\,\frac{1+\sqrt{5}}{2} - 4].$$

We first evaluate $(\sqrt{5}+1) \div 2$ and store the result for future use. The grid shows decimal values correct to two places.

Key	X	Y	Z	T	Remarks
5	5				
√x̄	2.23				
1	1	2.23			
+	3.23				
2	2	3.23			
÷	1.61				$(\sqrt{5}+1) \div 2$ in X
STO 1	1.61				$(\sqrt{5}+1) \div 2$ stored in R_1 and still in X
x²	2.61				Square of $(\sqrt{5}+1) \div 2$
7	7	2.61			
×	18.32				Numerator in X
RCL 1	1.61	18.32			$(\sqrt{5}+1) \div 2$ recalled and numerator moved to Y
3	3	1.61	18.32		
×	4.85	18.32			
4	4	4.85	18.32		
−	0.85	18.32			Denominator in X and numerator in Y
÷	21.4567				Answer

⚠️2 Evaluate $\dfrac{1}{\sqrt{2}} - \dfrac{1}{\sqrt{3}}$.

Solution Here we use the 1/x key since this is simpler than using the ÷ key to evaluate $1 \div \sqrt{2}$ and $1 \div \sqrt{3}$. The grid shows numbers to four decimal places.

Key	X	Y	Z	T	Remarks
2	2				
$\sqrt{x}$	1.4142				$\sqrt{2}$ in X
$1/x$	0.7071				$1/\sqrt{2}$ in X
3	3	0.7071			
$\sqrt{x}$	1.7321	0.7071			$\sqrt{3}$ in X
$1/x$	0.5774	0.7071			$1/\sqrt{3}$ in X and $1/\sqrt{2}$ in Y
$-$	0.1298				Answer (to four places)

$\triangle{3}$ Evaluate $\dfrac{3.52}{\sqrt{1.63^2 + 3.75^2}}$.

Solution   We begin by evaluating the denominator and then use the $\boxed{1/x}$ key.

Key	X	Y	Z	T	Remarks
1.63	1.63				
x^2	2.6569				1.63^2 in X
3.75	3.75	2.6569			
x^2	14.0625	2.6569			3.75^2 in X; 1.63^2 in Y
$+$	16.7194				
$\sqrt{x}$	4.0889				Denominator in X
$1/x$	0.2446				Reciprocal of denominator
3.52	3.52	0.2446			
x	0.8609				Answer (to four places)

▌

Another convenience for evaluating polynomial functions of degree greater than two and exponential functions in general is the $\boxed{y^x}$ key. This key raises the number in the Y register to the power given in the X register. The use of this key is restricted to $y > 0$, while x can be any real number (see Chapter 10 for a detailed discussion of exponential functions).

We continue with an example where the $\boxed{y^x}$ key is used.

$\triangle{4}$ Evaluate $f(x) = 4x^3 + 5x^2 - 7$ at $x = 3 - \sqrt{2}$.

Solution   The problem is to evaluate $4(3 - \sqrt{2})^3 + 5(3 - \sqrt{2})^2 - 7$. We first evaluate $3 - \sqrt{2}$, store the result, and recall it when needed.

Key	X	Y	Z	T	Remarks
3	3				
ENT	3	3			
2	2	3			
√x	1.41...	3			
−	1.58...				$3 - \sqrt{2}$ in X
STO 4	1.58...				$3 - \sqrt{2}$ in X and stored in R$_4$
3	3	1.58...			
yˣ	3.98...				$(3 - \sqrt{2})^3$ in X
4	4	3.98...			
×	15.95...				
RCL 4	1.58...	15.95...			$3 - \sqrt{2}$ recalled to X
x²	2.51...	15.95...			$(3 - \sqrt{2})^2$ in X
5	5	2.51...	15.95...		
×	12.57...	15.95...			$5(3 - \sqrt{2})^2$ in X
+	28.52...				$4(3 - \sqrt{2})^3 + 5(3 - \sqrt{2})^2$
7	7	28.52...			
−	21.5248				Answer (to four places)

EXERCISE A.2 (Continued)

Evaluate the following expressions to three decimal places. Check your answers; in case of disagreement, complete a grid to determine whether your answer or the author's (or neither) is correct.

1. If $f(x) = 3x^2 - 2x + 1$, find $f(2.13)$.

2. Evaluate $f(x) = 1.6x^2 - 2.4x + 4.1$ at $x = 2.46$.

3. Find the value of $g(x) = 5x^2 + \dfrac{1}{x}$ at $x = -1.57$.

4. Evaluate $\dfrac{1}{2} + \dfrac{1}{3} + \dfrac{1}{4} + \dfrac{1}{5} + \dfrac{1}{6}$.

5. If $f(x) = 1 + \cfrac{1}{1 + \cfrac{1}{1 + 1/x}}$, find: a) $f(2)$ b) $f(-1.48)$

6. Evaluate the following expressions by using the $\boxed{\pi}$ key on your calculator:

   a) $(24.67)\left(64 + \dfrac{27}{60}\right)\dfrac{\pi}{180}$ b) $\dfrac{1}{2}(24.67)^2\left(64 + \dfrac{27}{60}\right)\left(\dfrac{\pi}{180}\right)$

7. If $u = 2.21$, $v = \frac{7\pi}{10}$, $t = 126.43\left(\frac{\pi}{180}\right)$, order these three numbers from smallest to largest.

8. Evaluate:

   a) $(34.63)\left(\frac{\pi}{180}\right)\sqrt{\dfrac{2(35.61)(180)}{34.63\pi}}$ b) $\sqrt{\dfrac{2(35.61)(34.63)\pi}{180}}$

9. Evaluate:

   a) $\dfrac{1+\sqrt{7}}{3}$ b) $\left(\dfrac{1+\sqrt{7}}{3}\right)^2$ c) $\left(\dfrac{1+\sqrt{7}}{3}\right)^3$

10. The following numbers may be used as rational approximations of π. Calculate each number and use the $\boxed{\pi}$ key on your calculator to determine the decimal-place accuracy:

   a) $\frac{22}{7}$ b) $\frac{333}{106}$ c) $\frac{355}{113}$ d) $\frac{208341}{66317}$

11. Evaluate: 12. Evaluate:

   a) $\left(\sqrt{5.38}\right)^3$ b) $\sqrt{5.38^3}$ a) $\sqrt{24.3 + 36.8}$ b) $\sqrt{24.3} + \sqrt{36.8}$

13. Evaluate: 14. If $f(x) = 3x^4 - 8x^2 + 12$, find $f(1.43)$

   a) $\dfrac{\sqrt{3}-1}{\sqrt{3}+1}$ b) $2 - \sqrt{3}$

15. If $f(x) = \dfrac{x^6 - 1}{x - 1}$, find

   a) $f(3)$ b) $f(2.3)$ c) $f(-1.8)$ d) $f(1)$

16. If $g(x) = x^5 + x^4 + x^3 + x^2 + x + 1$, find:
   a) $g(3)$ b) $g(2.3)$ c) $g(-1.8)$ d) $g(1)$

   Compare these results with the answers in Problem 15. What conclusions can you draw about the functions f and g?

17. Evaluate   a) $\sqrt{24.7} - \sqrt{36.8}$ b) $\sqrt{24.7 - 36.8}$

18. Evaluate $\left(\dfrac{1-\sqrt{5}}{2}\right)^3$ 19. Evaluate $\sqrt{\left(1-\sqrt{3}\right)^2 - 1}$

20. If $f(x) = 3x^4 - 4x^3 + x - 5$, find:
   a) $f(3)$ b) $f(-1.2)$ c) $f(\pi)$ d) $f\left(\dfrac{1+\sqrt{5}}{2}\right)$

APPROXIMATE NUMBERS

That is, all nonzero digits are significant, while zeros that merely serve the purpose of locating the decimal point are not, but all other zeros are. In cases when it is not clear whether a zero merely indicates the place of the decimal point (as in *d* above), scientific notation is useful. To represent a number in *scientific notation* we write it as a product of a number between 1 and 10 and a power of 10; all digits of the factor between 1 and 10 are significant.

Examples

 Determine which digits are significant in the following numbers:

a) 37.543   b) 136.1030   c) 240.00
d) 0.0048   e) 0.00480   f) 70 400

Solution

a) All five digits are significant.

b) All seven digits are significant (including the zero at the end).

c) The three zeros are significant, and so the number has five significant digits.

d) Only the 4 and 8 are significant digits.

e) The 4, 8, and the final 0 are significant digits.

f) The digits 7, 0, 4 are significant but we cannot say without further information whether the last two zeros are significant.   ∎

⚠️2 Write each of the numbers given in Example 1 in scientific notation.

Solution

a) $37.543 = 3.7543 \times 10$

b) $136.1030 = 1.361030 \times 10^2$

c) $240.00 = 2.4000 \times 10^2$

d) $0.0048 = 4.8 \times 10^{-3}$

e) $0.00480 = 4.80 \times 10^{-3}$

f) $70\ 400 = 7.04 \times 10^4$ would indicate that only 7, 0, 4 are significant digits.
$70\ 400 = 7.040 \times 10^4$ would imply that 7, 0, 4, 0 are significant digits.
$70\ 400 = 7.0400 \times 10^4$ would tell us that all five digits are significant.∎

⚠️3 The following numbers are expressed in scientific notation. Write them in ordinary decimal form:

a) 2.78×10^4 b) 3.47×10^{-4} c) 3.40×10^3 d) 4.800×10^{-1}

Solution

a) 27 800   b) 0.000347   c) 3400   d) 0.4800   ∎

B.2 ROUNDING OFF NUMBERS

When a number is given in decimal form it is frequently necessary to express it as an approximate number with fewer significant digits. We describe this as the process of *rounding off a number* and illustrate with the following examples.

⚠ Round off the following numbers to three significant digits:
  a) 3476   b) 24.74   c) 73.80   d) 0.473501
  e) 2435   f) 69.95   g) π h) $\pi/2$

Solution

  a) The number $3480 = 3.48 \times 10^3$ has three significant digits and it is an approximation to a number between 3475 and 3485. Since the given number 3476 is in this range, we say that 3476 rounded off to three significant digits is 3.48×10^3.

  Similarly for b), c), d) we get:

  b) 24.7   c) 73.8   d) 0.474

  e) Here we encounter a borderline case in which it is not clear whether we should round off to 2430 or 2440. Both appear to be equally good and so we shall adopt the rule that we round *up* and use $2440 = 2.44 \times 10^3$ as the answer.*

  f) This is similar to (e), and so 70.0 is the approximation of 69.95 with three significant digits.

  g) Since $\pi = 3.14159 \ldots$, we round off to 3.14.

  h) $\pi/2 = 1.57079 \ldots$ rounded off to three significant digits is 1.57.   ▌

B.3 COMPUTATIONS WITH APPROXIMATE NUMBERS

When approximate numbers are used in computations it is natural to ask: "How many significant digits should we retain in the final result?" To give an answer it is helpful to consider some examples. We first take the problem of multiplying or dividing two approximate numbers and then we study addition and subtraction of such numbers.†

1. Multiplication and Division of Approximate Numbers

Suppose the length and width of a rectangular object are measured with a ruler marked in millimeters and are found to be $l \doteq 16.4$ cm, $w \doteq 8.6$ cm. We wish to

---

*Some textbooks give a slightly different rule in which the number is sometimes rounded up and other times it is rounded down.

†The general problem of accuracy in computations involving other operations (such as square root, logarithm, etc.) is a topic for numerical-analysis courses.

find the area of the rectangle. Since Area $= l \times w$, we get

$$\text{Area} \doteq (16.4 \times 8.6) \text{ cm}^2 \doteq 141.04 \text{ cm}^2.$$

This is a computed value based upon the measurements of l and w expressed as approximate numbers. How many of the five digits in 141.04 are really meaningful and not misleading in terms of stating the actual area of the object?

Based upon the given information about l and w, all we can say is that

$$16.35 < l < 16.45 \text{ cm} \qquad \text{and} \qquad 8.55 < w < 8.65 \text{ cm}.$$

This implies that

$$16.35 \times 8.55 < A < 16.45 \times 8.65 \text{ cm}^2.$$

That is, all we can really say about the actual area is:

$$139.7925 < A < 142.2925 \text{ cm}^2. \tag{B.1}$$

This is the best claim we can make about the area on the basis of the given measurements.

Our computed value of $A \doteq 141.04$ cm² is certainly in the range given by expression (B.1), but stating that $A \doteq 141.04$ cm² implies that we know $141.035 < A < 141.045$ cm². This says considerably more than what we actually do know.

Suppose we round off the computed value to three significant digits: $A \doteq 141$ cm². This implies that $140.5 < A < 141.5$ cm², and clearly this still claims more than the inequality given in (B.1). Therefore, we try rounding off to two significant digits: $A \doteq 140$ cm² $= 1.4 \times 10^2$ cm². This means that $135 < A < 145$ cm², and making such a statement is consistent with the inequality given by (B.1).

In conclusion, rounding off the computed value of the area to two significant digits results in the best statement we can make that is consistent with what the given measurements tell us about the actual area. Since l was measured to three significant digits and w to two significant digits, this suggests that we should round off the product to the smaller number of significant digits of the measured values.

The problem of dividing two approximate numbers is similar. Suppose $a \doteq 34.6$ and $b \doteq 8.4$ are approximate numbers and we wish to determine $c = a \div b$. Using a calculator to evaluate c, we get

$$c = \frac{34.6}{8.4} = 4.1190 \ldots .$$

How many digits should we retain in the answer? Since $34.55 < a < 34.65$ and $8.35 < b < 8.45$, we obtain

$$\frac{34.55}{8.45} < \frac{a}{b} < \frac{34.65}{8.35}$$

Thus, all we know about c is that

$$4.0888 < c < 4.1497 \quad \text{(to four decimal places)} \tag{B.2}$$

If we round off c to three significant digits ($c \doteq 4.12$), then we are saying that $4.115 < c < 4.125$, and this is not consistent with what we know about c as given by (B.2). If we round off to two significant digits ($c \doteq 4.1$), then we imply that $4.05 < c < 4.15$, which is in agreement with statement (B.2). Since $a = 34.6$ has three significant digits and $b = 8.4$ has two significant digits, this example suggests that the quotient of two approximate numbers should be rounded off to the smaller number of significant digits of the two measured values.

The above examples suggest the following

Rule for multiplying and dividing approximate numbers
In the multiplication and division of approximate numbers the result should be rounded off to the least number of significant digits in the data used.

For example, suppose $x \doteq 47.36$, $y \doteq 17.5$, $z \doteq 5.2$ and we wish to evaluate $u = (xy) \div z$. Since the numbers of significant digits in x, y, z are four, three, two, respectively, we should retain two significant digits for u. Thus

$$u \doteq (47.36 \times 17.5) \div 5.2 = 159.3846 \ldots$$

and so we have $u \doteq 160 = 1.6 \times 10^2$. If this value is to be used in subsequent computations, then we should use one more significant digit ($u \doteq 159$) for that purpose, but we must remember that in the final round off, u is accurate to only two significant digits.

2. Addition and Subtraction of Approximate Numbers

When adding or subtracting approximate numbers the situation is a little different from that of multiplying or dividing. For example, suppose a bank reports that a certain fund has \$248,000 in it, where this is accurate to the nearest thousand dollars. Now suppose that \$72.35 is added to this fund. It would be misleading to say that the fund now has \$248,072.35 in it. We would say that the fund still has \$248,000 in it to the nearest thousand dollars (based on the given information). That is, we would write $248,000 + 72.35 \doteq 248,000$.

It is clear from this example that when we add two approximate numbers, we are not interested in the number of significant digits each has, but we are primarily interested in the *level of precision* of each number. We say that the level of precision of 248,000 is the nearest thousand while that of 72.35 is the nearest hundredth; thus the level of precision of 72.35 is greater than that of 248,000.

As another example, suppose x, y, and z are approximate numbers given by $x \doteq 24.65$, $y \doteq 0.036$, $z \doteq 132.4$. The levels of precision of x, y, z are hundredths, thousandths, tenths, respectively. Common sense would suggest that the sum

$$x + y + z \doteq 24.65 + 0.036 + 132.4 = 157.086$$

should be rounded off to the nearest tenth, since z is no more accurate than the nearest tenth and we cannot expect $x + y + z$ to be more accurate. Thus,

$$x + y + z \doteq 157.1.$$

The above examples lead us to the following common-sense rule.

Rule for adding and subtracting approximate numbers
In the addition and subtraction of approximate numbers the result should be rounded off to the least level of precision in the data used.

---

3. Linear and Angle Measurements

In solving triangles the angle and length measurements are usually given as approximate numbers. Therefore, it is desirable to have a guide that can be used to determine the angle measurements with an accuracy corresponding to that of the length measurements. For angles that are not too close to $0°$ or $90°$, the following table provides a satisfactory rule:

Lengths accurate to	Corresponding angles accurate to
Two significant digits	Nearest degree
Three significant digits	Nearest 10′
Four significant digits	Nearest minute
Five significant digits	Nearest tenth of a minute

Examples

In the following examples, suppose x, y, z, u, v, t are approximate numbers given by:

$$x \doteq 3.48, \quad y \doteq 0.0360, \quad z \doteq 3251, \quad u \doteq 5.004,$$
$$v \doteq 84{,}000 \quad \text{(only 8 and 4 are significant)},$$
$$t \doteq 24{,}800 \quad \text{(the tens 0 is significant)}.$$

⚠ Write the above numbers in scientific notation.

Solution

$$x \doteq 3.48 \times 10^0, \qquad y \doteq 3.60 \times 10^{-2}, \qquad z \doteq 3.251 \times 10^3,$$
$$u \doteq 5.004 \times 10^0, \qquad v \doteq 8.4 \times 10^4, \qquad t \doteq 2.480 \times 10^4. \qquad ∎$$

△2 Give the number of significant digits in each of the above numbers.

Solution

x has three; y has three; z has four; u has four; v has two; t has four. ❙

△3 State the level of precision of the given numbers.

Solution The level of precision of x is hundredths, of y is ten thousandths, of z is units, of u is thousandths, of v is thousands, and of t is tens. ❙

△4 Using the rule for multiplication and division of approximate numbers, evaluate the following:

a) $x \cdot z$ b) $\dfrac{yv}{x}$ c) $u \cdot t$

Solution

a) $x \cdot z \doteq (3.48)(3251) = 11313.48$. Since x has three and z has four significant digits, the result should be rounded off to three significant digits. Thus

$$x \cdot z \doteq 11300 = 1.13 \times 10^4.$$

b) $\dfrac{y \cdot v}{x} \doteq \dfrac{(0.0360)(84000)}{3.48} = 868.9655 \ldots$

The smallest number of significant digits of x, y, and v is two, and so the answer should be rounded off to two significant digits. That is,

$$\frac{y \cdot v}{x} \doteq 870 = 8.7 \times 10^2.$$

c) Both u and t have four significant digits and so $u \cdot t$ should be rounded off to four significant digits:

$$u \cdot t \doteq (5.004)(24800) \doteq 1.241 \times 10^5. \qquad ❙$$

△5 Using the rule for addition and subtraction of approximate numbers, evaluate the following:

a) $x + y$ b) $z + t$ c) $u - x$
d) $v + t$ e) $x + z - u$

Solution

a) $x + y \doteq 3.48 + 0.0360 = 3.516$.
Since the level of precision of x is hundredths and that of y is ten thousandths, we round off the sum to hundredths:

$$x + y \doteq 3.52.$$

b) $z + t \doteq 3251 + 24{,}800 = 28{,}051.$

The level of precision of z is units and that of t is tens, and so we round off the sum to tens:

$$z + t \doteq 28050 = 2.805 \times 10^4.$$

c) $u - x \doteq 5.004 - 3.48 = 1.524.$

The result should be rounded off to the nearest hundredth and so we have

$$u - x \doteq 1.52.$$

d) $v + t \doteq 84{,}000 + 24{,}800 = 108{,}800.$

Since v is correct to the nearest thousand and t is accurate to the nearest tens, we round off the sum to the nearest thousand:

$$v + t \doteq 109{,}000 = 1.09 \times 10^5.$$

e) $x + z - u \doteq 3.48 + 3251 - 5.004 = 3249.476.$

Since the least precise of x, z, u is z (to the nearest unit), we round off the result to the nearest unit:

$$x + z - u \doteq 3249. \qquad \blacksquare$$

$\boxed{6}$ Using the rules for computation with approximate numbers, evaluate the following:

a) $z - xu$

b) $\dfrac{v - t}{x}$

Solution

a) We first evaluate xu:

$$xu \doteq (3.48)(5.004) = 17.41392 \doteq 17.41.$$

Therefore,

$$z - xu \doteq 3251 - 17.41 = 3233.59 \doteq 3234.$$

Note that in the final computation we used an extra digit for xu.

b) We first evaluate $v - t$:

$$v - t \doteq 84{,}000 - 24{,}800 = 59{,}200 \doteq 59{,}000 = 5.9 \times 10^4.$$

Thus,

$$\frac{v - t}{x} \doteq \frac{59200}{3.48} = 17011.494 \ldots \doteq 17{,}000 = 1.7 \times 10^4.$$

Note that in the final computation we used $v - t = 59{,}200$ (an extra significant digit), but we rounded off the final result to two significant digits. $\blacksquare$

⚠ The radius of a circle is measured as $r \doteq 6.41$ cm. Find the area of the circle.

Solution We use the formula Area $= \pi r^2$. Since r is measured to three significant digits, the result should be rounded off to three significant digits. We use π as given by the calculator and find that

$$\text{Area} \doteq \pi(6.41)^2 = 129.082 \ldots \text{ cm}^2 \doteq 129 \text{ cm}^2.$$ ∎

EXERCISES

In Problems 1 through 7, suppose x, y, z, u, v, t are approximate numbers given by

$$x \doteq 64.75, \qquad y \doteq 4830, \qquad z \doteq 0.0045, \qquad u \doteq 0.0370, \qquad v \doteq 3005.2,$$

$$t \doteq 3100 \quad \text{(the tens 0 is significant and the units 0 is not)}.$$

1. Write each of the above numbers in scientific notation.

2. Determine the number of significant digits in each of the above numbers.

3. State the level of precision of each of the above numbers.

4. Round off the above numbers to two significant digits.

Using the rules for computing with approximate numbers, evaluate the expressions given in Problems 5 through 7.

5. a) xu b) vz c) $t \div y$ d) $(uy) \div z$

6. a) $x + y$ b) $u - z$ c) $y - t$ d) $y - x - v$

7. a) $xz - u$ b) $\dfrac{y - v}{t}$ c) $y + ut$

8. The radius of a circle (measured accurately to the nearest millimeter) is found to be $r \doteq 2.476$ m. Find the circumference and area of the circle.

9. The radius of a sphere is measured as $r \doteq 3.47$ cm. Find the surface area and volume of the sphere.

10. The lengths of the edges of a rectangular box are measured to the nearest millimeter and found to be

$$a \doteq 23.4 \text{ cm}, \qquad b \doteq 12.8 \text{ cm}, \qquad c \doteq 8.4 \text{ cm}.$$

Determine the volume and the total surface area of the box.

11. The speed of light is approximately 3×10^5 km/sec. A light-year is defined as the distance travelled by light in one year. Assuming 365 days in a year, find the number of kilometers in a light-year. Express your answer in scientific notation.

12. The hypotenuse and an angle of a right triangle are measured and found to be 32.4 cm and $23°40'$, respectively. Calculate the area and the perimeter of the triangle.

TABLES

t	t degrees	$\sin t$	$\cos t$	$\tan t$	$\cot t$	$\sec t$	$\csc t$		
.0000	**0° 00′**	.0000	1.0000	.0000	—	1.000	—	**90° 00′**	1.5708
.0029	10	.0029	1.0000	.0029	343.8	1.000	343.8	50	1.5679
.0058	20	.0058	1.0000	.0058	171.9	1.000	171.9	40	1.5650
.0087	30	.0087	1.0000	.0087	114.6	1.000	114.6	30	1.5621
.0116	40	.0116	.9999	.0116	85.94	1.000	85.95	20	1.5592
.0145	50	.0145	.9999	.0145	68.75	1.000	68.76	10	1.5563
.0175	**1° 00′**	.0175	.9998	.0175	57.29	1.000	57.30	**89° 00′**	1.5533
.0204	10	.0204	.9998	.0204	49.10	1.000	49.11	50	1.5504
.0233	20	.0233	.9997	.0233	42.96	1.000	42.98	40	1.5475
.0262	30	.0262	.9997	.0262	38.19	1.000	38.20	30	1.5446
.0291	40	.0291	.9996	.0291	34.37	1.000	34.38	20	1.5417
.0320	50	.0320	.9995	.0320	31.24	1.001	31.26	10	1.5388
.0349	**2° 00′**	.0349	.9994	.0349	28.64	1.001	28.65	**88° 00′**	1.5359
.0378	10	.0378	.9993	.0378	26.43	1.001	26.45	50	1.5330
.0407	20	.0407	.9992	.0407	24.54	1.001	24.56	40	1.5301
.0436	30	.0436	.9990	.0437	22.90	1.001	22.93	30	1.5272
.0465	40	.0465	.9989	.0466	21.47	1.001	21.49	20	1.5243
.0495	50	.0494	.9988	.0495	20.21	1.001	20.23	10	1.5213
.0524	**3° 00′**	.0523	.9986	.0524	19.08	1.001	19.11	**87° 00′**	1.5184
.0553	10	.0552	.9985	.0553	18.07	1.002	18.10	50	1.5155
.0582	20	.0581	.9983	.0582	17.17	1.002	17.20	40	1.5126
.0611	30	.0610	.9981	.0612	16.35	1.002	16.38	30	1.5097
.0640	40	.0640	.9980	.0641	15.60	1.002	15.64	20	1.5068
.0669	50	.0669	.9978	.0670	14.92	1.002	14.96	10	1.5039
.0698	**4° 00′**	.0698	.9976	.0699	14.30	1.002	14.34	**86° 00′**	1.5010
.0727	10	.0727	.9974	.0729	13.73	1.003	13.76	50	1.4981
.0756	20	.0756	.9971	.0758	13.20	1.003	13.23	40	1.4952
.0785	30	.0785	.9969	.0787	12.71	1.003	12.75	30	1.4923
.0814	40	.0814	.9967	.0816	12.25	1.003	12.29	20	1.4893
.0844	50	.0843	.9964	.0846	11.83	1.004	11.87	10	1.4864
.0873	**5° 00′**	.0872	.9962	.0875	11.43	1.004	11.47	**85° 00′**	1.4835
.0902	10	.0901	.9959	.0904	11.06	1.004	11.10	50	1.4806
.0931	20	.0929	.9957	.0934	10.71	1.004	10.76	40	1.4777
.0960	30	.0958	.9954	.0963	10.39	1.005	10.43	30	1.4748
.0989	40	.0987	.9951	.0992	10.08	1.005	10.13	20	1.4719
.1018	50	.1016	.9948	.1022	9.788	1.005	9.839	10	1.4690
.1047	**6° 00′**	.1045	.9945	.1051	9.514	1.006	9.567	**84° 00′**	1.4661
.1076	10	.1074	.9942	.1080	9.255	1.006	9.309	50	1.4632
.1105	20	.1103	.9939	.1110	9.010	1.006	9.065	40	1.4603
.1134	30	.1132	.9936	.1139	8.777	1.006	8.834	30	1.4573
.1164	40	.1161	.9932	.1169	8.556	1.007	8.614	20	1.4544
.1193	50	.1190	.9929	.1198	8.345	1.007	8.405	10	1.4515
.1222	**7° 00′**	.1219	.9925	.1228	8.144	1.008	8.206	**83° 00′**	1.4486
		$\cos t$	$\sin t$	$\cot t$	$\tan t$	$\csc t$	$\sec t$	t degrees	t

t	t degrees	$\sin t$	$\cos t$	$\tan t$	$\cot t$	$\sec t$	$\csc t$		
.1222	7° 00′	.1219	.9925	.1228	8.144	1.008	8.206	83° 00′	1.4486
.1251	10	.1248	.9922	.1257	7.953	1.008	8.016	50	1.4457
.1280	20	.1276	.9918	.1287	7.770	1.008	7.834	40	1.4428
.1309	30	.1305	.9914	.1317	7.596	1.009	7.661	30	1.4399
.1338	40	.1334	.9911	.1346	7.429	1.009	7.496	20	1.4370
.1367	50	.1363	.9907	.1376	7.269	1.009	7.337	10	1.4341
.1396	8° 00′	.1392	.9903	.1405	7.115	1.010	7.185	82° 00′	1.4312
.1425	10	.1421	.9899	.1435	6.968	1.010	7.040	50	1.4283
.1454	20	.1449	.9894	.1465	6.827	1.011	6.900	40	1.4254
.1484	30	.1478	.9890	.1495	6.691	1.011	6.765	30	1.4224
.1513	40	.1507	.9886	.1524	6.561	1.012	6.636	20	1.4195
.1542	50	.1536	.9881	.1554	6.435	1.012	6.512	10	1.4166
.1571	9° 00′	.1564	.9877	.1584	6.314	1.012	6.392	81° 00′	1.4137
.1600	10	.1593	.9872	.1614	6.197	1.013	6.277	50	1.4108
.1629	20	.1622	.9868	.1644	6.084	1.013	6.166	40	1.4079
.1658	30	.1650	.9863	.1673	5.976	1.014	6.059	30	1.4050
.1687	40	.1679	.9858	.1703	5.871	1.014	5.955	20	1.4021
.1716	50	.1708	.9853	.1733	5.769	1.015	5.855	10	1.3992
.1745	10° 00′	.1736	.9848	.1763	5.671	1.015	5.759	80° 00′	1.3963
.1774	10	.1765	.9843	.1793	5.576	1.016	5.665	50	1.3934
.1804	20	.1794	.9838	.1823	5.485	1.016	5.575	40	1.3904
.1833	30	.1822	.9833	.1853	5.396	1.017	5.487	30	1.3875
.1862	40	.1851	.9827	.1883	5.309	1.018	5.403	20	1.3846
.1891	50	.1880	.9822	.1914	5.226	1.018	5.320	10	1.3817
.1920	11° 00′	.1908	.9816	.1944	5.145	1.019	5.241	79° 00′	1.3788
.1949	10	.1937	.9811	.1974	5.066	1.019	5.164	50	1.3759
.1978	20	.1965	.9805	.2004	4.989	1.020	5.089	40	1.3730
.2007	30	.1994	.9799	.2035	4.915	1.020	5.016	30	1.3701
.2036	40	.2022	.9793	.2065	4.843	1.021	4.945	20	1.3672
.2065	50	.2051	.9787	.2095	4.773	1.022	4.876	10	1.3643
.2094	12° 00′	.2079	.9781	.2126	4.705	1.022	4.810	78° 00′	1.3614
.2123	10	.2108	.9775	.2156	4.638	1.023	4.745	50	1.3584
.2153	20	.2136	.9769	.2186	4.574	1.024	4.682	40	1.3555
.2182	30	.2164	.9763	.2217	4.511	1.024	4.620	30	1.3526
.2211	40	.2193	.9757	.2247	4.449	1.025	4.560	20	1.3497
.2240	50	.2221	.9750	.2278	4.390	1.026	4.502	10	1.3468
.2269	13° 00′	.2250	.9744	.2309	4.331	1.026	4.445	77° 00′	1.3439
.2298	10	.2278	.9737	.2339	4.275	1.027	4.390	50	1.3410
.2327	20	.2306	.9730	.2370	4.219	1.028	4.336	40	1.3381
.2356	30	.2334	.9724	.2401	4.165	1.028	4.284	30	1.3352
.2385	40	.2363	.9717	.2432	4.113	1.029	4.232	20	1.3323
.2414	50	.2391	.9710	.2462	4.061	1.030	4.182	10	1.3294
.2443	14° 00′	.2419	.9703	.2493	4.011	1.031	4.134	76° 00′	1.3265
		$\cos t$	$\sin t$	$\cot t$	$\tan t$	$\csc t$	$\sec t$	t degrees	t

t	t degrees	$\sin t$	$\cos t$	$\tan t$	$\cot t$	$\sec t$	$\csc t$		
.2443	**14° 00′**	.2419	.9703	.2493	4.011	1.031	4.134	**76° 00′**	1.3265
.2473	10	.2447	.9696	.2524	3.962	1.031	4.086	50	1.3235
.2502	20	.2476	.9689	.2555	3.914	1.032	4.039	40	1.3206
.2531	30	.2504	.9681	.2586	3.867	1.033	3.994	30	1.3177
.2560	40	.2532	.9674	.2617	3.821	1.034	3.950	20	1.3148
.2589	50	.2560	.9667	.2648	3.776	1.034	3.906	10	1.3119
.2618	**15° 00′**	.2588	.9659	.2679	3.732	1.035	3.864	**75° 00′**	1.3090
.2647	10	.2616	.9652	.2711	3.689	1.036	3.822	50	1.3061
.2676	20	.2644	.9644	.2742	3.647	1.037	3.782	40	1.3032
.2705	30	.2672	.9636	.2773	3.606	1.038	3.742	30	1.3003
.2734	40	.2700	.9628	.2805	3.566	1.039	3.703	20	1.2974
.2763	50	.2728	.9621	.2836	3.526	1.039	3.665	10	1.2945
.2793	**16° 00′**	.2756	.9613	.2867	3.487	1.040	3.628	**74° 00′**	1.2915
.2822	10	.2784	.9605	.2899	3.450	1.041	3.592	50	1.2886
.2851	20	.2812	.9596	.2931	3.412	1.042	3.556	40	1.2857
.2880	30	.2840	.9588	.2962	3.376	1.043	3.521	30	1.2828
.2909	40	.2868	.9580	.2994	3.340	1.044	3.487	20	1.2799
.2938	50	.2896	.9572	.3026	3.305	1.045	3.453	10	1.2770
.2967	**17° 00′**	.2924	.9563	.3057	3.271	1.046	3.420	**73° 00′**	1.2741
.2996	10	.2952	.9555	.3089	3.237	1.047	3.388	50	1.2712
.3025	20	.2979	.9546	.3121	3.204	1.048	3.356	40	1.2683
.3054	30	.3007	.9537	.3153	3.172	1.049	3.326	30	1.2654
.3083	40	.3035	.9528	.3185	3.140	1.049	3.295	20	1.2625
.3113	50	.3062	.9520	.3217	3.108	1.050	3.265	10	1.2595
.3142	**18° 00′**	.3090	.9511	.3249	3.078	1.051	3.236	**72° 00′**	1.2566
.3171	10	.3118	.9502	.3281	3.047	1.052	3.207	50	1.2537
.3200	20	.3145	.9492	.3314	3.018	1.053	3.179	40	1.2508
.3229	30	.3173	.9483	.3346	2.989	1.054	3.152	30	1.2479
.3258	40	.3201	.9474	.3378	2.960	1.056	3.124	20	1.2450
.3287	50	.3228	.9465	.3411	2.932	1.057	3.098	10	1.2421
.3316	**19° 00′**	.3256	.9455	.3443	2.904	1.058	3.072	**71° 00′**	1.2392
.3345	10	.3283	.9446	.3476	2.877	1.059	3.046	50	1.2363
.3374	20	.3311	.9436	.3508	2.850	1.060	3.021	40	1.2334
.3403	30	.3338	.9426	.3541	2.824	1.061	2.996	30	1.2305
.3432	40	.3365	.9417	.3574	2.798	1.062	2.971	20	1.2275
.3462	50	.3393	.9407	.3607	2.773	1.063	2.947	10	1.2246
.3491	**20° 00′**	.3420	.9397	.3640	2.747	1.064	2.924	**70° 00′**	1.2217
.3520	10	.3448	.9387	.3673	2.723	1.065	2.901	50	1.2188
.3549	20	.3475	.9377	.3706	2.699	1.066	2.878	40	1.2159
.3578	30	.3502	.9367	.3739	2.675	1.068	2.855	30	1.2130
.3607	40	.3529	.9356	.3772	2.651	1.069	2.833	20	1.2101
.3636	50	.3557	.9346	.3805	2.628	1.070	2.812	10	1.2072
.3665	**21° 00′**	.3584	.9336	.3839	2.605	1.071	2.790	**69° 00′**	1.2043
		$\cos t$	$\sin t$	$\cot t$	$\tan t$	$\csc t$	$\sec t$	t degrees	t

t	t degrees	$\sin t$	$\cos t$	$\tan t$	$\cot t$	$\sec t$	$\csc t$		
.3665	**21° 00′**	.3584	.9336	.3839	2.605	1.071	2.790	**69° 00′**	1.2043
.3694	10	.3611	.9325	.3872	2.583	1.072	2.769	50	1.2014
.3723	20	.3638	.9315	.3906	2.560	1.074	2.749	40	1.1985
.3752	30	.3665	.9304	.3939	2.539	1.075	2.729	30	1.1956
.3782	40	.3692	.9293	.3973	2.517	1.076	2.709	20	1.1926
.3811	50	.3719	.9283	.4006	2.496	1.077	2.689	10	1.1897
.3840	**22° 00′**	.3746	.9272	.4040	2.475	1.079	2.669	**68° 00′**	1.1868
.3869	10	.3773	.9261	.4074	2.455	1.080	2.650	50	1.1839
.3898	20	.3800	.9250	.4108	2.434	1.081	2.632	40	1.1810
.3927	30	.3827	.9239	.4142	2.414	1.082	2.613	30	1.1781
.3956	40	.3854	.9228	.4176	2.394	1.084	2.595	20	1.1752
.3985	50	.3881	.9216	.4210	2.375	1.085	2.577	10	1.1723
.4014	**23° 00′**	.3907	.9205	.4245	2.356	1.086	2.559	**67° 00′**	1.1694
.4043	10	.3934	.9194	.4279	2.337	1.088	2.542	50	1.1665
.4072	20	.3961	.9182	.4314	2.318	1.089	2.525	40	1.1636
.4102	30	.3987	.9171	.4348	2.300	1.090	2.508	30	1.1606
.4131	40	.4014	.9159	.4383	2.282	1.092	2.491	20	1.1577
.4160	50	.4041	.9147	.4417	2.264	1.093	2.475	10	1.1548
.4189	**24° 00′**	.4067	.9135	.4452	2.246	1.095	2.459	**66° 00′**	1.1519
.4218	10	.4094	.9124	.4487	2.229	1.096	2.443	50	1.1490
.4247	20	.4120	.9112	.4522	2.211	1.097	2.427	40	1.1461
.4276	30	.4147	.9100	.4557	2.194	1.099	2.411	30	1.1432
.4305	40	.4173	.9088	.4592	2.177	1.100	2.396	20	1.1403
.4334	50	.4200	.9075	.4628	2.161	1.102	2.381	10	1.1374
.4363	**25° 00′**	.4226	.9063	.4663	2.145	1.103	2.366	**65° 00′**	1.1345
.4392	10	.4253	.9051	.4699	2.128	1.105	2.352	50	1.1316
.4422	20	.4279	.9038	.4734	2.112	1.106	2.337	40	1.1286
.4451	30	.4305	.9026	.4770	2.097	1.108	2.323	30	1.1257
.4480	40	.4331	.9013	.4806	2.081	1.109	2.309	20	1.1228
.4509	50	.4358	.9001	.4841	2.066	1.111	2.295	10	1.1199
.4538	**26° 00′**	.4384	.8988	.4877	2.050	1.113	2.281	**64° 00′**	1.1170
.4567	10	.4410	.8975	.4913	2.035	1.114	2.268	50	1.1141
.4596	20	.4436	.8962	.4950	2.020	1.116	2.254	40	1.1112
.4625	30	.4462	.8949	.4986	2.006	1.117	2.241	30	1.1083
.4654	40	.4488	.8936	.5022	1.991	1.119	2.228	20	1.1054
.4683	50	.4514	.8923	.5059	1.977	1.121	2.215	10	1.1025
.4712	**27° 00′**	.4540	.8910	.5095	1.963	1.122	2.203	**63° 00′**	1.0996
.4741	10	.4566	.8897	.5132	1.949	1.124	2.190	50	1.0966
.4771	20	.4592	.8884	.5169	1.935	1.126	2.178	40	1.0937
.4800	30	.4617	.8870	.5206	1.921	1.127	2.166	30	1.0908
.4829	40	.4643	.8857	.5243	1.907	1.129	2.154	20	1.0879
.4858	50	.4669	.8843	.5280	1.894	1.131	2.142	10	1.0850
.4887	**28° 00′**	.4695	.8829	.5317	1.881	1.133	2.130	**62° 00′**	1.0821
		$\cos t$	$\sin t$	$\cot t$	$\tan t$	$\csc t$	$\sec t$	t degrees	t

t	t degrees	$\sin t$	$\cos t$	$\tan t$	$\cot t$	$\sec t$	$\csc t$		
.4887	**28° 00′**	.4695	.8829	.5317	1.881	1.133	2.130	**62° 00′**	1.0821
.4916	10	.4720	.8816	.5354	1.868	1.134	2.118	50	1.0792
.4945	20	.4746	.8802	.5392	1.855	1.136	2.107	40	1.0763
.4974	30	.4772	.8788	.5430	1.842	1.138	2.096	30	1.0734
.5003	40	.4797	.8774	.5467	1.829	1.140	2.085	20	1.0705
.5032	50	.4823	.8760	.5505	1.816	1.142	2.074	10	1.0676
.5061	**29° 00′**	.4848	.8746	.5543	1.804	1.143	2.063	**61° 00′**	1.0647
.5091	10	.4874	.8732	.5581	1.792	1.145	2.052	50	1.0617
.5120	20	.4899	.8718	.5619	1.780	1.147	2.041	40	1.0588
.5149	30	.4924	.8704	.5658	1.767	1.149	2.031	30	1.0559
.5178	40	.4950	.8689	.5696	1.756	1.151	2.020	20	1.0530
.5207	50	.4975	.8675	.5735	1.744	1.153	2.010	10	1.0501
.5236	**30° 00′**	.5000	.8660	.5774	1.732	1.155	2.000	**60° 00′**	1.0472
.5265	10	.5025	.8646	.5812	1.720	1.157	1.990	50	1.0443
.5294	20	.5050	.8631	.5851	1.709	1.159	1.980	40	1.0414
.5323	30	.5075	.8616	.5890	1.698	1.161	1.970	30	1.0385
.5352	40	.5100	.8601	.5930	1.686	1.163	1.961	20	1.0356
.5381	50	.5125	.8587	.5969	1.675	1.165	1.951	10	1.0327
.5411	**31° 00′**	.5150	.8572	.6009	1.664	1.167	1.942	**59° 00′**	1.0297
.5440	10	.5175	.8557	.6048	1.653	1.169	1.932	50	1.0268
.5469	20	.5200	.8542	.6088	1.643	1.171	1.923	40	1.0239
.5498	30	.5225	.8526	.6128	1.632	1.173	1.914	30	1.0210
.5527	40	.5250	.8511	.6168	1.621	1.175	1.905	20	1.0181
.5556	50	.5275	.8496	.6208	1.611	1.177	1.896	10	1.0152
.5585	**32° 00′**	.5299	.8480	.6249	1.600	1.179	1.887	**58° 00′**	1.0123
.5614	10	.5324	.8465	.6289	1.590	1.181	1.878	50	1.0094
.5643	20	.5348	.8450	.6330	1.580	1.184	1.870	40	1.0065
.5672	30	.5373	.8434	.6371	1.570	1.186	1.861	30	1.0036
.5701	40	.5398	.8418	.6412	1.560	1.188	1.853	20	1.0007
.5730	50	.5422	.8403	.6453	1.550	1.190	1.844	10	.9977
.5760	**33° 00′**	.5446	.8387	.6494	1.540	1.192	1.836	**57° 00′**	.9948
.5789	10	.5471	.8371	.6536	1.530	1.195	1.828	50	.9919
.5818	20	.5495	.8355	.6577	1.520	1.197	1.820	40	.9890
.5847	30	.5519	.8339	.6619	1.511	1.199	1.812	30	.9861
.5876	40	.5544	.8323	.6661	1.501	1.202	1.804	20	.9832
.5905	50	.5568	.8307	.6703	1.492	1.204	1.796	10	.9803
.5934	**34° 00′**	.5592	.8290	.6745	1.483	1.206	1.788	**56° 00′**	.9774
.5963	10	.5616	.8274	.6787	1.473	1.209	1.781	50	.9745
.5992	20	.5640	.8258	.6830	1.464	1.211	1.773	40	.9716
.6021	30	.5664	.8241	.6873	1.455	1.213	1.766	30	.9687
.6050	40	.5688	.8225	.6916	1.446	1.216	1.758	20	.9657
.6080	50	.5712	.8208	.6959	1.437	1.218	1.751	10	.9628
.6109	**35° 00′**	.5736	.8192	.7002	1.428	1.221	1.743	**55° 00′**	.9599
		$\cos t$	$\sin t$	$\cot t$	$\tan t$	$\csc t$	$\sec t$	t degrees	t

t	t degrees	$\sin t$	$\cos t$	$\tan t$	$\cot t$	$\sec t$	$\csc t$		
.6109	**35° 00′**	.5736	.8192	.7002	1.428	1.221	1.743	**55° 00′**	.9599
.6138	10	.5760	.8175	.7046	1.419	1.223	1.736	50	.9570
.6167	20	.5783	.8158	.7089	1.411	1.226	1.729	40	.9541
.6196	30	.5807	.8141	.7133	1.402	1.228	1.722	30	.9512
.6225	40	.5831	.8124	.7177	1.393	1.231	1.715	20	.9483
.6254	50	.5854	.8107	.7221	1.385	1.233	1.708	10	.9454
.6283	**36° 00′**	.5878	.8090	.7265	1.376	1.236	1.701	**54° 00′**	.9425
.6312	10	.5901	.8073	.7310	1.368	1.239	1.695	50	.9396
.6341	20	.5925	.8056	.7355	1.360	1.241	1.688	40	.9367
.6370	30	.5948	.8039	.7400	1.351	1.244	1.681	30	.9338
.6400	40	.5972	.8021	.7445	1.343	1.247	1.675	20	.9308
.6429	50	.5995	.8004	.7490	1.335	1.249	1.668	10	.9279
.6458	**37° 00′**	.6018	.7986	.7536	1.327	1.252	1.662	**53° 00′**	.9250
.6487	10	.6041	.7969	.7581	1.319	1.255	1.655	50	.9221
.6516	20	.6065	.7951	.7627	1.311	1.258	1.649	40	.9192
.6545	30	.6088	.7934	.7673	1.303	1.260	1.643	30	.9163
.6574	40	.6111	.7916	.7720	1.295	1.263	1.636	20	.9134
.6603	50	.6134	.7898	.7766	1.288	1.266	1.630	10	.9105
.6632	**38° 00′**	.6157	.7880	.7813	1.280	1.269	1.624	**52° 00′**	.9076
.6661	10	.6180	.7862	.7860	1.272	1.272	1.618	50	.9047
.6690	20	.6202	.7844	.7907	1.265	1.275	1.612	40	.0918
.6720	30	.6225	.7826	.7954	1.257	1.278	1.606	30	.8988
.6749	40	.6248	.7808	.8002	1.250	1.281	1.601	20	.8959
.6778	50	.6271	.7790	.8050	1.242	1.284	1.595	10	.8930
.6807	**39° 00′**	.6293	.7771	.8098	1.235	1.287	1.589	**51° 00′**	.8901
.6836	10	.6316	.7753	.8146	1.228	1.290	1.583	50	.8872
.6865	20	.6338	.7735	.8195	1.220	1.293	1.578	40	.8843
.6894	30	.6361	.7716	.8243	1.213	1.296	1.572	30	.8814
.6923	40	.6383	.7698	.8292	1.206	1.299	1.567	20	.8785
.6952	50	.6406	.7679	.8342	1.199	1.302	1.561	10	.8756
.6981	**40° 00′**	.6428	.7660	.8391	1.192	1.305	1.556	**50° 00′**	.8727
.7010	10	.6450	.7642	.8441	1.185	1.309	1.550	50	.8698
.7039	20	.6472	.7623	.8491	1.178	1.312	1.545	40	.8668
.7069	30	.6494	.7604	.8541	1.171	1.315	1.540	30	.8639
.7098	40	.6517	.7585	.8591	1.164	1.318	1.535	20	.8610
.7127	50	.6539	.7566	.8642	1.157	1.322	1.529	10	.8581
.7156	**41° 00′**	.6561	.7547	.8693	1.150	1.325	1.524	**49° 00′**	.8552
.7185	10	.6583	.7528	.8744	1.144	1.328	1.519	50	.8523
.7214	20	.6604	.7509	.8796	1.137	1.332	1.514	40	.8494
.7243	30	.6626	.7490	.8847	1.130	1.335	1.509	30	.8465
.7272	40	.6648	.7470	.8899	1.124	1.339	1.504	20	.8436
.7301	50	.6670	.7451	.8952	1.117	1.342	1.499	10	.8407
.7330	**42° 00′**	.6691	.7431	.9004	1.111	1.346	1.494	**48° 00′**	.8378
		$\cos t$	$\sin t$	$\cot t$	$\tan t$	$\csc t$	$\sec t$	t degrees	t

t	t degrees	$\sin t$	$\cos t$	$\tan t$	$\cot t$	$\sec t$	$\csc t$		
.7330	**42° 00′**	.6691	.7431	.9004	1.111	1.346	1.494	**48° 00′**	.8378
.7359	10	.6713	.7412	.9057	1.104	1.349	1.490	50	.8348
.7389	20	.6734	.7392	.9110	1.098	1.353	1.485	40	.8319
.7418	30	.6756	.7373	.9163	1.091	1.356	1.480	30	.8290
.7447	40	.6777	.7353	.9217	1.085	1.360	1.476	20	.8261
.7476	50	.6799	.7333	.9271	1.079	1.364	1.471	10	.8232
.7505	**43° 00′**	.6820	.7314	.9325	1.072	1.367	1.466	**47° 00′**	.8203
.7534	10	.6841	.7294	.9380	1.066	1.371	1.462	50	.8174
.7563	20	.6862	.7274	.9435	1.060	1.375	1.457	40	.8145
.7592	30	.6884	.7254	.9490	1.054	1.379	1.453	30	.8116
.7621	40	.6905	.7234	.9545	1.048	1.382	1.448	20	.8087
.7650	50	.6926	.7214	.9601	1.042	1.386	1.444	10	.8058
.7679	**44° 00′**	.6947	.7193	.9657	1.036	1.390	1.440	**46° 00′**	.8029
.7709	10	.6967	.7173	.9713	1.030	1.394	1.435	50	.7999
.7738	20	.6988	.7153	.9770	1.024	1.398	1.431	40	.7970
.7767	30	.7009	.7133	.9827	1.018	1.402	1.427	30	.7941
.7796	40	.7030	.7112	.9884	1.012	1.406	1.423	20	.7912
.7825	50	.7050	.7092	.9942	1.006	1.410	1.418	10	.7883
.7854	**45° 00′**	.7071	.7071	1.0000	1.0000	1.414	1.414	**45° 00′**	.7854
		$\cos t$	$\sin t$	$\cot t$	$\tan t$	$\csc t$	$\sec t$	t degrees	t

Common logarithms

N	0	1	2	3	4	5	6	7	8	9
1.0	.0000	.0043	.0086	.0128	.0170	.0212	.0253	.0294	.0334	.0374
1.1	.0414	.0453	.0492	.0531	.0569	.0607	.0645	.0682	.0719	.0755
1.2	.0792	.0828	.0864	.0899	.0934	.0969	.1004	.1038	.1072	.1106
1.3	.1139	.1173	.1206	.1239	.1271	.1303	.1335	.1367	.1399	.1430
1.4	.1461	.1492	.1523	.1553	.1584	.1614	.1644	.1673	.1703	.1732
1.5	.1761	.1790	.1818	.1847	.1875	.1903	.1931	.1959	.1987	.2014
1.6	.2041	.2068	.2095	.2122	.2148	.2175	.2201	.2227	.2253	.2279
1.7	.2304	.2330	.2355	.2380	.2405	.2430	.2455	.2480	.2504	.2529
1.8	.2553	.2577	.2601	.2625	.2648	.2672	.2695	.2718	.2742	.2765
1.9	.2788	.2810	.2833	.2856	.2878	.2900	.2923	.2945	.2967	.2989
2.0	.3010	.3032	.3054	.3075	.3096	.3118	.3139	.3160	.3181	.3201
2.1	.3222	.3243	.3263	.3284	.3304	.3324	.3345	.3365	.3385	.3404
2.2	.3424	.3444	.3464	.3483	.3502	.3522	.3541	.3560	.3579	.3598
2.3	.3617	.3636	.3655	.3674	.3692	.3711	.3729	.3747	.3766	.3784
2.4	.3802	.3820	.3838	.3856	.3874	.3892	.3909	.3927	.3945	.3962
2.5	.3979	.3997	.4014	.4031	.4048	.4065	.4082	.4099	.4116	.4133
2.6	.4150	.4166	.4183	.4200	.4216	.4232	.4249	.4265	.4281	.4298
2.7	.4314	.4330	.4346	.4362	.4378	.4393	.4409	.4425	.4440	.4456
2.8	.4472	.4487	.4502	.4518	.4533	.4548	.4564	.4579	.4594	.4609
2.9	.4624	.4639	.4654	.4669	.4683	.4698	.4713	.4728	.4742	.4757
3.0	.4771	.4786	.4800	.4814	.4829	.4843	.4857	.4871	.4886	.4900
3.1	.4914	.4928	.4942	.4955	.4969	.4983	.4997	.5011	.5024	.5038
3.2	.5051	.5065	.5079	.5092	.5105	.5119	.5132	.5145	.5159	.5172
3.3	.5185	.5198	.5211	.5224	.5237	.5250	.5263	.5276	.5289	.5302
3.4	.5315	.5328	.5340	.5353	.5366	.5378	.5391	.5403	.5416	.5428
3.5	.5441	.5453	.5465	.5478	.5490	.5502	.5514	.5527	.5539	.5551
3.6	.5563	.5575	.5587	.5599	.5611	.5623	.5635	.5647	.5658	.5670
3.7	.5682	.5694	.5705	.5717	.5729	.5740	.5752	.5763	.5775	.5786
3.8	.5798	.5809	.5821	.5832	.5843	.5855	.5866	.5877	.5888	.5899
3.9	.5911	.5922	.5933	.5944	.5955	.5966	.5977	.5988	.5999	.6010
4.0	.6021	.6031	.6042	.6053	.6064	.6075	.6085	.6096	.6107	.6117
4.1	.6128	.6138	.6149	.6160	.6170	.6180	.6191	.6201	.6212	.6222
4.2	.6232	.6243	.6253	.6263	.6274	.6284	.6294	.6304	.6314	.6325
4.3	.6335	.6345	.6355	.6365	.6375	.6385	.6395	.6405	.6415	.6425
4.4	.6435	.6444	.6454	.6464	.6474	.6484	.6493	.6503	.6513	.6522
4.5	.6532	.6542	.6551	.6561	.6571	.6580	.6590	.6599	.6609	.6618
4.6	.6628	.6637	.6646	.6656	.6665	.6675	.6684	.6693	.6702	.6712
4.7	.6721	.6730	.6739	.6749	.6758	.6767	.6776	.6785	.6794	.6803
4.8	.6812	.6821	.6830	.6839	.6848	.6857	.6866	.6875	.6884	.6893
4.9	.6902	.6911	.6920	.6928	.6937	.6946	.6955	.6964	.6972	.6981
5.0	.6990	.6998	.7007	.7016	.7024	.7033	.7042	.7050	.7059	.7067
5.1	.7076	.7084	.7093	.7101	.7110	.7118	.7126	.7135	.7143	.7152
5.2	.7160	.7168	.7177	.7185	.7193	.7202	.7210	.7218	.7226	.7235
5.3	.7243	.7251	.7259	.7267	.7275	.7284	.7292	.7300	.7308	.7316
5.4	.7324	.7332	.7340	.7348	.7356	.7364	.7372	.7380	.7388	.7396

N	0	1	2	3	4	5	6	7	8	9
5.5	.7404	.7412	.7419	.7427	.7435	.7443	.7451	.7459	.7466	.7474
5.6	.7482	.7490	.7497	.7505	.7513	.7520	.7528	.7536	.7543	.7551
5.7	.7559	.7566	.7574	.7582	.7589	.7597	.7604	.7612	.7619	.7627
5.8	.7634	.7642	.7649	.7657	.7664	.7672	.7679	.7686	.7694	.7701
5.9	.7709	.7716	.7723	.7731	.7738	.7745	.7752	.7760	.7767	.7774
6.0	.7782	.7789	.7796	.7803	.7810	.7818	.7825	.7832	.7839	.7846
6.1	.7853	.7860	.7868	.7875	.7882	.7889	.7896	.7903	.7910	.7917
6.2	.7924	.7931	.7938	.7945	.7952	.7959	.7966	.7973	.7980	.7987
6.3	.7993	.8000	.8007	.8014	.8021	.8028	.8035	.8041	.8048	.8055
6.4	.8062	.8069	.8075	.8082	.8089	.8096	.8102	.8109	.8116	.8122
6.5	.8129	.8136	.8142	.8149	.8156	.8162	.8169	.8176	.8182	.8189
6.6	.8195	.8202	.8209	.8215	.8222	.8228	.8235	.8241	.8248	.8254
6.7	.8261	.8267	.8274	.8280	.8287	.8293	.8299	.8306	.8312	.8319
6.8	.8325	.8331	.8338	.8344	.8351	.8357	.8363	.8370	.8376	.8382
6.9	.8388	.8395	.8401	.8407	.8414	.8420	.8426	.8432	.8439	.8445
7.0	.8451	.8457	.8463	.8470	.8476	.8482	.8488	.8494	.8500	.8506
7.1	.8513	.8519	.8525	.8531	.8537	.8543	.8549	.8555	.8561	.8567
7.2	.8573	.8579	.8585	.8591	.8597	.8603	.8609	.8615	.8621	.8627
7.3	.8633	.8639	.8645	.8651	.8657	.8663	.8669	.8675	.8681	.8686
7.4	.8692	.8698	.8704	.8710	.8716	.8722	.8727	.8733	.8739	.8745
7.5	.8751	.8756	.8762	.8768	.8774	.8779	.8785	.8791	.8797	.8802
7.6	.8808	.8814	.8820	.8825	.8831	.8837	.8842	.8848	.8854	.8859
7.7	.8865	.8871	.8876	.8882	.8887	.8893	.8899	.8904	.8910	.8915
7.8	.8921	.8927	.8932	.8938	.8943	.8949	.8954	.8960	.8965	.8971
7.9	.8976	.8982	.8987	.8993	.8998	.9004	.9009	.9015	.9020	.9025
8.0	.9031	.9036	.9042	.9047	.9053	.9058	.9063	.9069	.9074	.9079
8.1	.9085	.9090	.9096	.9101	.9106	.9112	.9117	.9122	.9128	.9133
8.2	.9138	.9143	.9149	.9154	.9159	.9165	.9170	.9175	.9180	.9186
8.3	.9191	.9196	.9201	.9206	.9212	.9217	.9222	.9227	.9232	.9238
8.4	.9243	.9248	.9253	.9258	.9263	.9269	.9274	.9279	.9284	.9289
8.5	.9294	.9299	.9304	.9309	.9315	.9320	.9325	.9330	.9335	.9340
8.6	.9345	.9350	.9355	.9360	.9365	.9370	.9375	.9380	.9385	.9390
8.7	.9395	.9400	.9405	.9410	.9415	.9420	.9425	.9430	.9435	.9440
8.8	.9445	.9450	.9455	.9460	.9465	.9469	.9474	.9479	.9484	.9489
8.9	.9494	.9499	.9504	.9509	.9513	.9518	.9523	.9528	.9533	.9538
9.0	.9542	.9547	.9552	.9557	.9562	.9566	.9571	.9576	.9581	.9586
9.1	.9590	.9595	.9600	.9605	.9609	.9614	.9619	.9624	.9628	.9633
9.2	.9638	.9643	.9647	.9652	.9657	.9661	.9666	.9671	.9675	.9680
9.3	.9685	.9689	.9594	.9699	.9703	.9708	.9713	.9717	.9722	.9727
9.4	.9731	.9736	.9741	.9745	.9750	.9754	.9759	.9763	.9768	.9773
9.5	.9777	.9782	.9786	.9791	.9795	.9800	.9805	.9809	.9814	.9818
9.6	.9823	.9827	.9832	.9836	.9841	.9845	.9850	.9854	.9859	.9863
9.7	.9868	.9872	.9877	.9881	.9886	.9890	.9894	.9899	.9903	.9908
9.8	.9912	.9917	.9921	.9926	.9930	.9934	.9939	.9943	.9948	.9952
9.9	.9956	.9961	.9965	.9969	.9974	.9978	.9983	.9987	.9991	.9996

ANSWERS TO ODD-NUMBERED EXERCISES

ANSWERS TO ODD-NUMBERED EXERCISES

Chapter 1

Exercise 1.3 (page 5)

1. a) 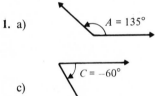 $A = 135°$

b) 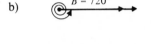 $B = 720°$

c)  $C = -60°$

d)  $D = -540°$

e) 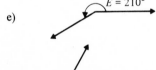 $E = 210°$

f) $F = 10°$

g) 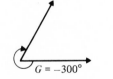 $G = -300°$

h) $H = 22°\ 30'$

3. a) $A = 2\pi$

b) $B = \dfrac{17\pi}{6}$

c) $C = \dfrac{\pi}{2}$

d) $D = \dfrac{\pi}{4}$

e)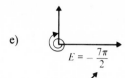
$E = -\dfrac{7\pi}{2}$

f)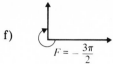
$F = -\dfrac{3\pi}{2}$

g)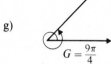
$G = \dfrac{9\pi}{4}$

h)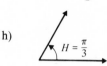
$H = \dfrac{\pi}{3}$

5. a)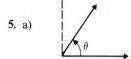

b)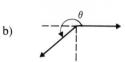

c)

d)

e)

f)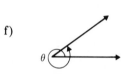

7. a) 48.6617°   b) −75.2114°

9. a) 37°34′59″   b) 321°34′35″

Exercise 1.4 (page 9)

1. a) $\dfrac{\pi}{3}$; 1.047   b) $-\dfrac{3\pi}{4}$; −2.356   c) $\dfrac{5\pi}{4}$; 3.927   d) 4π; 12.566

3. a) 0.411   b) −0.849   c) 4.150   d) 2.124   e) 7.634

5. a) 30°   b) 120°   c) 270°   d) 92°   e) 70°

7. a) 65.890°; 65°53′25″   b) 142.094°; 142°05′37″

   c) 2.825°; 2°49′29″   d) −330.024°; −330°01′25″

   e) 3666.930°; 3666°55′48″

9. 3.141592920 (to nine decimal places); approximates π correctly to six decimal
   places.

Exercise 1.5 (page 14)

1. a) 23.52 cm   b) 47.94 cm   c) 134.00 cm

3. a) 0.49   b) 2.39   c) 1.16

5. a) 16.01 m   b) 89.72 m   c) 50.47 m   d) 392.54 m

7. a) 131.60 cm/sec   b) 30389.39 cm/min

   c) 9723.20 cm/min   d) 52.74 cm/sec

9. a) 1 rev/hr   b) 1/60 rev/min   c) 6 deg/min   d) 0.1047 rad/min

11. a) 40.8407 cm/hr   b) 0.6807 cm/min   c) 0.0113 cm/sec

13. 9972.67 m/min   15. 1675.52 km/hr   17. 10109 km/hr

19. a) 1.10 rad b) 63.26° **21.** a) 11589.54° b) 202.28

23. a) 0.0172 rad/day b) 0.000717 rad/hr c) 106798 km/hr

25. 136.35 cm/sec; 1090.76 cm **27.** 7.52 m

29. 17 minutes after one o'clock **31.** About 35 m³

Review Exercises (page 18)

 1. a) 37.70° b) – 321.29° c) 81.93° d) 117.39°

3. a)  b) 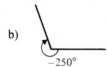 c)

 d) 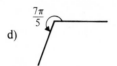 e)  f)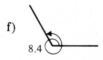

 5. 340.4 cm² **7.** $\theta < \beta < \alpha < \gamma$ **9.** 232.74 m² **11.** 6.56 cm **13.** 8 **15.** 19/17

Chapter 2

Exercise 2.1 (page 27)

1. a) $\dfrac{\sqrt{2}}{2}$ b) 1 c) 1 d) $\sqrt{2}$ e) $\sqrt{2}$

3. a) $\dfrac{4}{3}$ b) $\dfrac{3}{4}$ c) $\dfrac{5}{4}$ **5.** a) 0.66 b) 1.13

7. a) $\dfrac{15}{8}$ b) $\dfrac{8}{15}$ c) $\dfrac{17}{15}$ d) $\dfrac{17}{15}$

9. $\sin \theta = 0.78$; $\tan \theta = 1.23$; $\cot \theta = 0.81$; $\sec \theta = 1.59$; $\csc \theta = 1.29$

11. a) 6.10 b) 0.39 c) 0.42 **13.** 167 m

Exercise 2.2 (page 30)

1. 0.4695	**3.** 0.3090	**5.** 1.2208	**7.** 0.6865
9. 0.9758	**11.** 0.3153	**13.** 0.4142	**15.** 1.0000
17. 1.99	**19.** 95.48	**21.** 9.94	**23.** 8.67
25. 1.17	**27.** 1.31	**29.** – 0.33	**31.** 17.33 m

Exercise 2.3 (page 35)

 1. a) 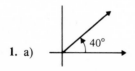 b) 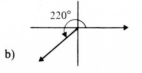 c)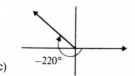

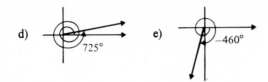

3. a) I   **b)** IV   **c)** III   **d)** III   **e)** III

5. a) 260°   **b)** 180°   **c)** 180°   **d)** $\dfrac{5\pi}{4}$ **e)** 1.96

7. Any angle of the form 90° + k · 360°, where k is an integer

9. $\left\{-\dfrac{2\pi}{3} + k \cdot 2\pi \,\middle|\, k \text{ is any integer}\right\}$

11. a) {45° + k · 360° | k is an integer}
   b) {225° + k · 360° | k is an integer}
   c) {120° + k · 360° | k is an integer}

Exercise 2.4 (page 42)

1. $\sin \theta = -\dfrac{3}{5} = -0.6000;$ $\tan \theta = -\dfrac{3}{4} = -0.7500;$ $\sec \theta = \dfrac{5}{4} = 1.2500;$

$\cos \theta = \dfrac{4}{5} = 0.8000;$ $\cot \theta = -\dfrac{4}{3} = -1.3333;$ $\csc \theta = -\dfrac{5}{3} = -1.6667$

3. a) $\dfrac{\sqrt{3}}{2}$ **b)** $\dfrac{1}{2}$ **c)** $-\dfrac{1}{2}$ **d)** $-\dfrac{\sqrt{3}}{2}$

5. a) -1 **b)** $-\sqrt{2}$ **c)** 1   **d)** $\sqrt{2}$

7. a) $\dfrac{1}{2}$ **b)** $-\dfrac{1}{\sqrt{3}}$ **c)** $\dfrac{1}{2}$ **d)** $-\dfrac{1}{2}$

9. a) 1   **b)** 1   **c)** Undefined   **d)** -1

11. a) 2   **b)** -1 **c)** $\dfrac{1}{\sqrt{3}}$ **d)** $-\dfrac{1}{2}$

13. $\sin \theta = \dfrac{4}{5} = 0.800;$ $\tan \theta = -\dfrac{4}{3} = -1.333;$ $\cot \theta = -\dfrac{3}{4} = -0.750;$

$\sec \theta = -\dfrac{5}{3} = -1.667;$ $\csc \theta = \dfrac{5}{4} = 1.250$

15. $\sin \beta = -\dfrac{4}{5} = -0.800;$ $\cos \beta = -\dfrac{3}{5} = -0.600;$ $\tan \beta = \dfrac{4}{3} = 1.333;$

$\sec \beta = -\dfrac{5}{3} = -1.667;$ $\csc \beta = -\dfrac{5}{4} = -1.250$

17. $\cos \theta = \dfrac{\sqrt{15}}{4} = 0.968;$ $\tan \theta = -\dfrac{1}{\sqrt{15}} = -0.258;$ $\cot \theta = -\sqrt{15} = -3.873;$

$\sec \theta = \dfrac{4}{\sqrt{15}} = 1.033;$ $\csc \theta = -4 = -4.000$

19. $\dfrac{2 + \sqrt{3}}{2} = 1.866$

Exercise 2.5 (page 45)

1. 0.75471   **3.** − 0.90040   **5.** 0.12278   **7.** − 1.19236

9. − 0.61232   **11.** 0.00140   **13.** 0.59720   **15.** − 11.32603

17. − 7.01525   **19.** − 0.13449   **21.** − 2.82674   **23.** 0.9903

25. 0.971 337 975 (four terms); 0.971 337 975 (directly)

Exercise 2.6 (page 52)

Problem	s	Point P	sin s	cos s	tan s	cot s	sec s	csc s
1	$\pi/2$	(0, 1)	1	0	undef.	0	undef.	1
3	$-3\pi/4$	$\left(-\dfrac{\sqrt{2}}{2}, -\dfrac{\sqrt{2}}{2}\right)$	$-\dfrac{\sqrt{2}}{2}$	$-\dfrac{\sqrt{2}}{2}$	1	1	$-\sqrt{2}$	$-\sqrt{2}$
5	$9\pi/4$	$\left(\dfrac{\sqrt{2}}{2}, \dfrac{\sqrt{2}}{2}\right)$	$\dfrac{\sqrt{2}}{2}$	$\dfrac{\sqrt{2}}{2}$	1	1	$\sqrt{2}$	$\sqrt{2}$
7	$3\pi/2$	(0, −1)	− 1	0	undef.	0	undef.	− 1
9	$17\pi/4$	$\left(\dfrac{\sqrt{2}}{2}, \dfrac{\sqrt{2}}{2}\right)$	$\dfrac{\sqrt{2}}{2}$	$\dfrac{\sqrt{2}}{2}$	1	1	$\sqrt{2}$	$\sqrt{2}$
11	$7\pi/3$	$\left(\dfrac{1}{2}, \dfrac{\sqrt{3}}{2}\right)$	$\dfrac{\sqrt{3}}{2}$	$\dfrac{1}{2}$	$\sqrt{3}$	$\dfrac{1}{\sqrt{3}}$	2	$\dfrac{2}{\sqrt{3}}$
13	1	(0.540, 0.841)	0.84	0.54	1.56	0.64	1.85	1.19
15	7.3	(0.526, 0.850)	0.85	0.53	1.62	0.62	1.90	1.18
17	$\sqrt{2}$	(0.156, 0.988)	0.99	0.16	6.33	0.16	6.41	1.01
19	− 12	(0.844, 0.537)	0.54	0.84	0.64	1.57	1.18	1.86

21. $\dfrac{2\pi}{3} + k \cdot 2\pi$ **23.** $\dfrac{5\pi}{4} + k \cdot 2\pi$ **25.** $k \cdot 2\pi$

In problems 27–31, if P: (a, b) is the point on the unit circle associated with arc length s, then:

27. $(-a, b)$ is associated with $\pi - s$ **29.** $(-b, a)$ is associated with $\dfrac{\pi}{2} + s$

31. $(-b, a)$ is associated with $s + \dfrac{\pi}{2}$

33. (a) Yes (b) Yes **35.** (a) No (b) No

37. (a) Yes (b) Yes **39.** (a) Yes (b) No

Review Exercises (page 60)

1. a)  b) 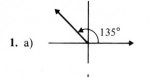 c)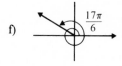

d) 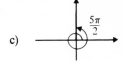 e)  f)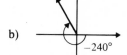

3. a) 1   b) $\dfrac{1}{\sqrt{3}}$ c) $-\dfrac{2}{\sqrt{3}}$ d) $-\dfrac{1}{2}$ e) 0   f) 1   g) 1   h) -1

5. a) $-\dfrac{4}{5}$ b) $-\dfrac{5}{3}$ c) $\dfrac{3}{5}$ d) $\dfrac{4}{3}$ e) $\dfrac{5}{3}$ f) $\dfrac{4}{5}$

7. a) $270°$ b) $30°$ c) $135°$ d) $-45°$

9. a) $-\dfrac{\sqrt{3}}{2}$ b) 0   c) $\dfrac{1}{2}$ d) $\dfrac{\sqrt{3}}{2}$ e) $\sqrt{3}$ f) $\dfrac{2}{\sqrt{3}}$

11. a) 0.6820   b) -0.4877 c) 0.5407   d) 0.9004   e) 1.1897   f) 0.7771

13. a) 0.7880   b) 1.7646   **15.** a) 1   b) 1

17. a) True   b) False   c) True   d) False

Chapter 3

Exercise 3.1 (page 69)

1. $b = 4.60$ cm; $c = 5.64$ cm; $\beta = 54°36'$

3. $b = 288.00$ cm; $\alpha = 31°17'$; $\beta = 58°43'$

5. $a = 25.90$ cm; $b = 50.21$ cm; $\beta = 62°43'$; Area = 650.25 cm²

7. $c = 26\ 417.00$ m; $\alpha = 66°24'$; $\beta = 23°36'$

9. $b = 175.00$ km, $c = 337.00$ km; $\alpha = 58°43'$

11. $b = 11.27$ cm; $\alpha = 25°26'$; $\beta = 64°34'$; Area = 30.20 cm²

13. $a = 39.24$ cm; $b = 51.27$ cm; $\beta = 52°34'$; Area = 1005.83 cm²

15. $c = 2.93$ cm; $\alpha = 59°40'$; $\beta = 30°20'$ **17.** $77°00'$

19. 573.04 m   **21.** 3.03 m²   **23.** 2243.11 cm²   **25.** 25.85 cm

27. $|\overline{CE}| = 13.61$; $|\overline{CF}| = 9.98$ m   **31.** $|\overline{BC}| = 19.22$ cm; $|\overline{CD}| = 14.37$ cm

33. 25.34 m   **35.** 1799.83 cm³   **37.** 174.27 cm   **39.** 5.32 cm   **41.** 10.25 cm²

Exercise 3.2 (page 80)

1. $c = 48$, $\alpha = 31°07'$, $\beta = 105°53'$ **3.** $b = 90$, $\alpha = 69°06'$, $\gamma = 27°30'$

5. No solution   **7.** $\alpha = 58°43'$, $\beta = 31°17'$, $\gamma = 90°$

9. $\alpha = 56°05'$, $\beta = 34°12'$, $\gamma = 89°43'$

11. Two solutions: $c_1 = 46.37$, $\beta_1 = 46°59'$, $\gamma_1 = 101°46'$
$\qquad\qquad\qquad c_2 = 12.84$, $\beta_2 = 133°01'$, $\gamma_2 = 15°44'$

13. $a = 32$, $\alpha = 56°48'$, $\gamma = 55°12'$ **17.** 85.5 km   **19.** $90°00'$

21. Altitude 29.43;   Area = 1130.18   **23.** 41.59   **25.** 52°   **29.** 22.75 m

Exercise 3.3 (page 85)

1. $\gamma = 80°$, $b = 34$, $c = 35$ **3.** $\beta = 21°$, $a = 64$, $b = 31$
5. $\gamma = 92°31'$, $b = 50.0$, $c = 60.8$ **7.** $\gamma = 80°47'$, $a = 4.734$, $b = 2.146$
9. 140.1 m   **11.** 57.5 cm   **13.** 151.87

15. Same answers as to Problem 11 of Exercise 3.2.

17. 22.9 m   **19.** 388 m   **21.** 31 m   **25.** 428 m

Exercise 3.4 (page 91)

1. 877.7   **3.** 1010.1   **5.** 2110.7   **9.** 4.394
11. Area = 49320 m²;   Perimeter = 1188 m   **13.** 43 200 m²
15. $a = 6.85$ m, $b = 9.43$ m, $c = 7.51$ m   **17.** $b = 27.69$ cm, $a = 28.73$ cm

Exercise 3.5 (page 99)

1. 2.8 km in the direction of 32.01° west of north
3. a) 3.5 cm; 70° east of north   b) 2.6 cm; 83° west of south
   c) 8.4 cm; 67° east of north
5. 943 km in the direction of 4.93° west of south
7. 36.20 m in the direction of 17°02' east of north
9. 4.33 m in the direction of 33°42' east of north
11. a) 5.39   b) 7.62   c) 13
13. a) Same direction   b) Opposite direction   c) Perpendicular to each other
15. (732, −217)

Exercise 3.6 (page 105)

1. $3i - 4j$ **3.** $-4i + 5j$ **5.** $-9i + 17j$ **7.** $-4i + 6j$ **9.** 17.46
11. θ for *A* is 30°; θ for *B* is 110°
13. $A + B = 0.205i + 3.757j$; magnitude 3.76 cm; direction 3.12° east of north
15. $487i - 282j$ **17.** $550i - 1741j$; 1826 km in the direction of 17.53° east of south
19. 39°54′ east of north   **21.** 1.98 km in the direction of 53°15′ east of north
23. $\dfrac{3}{\sqrt{10}} i + \dfrac{1}{\sqrt{10}} j$ **25. a)** 60°15′   **b)** 60°15′
27. Sum of $2.50i + 1.83j$ and $0.50i + 2.17j$ **29. b)** $6i + 22j$ **c)** $17i + 25j$
31. 1052 km in the direction of 62°22′ east of south

Exercise 3.7 (page 109)

1. a) 360 km/hr due east   **b)** 270 km
3. a) 234 km/hr, 49°50′ east of north   **b)** 176 km
5. Compass reading 11°32′ west of north; ground speed 392 km/hr
7. 1 hour and 23 minutes   **9.** 2 hours and 35 minutes
11. 35 km/hr in the direction of 80°39′ east of south   **13.** 0.18 km
15. 48 km/hr in the direction of 4°36′ west of south

Exercise 3.8 (page 114)

1. 113 kg; 53 kg   **3.** 91 kg   **5.** 44 kg   **7.** 55 kg
9. 89 kg   **11.** 81 kg; 52 kg   **13.** 93 kg   **15.** 135 kg
17. Less than 74°56′   **19.** 22 kg   **21.** Less than 60°

Review Exercises (page 117)

1. 27.90 cm; 24.94 cm   **3.** 18.8 cm; 39°20′; 50°40′   **5.** 14 cm   **7.** No triangle
9. $\alpha = 46°50′$; $\beta = 80°40′$; $\gamma = 52°30′$ **11.** No triangle   **13.** No triangle
15. $|\overline{AB}| = 53$ m; $|\overline{AC}| = 197$ m   **17.** 9.17 cm   **19.** 8.1
21. a) $12i - 7j$ **b)** $4i - 4j$ **23. a)** 58.67°   **b)** 6.34°
25. a) $-1074i + 953j$
    b) Salt Lake City is 605 km from Denver in the direction of 77°36′ west of north
27. 9°36′ west of south; 473 km   **29.** 111.39 kg

Chapter 4

Exercise 4.2 (page 128)

1. Yes   **3.** No   **5.** No   **7.** No   **9.** Yes
11. No   **13.** No   **15.** No   **17.** No   **19.** Yes

Exercise 4.3 (page 131)

5. a) $\dfrac{\sqrt{6}-\sqrt{2}}{4}$ 　　　 b) $\dfrac{\sqrt{2}-\sqrt{6}}{4}$ 　　　 c) $-\left(2+\sqrt{3}\right)$

   d) $2+\sqrt{3}$ 　　　 e) $-(\sqrt{6}+\sqrt{2})$ 　　　 f) $\sqrt{2}-\sqrt{6}$

7. $\dfrac{1}{7}$ 　　　 9. $1/2$ 　　　 11. Identity 　　　 13. Identity

15. Identity 　　　 17. Identity 　　　 19. $\dfrac{\sqrt{10+2\sqrt{5}}}{4}$

23. a) $\dfrac{\sqrt{2}}{2}$ (sin x − cos x) 　 b) −cos x 　 c) $\dfrac{\sqrt{2}}{2}$ (sin x + cos x)

   d) 2 sin x cos x 　 e) $\cos^2 x - \sin^2 x$ 　 f) sin x cos $x - \dfrac{\sqrt{3}}{2}\cos^2 x + \dfrac{\sqrt{3}}{2}$ $\sin^2 x$

Exercise 4.4 (page 136)

25. a) $-\dfrac{120}{169}$ 　 b) $\dfrac{119}{169}$ 　 c) $-\dfrac{120}{119}$

27. a) 0.9507 　 b) −0.3102 　 c) −3.0652

29. a) $\dfrac{1}{4}$ 　 b) $\dfrac{\sqrt{3}}{2}$ 　 c) $-\dfrac{\sqrt{3}}{2}$ 　　　 31. Identity

33. Identity 　　　 35. Identity 　　 37. Not an identity 　　　 39. Identity

Exercise 4.5 (page 141)

1. a) $\dfrac{1}{2}\sqrt{2+\sqrt{2}}$ 　 b) $\dfrac{1}{2}\sqrt{2+\sqrt{2}}$ 　 c) $\dfrac{1}{2}\sqrt{2+\sqrt{3}}$ 　 d) $-\dfrac{1}{2}\sqrt{2-\sqrt{3}}$

3. a) $\dfrac{1}{2}\sqrt{2-\sqrt{3}}$ 　 b) $-\dfrac{1}{2}\sqrt{2-\sqrt{2}}$ 　 c) $-\dfrac{1}{2}\sqrt{2+\sqrt{2}}$ 　 d) $2-\sqrt{3}$

5. a) $\dfrac{3\sqrt{13}}{13}$ 　 b) $\dfrac{2\sqrt{13}}{13}$ 　 c) $\dfrac{3}{2}$ 　 d) $\dfrac{\sqrt{13}}{2}$

7. $\cos\dfrac{\theta}{2} = -\dfrac{1}{2}\sqrt{2+\sqrt{3}}$; 　 $\tan\dfrac{\theta}{2} = 2-\sqrt{3}$

9. a) $-\dfrac{5\sqrt{26}}{26}$ 　 b) $\sqrt{\dfrac{\sqrt{26}+1}{2\sqrt{26}}}$ 　 c) $\dfrac{5}{13}$ 　 d) $-\dfrac{\sqrt{26}+1}{5}$

11. $-\dfrac{1}{8}$ 　　 13. a) 0.2683 　 b) 0.9581 　 c) 0.2988

23. $-\dfrac{\sqrt{6}+\sqrt{2}}{4}$; 　 $-\dfrac{\sqrt{2+\sqrt{3}}}{2}$

Review Exercises (page 142)

27. Identity 　　　 29. Not an identity 　　　 31. Not an identity

33. $-\dfrac{4}{5}$ 　 35. $1/\sqrt{10}$ 　 37. $-56/33$ 　 39. $119/169$ 　 41. $-116/845$

43. $9/25$ 　　 45. $-5/12$ 　　 47. $-4/5$ 　　 49. $-3696/4225$

Chapter 5

Exercise 5.1 (page 149)

Let R be the set of real numbers.

1. a) R b) R c) $f^{-1}(x) = \dfrac{3-x}{5}$; f^{-1} is a function

3. a) R b) $\{y \mid y \geq 0\}$ c) $y = \pm\dfrac{1}{2}\sqrt{x}$; f^{-1} is not a function

5. a) R b) $\{y \mid y \geq 0\}$ c) $f^{-1}(x) = 1 \pm \sqrt{x}$; f^{-1} is not a function

7. a) $\{x \mid x \neq 0\}$ b) $\{y \mid y \neq -1\}$ c) $f^{-1}(x) = \dfrac{2}{x+1}$; f^{-1} is a function

9. a) $\{x \mid x \geq 0\}$ b) $\{y \mid y \geq 4\}$ c) $f^{-1}(x) = (x-4)^2$, $x \geq 4$; f^{-1} is a function

11. a) $f^{-1}(x) = \dfrac{x+4}{3}$ b) $f(f^{-1}(x)) = x$ **13.** a) $f^{-1}(x) = \dfrac{2}{x-1}$ b) $f(f^{-1}(x)) = x$

15. $f^{-1}(x) = \dfrac{x-3}{5}$; f^{-1} is a function   **17.** $y = \pm\dfrac{1}{3}\sqrt{x}$; not a function

19. $y = \pm(x-1)$ and $x \geq 1$; not a function

Exercise 5.2 (page 158)

3. $\dfrac{\pi}{4}$ **5.** $-\dfrac{\pi}{6}$ **7.** Not defined   **9.** π **11.** $-\dfrac{\pi}{4}$

13. $\{\theta \mid \theta = \dfrac{\pi}{4} + 2k\pi \text{ or } \theta = \dfrac{3\pi}{4} + 2k\pi\}$;

$\{\theta \mid \theta = 45° + k \cdot 360° \text{ or } \theta = 135° + k \cdot 360°\}$

15. $\{\theta \mid \theta = \pi + 2k\pi\}$; $\{\theta \mid \theta = 180° + k \cdot 360°\}$

17. 0.39; 22.14°   **19.** -0.57; $-32.48°$ **21.** Not defined

23. 2.64; 151.27°   **25.** Not defined   **27.** Not defined

29. 2.00; 114.34°   **31.** 3/4   **33.** -1 **35.** Not defined

37. $-\dfrac{\sqrt{7}}{21}$ **39.** $\dfrac{\sqrt{3}}{2}$ **41.** π **43.** $\dfrac{\sqrt{3}}{2}$ **45.** 0.97   **47.** Not defined

49. 0.24   **51.** Yes   **53.** Yes   **55.** Yes   **57.** 0.0707   **59.** No solution

Exercise 5.3 (page 166)

3. 60°; $\dfrac{\pi}{3}$ **5.** $-60°$; $-\dfrac{\pi}{3}$ **7.** $-180°$; $-\pi$

9. $\{\theta \mid \theta = 30° + k \cdot 180°\}$; $\{\theta \mid \theta = \dfrac{\pi}{6} + k \cdot \pi\}$

11. $\{\theta \mid \theta = 150° + k \cdot 180°\}$; $\{\theta \mid \theta = \dfrac{5\pi}{6} + k \cdot \pi\}$

13. 0.6358; 36.43°   **15.** 0.8361; 47.91°

17. 2.7490; 157.51°   **19.** -0.1887; $-10.81°$

21. $\{\theta \mid \theta = 1.1787 + k\pi\}$ (numbers should be rounded off to two decimal places)

23. $\{\theta \mid \theta = 69.86° + k \cdot 180°\}$ **25.** $4/3$ **27.** $-\dfrac{20}{29}$

29. $\dfrac{3}{5}$ **31.** $\sqrt{\dfrac{2\sqrt{13}}{\sqrt{13}-3}}$ **37.** Yes   **39.** No   **41.** Yes

49. b)

x, m	40	25	20	10	8	6	5	4
$\theta°$	2.14	3.40	4.22	7.98	9.59	11.82	13.19	14.62

3.5	3.2	3.1	3.0	2.8	2.5	2.0	1.5	1.0	0.5
15.26	15.56	15.64	15.71	15.80	15.80	15.26	13.67	10.62	5.91

    c) The maximum value of θ is 15.80° and is given by x between 2.5 and 2.8. Try more values of x in this interval: $x = 2.66$ m, $\theta = 15.82640°$; $x = 2.65$ m, $\theta = 15.82660°$; $x = 2.64$ m, $\theta = 15.82658°$. We conclude that $x = 2.65$ m (to two decimal places) gives the maximum value of θ: $\theta_{max} = 15.82660°$.

51. 1.5574   **53.** $\left\{x \mid -\dfrac{\pi}{2} < x < \dfrac{\pi}{2}\right\}$ **55.** $\{x \mid x \geq 0.9316\}$

Exercise 5.4 (page 172)

1. a) 60°   b) 45°   c) $-60°$ d) 135°   e) $-90°$

3 a) $\dfrac{\sqrt{7}}{4}$;   0.6614   b) $\dfrac{3\sqrt{7}-12}{20}$; -0.2031

    c) Not defined since $1/3$ is not in the domain of function Csc^{-1}

    d) 90° or $\dfrac{\pi}{2}$ e) $\dfrac{12\left(\sqrt{15}+\sqrt{8}\right)}{7}$;   11.4881

5. a) 0.8277   b) 2.3761
    c) Not defined since $(1-\sqrt{5})/3$ is not in the domain of function Sec^{-1}
    d) -0.2916 e) 0.7155

7. a) 73.92°
    b) Not defined since $\sin 47°$ is not in the domain of function Csc^{-1}
    c) 106.75°
    d) Not defined since $(2+\sqrt{5})/8$ is not in the domain of function Csc^{-1}
    e) $-42.42°$

9. a) $\{\theta \mid \theta = 150° + k \cdot 360°$ or $\theta = 210° + k \cdot 360°\}$
    b) $\{\theta \mid \theta = 270° + k \cdot 360°\}$

Review Exercises (page 173)

1. 90°, $\pi/2$ **3.** $-45°$, $-\pi/4$ **5.** 150°, $5\pi/6$ **7.** 90°, $\pi/2$

9. 225°, $5\pi/4$ **11.** π **13.** $-24/25$ **15.** $-5/\sqrt{26}$

17. $-16/63$ **19.** 120/119   **21.** 0.436   **23.** 3

25. 0.890   **27.** Undefined   **29.** $\sqrt{\dfrac{\sqrt{17}+4}{2\sqrt{17}}} = 0.993$ **31.** Undefined

33. Undefined   **35.** Undefined   **37.** -1.075 **39.** 0.422

41. 0   **43.** 2.034   **45.** $\sqrt{3}/2$ **47.** False

49. False   **51.** True   **53.** False   **55.** False

Chapter 6

Exercise 6.1 (page 178)

Let S represent the solution set for the given equation.

1. $S = \{x \mid x = 120° + k \cdot 360°$ or $x = 240° + k \cdot 360°\}$

3. $S = \{x \mid x = 30° + k \cdot 180°\}$

5. $S = \{x \mid x = 64.62° + k \cdot 360°$ or $x = -64.62° + k \cdot 360°\}$

7. $S = \emptyset$, empty set   **9.** $S = \left\{\dfrac{5\pi}{6}, \dfrac{7\pi}{6}\right\}$

11. $S = \left\{\dfrac{5\pi}{36}, \dfrac{13\pi}{36}, \dfrac{29\pi}{36}, \dfrac{37\pi}{36}, \dfrac{53\pi}{36}, \dfrac{61\pi}{36}\right\}$

13. $S = \left\{\dfrac{\pi}{6}, \dfrac{11\pi}{6}\right\}$ **15.** $S = \left\{\dfrac{5\pi}{6}, \dfrac{11\pi}{6}\right\}$ **17.** $S = \{0.13, 3.27\}$

19. $S = \{1.72, 4.86\}$ **21.** $S = \{0.68\}$ **23.** $S = \{0.87\}$

25. $\left\{x \mid x = \dfrac{3\pi}{4} + k \cdot 2\pi\right\}$

Exercise 6.2 (page 181)

Let S represent the solution set for the given equation.

1. $S = A \cup B$, where
$A = \{x \mid x = 221.81° + k \cdot 360°$ or $x = 318.19° + k \cdot 360°\}$
$B = \{x \mid x = 90° + k \cdot 360°\}$

3. $S = \{x \mid x = 180° + k \cdot 360°\}$

5. $S = \{x \mid x = 30° + k \cdot 180°$ or $x = 150° + k \cdot 180°\}$

7. $S = \{x \mid x = 60° + k \cdot 360°$ or $x = 300° + k \cdot 360°\}$

9. $S = \left\{\dfrac{7\pi}{6}, \dfrac{11\pi}{6}\right\}$ **11.** $S = \{0.84, 5.44, \pi\}$

13. $S = \left\{ \dfrac{3\pi}{4}, \dfrac{7\pi}{4} \right\}$

15. $S = \left\{ \dfrac{\pi}{3}, \dfrac{2\pi}{3}, \dfrac{4\pi}{3}, \dfrac{5\pi}{3} \right\}$

17. $S = \left\{ \dfrac{\pi}{2}, \dfrac{3\pi}{2} \right\}$

19. $S = \left\{ \dfrac{3\pi}{2} \right\}$

21. $S = \left\{ \dfrac{7\pi}{6}, \dfrac{11\pi}{6} \right\}$

23. $S = \left\{ \dfrac{\pi}{4}, \dfrac{3\pi}{4}, \dfrac{5\pi}{4}, \dfrac{7\pi}{4} \right\}$

25. $S = \left\{ \dfrac{\pi}{3}, \dfrac{2\pi}{3}, \dfrac{4\pi}{3}, \dfrac{5\pi}{3} \right\}$

27. $S = \{0.97, 5.31\}$

29. $S = \{1.88, 4.40\}$

31. $S = \{3.72, 5.70\}$

33. $S = \emptyset$, empty set

35. $S = \{0.32, 1.08, 2.06, 2.82\}$

37. $S = \{1.17, 2.41, 4.32, 5.55\}$

39. $S = \emptyset$, empty set

Exercise 6.3 (page 184)

Let S represent the solution set for the given equation.

1. $S = \{2.30, 5.84\}$ **3.** $S = \{4.71, 5.64\}$ **5.** $S = \emptyset$, empty set

7. $S = \{2.09, 6.05\}$ **9.** $S = \{0.79\}$ **11.** $S = \{90°, 180°\}$

13. $S = \{131°36', 334°40'\}$ **15.** $S = \{63°26', 90°, 243°26', 270°\}$

17. $S = \{90°, 216°52', 270°\}$ **19.** $S = \{45°, 98°08', 225°, 278°08'\}$

Exercise 6.4 (page 187)

Let S represent the solution set for the given equation.

1. $S = \{0.23, 1.80, 3.37, 4.94\}$ **3.** $S = \left\{ \dfrac{\pi}{2}, \dfrac{3\pi}{2} \right\}$

5. $S = \left\{ \dfrac{\pi}{3}, \pi, \dfrac{5\pi}{3} \right\}$ **7.** $S = \{0, 2\pi\}$ **9.** $S = \{0, \pi, 2\pi\}$

11. $S = \left\{ \dfrac{3\pi}{4}, \dfrac{7\pi}{4} \right\}$ **13.** $S = \left\{ \dfrac{\pi}{12}, \dfrac{5\pi}{12}, \dfrac{13\pi}{12}, \dfrac{17\pi}{12} \right\}$

15. $S = \left\{ \dfrac{\pi}{24}, \dfrac{5\pi}{24}, \dfrac{13\pi}{24}, \dfrac{17\pi}{24}, \dfrac{25\pi}{24}, \dfrac{29\pi}{24}, \dfrac{37\pi}{24}, \dfrac{41\pi}{24} \right\}$

17. $S = \{210°, 330°\}$ **19.** $S = \{14.48°, 90°, 165.52°, 270°\}$

21. $S = \{0°, 120°, 180°, 240°, 360°\}$ **23.** $S = \emptyset$, empty set

25. $S = \{54.74°, 125.26°, 234.74°, 305.26°\}$ **27.** $S = \{0°, 180°, 360°\}$

29. $S = \{0°, 20°, 60°, 100°, 120°, 140°, 180°, 220°, 240°, 260°, 300°, 340°, 360°\}$

Exercise 6.5 (page 190)

1. 0   **3.** -0.74 **5.** 1.17   **7.** 1.76   **9.** 1.18   **11.** 1.11

Exercise 6.6 (page 193)

Let S represent the solution set for the given equation.

1. $S = \{15°, 75°, 195°, 255°\}$ **3.** $S = \{60°, 180°, 300°\}$

5. $S = \{0°, 90°, 180°, 270°, 360°\}$ **7.** $S = \{0, 2\pi/3, \pi, 4\pi/3, 2\pi\}$

9. $S = \{\pi/4, 5\pi/4\}$ **11.** $S = \{0.36, 1.21, 3.51, 4.35\}$

13. $S = \{0, \pi/3, 5\pi/3, 2\pi\}$ **15.** $S = \{0.62, 2.53, 3.76, 5.67\}$

Review Exercises (page 193)

1. $\pi/3$; $5\pi/3$ **3.** No solution   **5.** 0.927;   4.069

7. $\pi/6$; $5\pi/6$ **9.** 2.498   **11.** $\pi/2$; $3\pi/2$

13. No solution   **15.** 1.122;   2.446;   3.837;   5.162

17. All values of x in the interval $0 \leq x \leq 2\pi$

19. 1.946;   4.338   **21.** No solution   **23.** $\pi/4$; $3\pi/4$; $5\pi/4$; $7\pi/4$

25. All values of x in the internal $0 \leq x \leq 1$

27. 0.786   **29.** All values of x in the interval $0 \leq x \leq 2\pi$

31. No solution   **33.** 1.170   **35.** 1.283

37. $\pi/2$; $3\pi/2$ **39.** $\pi/2$; $3\pi/2$;   1.274;   5.009

41. No solutions   **43.** -0.841 **45.** $\pi/6$; $5\pi/6$

47. $-1 \leq x \leq 0.479$ **49.** $x = (2k - 1)\pi$, where k is an integer

Chapter 7

Exercise 7.1 (page 203)

Let P represent the period and A the amplitude of the given function.

1. $P = 2\pi$, $A = 2$ **3.** $P = 2\pi$, $A = 4$ **5.** $P = 2\pi$, $A = 1/2$

7. $P = 2\pi/3$, $A = 1$ **9.** $P = 2\pi/3$, $A = 2$ **11.** $P = 2\pi$, $A = 4$

13. $P = 4$, $A = 3$ **15.** $P = 2$, $A = 2$ **17.** $P = 2\pi$, $A = 1$

19. $P = 2\pi/3$, $A = 1$ **21.** $P = 2\pi/3$, $A = 4$ **23.** $P = \pi$, $A = 2$

25. $P = 1$, $A = 3$ **27.** $P = 1$, $A = 3$ **29.** $P = 1$, $A = 3$

Exercise 7.2 (page 206)

In each of the following a) *P* represents the period; b) a *suggested* interval is given (for which one branch of the curve might be drawn) along with some key values of *x* that can be used; the table should include other in-between values of *x*.

1. a) $P = \pi$ b) $-\frac{\pi}{2} < x < \frac{\pi}{2}$; values of *x*: $-1.56, -\frac{\pi}{4}, 0, \frac{\pi}{4}, 1.56$

3. a) $P = \pi$ b) $0 < x < \pi$; values of *x*: $0.1, \frac{\pi}{4}, \frac{\pi}{2}, \frac{3\pi}{4}, 3.1$

5. a) $P = 2\pi$ b) $-\pi < x < \pi$; values of *x*: $-3.1, \quad -\frac{\pi}{2}, 0, \frac{\pi}{2}, 3.1$

7. a) $P = \frac{\pi}{2}$ b) $0 < x < \frac{\pi}{2}$; values of *x*: $0.1, \frac{\pi}{8}, \frac{\pi}{4}, \frac{3\pi}{8}, 1.56$

9. a) $P = 1$ b) $0 < x < 1$; values of *x*: $0.05, 0.25, 0.50, 0.75, 0.95$

11. a) $P = 1$ b) $0 < x < 1$; values of *x*: $0.05, 0.25, 0.50, 0.75, 0.95$

Exercise 7.3 (page 207)

In each of the following a) *P* represents the period; b) a *suggested* interval is given (for which one branch of the curve might be drawn) along with some key values of *x* that can be used; the table should include other in-between values of *x*.

1. a) $P = \pi$

   b) $-\frac{\pi}{2} < x < \frac{3\pi}{2}$; values of *x*: $-1.56, -\frac{\pi}{4}, 0, \frac{\pi}{4}, 1.56, 1.60, \frac{3\pi}{4}, \pi, \frac{5\pi}{4}, 2.35$

3. a) $P = \pi$

   b) $-\frac{\pi}{4} < x < \frac{3\pi}{4}$; values of *x*: $-0.78, -\frac{\pi}{8}, 0, \frac{\pi}{8}, 0.78, 0.80, \frac{3\pi}{8}, \frac{\pi}{2}, \frac{5\pi}{8}, 1.17$

5. a) $P = 2/3$

   b) $-\frac{1}{3} < x < \frac{1}{3}$; values of *x*: $-0.33, -\frac{1}{4}, -\frac{1}{6}, -\frac{1}{12}, -0.01, 0.01,$

                                  $\frac{1}{12}, \frac{1}{6}, \frac{1}{4}, 0.33$

7. a) $P = 1$

   b) $-\frac{1}{2} < x < \frac{1}{2}$; values of *x*: $-0.49, -\frac{3}{8}, -\frac{1}{4}, -\frac{1}{8}, -0.01, 0.01, \frac{1}{8},$

                                  $\frac{1}{4}, \frac{3}{8}, 0.49$

9. a) $P = \pi$

   b) $-\frac{\pi}{2} < x < \frac{\pi}{2}$; values of *x*: $-1.56, -\frac{3\pi}{8}, -\frac{\pi}{4}, -\frac{\pi}{8}, -0.01, 0.01, \frac{\pi}{8},$

                                  $\frac{\pi}{4}, \frac{3\pi}{8}, 1.56$

Exercise 7.4 (page 211)

In each of the following, a procedure is suggested for drawing the graph of the given equation. Draw the graphs of the two equations on the same set of coordinates and then use the method of adding or multiplying the ordinates, as indicated.

1. $y = 1$ and $y = \sin x$;   add   3. $y = x/2$ and $y = 2 \sin x$;   add

5. $y = 2x$ and $y = \cos x$;   add   7. $y = \sin x$ and $y = -1$;   add

9. $y = x$ and $y = \sin x$;   multiply

11. $y = -x$ and $y = \cos x$;   multiply

13. $y = \sqrt{x}$ and $y = \sin x$;   multiply

15. $y = \sqrt{x}$ and $y = \sin(-x)$;   add

Exercise 7.5 (page 214)

Let R, $D(f)$, and $R(f)$ denote the set of real numbers, the domain, and the range of f, respectively.

1. a) $D(f) = R$
   b) Equation is equivalent to $y = 1 - \sin 2x$
   c) $R(f) = \{y \mid 0 \leq y \leq 2\}$

3. a) $D(f) = \{x \mid x \in R$ and $x \neq (2k + 1) \cdot \frac{\pi}{2}$, where k is any integer$\}$
   b) Equation is equivalent to $y = 2 \sin x$, where x is restricted to values in $D(f)$. That is, draw a graph of $y = 2 \sin x$ without the points corresponding to $x = (2k + 1)\pi/2$.
   c) $R(f) = \{y \mid -2 < y < 2\}$

5. a) $D(f) = \{x \mid x \in R$ and $x \neq k\pi$, where k is any integer$\}$
   b) Equation is equivalent to $y = \sin 2x$, where x is restricted to values in $D(f)$. Draw a graph of $y = \sin 2x$ without the points corresponding to
   $$x = 0, \pm \pi, \pm 2\pi, \pm 3\pi, \ldots$$
   c) $R(f) = \{y \mid -1 \leq y < 0$ or $0 < y \leq 1\}$

7. a) $D(f) = R$
   b) Equation is equivalent to $y = \sqrt{2} \sin (x + \pi/4)$
   c) $R(f) = \{y \mid -\sqrt{2} \leq y \leq \sqrt{2}\}$

9. a) $D(f) = R$
   b) Equation is equivalent to $y = \sqrt{2} \cos\left(x + \frac{\pi}{4}\right)$
   c) $R(f) = \{y \mid -\sqrt{2} \leq y \leq \sqrt{2}\}$

11. a) $D(f) = \{x \mid x \in R$ and $x \neq (2k + 1) \cdot \frac{\pi}{4}$, where k is any integer$\}$.
    b) Equation is equivalent to $y = 1$, where x is restricted to values in $D(f)$. Graph of the given equation is the same as the graph of $y = 1$ except there are "holes" at points $[(2k + 1)\pi/4, 1]$
    c) $R(f) = \{1\}$

13. a) $D(f) = R$
    b) Equation is equivalent to $y = 2 \cos\left(2x + \frac{\pi}{3}\right)$
    c) $R(f) = \{y \mid -2 \leq y \leq 2\}$

15. a) $D(f) = \{x \mid -1 \leq x \leq 1\}$
    b) Equation is equivalent to $y = x$, where x is restricted to $-1 \leq x \leq 1$. That is, the graph is a line segment.
    c) $R(f) = \{y \mid -1 \leq y \leq 1\}$

17. a) $D(f) = R$
    b) Equation is equivalent to $y = 1$
    c) $R(f) = \{1\}$

19. a) $D(f) = R$
    b) Equation is equivalent to $y = x$
    c) $R(f) = R$

Review Exercises (page 214)

Let D and R denote the domain and range of the given function, respectively, and R the set of real numbers.

1. a) Yes; $p = 2\pi$ b) $D = R$ d) $R = \{y \mid -2 \leq y \leq 2\}$

3. a) Yes; $p = \pi$ b) $D = \{x \mid x \in R \text{ and } x \neq (2k - 1)\pi/2, \ k \text{ is an integer}\}$ d) $R = R$

5. a) Yes; $p = 2\pi$ b) $D = R$ d) $R = \{y \mid 0 \leq y \leq 2\}$

7. a) Yes; $p = \pi$ b) $D = \{x \mid x \in R \text{ and } x \neq k\pi, \ k \text{ is an integer}\}$ d) $R = R$

9. a) Yes; $p = \pi$ b) $D = R$ d) $R = \{y \mid -3 \leq y \leq 3\}$

11. a) Yes; $p = \pi$ b) $D = R$ d) $R = \{y \mid -2 \leq y \leq 2\}$

13. a) No   b) $D = R$ d) $R = R$

15. a) Yes; $p = 2\pi$ b) $D = \{x \mid x = (4k + 1)\pi/2, \ k \text{ an integer}\}$
    c) Graph consists of isolated points $[(4k + 1)\pi/2, 0]$, k an integer   d) $R = \{0\}$

17. a) Yes; $p = \pi$ b) $D = R$ d) $R = \{y \mid -1 \leq y \leq 1\}$

19. a) No   b) $D = \{x \mid -1 \leq x \leq 1\}$
    c) Graph is the line segment joining points $(-1, -1)$ and $(1, 1)$
    d) $R = \{y \mid -1 \leq y \leq 1\}$

Chapter 8

Exercise 8.1 (page 222)

1. a) $-i$ b) -1 c) 1 d) i e) i f) $-i$ g) 1 h) $-i$

3. a) 12 b) $12i$ c) -12 d) $-\frac{3}{4} i$ e) $\frac{3}{4} i$ f) $\frac{3}{4}$

5. a) 4 b) $-1 - 5i$ c) $\dfrac{4 - 3\sqrt{2}}{2} - \dfrac{2 + 3\sqrt{2}}{2} i$

9. a) $3 - 8i$ b) $2 + \sqrt{3} i$ c) $-4 + 4\sqrt{2} i$
    d) 9 e) $\dfrac{1}{10} + \dfrac{3}{10} i$ f) $\dfrac{4}{17} + \dfrac{3\sqrt{2}}{17} i$

11. a) $2i$; $-\dfrac{1}{2} i$ b) i; $-3i$ c) $\dfrac{\sqrt{13} - 3}{2} i$; $-\dfrac{\sqrt{13} + 3}{2} i$ d) i; $-\dfrac{1}{2} i$

13. $x = -1, y = 2$ **15.** $x = -5, y = 13$ or $x = 2, y = 6$

17. Yes   **19.** a) No   b) No

Exercise 8.2 (page 226)

1. $(3, 5)$ **3.** $(0, 4)$ **5.** $(-\sqrt{3}, 2)$ **7.** $(0, 0)$ **9.** $-4i$ **11.** $-4 - 3i$

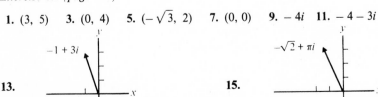

13.

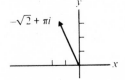

15.

17.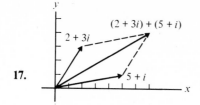

19.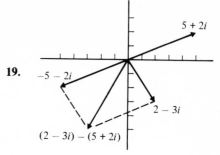

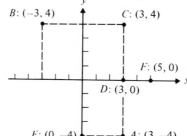

21. a) $3 - 4i$
b) $-3 + 4i$
c) $3 + 4i$
d) 3
e) $-4i$
f) 5

23. a) $-\dfrac{1}{2} + \dfrac{\sqrt{3}}{2} i$ b) $-\dfrac{1}{2} - \dfrac{\sqrt{3}}{2} i$ c) $-\dfrac{1}{2} - \dfrac{\sqrt{3}}{2} i$ d) 1

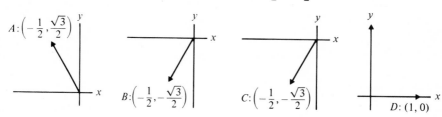

Exercise 8.3 (page 231)

3. a) $\pi(\cos 0° + i \sin 0°)$ b) $5(\cos 306.87° + i \sin 306.87°)$
c) $\sqrt{2}(\cos 135° + i \sin 135°)$ d) $13(\cos 337.38° + \sin 337.38°)$

5. a) $\dfrac{3\sqrt{2}}{2} + \dfrac{3\sqrt{2}}{2} i$ b) -5 c) $-\dfrac{1}{2} - \dfrac{\sqrt{3}}{2} i$

7. a) $4(\cos 315° + i \sin 315°)$ b) $3(\cos 120° + i \sin 120°)$
c) $\cos \dfrac{\pi}{6} + i \sin \dfrac{\pi}{6}$

9. a) $\cos 45° + i \sin 45°$ b) $\dfrac{\sqrt{2}}{2} + \dfrac{\sqrt{2}}{2} i$

11. a) $2(\cos 120° + i \sin 120°)$ b) $-1 + \sqrt{3} i$

13. $18(\cos 180° + i \sin 180°) = -18$

9. $r = \sin 2\theta$

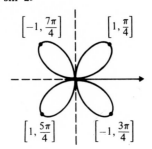

11. $r = \cos^2\theta - \sin^2\theta = \cos 2\theta$

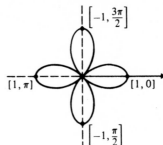

13. $r = \cos \theta \tan \theta$

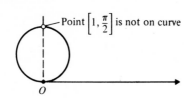

15. $r = \sin\left(\theta + \frac{\pi}{4}\right)$

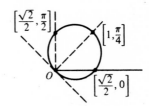

17. $r = 1 + 2 \cos \theta$

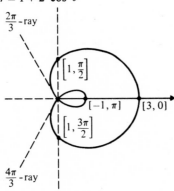

19. $r = \theta, \ \theta \geq 0$

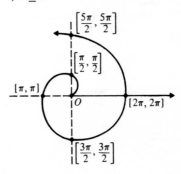

Exercise 9.3 (page 256)

1. a) $\left[\sqrt{2}, \ 135°\right]$ b) $[2, \ 240°]$ c) $[5.09, \ 51.85°]$ d) $[2.89, \ 122.87°]$

3. a) $\left[3\sqrt{2}, \ \frac{3\pi}{4}\right]$ b) $\left[\sqrt{10}, \ 5.03\right]$ c) $[3.53, \ 0.48]$

5. a) $(0, \ 2)$ b) $\left(\frac{3\sqrt{2}}{2}, \ \frac{3\sqrt{2}}{2}\right)$ c) $(2.09, \ -0.81)$

7. a) Yes   b) No   c) Yes   d) No   e) No

11. $x = 3$ **13.** $x^2 = 2v + 4$

15. $x^2 + y^2 = 1,$ $r = 1$

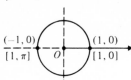

17. $3x - y = 0,$ $\theta = \text{Tan}^{-1}3 = 1.25$

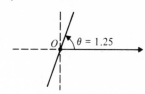

19. No; the origin is on $r = \sin \theta$ but there is no value of θ and $r = 0$ that will satisfy the equation $r \csc \theta = 1$.

Review Exercises (page 258)

1. Each of the following represents only one of an infinite number of possible answers:

   a) $[1, 0]$ b) $[3, \pi]$ c) $[4\sqrt{2}, \pi/4]$ d) $[2\sqrt{2}, 3\pi/4]$

   e) $[2, 7\pi/6]$ f) $[2, -\pi/4]$ g) $[4, \pi/2]$ h) $[3, 3\pi/2]$

3. a) $(2, 2\sqrt{3})$ b) $(\sqrt{3}, -1)$ c) $(-4, 0)$

   d) $\left(-\dfrac{1}{\sqrt{2}}, -\dfrac{1}{\sqrt{2}}\right)$ e) $\left(\dfrac{3}{\sqrt{2}}, \dfrac{3}{\sqrt{2}}\right)$

5. The graph is a circle of radius $1/2$ **7.** The graph is a circle of radius 1

9. The graph is a vertical line three units to the right of the polar origin

11. The graph is a spiral   **13.** $r^2 = 4$; this is a circle with center at 0 and radius 2

15. $y^2 + 2x - 1 = 0$; this represents a parabola

Chapter 10

Exercise 10.1 (page 264)

1. 729   **3.** 16   **5.** 1/729   **7.** 1/5   **9.** 1/3

11. 25/3   **13.** 7/3   **15.** 256   **17.** 18   **19.** 13

21. -1 **23.** 928   **25.** 140   **27.** 3.07   **29.** -0.02

31. Undefined **33.** 2.89   **35.** 0.89   **37.** 2.03   **39.** 7.39

41. 1.65   **43.** 1.20   **45.** a) $\dfrac{1}{2(\sqrt{3}-1)}$ b) $\dfrac{4}{3-\sqrt{5}}$ c) $-\dfrac{4}{1+\sqrt{17}}$

47. 1   **49.** x^3 **51.** x^7 **53.** $\dfrac{1}{x}$ **55.** $\dfrac{x-1}{x}$ **57.** a) 0.63   b) 3.17   c) 2

59. a) 1.84   b) 2.73   c) 0.25   **61.** a) 27   b) 6.84

63. a) 1   b) 0.73   c) Undefined   **65.** a) 3.12   b) 2.43

67. True   **69.** True

Exercise 10.2 (page 269)

1.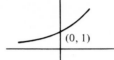

3.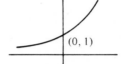

5.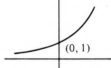

7.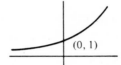

9.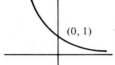

11.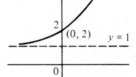

13.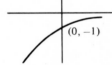

15.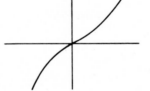

17. a) 0.50   b) 0.27   c) 0.12   d) 0.95   e) 0.65

19.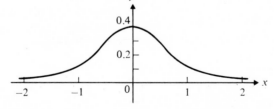

Exercise 10.3 (page 275)

1. 5   **3.** $\dfrac{5}{2}$ **5.** 2

7. $-8/3$ **9.** -1 **11.** Undefined

13. Undefined

15. $\dfrac{5}{2}$

17. $\dfrac{3}{2} \log_b p - 2 \log_b q$

19. $\dfrac{9}{4} \log_b p + \dfrac{1}{2} \log_b q$

21. 0

23. $\log_b p + \log_b q - 1$

25. 1.1133

27. 2.6826

29. 3.8136

31. 1.8155

33. 0.4729

35. 1.4610

37. 0.4307

39. 1.1656

41. $\log_3 100$

43. $\log_7 9$

45. $\log_2(3/2)$

47. 4

49. 2

51. 1

53. 2

55. 2

57. True

59. Meaningless

61. False

63. Meaningless

Exercise 10.4 (page 282)

1. 1.6094
3. 0.2718
5. 2.2912
7. Undefined
9. Undefined
11. 1.6309
13. -0.1603
15. 0.8932
17. 0.4752
19. 0
21. 1.43
23. -0.42
25. 0.5
27. 3.0061
29. 4.6274
31. 0.4246
33. 0.4809
35. No solution
37. -0.2135
39. -0.1392
41. 0.3446
43. 0.3388
45. 4.1787
47. 22.9087
49. 0.6545
51. No solution
53. 42.2561
55. 28.7685
57. 2
59. 3
61. 0.9423
63. 3.5920
65. True
67. Meaningless
69. True
71. False

Exercise 10.5 (page 286)

1. 1.29
3. -0.74
5. 0.66
7. 0.22
9. 0.06
11. 2.32
13. 1.89
15. 2
17. 4
19. 27.40
21. -0.22
23. 0.35
25. 0.27
27. $x = 3, y = 0$
29. $x = 2.28, y = -0.26$
31. 0.56714329 (to eight decimal places)

Review Exercises (page 288)

1. 0.903
3. 3.135
5. 10.751
7. 0.520
9. 1.292
11. 0.166
13. Undefined
15. $\dfrac{7}{2}$
17. Undefined
19. 12.265
21. 24.799
23. 6.167
25. 3
27. -0.432
29. 522.735
31. 0.434
33. 2.262
35. No solution

37.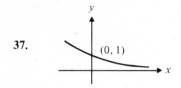

39.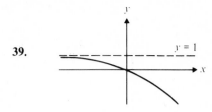

Appendix A

Exercise A.2 (continued) (page 309)

1. 10.351   **2.** 7.879   **3.** 11.688   **4.** 1.450   **5.** a) 1.600   b) 1.245

6. a) 27.750   b) 342.301   **7.** $u = 2.210$, $v = 2.199$, $t = 2.207$; thus $v < t < u$

8. a) 6.561   b) 6.561   **9.** a) 1.215   b) 1.477   c) 1.795

10. The number agrees with π through
   a) two decimal places   b) four decimal places
   c) six decimal places   d) at least eight decimal places

11. a) 12.479   b) 12.479   **12.** a) 7.817   b) 10.996

13. a) 0.268   b) 0.268   **14.** 8.186

15. a) 364   b) 113.105   c) -11.790; use $(-1.8)^6 = 1.8^6$
   d) Calculator indicates Error. Why?

16. a) 364   b) 113.105   c) -11.790 d) 6

17. a) -1.096 b) Calculator indicates Error. Why?

18. -0.236, since $\dfrac{1-\sqrt{5}}{2}$ is negative; use $\left(\dfrac{1-\sqrt{5}}{2}\right)^3 = -\left(\dfrac{\sqrt{5}-1}{2}\right)^3$

19. The calculator indicates Error. Why?

20. a) 133   b) 6.933. Use $3(-1.2)^4 - 4(-1.2)^3 + (-1.2) - 5$
$$= 3(1.2)^4 + 4(1.2)^3 - 1.2 - 5.$$
   c) 166.344   d) 0.236

Appendix B

Exercise B (page 320)

1. $x \doteq 6.475 \times 10$; $y \doteq 4.83 \times 10^3$; $z \doteq 4.5 \times 10^{-3}$;
   $u \doteq 3.70 \times 10^{-2}$; $v \doteq 3.0052 \times 10^3$; $t \doteq 3.10 \times 10^3$

3. x, hundredths; y, tens; z, ten thousandths; u, ten thousandths; v, tenths; t, tens

5. a) 2.40   b) 14   c) 0.642   d) 4.0×10^5

7. a) 0.25   b) 0.589   c) 4.94×10^3 **9.** 37.8 cm²; 175 cm³   **11.** 9×10^{12} km

INDEX

INDEX